Ethnography for Designers

Ethnography for Designers teaches architects and designers how to listen actively to the knowledge people have about their own culture. This approach gives structure to values and qualities. It does this by noting the terms and underlying structure of thought people use to describe aspects of their culture. By responding to underlying cognitive patterns, the architect can both respond to the user and interpret creatively. Thus, ethno-semantic methods can help designers enhance their professional responsibility to users and, at the same time, feel fulfilled creatively. This book is a practical guide for those teaching social factors and social research methods to designers *and* for those using these methods in practice.

Galen Cranz is Professor of Architecture at the University of California at Berkeley, a Ph.D. sociologist from the University of Chicago, and a certified teacher of the Alexander Technique. She teaches social and cultural approaches to architecture and urban design. Emphasizing ethnography as a research method, she brings users' as well as creators' perspectives to our understanding of built environments.

"Cranz draws upon three decades of teaching semantic ethnography in this thoughtful guide to doing research for design. The ethnographic approach is uniquely suited to sensitive and nuanced study of spaces of micro-cultures. Designers will find it an effective tool in envisioning places that are supportive of local cultures."

Amita Sinha, Professor of Landscape Architecture, University of Illinois at Urbana Champaign, USA

"The outcome of design activity typically implies the involvement of an audience. This much-needed text arms the designer with the cultural awareness and specific skills needed to approach projects in a refreshingly unbiased way. Noted sociologist Professor Galen Cranz who, for many years, has been deeply engaged with the education of designers, clarifies the ethnographic process and particularizes it for design. *Ethnography for Designers* provides designers with what they need to know about their audience and users as they inhabit the various research phases of any project."

Leslie Becker, Ph.D. Professor, Graphic Design and Visual Studies, California College of the Arts, San Francisco, California, USA

"In *Ethnography for Designers* architects and architecture students will find an invaluable guide to conducting research projects that reveal culturally significant aspects of the built environment and that generate thoughtful design proposals. With an abundance of clear directives and excellent exemplars, Professor Cranz demonstrates how architects can be researchers *and* designers. As many become increasingly entranced with collecting large amounts of data, nearly mechanically with digital tools, the careful attention Cranz pays to listening and learning, to analyzing and imagining, is particularly welcome."

Karen A. Franck, Professor, New Jersey Institute of Technology and co-author of *Design Through Dialogue* and *Architecture from the Inside Out*

"*Ethnography for Designers* is a tour de force away from common notions of science focused on deterministic hypothesis testing. Discovery science, so important to physical and biological sciences, is a welcome paradigm shift in the social sciences. Ethno-semantic methods empower creative architects to acquire cultural knowledge inspiring innovative new building forms to enhance their professional responsibility to users. This important book also thoughtfully acknowledges limitations of verbal interviews in accessing environmental meaning, suggesting a follow-up volume addressing the visual."

Eleftherios Pavlides Ph.D., AIA, Professor of Architecture, School of Architecture, Art and Historic Preservation, Roger Williams University, USA

Ethnography for Designers

Galen Cranz

LONDON AND NEW YORK

First published 2016
by Routledge
2 Park Square, Milton Park, Abingdon, Oxon OX14 4RN

and by Routledge
711 Third Avenue, New York, NY 10017

Routledge is an imprint of the Taylor & Francis Group, an informa business

British Library Cataloguing-in-Publication Data
A catalogue record for this book is available from the British Library

Library of Congress Cataloging-in-Publication Data
Cranz, Galen, author.
Ethnography for designers / Galen Cranz.
pages cm
Includes bibliographical references and index.
ISBN 978-1-138-12108-9 (hb : alk. paper) -- ISBN 978-1-138-12109-6 (pb : alk. paper) --
ISBN 978-1-315-65126-2 (ebook) 1. Architects and community. 2. Architectural practice--Social aspects. 3. Applied anthropology. I. Title.
NA2543.S6C74 2016
720'.47--dc23
2015035195

ISBN: 978-1-138-12108-9 (hbk)
ISBN: 978-1-138-12109-6 (pbk)
ISBN: 978-1-315-65126-2 (ebk)

Typeset in Sabon by
Servis Filmsetting Ltd, Stockport, Cheshire

Printed and bound in the United States of America by Publishers Graphics, LLC on sustainably sourced paper.

Contents

Preface

Background

Ethnography for Designers helps architecture and design students learn how to listen actively and deeply to clients and users. Listening is profound and simple, useful to professionals and to all of us as people. This book provides practical tips for applying ethnography to architectural and other types of design.

I have been introduced to design thinking primarily through architecture, but this book is addressed to all designers of the material world. Architects have been thinking about the social meaning of their work for centuries. The Roman architect and theorist Vitruvius named three facets of architecture: firmness, commodity, and delight. He thought that a building should stand up, accommodate people's activities, and be artistic. All design could be said to be the union of these three concerns: social purpose, structure, and aesthetics. An architect is not just a structural engineer, nor only a sociologist, nor solely an artist. Over time, however, the artistic function of architecture has come to have most of the emotional hold on both faculty and students in architecture schools. In the 1970s some architects were concerned that they had erred on the artistic side of the equation, and so they recruited social scientists to architecture faculties to rebalance a previous weight on structure and appearance.

One of the reasons that architects decided to bring sociologists and psychologists into their field was that the architecture profession had been embarrassed by social failures of some notable buildings, the most infamous having been the prize-winning public housing complex, Pruitt Igoe in St. Louis, Missouri. Together the planners and architects of those high-rises imagined that they could support neighborliness if they created an elevator system that stopped only on every other floor, thereby encouraging people on different floors to meet one another. Instead, this building became notorious for crime in the stairwells. For several reasons like this, the building was deemed unsuitable for single-parent families and eventually was blown up in 1972.[1] At least one architectural critic has pinpointed the demolition of these buildings as the "end of Modernism."[2]

For me those various failures marked the beginning of a career as a sociologist in an academic department of architecture. I was hired to teach at Princeton University's School of Architecture and Urban Planning in 1971. As a graduate student at the University of Chicago in Sociology I had specialized in "the social use of space." I had studied a middle-class high-rise housing project, and later a summer job designing playgrounds led me to study the history of city parks in Chicago.[3] At Princeton I received an "on-the-job education" in architecture and urbanism, thanks to the students there and my colleagues Lance Brown, Harrison Fraker, Bob Geddes,

Michael Graves, Robert Gutman, Suzanne Keller, Heath Licklider, Aaron Marcus, Tom Schumacher, and Tony Vidler. I learned by listening to the propositions they made about the nature of architecture and the questions they asked.

How can designers understand users?

One of the questions they asked was, if we're supposed to design with the user in mind, exactly how do we do that? Listen to the user? Pay attention to the user? The trouble is, they pointed out, users don't always know what they want, so paying attention to them might give you little or no direction. Even worse, paying attention to the user might direct you only in tried and true directions because people like what they have already experienced. A stale conservatism would be perpetuated. Where is the artistic creativity and innovation in that? What if circumstances change and require new arrangements?

Such questions echoed general concerns in architectural education. Recognizing the need to understand and design in a way that respects and accommodates user needs, in 1974 the *Journal of Architectural Education* posed a series of questions: How does one get inside the head of the user? How do you find out the attitudes, basic needs, and interests of users? And how can these answers be applied to design?[4]

Paying attention to the user could mean extrapolating from your own feelings outwards, which might be effective if you are the same as the people who will live in your buildings. Tellingly, one of my colleagues at Princeton went so far as to argue that no special effort was needed to program (that is, define the social purposes of) a house because everybody knows what a house is. He claimed that the cultural program was set. But, our ***culture*** is not unified, but rather, diverse. A "normal house" in New Jersey is not the same in California or New Mexico—nor Florida or Minnesota. Besides regional differences, there are class and cultural differences, and even within the same social class or culture there are age and gender differences; think toddler, wife, grandfather. And of course even the smallest organization, the family, has different roles—parent, child, guest, service technician. Extrapolating from your own idea of a house to others' ideas might not be a surefire recipe for architectural success. Today design ethnographer Steve Portigal cautions that designing according to one's own ideas—also known as "self-design"—is inherently limited: even if you consider yourself a user of the space or product you are designing, your view is inherently limited, as is your potential to innovate.[5]

So where to go from here? Participatory approaches have been advocated. They require that the architect pay attention by bringing members of the community into the design process in meetings and focus groups. That approach seems flawed, too, by virtue of the fact that the people who choose to come to these meetings may or may not be the most representative of the future users of the building. Their personalities may be more outgoing and more specific in their demands than the average user. Further, they are usually only surrogates for those who will eventually use the building, because the specific future users are not known, only the general type.

In listening to these proposals and critiques I was always struck by what seemed to me the obvious answer: that anthropologists should be involved in participatory approaches because they practice what is called ***participant observation***. They become part of the community and can speak for it. But this obvious link between anthropology and architecture has been slow in coming. Admittedly, architecture works at a faster pace than anthropology. By the time someone has been able to become a member of the community, the building could have been planned, financed, designed, built, and occupied! The more one thinks about it, the more one realizes that it's not so obvious what "paying attention" to the user might mean. It's not at all obvious what the most practical way to pay attention is.

Few social research methods are adapted to the way architects and designers work. In reality, architects and other types of designers mostly just talk with clients; they don't have the time or inclination to spend time in the field doing participant observation, making systematic observations, or administering questionnaires.

Why ethnography

Halfway through my four years at Princeton I discovered semantic ethnography as described by James Spradley and David McCurdy in *The Cultural Experience: Ethnography in Complex Societies*.[6] Here I felt that I had found a good compromise between an uninventive, literal response to the user, on the one hand, and a projection of one's own ideals onto the user, on the other. ***Semantic ethnography*** teaches one how to listen actively to the knowledge people have about their own culture. By listening to the vocabulary terms and the underlying structure of thought that people use to describe aspects of their culture, the architect has access to something profound. By responding to the underlying cognitive structure (or pattern), the architect can both respond to the user *and* interpret creatively. For example, when describing what they want in a house, clients might say that they want a fireplace, whereas you as an architect know that this is an inefficient way to heat a space, since most heat goes up the chimney, and that burning contributes to air pollution. The fireplace is one of the client's ideal features, but you might consider it ecologically immoral. Who do you please—your client or your professional self?

I hold out the hope that if you were to listen to all the terms the client uses to describe the ideal house and to the underlying structure you can find the place of the fireplace in the user's worldview and thereby gain access to an alternative expression of the same value. The fireplace could be a part of a larger category of ways to heat a room, facilitate romance and seduction, bring the family together, create psychological warmth, or conform to cultural conventions about what a living room is for that social class. After you identify the larger category that the fireplace is a part of, you have access to alternative ways to express that same purpose. For example, you can reinterpret romance, family togetherness, and psychological warmth as ways to offer relaxation and pleasure in one another's company with a focal point of perception (the flames). A circle of couches warmed by the sun and focused on a fish tank or a sculpture that holds candles to be lit on special occasions might meet people's desire for pleasure and connection. A freestanding metal Swedish, German, or Austrian stove that heats the room, holds a teakettle, and bakes bread is an engineered alternative that is close to the original built-in brick fireplace but with less pollution and wasted heat.

The same can be argued for other quotidian objects including kitchen tables, refrigerators, and lawns. Is a table simply an eating surface, or can it also be the social center of the home? Similarly, is a refrigerator seen as a device to cool food items, or is it a message center for a busy family of four? [7] And what are the implications of these—and other—possibilities? Lawns—though ecologically dubious—are conventionally desired and often socially useful for picnics and children's play; [8] if you find out that the lawn is desired as a symbol of conformity, that is very different from learning that it is desired as a ground cover, or place to play, or a visual field of green. The design implications are quite different. As a ground cover, it could be transformed entirely with less maintenance-intensive plants; as a place to play it could be reduced to blanket size with surrounding borders of meadow, herb garden, or orchard. You can practice this kind of analysis with many of the elements in a home—the car, the clothesline, storage, the bathroom, the toilet, trash, home office, television, and chairs. These items might be subsets of different categories for different people, and they might be linked to each other in many different ways. Understanding how clients and users assemble their world will help you help them put it together in new and interesting ways. I would go so far as to say that acquiring this kind of cultural knowledge is a way to create *new* types of buildings and *new* artistic forms, exactly the innovation prized by those most interested in the aesthetic side of architecture.

BOX 0.1: COMMUNICATION THEORY AND SEMANTIC ETHNOGRAPHY

The anthropologist Edward T. Hall's work on space proved useful to me as a student, researcher, and teacher. In *The Silent Language* (1959) and *The Hidden Dimension* (1966), Hall showed how space communicates. He used communication theory to account for the relationship between material and nonmaterial culture. This theory is profound, simple, and broadly applicable. Both material and nonmaterial things carry meaning, and they intertwine, sometimes reinforcing one another and sometimes "speaking out of two sides of their mouths." That is, if the nonmaterial world says one thing, the material world may restate the message at a different level of consciousness or sometimes reveal the "lie" behind what people claim. For example, verbally Americans claim to be classless, but spatially our residences are separated. Thus, communication between the physical and the nonphysical can be complex. Hall's work tells us that space is as important as built form in organizing social life.

Communication theory best describes the relationship between environment and behavior, because it sidesteps the problems of ***environmental determinism*** and the more general problem of the direction of causality. Environment and behavior are often in a mutual cause-and-effect relationship. That is, behavior can be both the cause and the effect of the physical arrangement. Therefore, understanding what they communicate to one another is easier and more relevant than deciding what came first. Semantic ethnography is consistent with a communication theory perspective because it helps us understand systems of meaning and similarly avoids having to impute one-way cause and effect. The method does not lend itself to easy reductionist approaches that identify cause-and-effect variables. It is closer to phenomenological approaches, which are notoriously ambiguous and hard to standardize; semantic ethnography offers structured procedures without resorting to standardization.

Understanding that buildings and other designed spaces are encoded with social values will help sociologists understand from yet one more perspective—spatial and physical—how social order is constructed, maintained, and challenged.

Of course, architecture, space, and place can be studied in many different ways, using many different methods. This text focuses on semantic ethnography, not only because it is practical for architectural practice, but also because its open-ended, inductive approach is appropriate to the social study of new topics. The changing meanings of the built environment, its multiple and various roles in social life, and the relative newness of the field with its emergent theories and hypotheses require a qualitative method that keeps us in the role of learners.

Even established fields like architectural history can benefit from learning to "listen" ethnographically; the documents and texts left to us in various archives can be treated as conversations with specialized vocabulary and an underlying hierarchy of meaning. For example, my own archival research on urban parks, using the cognitive ethnographer's awareness, revealed that the terms pleasure, amusement, and didactic were implicitly organized along a continuum with pleasure being the balanced middle point between the two negative extremes of "mere amusement" and "overly didactic."[i]

Notes

i Galen Cranz, *The Politics of Park Design: A History of Urban Parks in America* (Cambridge, MA: The MIT Press, 1982).

Semantic ethnography probably works better than any other ***social research method*** for the kind of contact architects typically have with clients, that of an interview-like situation. Semantic ethnography does not require a large sample of respondents, nor even being in the field to observe. It does not distort the respondent's reality by asking them to respond to pre-established questions. It does not require extensive travel. Accordingly, I see it as better than questionnaires and surveys, more practical than observation, and more practical than participant observation. Semantic ethnography allows the architect to take advantage of conventional client interviews to listen deeply and maximize understanding of the situation. Grant McCracken explains that: "Ethnography helps us make sense of unfamiliar places . . . [such that] we can recognize, enter, and participate in it." And, of particular importance to designers, through such insights, "we can innovate for it, speak to it, serve it."[9]

Designers do value being cultural creatives, and semantic ethnography is a way of involving them in culture. This approach teaches the architect how to listen actively to the knowledge people have about their own culture. It gives structure to values and qualities. It does this by noting the terms and underlying structure of thought people use to describe aspects of their culture. By responding to the underlying cognitive pattern, the architect can both respond to the user *and* interpret creatively. Thus, ethnosemantic methods allow designers to fulfill their professional responsibility to users and, at the same time, to feel fulfilled creatively.

How ethnography works

Semantic ethnography is both a theory and a method. Its practitioners argue that theory *emerges from* the ***informant*** and offers a method for listening to the informant and structuring their knowledge.[10] Thus, this book is both a treatise and a manual. Ethnography transcends the dichotomy between theory and method because it is both.[11]

Ethnography is ***inductive*** rather than ***deductive.*** It does not start out with a hypothesis or generalization as the beginning point of research. Rather, it may produce a generalization or even a hypothesis by studying details. Thus, ethnography is opposite of common notions of science, focused on *hypothesis testing*. Instead, ethnography plays an important role in *discovery science*, the creative part of science that is concerned with insights, hypothesis formation (not yet hypothesis testing), and new ideas about the relationship among things (aka theory).

Semantic ethnography emphasizes the importance of what people can tell you in words, which means it emphasizes what people know that they know. It does not deal with the unconscious (except very indirectly). For example, people may not be conscious of *why* they think of chairs and beds as a subset of furniture. The method does not work well for unconscious and latent functions directly, but indirectly we can see that an assumption has been made about the taken-for-granted category, furniture. But admittedly language has its limits. The anthropologist Edward T. Hall has noted that humans learn before they have language by seeing how things are done by others. Architecture also communicates through form rather than language.

Finally, semantic ethnography is useful not only in programming or designing new environments, but also in evaluating the extent to which existing environments support the activities, values, and interests of users. The methodologies we propose to guide you through an ethnography project acknowledge both purposes: you will evaluate an existing site to inform the program and design of another.

There are many kinds of ethnographies, of which cognitive or semantic ethnography is only one. Norman Denzin has summarized them as traditional (1900–World War II), modernist (WWII to the mid-1970s), blurred genres (1970–1986), representational (1986 to the present), and the present. He argues that all ethnography is mediated and that even language is a media, so ethnography should be recognized as interpretive. This means that a writer should write about him- or herself as well as those being written about.[12] Paradoxically, identifying the subjective makes one's ethnography more objective.

Semantic ethnography has similarities to other approaches to social research. Semantic ethnography is similar to other qualitative methods that take the subject's point of view.[13] The radical Brazilian educator Paolo Freire is opposed to a "banking theory of education" in which knowledge is distributed to the ignorant. He believes that ordinary people have knowledge, and that it needs to be elicited by a skilled listener and interpreter through dialogue, a two-way flow of information. In *Pedagogy of the Oppressed,* Freire emphasized the importance of ordinary peoples' direct experience. He believed that investigators should not come in to study a culture with a theory because theories predefine your position.[14] Like this tradition, semantic ethnography seeks to discover and interpret, rather than test pre-existing ideas.

Anselm Strauss developed an approach to qualitative research that he called grounded theory, which he claimed is the most scientific of the qualitative methods because after the researcher gathers, codes, edits, and analyzes, he or she compares findings to other published findings. The kind of ethnography taught here lends itself to this important last step as well. After you have done the bulk of your study you will be asked to review other published ***literature*** on your topic to see how your findings compare and contrast with others. In this way you will be contributing to and helping create a public body of knowledge.

The use of semantic ethnography in design has many similarities to applied ethnography as well, a practice that has become increasingly important in market research, service design, and industrial design professions wherein user needs and experiences are actively researched—using a combination of ethnographic methods including observation and interviews—to create products and designs that are directly relevant to consumer needs.[15] The burgeoning field of user experience (UX) in New Media involves close study of the relationship between people and their computer equipment and has proliferated many experts who are interested in both online behaviors and how people think about online tasks. This is where semantic ethnography is particularly helpful.[16]

This book is a practical guide for practicing professionals. It can also be used by those teaching social factors and social research methods to designers. It showcases a method that tunes the designer into the needs and aspirations of the client and user.

Acknowledgments

I started to assign ***semantic ethnographic research projects*** to seniors in architecture at Princeton in 1973. The method built upon my earlier education with Gerald Suttles who had renewed the teaching of participant observation in sociology at the University of Chicago. When I moved to the University of California at Berkeley in 1975, I brought Spradley and McCurdy's semantic approach with me. Now I have accumulated decades of ethnographies from undergraduates and a handful from graduate students.

The chief complaint that students have had about using the Spradley and McCurdy textbook was that the examples apply to anthropology rather than to architecture. Therefore, in the early 1990s I decided to rewrite the book with architectural examples. Over the years I have enlisted the help of able Graduate Student Instructors (GSI)—Dana Cuff, Carolyn Francis, and Amita Sinha—who helped by reading previous case studies—and Janice Bissell, who suggested the literature review component of the project. I was able to hire Annemarie Broudehoux and Jess Wendover Zimbabwe with the help of Teaching Improvement and research grants from the University of California at Berkeley. At this stage, in order to sidestep the sexism that some writers feel is built into our language when we use the pronoun "he" to cover both male and female students, readers, or architects, we decided to alternate using the pronouns "he" and "she" in the text. We chose not to use the graphic device s/he or she/he, because we find it more awkward than using the two pronouns alternately. In the spring of 2004, the students in the graduate seminar "Ethnography: A Closer Look" helped evaluate this text: Leslie Becker, Eunah Cha, Buzz Chen, Jaehee Chung, Inbo Kang, Mora Nabi, Pam Treetipbut, and Charlene Young. They reviewed a draft of this material and highlighted the sentences or phrases that they felt were particularly important. Those same lines, added to by undergraduate student Fernanda Roveri, now comprise the "chapter reviews" at the end of most chapters. Corey Schnobrich reviewed the manuscript as a GSI. Hans Sagan, Jonathan Bean, and Georgia Lindsay have helped by editing the text based on their experiences teaching the material. With the aid of another Instructional Improvement Grant in 2013, I hired Caitlin DeClercq to write the "skill spotlight" sections based on her experience with this textbook as both a student and teacher; integrate new, illustrative examples of student ethnographies from each decade into the text and append sample ethnographic reports to the back of the book; compile the glossary and chapter reviews; format the text for ease of use; and contribute a final round of editing. Over the years many students have written ethnographic reports from which we have used quotations throughout the text; those quotations have been made anonymous, but twelve reports have been printed in their entirety and these are identified with their authors' names. Anonymous Routledge reviewers asked me to emphasize the global relevance of this method and to indicate how it complements other methods of social research in design. Finally, Professor Leonardo Chiesi has helped clarify writing and thinking. Thea Maris proofread ultra-carefully. My thanks to all for helping develop this cultural approach to design.

Notes

1 Roger Montgomery and Katharine Bristol have shown that Pruitt-Igoe's problems did not stem from architectural design but rather from changes in social policy, but nevertheless this example continues to hold a mythical place in architectural history as a "turning point." See Roger Montgomery, "Pruitt-Igoe: Policy Failure or Societal Symptom," in Barry Checkoway and Carl V. Patton, Eds. *Metropolitan Midwest: Policy Problems and Prospects for Change* (Champaign: University of Illinois Press, 1985); and Katharine G. Bristol, "The Pruitt-Igoe Myth," *Journal of Architectural Education* 44, no. 3 (1991): 163–71. See also Chad Freidrichs, Director, *The Pruitt Igoe Myth* (Unicorn Stencil Films, 2011).

2 Charles Jencks, *The Language of Post-modern Architecture* (New York: Rizzoli, 1987).

3 Galen Cranz, *The Politics of Park Design: A History of Urban Parks in America* (Cambridge, MA: The MIT Press, 1982).

4 AIA/ACSA "Teachers Seminar Program Notes," *Journal of Architectural Education* 28, no. 1/2, Part 1. (1976): 4–9.

5 Steve Portigal, *Interviewing Users* (Brooklyn, NY: Rosenfeld Media, 2013).

6 E.T. Hall explained the origins of an inductive approach to theory building in anthropology in an online interview: "[Edward] Sapir was the one who really started this. We went out, the Europeans went out and taught languages in terms of the European paradigms. And the American Indian's languages were so different. There was no way on God's green earth to fit these languages together with our European paradigms. So Sapir said in effect, you have to start out afresh every time. Get your information from the system not from some background data. This is an earth-shaking idea. It was so revolutionary. It still has not caught on. I don't know how many years it's been since then . . . seventy or eighty years. So, you are after the reality of the culture as defined by the people who share it. Not really anything else." ("Gifts of Wisdom: An Interview with Dr. Edward T. Hall," interviewed by Kathryn Sorrells, Associate Editor, *The Edge* http://people.umass.edu/~leda/comm494r/The%20Edge%20Interview%20Hall.htm).

7 Tony Salvador, Genevieve Bell, and Ken Andersen, "Design Ethnography," *Design Management Journal* 10, no. 4 (1999).

8 Laura Jackson offers a brief review of the deleterious ecological and health implications of lawns. See Laura E. Jackson, "The Relationship of Urban Design to Human Health," *Landscape and Urban Planning* 64 (2003).

9 Grant McCracken, "Foreword," in Portigal, *Interviewing Users*, xiii–xiv.

10 Anselm Strauss and Juliet Corbin, "Grounded Theory Methodology: An Overview,"in *Handbook of Qualitative Research*, ed. Norman K. Denzin and Yvonna S. Lincoln (Thousand Oaks, CA: Sage, 1994); Paolo Freire, *Pedagogy of the Oppressed* (New York: Bloomsbury, 1970, 2012); James Spradley and David McCurdy, *The Cultural Experience* (Chicago, IL: Science Research Associates, 1972).

11 Elsewhere I have argued that we should transcend the conventional dichotomy between ideas (thinking) and self-help (how-to). Theory shows us *how to* think about something

in a new way; in this sense theory is "how-to" think. Galen Cranz, *The Chair: Rethinking Culture, Body, and Design* (New York: W.W. Norton, 2000).

12 Norman K. Denzin, *Interpretive Ethnography: Ethnographic Practices for the 21st-century* (Thousand Oaks, CA: Sage, 1997).

13 In contrast, quantitative research treats phenomenon as objects that can be counted. For example, qualitative methods study buildings in terms of their aesthetic values and people's reactions to them, rather than in terms of their objective measurements. Of course, the distinction is not hard and fast, because, once described, feelings too can be counted. Note that qualitative is "subjective" rather than "objective," only in the sense of point of view; qualitative methods seek to be as "objective" as quantitative methods in the sense of being accurate and descriptive.

14 In the 2004 seminar on semantic ethnography one graduate student, a woman from Korea, felt that his opinionated style paradoxically stops dialogue with the reader because it dominates the reader.

15 See for example: Portigal, *Interviewing Users*; Salvador et al. "Design Ethnography"; Donna Kelly and Michael Gibbons, "Marketing Methodologies Ethnography," *Journal of Medical Marketing* 8, no. 279 (2008); Julien Cayla and Eric J. Arnould, "Ethnographic Stories for Learning,"*Journal of Marketing* 77, no. 4 (2013); Eric J. Arnould and Melanie Wallendorf, "Market-Oriented Ethnography," *Journal of Marketing Research* 31 (1994).

16 A blog called anthrodesign.com is an online discussion forum on the role of applied anthropology in design, and it has a global following (in particular in the UK, the US, Hong Kong and Singapore).

Part 1

The ethnographic design project

1 Introduction to design ethnography

1.1 The responsibility of the designer

The built environment affects people. People look at, drive by, walk through, and clean buildings. They rest, work, study, meet others, learn, and buy things in them. They take away ideas about proper ways to do those things from the cues architects use in buildings and landscapes. These ***cues*** tell us where and how to move: sit over here; never run in church; jump and run in the gym. How do we know these things? By the shape of and relationship between spaces, not just by words, letters, or diagrams.[1] Not only do buildings influence behavior, but also they carry ***symbolic meanings***. For example, columns can signal that a place is stately. Other cues signal glamour or hominess. People spend most of their lives in buildings, so architects, developers, and builders have a special opportunity to think carefully about how their work will influence people's behaviors now and in the future. This book offers a way to help design professionals create buildings that respond to people's practical needs and wants and that are artistic, creative, and delightful as well. Additionally, it helps social scientists understand the social significance of buildings.

Buildings, spaces, and objects should be designed and evaluated based on a deep understanding of ***cultural practice***. Cultural practice is defined as the information and ideas people use to guide their everyday behavior. Designers' understanding of how people use and conceive of their physical environment will help them design environments that resonate with cultural practices. In the words of one architecture student, "[T]he role of the designer is not to interpret what he himself deems important and exciting into physical sculptures, but rather, listen to the world view of the users . . . and to translate . . . the needs and passions of the users into physical solutions."[2] Some of the most famous designers have incorporated information about users into their designs: Frank Lloyd Wright and Alvar Aalto relied on a close observation of the symbolic life and movements of people for whom they imagined their designs, and Richard Neutra used questionnaires that detailed users' perspectives.

Ethnosemantic methods allow designers to fulfill their professional responsibility to users and, at the same time, to feel fulfilled creatively. The ultimate purpose of design ethnography is to inspire designers to respond to users, and the immediate goal of this workbook is two-fold: first to alert practitioners to the need for a new kind of architectural (and other kinds of environmental) programming, based in part on users' assessments of their prior experience with buildings, and then to guide beginners in undertaking an ethnographic research project to enable them to develop skills in collecting and responding to user data.

BOX 1.1: ETHNOGRAPHY AND NEW MODELS FOR ARCHITECTURAL CRITICISM AND PRACTICE

In a recent article, Nancy Levinson, Editor of *Places*, problematizes the role of the architectural critic, which she notes increasingly has taken on an art-critique model and, in so doing, has led to significant implications for the architecture profession—as well as its clients (those of us who occupy buildings). This model "tends to view works of architecture almost entirely as objects and hardly at all as environments" and in so doing preferences formal qualities over experience and aesthetics over function. In short, architectural criticism often is about "how a building *looks* more than how it *works.*"

Levinson continues by noting that a further limitation of this art-critique model is its investment in—and perpetuation of—what she terms the "boring star system" in which "critical validation leads to major commissions which in turn lead to more critical validation . . . creating an ever-constricting favored circle." This self-perpetuating, closed circle is all the more problematic given the limited voices and points of view it allows within its reach.

Finally, the object-focused, star-driven facets of the architectural profession have created "the global critic, the critic with the world beat" who flies from country to country, "wherever the newest icon or star is being born."

Though we want our critics to be well-traveled—after all, Levinson notes, seeing other places helps us understand those we live in all the better—we must ask "how . . . a critic [can] attain deep experience and comprehensive knowledge in a global field" including the connections to place, culture, and experience that are so essential for not only good architecture but good criticism as well.

Ultimately, Levinson concludes by suggesting that critics could develop specialty points of view from which to assess buildings. Our specialty, the experience of those who use buildings—as individuals, groups, institutions, and cultures—does take time; yet our careful work deserves a broad audience, not only among academic and professional circles, but for the general public as well, the people—sometimes called the nonpaying clients—who experience the building either as an occupant, a passer-by, or a neighbor.

Doing so can bring more—and diverse—view points into architectural discourse, reinforce the value of experience and culture in design, and change the profession of criticism and the practice of architecture.

Source: Nancy Levinson. "Critical Beats." *Places* (March 6, 2010). http://places.designobserver.com/feature/critical-beats/12948/.

1.2 Introduction to semantic ethnography

In this endeavor, we borrow from ***ethnography***, a research method used in cultural anthropology and sometimes in sociology, education, and business. Ethnography's main objective is the description of culture. Literally, ethnography means describing (graphing) people (ethno).[3] In general, ethnographers have been concerned with understanding how societies or cultural groups live, communicate, and conceive of the world. The main goal of ethnographic research is to be able to describe the culture of societies or cultural groups as an interrelated system of meanings from the point of view of those living in it; in other words, to articulate their implicit theory (rather than bring a formal theory to a social situation).

Though researchers and designers can utilize any number of methods to gain information about users—introspection, observation, surveys, interviews, census data, and participant observation—we see a variation of ethnography called semantic ethnography as most helpful for the jargon-filled world of design because it emphasizes meaning. [4] Based on verbal descriptions obtained through interviews, semantic ethnographic research puts the focus on a group's *learned* knowledge and how that group uses this knowledge to influence behavior. Semantic ethnography emphasizes how members inside the group experience culture. In addition to describing *what* a person is doing, semantic ethnography also asks *why* a person is doing something, and then *what* that action *means* in the group's larger system of meanings. As researcher, programmer, and designer you get to learn how the culture makes meaning for itself; this is the insider's point of view.

Over time with study you come to see a group as an insider sees it; thus, ethnographic research allows you to enter the world of an unfamiliar group. If, along the way, you become part of the scene you are studying, where you begin to see things as an insider yourself, then you have become what anthropologists call a participant observer. This term reflects a tradition within anthropology. Ethnographers—think of Margaret Mead, for example—spend months, even years "in the field" observing the behavior of the members of a culture, joining in daily routines, listening to stories and conversation, and recording their own interpretations. Because the participant observation method is so time-consuming, we have developed a method for using ethnographic principles in design that is more time-efficient, better adapted to the constraints of contemporary design practice, and focused on the social intentions built into the physical environment.

This book provides a distinctive version of ethnography for design students and practicing professionals to learn about people and their relationship to the built environment. Both students and seasoned professionals can use these skills. The skills you develop in ethnographic research are simple and useful in many situations ranging from redesigning an existing home to creating an entirely new setting for a corporate client. Ethnography can uncover both physical and conceptual problems within existing building conditions. We do not use checklists or surveys to anticipate "occupant satisfaction" or "user needs," because these methods do not fit well with the creative process: these are better used after a building has been built. We see ethnography as a key part of the creative process of design because it can happen at the same time as a designer develops a concept from initial idea to actual place.[5]

1.3 Ethnography in the design of places: programming and evaluation

The primary applications of ethnography to planning and design are ***programming*** and ***evaluation***. Programming begins at the initial stages of a project when the designers are determining the purpose of the building. Sanjoy Mazumdar notes that architectural programming arose in the 1960s in response to a "user needs gap," the disconnection between the needs of a paying client and the final users. He defines programming as: "A set of activities introduced into the design process [including] the description of the needs [and] wants of the occupants through the systematic and comprehensive collection and analyses of data [and] the specification of goals, objectives, and performance criteria."[6]

Mazumdar continues that the goals of programming include the development of "goal-oriented architecture" in which evidence—in other words, the data collected about users—forms the basis of design. In this way, programming is informed by a robust collection of data about user activities, needs, and interests, and ethnographic methods have been recognized by a number of fields beyond and including architecture as instrumental to that end.

A program can be explicit—as is the case with most commercial projects, which call for specific sizes and arrangements of interior spaces. For example, a hospital may require a certain number of treatment and examination rooms along with many other requirements. Other times, a program is implicit—as is the case with a contract for a house or a park.[7] In these cases, the overall purpose is known when the client comes to the architect, but further definition is required. Sometimes, the purpose of the project itself is challenged or slightly modified, or, upon closer examination, unconscious agendas and higher visions are revealed. Mazumdar notes the importance of using cultural research to understand a group's values and preferences, how they see themselves, and any social issues, divisions, or boundaries therein.[8] Thus, your study might reveal conflicts and even go on to help resolve different conceptions of what the project could be and whom it should serve.

Design solutions are sometimes fixed prematurely and using this method might help dislodge that tendency. If you appreciate the importance of research in the programming phase of the research-and-design cycle you might be able to suspend design activity until you have as much information as possible. Or, at least you might redesign frequently as new information emerges.

Evaluation research occurs after the building has been built and occupied in order to see how well the designer and client realized their intentions. What is learned can be used to plan remodels and inform the next building project as part of organizational learning.[9] Ideally, programming and evaluation research should be viewed as part of the design process, in an evolving cycle. We think *every* building should be evaluated so that the next time a similar building is designed it can be modified and refined in light of what was learned from past experience. Among other benefits, this approach could save millions of taxpayer dollars. Take, for example, the case of high-school design. Each year, governments spend large amounts on the construction of new high schools, but without regular evaluations going into data banks available to designers, design flaws are constantly repeated and leave their marks on generations of high-school students.[10] Ethnography is a user-oriented way to find out how buildings have been experienced in practice. Ideally, researchers and designers use this information to make improvements when programming the next building of a similar type.

1.4 The value of fieldwork and semantic analysis

The main idea behind design ethnography is to learn how to listen actively to the language of clients and users. Listening deeply for the structure underlying people's vocabulary will help you to see their world with new eyes. You may see design implications in the way people organize their world mentally.

In addition to the value of verbal descriptions, the physical scene is obviously important; thus, interviewing in the physical setting is ideal. Doing research at the site itself—"in the field," in the terms of anthropology—is called ***fieldwork***. Fieldwork gives you direct experience with the actual sites and practices of a particular group, giving you far better comprehension of the totality of experience than relying on strictly verbal or printed information.

Many students have found that doing fieldwork is an opportunity to get off their drafting stools in studio, away from the computer screen, into the material and social reality of the world for which they will be designing. Design ethnography takes students into places that they probably would not have encountered—or at least studied critically. We have seen insightful redesigns based on ethnographic research of local bars, temples, jails, dog shows, nail salons, wrestling venues, newspaper offices, ecological nongovernmental organizations, or scout troop meetings. Our students have volunteered to cook for a Sunday morning macrobiotic brunch, and joined the board members of a Montessori preschool.

Studying real places also provides a greater understanding of the theoretical relationship between people and the built environment. For example, concepts like privacy and territoriality, basic concepts in person–environment studies, emerge as common themes in many ethnographies. If you spend a few days, weeks, or months talking to customers of a local soup kitchen, you will have a better notion of territoriality and the problems and privacy needs of homeless and low-income people. If you describe the culture of a sixth grade classroom, you will bring back a wealth of information about learning theory, philosophy of education, and the sociology of schools for those designing learning environments. Such first-hand cultural investigation helps increase awareness of how design relates to social life and helps you understand people from different lifestyles and cultural backgrounds.

Despite these numerous values of fieldwork, you will not always be able to visit the site of a new commission. In this case, architectural ethnography, based on language, can still help you design in a way that responds to the cultural categories and distinctions held by the users. The most important advantage of the method is that off-site interviews—even those conducted in a sterile office—can become deeply informative. When projects are located far away, the informant's cultural knowledge could be acquired through a series of interviews and other exchanges via the Internet, fax, video, telephone, or Skype. While it is better to be physically present in the field, this is not always possible. If you cannot be in the field, then you can ask the insider to describe activities and events and thereby discover his cultural knowledge. You do not have to be a frequent business traveler yourself to find out about the frustration that travelers face in a foreign airport; simply listen to them.

Sometimes, however, even interviews may not be possible. If you are designing something that is radically new and innovative, there may not be a person to interview. In this situation, look to similar situations. If you are designing a new alternative to an established food bank, you might interview people who practice subsistence agriculture. If you are designing a new kind of doghouse, you might look online for people who have customized existing doghouses or built their own. If you are in a situation where privacy is a concern, or it is financially or logistically impossible to travel to the site of your project, novels, local magazines, and local websites can also provide insight into the insider's interpretation of a place. Even if you have an excellent informant, it's not a bad idea to consult these other sources. What you learn through literary sources and magazines will often contrast strongly with—or be a timely complement to—academic or expert sources.

One can also use the ethnographic mindset for doing historical architectural analysis. Recall from the Preface Box 0.1 that I diagrammed the language of nineteenth-century park planners to discover that for them "pleasure" was a term that fell midway between "amusement" and "didactic" and in their minds was preferable to either of the two extremes. Thus, we learn that pleasure was not a private sensation as we might think today, but rather an active social goal.

One can also use semantic ethnography to shape design. A significant example was my contribution to Bernard Tschumi's winning scheme for Parc de La Villette in Paris. My careful reading of the language of the brief for the park competition alerted me to the idea that the people who wrote the program for the park competition were looking for ways to transcend the traditional dichotomies of art versus science, popular versus elite culture, mind versus body. Whereas other designers used a bisecting canal to separate these polar opposites, Tschumi used the canal as a seam to bring them together, and I helped reviewers appreciate that difference. Earlier, I also had helped a small architecture firm compete successfully against large firms with track records of designing gymnasia by parsing the difference between recreation and leisure.

Further, the ethnographic approach improves one's skills in social organizing, including business. Past students, now colleagues, have reported using the method in sales; listening to the way customers think about their houses helped one person produce the highest volume of sales in a green building supply store in Portland, Oregon. Another student from New Jersey became an officer in the Zen Buddhist community in San Francisco and used these techniques to listen to everyone in her community in order to organize and lead well.

Finally, understanding others—through direct observation, semantic ethnographic interviewing, or reading—gives you a new awareness of your *own* values and the many implicit cultural premises that influence your design. This method will help you overcome the cultural biases that are invisible to you in your own design work, and thereby also help you become a more reflective and creative designer.

BOX 1.2: THE POWER OF SPATIAL AND SOCIAL ANALYSIS

As a graduate student in the Sociology Department at the University of Chicago I specialized in "the social use of space," a new field I was allowed to define for my Ph.D. exams. In preparing for them I noticed that the classics in sociology assume but leave out any explicit discussion of space. Few of the founding theorists—Max Weber, Émile Durkheim, Karl Marx—even mentioned the role of space in social life, and the next generation—Talcott Parsons, Edward Shils, Robert Merton—forgot about space and place altogether, even though actions presumably occurred in physical settings. Because they were generalizing beyond particular places their lack of attention to physical context was understandable. However, the classics in sociological field studies made a point of attending to the local and the particular, so why were the physical settings so thinly described? William F. Whyte's *Street Corner Society* (1943) even has a place type in the title, but little description of those street corners or clubhouses or any other setting can be found in that study. Similarly, Elliot Liebow's *Tally's Corner* (1966) is surprisingly devoid of physical variables in the analysis of how chronically underemployed men manage their lives.

Today, decades later, I am still surprised how few sociologists have included the physical world in their work.[1] By and large, the analysis of the social meaning of architecture has remained the domain of architectural historians, archaeologists, geographers, and environmental psychologists. After a long career in this field, variously called ***person–environment relations***, environmental design research, environment–behavior studies, and the social use of space, I want to invite social researchers to take a look at the power of physical and spatial analysis.

To begin, note that **architecture and space are treated almost synonymously** here because buildings create spaces; the two are inseparable. A solid cube is not a building; humans cannot inhabit a building that does not have empty space. And, of course, this space is not empty, socially speaking. It is filled with meaning, intention, and expectation. The size, shape, proportion, surfaces of walls, and the openings within them provide the cues to meaning and intentions about the use of each space. The built environment is a medium for communication through which social messages travel. Most of these architectural messages are silent, only occasionally needing signs, recorded messages, or hosts. Nonverbal communication is particularly powerful because it tells us where to go and what to do silently, below the level of conscious awareness. Subcortical persuasion is famously powerful. Because we are physical beings, we respond to the physical environment and its directives at deep levels in the brain.

The sheer size of a designed environment dictates the number of people that can be accommodated in a place, and so shapes experience. A nook for two creates a very different experience than a big warehouse for crowds of people.

The designed environment frames social interaction. Not only does it provide shelter and structure, but also it sets up the kinds of relationships that one can expect. It can connect people or separate them. Structures and places help define social groups, including families and workgroups, through homes and offices, classrooms, lecture halls, meeting halls, recreational groups, polling places.[2] Urban streets and buildings delineate boundaries of neighborhoods, both informally and formally (as in census tracks).

The physical environment influences emotional contact with others. Thereby, it has direct effects on alienation, crime, fear, and safety. For example, placing parking lots in front versus in back of the store or restaurant, coupled with lighting, influences how much fear people have, especially women alone in the dark. Whether or not you feel you can leave your house alone at night depends a lot on the design of the neighborhood.[3]

As an impediment or barrier **the physical environment creates boundaries between what is possible and not possible.** It shapes access and inaccessibility. Consequently, the physical environment is directly related to power because the control of space and territory create and reflect hierarchy. Powerful groups create and control spaces, and, conversely, spaces produce power for their users.

Buildings and landscapes reveal social history. Physical structure is data about social relations, a fact that is the basis of archaeology. For example, studying servants' quarters in historic homes allows us to understand early English

Colonial life in America. The physical environment is embodied data, ossified social relationships, especially revealing regarding class.

The physical environment can be studied for epidemiological purposes. For example, John Snow discovered the source of cholera in London by mapping the incidents of the disease and taking the pump handle off the pump to confirm that contaminated water at a particular well was the problem.[4]

The distribution of physical structures creates and exposes economic relationships and issues of environmental justice.[5] Where the polluting activities in a community are concentrated usually correlates with socioeconomic class, with poor people bearing a disproportionate share of the burden of environmental contamination. Resource distribution similarly correlates with socioeconomic class: for example, the term "food deserts" refers to areas—often where poor people reside—that are underserved by grocery stores, markets, and other places where healthy (and affordable) food can be purchased.

Finally, **the physical environment that humans build is important in regard to sustainability.** The embodied energy in building materials is an ecological issue, and, even more significantly, the amount of energy required to operate buildings is responsible for anywhere from one-third to one-half of all the energy consumed nationally. And, human behavior—regulation of windows, thermostats, and the like—accounts for about half of that. How and where we site facilities directly affects energy consumption. For example, how far away the grocery store is and whether or not there are bike lanes along nearby roads directly affects the amount of gasoline used. Recycling, composting—in fact our very understanding of waste—all depend on integrating places for these activities into the rounds of everyday life. What if we changed our view of trash from waste to simply material out of place?[6]

Social scientists need to appreciate that the designers, especially architects, aspire to synthesize several goals: structural soundness, social purpose, aesthetic satisfaction, and monetary profit. Not surprisingly, some focus more on one or two of the goals at the expense of the others. Some architects are more interested in form than in users. Many have no contact with the future users of their buildings and, consequently, such buildings were designed without deep knowledge of the ways future inhabitants will use the building. Yet those people will have to deal with design decisions for years to come. Technological and cultural change makes designing for the future risky, but even in the present designers are not always willing or able to take the point of view of ordinary users into account. Using our ethnographic approach to design may make it easier to do so.

Notes

1 One recent article is Thomas F. Gieryn, "A Space for Place in Sociology," *Annual Review of Sociology* 26 (2000): 463–96. Earlier, Robert Gutman and Magali Sarfati-Larson have each studied the architecture profession; Suzanne Keller and David Brain have studied new towns and new urbanism, respectively; Ron Smith has applied symbolic interactionism to architectural and planning issues; Harvey Moloch has studied industrial design; sociologist and urban planner Manuel Castells has considered the space of flows (*The Informational City: Information Technology, Economic Restructuring, and the Urban–Regional Process*, Oxford: Basil-Blackwell, 1989); David Halle (*Inside Culture: Art and Class in the American Home*, Chicago, IL: University of Chicago Press, 1993) studied the way art is displayed in homes; Mihali Csikzentmihali and Eugene Rochberg-Halton (*The Meaning of Things: Domestic Symbols and the Self*, Cambridge: Cambridge University Press, 1981) studied the meaning of objects in the home; Stuart Chapin used

mantelpiece display as an indicator of socioeconomic status (SES), followed up by Ed Laumann; Thorsten Veblen critiqued art and architecture as status symbols. In the several books by social psychologist Robert Sommer, one of the first environmental psychologists, I found help in thinking about the practical applications of social knowledge to architectural design. Anthropologist E. T. Hall was a seminal thinker about the role of space in interpersonal relationships and culture.

Leonardo Chiesi made a similar observation about many sociologists having forgotten space in *Il Doppio Espazio dell'architettura: Ricerca sociologica e progettazione* (Naples, Italy: Liguori Editions, 2010).

2 In the Richards Medical Building at the University of Pennsylvania, Louis Kahn thought that because scientists are part of a "scientific community" he would express this architecturally by creating open laboratories. However, when architectural sociologist Robert Gutman studied this building he observed that the scientists put up walls between their individual labs. Gutman learned that scientists work privately even if they publish their work for a larger scientific community. Perceptive interviewing and direct observation might have alerted Kahn to the difference between the need for privacy while actually doing scientific work and the need to share with a larger group by publishing the results of scientific work later. (Robert Gutman, Ed., *People and Buildings*, New York: Basic Books, 1972).

3 Research on the topic of public housing projects has been extrapolated to correcting the flaws of large-scale designs. Oscar Newman's research set a high standard for research that was used to shape policy regarding public housing and high-density housing more generally. Housing in Pruitt-Igoe in St. Louis is infamous in architectural history because it was intentionally demolished even though it originally won design awards. It was considered unsuitable for family life, and spaces that were intended to be common public spaces became sites for crime. Roger Montgomery ("Pruitt-Igoe: Policy Failure or Societal Symptom," 1985) and Katharine Bristol ("The Pruitt-Igoe Myth," *Journal of Architectural Education*, 1991) have argued that the building design was unfairly blamed for other larger social problems, specifically the fact that the building had been designed for nuclear families but ended up housing a disproportionate share of single-parent families. Research cannot anticipate last-minute changes in social policy.

4 Scott Crosier, "John Snow: The London Cholera Epidemic of 1854" (Center for Spatially Integrated Social Science, n.d.).

5 Sarah Lopez's study of "remittance homes" in Mexico revealed—in physical form—complex economic transactions both at the scale of multinational relationships and family members who moved between the US and Mexico to work and remit payments to families back home (Sarah Lopez, "The Remittance House," *Buildings and Landscapes* 17, no. 2 (2010)).

6 Cranz, Galen, keynote address, Environmental Design Research Association conference, Chicago, 1993.

1.5 Ethnography as an agent of change

If you want to facilitate social change through design, what can you do? First, your proposals are more likely to be built if they are supported by research. Proposals that emerge from systematic efforts to understand allow you to narrate your proposed design as the intelligent result of your analysis.

Second, ethnographic research in particular has the additional benefit of allowing designers access to the underlying mental structures of the peoples for whom they design. In general, people accept change more readily when the change is tied to something they already know or do. Therefore, showing how well your proposal matches up with how people are already using a particular place increases the likelihood of your final proposal being acted upon.

While you will likely be able to influence changes in behavior in the places that you design, it is not reasonable to expect that your ethnographic description of a small part of the environment will lead directly to changes in public policy. You *can* expect your study to make changes in how you will design that place. On the basis of your study you might formulate a hypothesis about how *other* such places could benefit. For example, one student researcher at a quick service restaurant observed the difficulty and the potential for injury a deep food prep counter caused, a finding which could be a problem in other such restaurants.[11] Thus, your study could be the beginning point for further qualitative or quantitative research with a larger sample of people who work at such restaurants, with possible improvements in design for employee health.

1.6 Limits of the ethnographic method

Despite its many advantages the ethnographic method has limits, including that it is time consuming. David McCurdy, one of the chief advocates of semantic ethnography, reports on some of the drawbacks of the method: "few anthropologists use the approach these days, claiming it is too structured and rigid, that it ignores behavioral observation and other field methods, and is limited to the discovery of ideal (rather than 'down to earth') culture." He thinks "they are wrong, especially because its structured approach is easier for students to understand and follow." He continues, "For students, however, it has been a successful way to teach what culture is and an appreciation for cross-cultural differences and misunderstanding."

Of interest to us in architecture and urbanism, McCurdy adds that this approach provides "a basis from which to add other field techniques as researchers pursue further fieldwork." Indeed, in my decades of experience teaching this approach, my teaching assistants and I have added other techniques to complement the user's understanding of a place. In our architecture and urban design research, we have added observation and literature reviews to complement the insider's view with outsiders' views.[12]

McCurdy reports that over the last few decades "a majority of users appear to be from other social science and human-centered disciplines. The structured nature of ethnosemantics and what it teaches about the importance of culture and cross-cultural misunderstanding seem to work for professionals outside of anthropology." Indeed, as architects, urban designers, and planners we confirm the value of the approach for environmental design. Understanding how users conceive of their lifeworlds helps our professions understand social life and literally embrace it with built form.

Social research over the decades has focused on research problems, not cultural discovery. McCurdy comments, "anthropologists of my and previous generations, conducted discovery research. We went to the field for years at a time to record whole cultures. We practiced participant observation. Problems and answers emerged from the data instead of limiting it. This is clearly not so today, as such studies are nearly impossible to do and as concerns over social justice and other problems focus research design. Instead of the fairly unstructured participatory field method of old, they use directed questions, focus groups, life histories, and observation as field methods." My architecture colleague Eleftherios Pavlides is adamant about the importance of discovery science in environmental design—in part because society changes so much that designers always have to be discovering new patterns, not just testing to see if older hypotheses about prior patterns are still true.[13]

McCurdy acknowledges yet another "reason many anthropologists fail to use ethnosemantics is their training. I and everyone I know who teaches with ethnosemantics had to learn the method by doing it ourselves and it usually took someone who already knew about the approach to teach us. Few learned the method in graduate school.

Learning takes time and commitment and . . . few wish to make the investment." We agree that few professionals can make the commitment to extensive fieldwork, but that is exactly why we think this approach to active, purely semantic listening can work for design professionals and social planners, even if they are not in the field but rather in an office interviewing others.[14] This text shares our decades of experience with the approach in order to encourage others to take advantage of its way of being objective about the subjective worlds in which people live.

Finally, let it be said that this is not the only way to study people's experience of the environment. Nonverbal experience is significant in our responses to the environment, and in this regard introspection, phenomenology, and somatics may be useful approaches, especially at the early stages of research about new experiences.[15] When one can describe an experience well for oneself, the next step is to learn how one's own experience compares and contrasts with others, and here again semantic ethnography becomes useful.

1.7 Chapter summary

The ethnographic method highlights the built environment as an active part of culture. People do not simply inhabit buildings and places; we change and modify them over time, and different people see different buildings in different ways. For some, a skyscraper is a symbol of freedom and possibility; for others, a symbol of oppression and control. Some see the home as a place of refuge from work, and others see the home as a place of backbreaking labor. The meanings we ascribe to the places we inhabit are always changing and always contingent on our position in society. In Chapter 3, we will examine the concept of culture in our complex society and its role in the design process, in order to set the stage for an ethnographic design project, introduced in Chapter 2.

BOX 1.3: EVIDENCE-BASED DESIGN: CREATING A COMPELLING NARRATIVE AND SUCCESSFUL DESIGN

The assertion that design proposals based on research are more likely to be built than those without a similar case to make assumes two conditions: first, that the evidence itself is relevant and robust; second, that the way the evidence is presented is compelling and creates a strong case. Through the ethnographic process described in this book, you will have the opportunity to present your design to a larger, *public* audience through the creation of a poster (or video). The goal of this poster is to convey the vision and logic of your proposed design to an audience that may not be familiar with your site, the needs of users, or the outcomes of your research. To both prepare for this milestone and think critically about the need to both collect data and convey high-quality results, we encourage you to look at the sample posters in the back of this text and assess the quality of data and presentation of evidence of each.

Ask yourself:

- Is the rationale for design made clear to someone unfamiliar with the site?
- Does the rationale make sense? Am I convinced by the author's argument? Why?
- What improvements could be made to articulate the rationale to a public audience better? To users of the site?

1. 8 Chapter review: main ideas

- Buildings should be designed based on a deep understanding of cultural practice (1.1).
- Ethnography's main objective is the description of culture. Literally, ethnography means describing (graphing) people (ethno) (1.2).
- The primary applications of ethnography to planning and design are programming and evaluation (1.3).
- Ideally semantic ethnography includes fieldwork, but if fieldwork is impossible one can still benefit from the careful asking and active listening skills of semantic ethnography (1.4).
- Your ethnographic study might reveal conflicts between the explicit and implicit program of a site and even go on to help resolve different conceptions of what the project could be and whom it should serve (1.5).

Notes

1 For example, in the temporary surge quarters of the College of Environmental Design (CED) on the UC Berkeley campus a single entrance to three departments framed a reception-like desk. It actually belonged to the Architecture Department but was often misread as the information desk for the CED as a whole because of the power of architectural configuration. Official signs hung from the ceiling in order to differentiate each department, but they were so small that they were barely visible. Sometimes unofficial signs were taped to the official ones, but neither the official nor the unofficial signs were adequate to orient newcomers. Architectural form (in this case, entry-door-reception desk) implicitly communicated more strongly than the explicit labels on signs. This misreading of the architecture reception desk underscores the power of architectural configuration.

2 Jeff Inaba, "An Architectural Redesign Based on Ethnographic Research" (1982).

3 Ethnography differs from ethnology, which involves more theory, hence the "logic" suffix.

4 Ethnography presumes and builds on introspection; thus, personal reflection is a necessary part of the ethnographic process though insufficient if used on its own for the same purpose.

5 In *Inquiry by Design,* John Zeisel demonstrates how research and design, both iterative processes, can work synergistically to promote collaborative, creative solutions. In this way, ethnographic research is a method to formulate a design hypothesis, and subsequent cycles of research and design serve, then, as means to test and refine your ideas. See John Zeisel, *Inquiry by Design: Environment/Behavior/Neuroscience in Architecture, Interiors, Landscape, and Planning.* Revised Edition (New York, W.W. Norton, 1981, 2006).

6 Sanjoy Mazumdar, "How Programming Can Become Counterproductive: An Analysis of Approaches to Programming," *Journal of Environmental Psychology* 12 (1992): 65.

7 Ibid.

8 Ibid.

9 Craig Zimring and Thierry Rosenheck, "Post-Occupancy Evaluations and Organizational Learning," in *Learning from Our Buildings: A State-of-the-Practice Summary of Post-Occupancy Evaluation* (Washington, DC: National Academies Press, 2002).

10 Janice Marie Bissell, "Teachers' Construction of Space and Place: A Study of School

Architectural Design as a Context of Secondary School Teachers' Work," Ph.D. dissertation, University of California, Berkeley, 2002.

11 Andrew Doan, "Ethnography Study of a Campus Café at UC Berkeley" (Fall 2006).

12 David McCurdy, email message to author, December 13, 2012.

13 Eleftherios Pavlides and Galen Cranz, "Three Theoretical Assumptions Needed to Create Useful Applied Social Science Research for Architecture," *International Journal of Interdisciplinary Social Sciences* 4, no. 10 (2009): 191–201.

14 For those who would like to learn more about the antecedents of this approach, an early example of an ethnosemantic ethnography is Spradley, *You Owe Yourself A Drunk* (1970), now a classic. Spradley also edited a reader, *Cognitive Anthropology*, and co-wrote with Brenda Mann, *The Cocktail Waitress* (1975). A more formal presentation of ethnosemantics was written by Oswald Werner, and an associate and Spradley also published *The Ethnographic Interview* (1979). According to David McCurdy, much of what he published in that book is incorporated in the second edition of *The Cultural Experience*.

15 In the realm of environmental design David Seamon has written consistently about phenomenology and edits a newsletter: *Architectural and Environmental Phenomenology Newsletter* (Manhattan: Kansas State University) Cumulative Index (Volumes 1–25, 1990–2015).

2 The ethnographic design project

A step-by-step overview

2.1 Project description overview

This chapter is designed to help you set up procedures for carrying out your ethnographic study. This project framework was developed for (and is directed to) students enrolled in a course that teaches the principles of ethnography and space; however, we also see the following steps as having value for those in other disciplines and for those in office practice.

General guidelines and project milestones are listed in Table 2.1. The project is divided into several parts intended to break the process into "bite-size" pieces. Once you have completed and sought feedback on all the parts, you will combine all of the parts into an edited, coherent report. In Table 2.1 you might want to fill in your own schedule for each of the parts.

Table 2.1 Overview of ethnographic design project

Part 1: Research Proposal. *Identifying and observing a cultural setting*
Research method: observation *Summary of project components*: • The setting and why you selected it • Visual and written description of the physical space as is, including photos and architectural drawings • Initial redesign of the space based on your ***personal perspective*** (personal observation) • *See also:* Box 2.5: Ethnography Project Guidelines—Part 1: Research Proposal *Relevant textbook sections:* 2.1–2.11, Box 2.4: Skill Spotlight—Conducting behavioral observations
Part 2: Cultural Informant. *Selecting and interviewing an informant*
Research method: semantic interviews *Summary of project components*: • Your informant, how you selected him or her, and an assessment of your rapport • Brief summary of your first interview • Coding of the interview notes or transcription • *See also:* Box 4.1: Ethnography Project Guidelines—Part 2: Cultural Informant, Interview, and Coding the Interview

Table 2.1 (continued)

Relevant textbook sections: 4.1–4.10, Box 4.2: Skill Spotlight—Quick tip for quick note taking: diagram your notes

Part 3: Taxonomy. *Creating and organizing vocabulary lists into a taxonomic structure*

Research methods: analysis and visual presentation of semantic data

Summary of project components:
- A vocabulary list and definitions
- A series of diagrams, charts, or tables to create a taxonomy of cultural terms
- Additional insights to further describe terms and taxonomy
- *See also:* Box 5.1: Ethnography Project Guidelines—Part 3: Taxonomy

Relevant textbook sections: 5.1–5.9

Part 4: Literature Review. *Researching the etic perspective and linking findings to your project*

Research method: literature review

Summary of project components:
- Annotated bibliography including at least ten sources with annotations and analysis (*maximum two sources can be websites; others are required to be peer-reviewed journals or books*)
- Written analysis of emic, etic, and personal perspectives
- Summary of how the three perspectives compare and contrast
- *See also:* Box 6.2: Ethnography Project Guidelines—Part 4: Literature Review

Relevant textbook sections: 6.1–6.7, Box 6.1: Skill Spotlight—Conducting and writing a literature review

Part 5: Redesign. *Programming and redesigning space to reflect cultural knowledge*

Design method: evidence-based design

Summary of project components:
- Revised program described with words and images
- Plans, sections, perspectives (as needed) for your final redesign
- Vision of and rationale for your final redesign
- Resubmission of initial redesign
- Visual and verbal analysis of how your initial and final redesign and revised program differ and the extent to which each aligns with your informant's perspective
- *See also:* Box 7.2: Ethnography Project Guidelines—Part 5: Program Development and Site Redesign

Relevant textbook sections: 7.1–7.5, Box 7.1: Skill Spotlight—Concepts: operational definitions and translation into design

Sharing Results: *The Design Board and Final Report*

Visual Presentation. *Creating poster or video to communicate research and design outcomes to the public*

Design research method: visual presentation of information

Summary of project components:
- Display board (or 90-second video) summarizing your design process and the major influences on it

Table 2.1 (continued)

- Board must include reference to your informant's cultural knowledge, a description of your proposed redesign, and a brief description of your research and design processes
- *See also:* Box 9.1: Ethnography Project Guidelines—Visual Presentation

Relevant textbook section: 9.1–9.3

Final Written Report. *Edited report of entire research process and conclusions*

Research methods and outcomes: presenting findings, writing about a systematic research project, contributing to shared knowledge

Summary of project components:

- 15–20-page, comprehensive, edited version of all previous written reports and compilation of visual media to convey your research process and conclusions
- Sections include the ethnography project, ***data collection*** processes, and a reflection on the project and the contribution your report makes to existing literature and the future design of similar buildings
- *See also:* Box 8.1: Ethnography Project Guidelines—Final Report

Relevant textbook sections: 8.1–8.8

2.2 Planning your study

Although ethnographic fieldwork requires a significant time commitment, it can be done in the course of a few months. All of the sample ethnographic design projects presented in this manual were completed by students in the course of one four-month semester. At a minimum, plan to spend about two and a half hours each week conducting research. You are welcome to spend more time than this; in fact, many students have become actively involved in their cultural settings.

Ethnographic methods require a significant amount of time for data collection. Such a length of time ensures immersion in the micro-cultures studied and gives access to large amounts of data, making later analysis more complete. You cannot expect to understand the full range of your cultural environment without having spent months, or years, studying it closely. As this is an introductory ethnographic project, you must take a different approach. The limits on your time require you to narrow your project to a manageable size. Instead of studying all the micro-cultures of a particular place, examine one facet of its use, or one group that uses it, or one social space within the larger site. Later in this chapter we will discuss strategies to structure your study so that it can be completed within the time you have available.

You may consider joining with one or two others to be able to study a larger setting or institution, for example a high school. If each person selects a different informant representing a different role (administrator, maintenance staff, teacher, etc.) or several different teachers from several different classes, your group can conduct a wider study. This option also offers a way to study an organization from an American Cultures perspective, that is, to compare how the organization works from the point of view of Hispanic users, Chinese, African-American, Anglo-American, etc. Even so, each student will need to define his or her own scope of study.

BOX 2.1: NOTE ON SAMPLE ETHNOGRAPHIES

In Part 2 of this textbook we have included a number of ethnographic reports written by students in the course we have taught in past years. Though each has its strengths and weaknesses, collectively these reports provide instructive examples of how to define, describe, and (re)design sites to meet the needs of sited micro-cultures.

2.3 Objectivity

In everyday life almost everyone thinks like an ethnographer. We all more or less consciously study human behavior and describe what people know and do. Children often act like ethnographers: they ask questions to discover what other people believe, what they mean by the words they use, and which forms of behavior are appropriate. And they are able to report their findings to their friends.

While both the everyday citizen and the ethnographer examine their worlds and try to make sense of the social behavior around them, the ethnographer is more systematic in both the collection of data and its analysis. When the purpose of ethnography is its application to design, the ethnographer is more concerned with the spatial implications of different behaviors. Thus, you will want to obtain from your research data that is not only interesting, but also useful to inform your design.[1]

The ethnographer also attempts to reflect on objectivity and bias, trying to represent as accurately as possible the culture being studied and account for the effects of studying it. In her description of an individual's cultural knowledge, the ethnographer always works to preserve human dignity and avoid caricature or stereotype. Instead of saying, "these superstitious people believe in a strange force that says sleeping with the head pointing north will make them live longer," the ethnographer would rather say something like "these people believe in the existence of magnetic fields which can be either beneficial or detrimental for their health and arrange furniture in space accordingly." A major component of objective observation and analysis is to write things as they really are, rather than what the ethnographer believes to be happening. Description is important in every science, and the goal of objectivity is an important component of research in general, including ethnography.

Although objectivity is desirable, we acknowledge that it is not possible to be entirely objective. Even "scientific" research cannot avoid distortion by what we call interpretation, which leads to intentional or nonintentional selective data collection, observation, and later interpretation. Any researcher decides, perhaps unconsciously, that some facts are more important than others and so the problem of selective observation introduces distortion early in the process. Further, interpretation can become interwoven with the facts so that they are inseparable from them. For example, a single type of behavior could be described as either "hardheaded" or "a person with strong commitments to his/her beliefs." For example, in 2004 Teresa Heinz Kerry, wife of the Democratic candidate for President of the United States, reframed a "fact" about her personality. She said that she has been called "opinionated" and that she looks forward to the day when that same quality would be considered "articulate and well-informed" as it is with men. The especially difficult aspect of seeking objectivity is that people, including researchers, are not always aware of their own selective processes. Even wanting to be aware does not guarantee it—all the more reason to *continually* question your own assumptions and to ask others to identify potential bias in your work. This is particularly important in ethnography, which—as Spradley and McCurdy remind us—is an *interpretive act.*

2.4 Making up for lack of objectivity

Researchers can make up for their lack of objectivity. The first step is to recognize the problems of selective observation and interpretation and to be aware of one's own personal and cultural prejudices by being conscious of what may influence data gathering. We all have had a variety of personal experiences that influence what we see; feminist scholar Donna Haraway calls these *situated knowledges.*[2]

Consider, for example, a person who grew up in a high-rise apartment building. He has many vivid memories of the fear of taking the elevator alone up many stories, and of having been beaten up by older kids in some hidden corner of the grounds. After years of study, this person becomes an architect and seeks to study residential high-rises; he will undoubtedly be influenced by his own earlier experience living in a similar environment. If he were to study more particularly preteen kids in public housing, his personal experiences as a child would be even more influential. He would select and interpret their behavior through the filter of his own personal experience, highlighting those aspects that resonate with his own past and neglecting other possibly valuable ones that he would consider to be of lesser significance. A person who grew up in a rural area and goes to a city only occasionally may be confused by what city people call natural; for her a park is artificial and not at all like the nature she has observed in the forest with its rotting logs, fungi, and ferns. A person who grew up in the suburbs may feel apartment living is cramped, while a person used to urban life might see apartment life as convenient, efficient, and close to "the action."

Being aware of your own personal biases is central to doing fieldwork. If you are afraid of flying, describing the culture of flight attendants and their working environment might be difficult for you without selecting facts on the basis of your own anxiety. If you are vegetarian, it will influence your observation, interpretation, and redesign of a grocery store—you would be unlikely to give the meat display much importance. Almost *any* personal experience can result in distortion of the data. When you do fieldwork in an environment you know well from personal experience, the prejudices are often intensified. You may be more critical of the design of a high school than that of a nuclear research center, or vice versa.

Another basis for selective observation is ***ethnocentrism***, the deeply ingrained attitude that our own culture is superior to others. If you grew up in a small town in the central valley, a San Francisco Chinatown food market might appear crowded, messy, and disorienting to you. But if you grew up in Beijing, the same market might make you feel comforted, welcomed—even homesick. Your cultural background will always influence your perception of the environment and become a source of bias and distortion.

In order to avoid personal bias and ethnocentrism, or at least reduce their effect, most researchers employ a second means for enhancing their objectivity: they consciously select their data on the basis of theory. Researchers seldom simply go out to "gather the facts." Rather, researchers take with them an implicit theory of what is important. Having a theory does not guarantee freeing oneself from bias, however. Theories can be used unsystematically, outside of awareness, and include the personal and cultural biases of the investigator that we have discussed. Design theories can be misused in these same ways and more: they are often used to present value judgments as objective facts. What we consider "well-designed" and as having aesthetic value is largely influenced by our education and by the canons established by the design profession at a particular time in history. A small-town diner considered to be "homey" by its owners may appear insignificantly quaint, "kitsch," or lacking design quality to a recently graduated architect. At the same time, Venturi, Rauch, Scott-Brown, and their postmodern followers may have praised it for its ordinariness, lack of pretension, and clear, bold communication.

Despite these pitfalls and ambiguities, researchers can use architectural concerns and theories to guide their research questions and the selection of data. For example, research on gender in rural Greece started by an architect and anthropologist team first described the homes in the village according to the criteria of interest to architects when they do measured drawings. Even though they started out with a theory that privileged material artifacts, they did eventually ask who was responsible—men or women—for each of the architectural features they had recorded. This line of questioning led the researchers to other aspects that had social and cultural significance for the inhabitants.[3] However, our approach to objectivity is different. We will not start out from previously established theories or interests, but rather build our understanding from how our informants see their worlds. For us, this is objective.

2.5 Taking notes

Before you visit your site for the first time as a part of this project, you should acquire a notebook or journal for use in recording information about the site.[4] You should not pre-edit what you put in the journal: you will never have to show it to anyone else, so you can always edit or redact its contents later for inclusion in your project report.

Creating the journal is a chance to put your creative energies to work. We place only one requirement on the journal: it should have a three-part division to reflect the three parts of the assignment (personal, emic, and etic). It could be as simple as buying a binder and three different colors of paper or pasting tabs into a pre-bound notebook.

2.6 Selecting a sited micro-culture

One of the most crucial steps in the ethnographic project is choosing the sited micro-culture you will study and redesign. You have many choices among settings in which to conduct your fieldwork. How do you select the right one for you? This choice is actually easily made: if you give yourself a little time to explore the different options, you are likely to end up having to choose between several appealing possibilities. A good way to start is by looking at your own natural inclinations.

For example, if you have always been crazy about horses, you might want to study the cultural knowledge of a riding teacher at a stable. Or perhaps you've dreamed of being a stand-up comedian, and would enjoy studying a local comedy club. Brainstorm a list of all possible projects. One of the best places to look is the Yellow Pages. (For now, libraries still have physical copies of these.) Or try Googling topics of interest to you.

Recall the times you've thought "*I wonder what this is like . . .*" or "*that sounds so strange*" to consider places where you find the culture especially fascinating or compelling, to identify place-based social concerns that you may want to address—an animal shelter, recycling centers, hospices—or to explore specific architectural settings such as an air traffic control tower or an oil refinery. Based on your own curiosity, you should be able to generate a list of potential study locations, each of which you find interesting. In Box 2.3 is a partial list of social situations and sited micro-cultures that are common to many urban settings.[5]

A social situation generally includes more than one sited micro-culture. In design terms, this means that a single room or building has different sets of user groups, each having its own specific cultural requirements. Consequently, designing to make the space functional and responsive to the patterns of all users would require an ethnographic study of *each* of the main sited micro-cultures or user groups. Differences,

BOX 2.2: ETHNOGRAPHY PROJECT GUIDELINES

Project Overview

This semester-long assignment is organized into seven parts and culminates with a final report; the structure of the project is intended to simulate the actual research and design processes you would use as a professional architect. Additionally, working in phases allows you to build upon the feedback you will receive from your instructor and classmates and gives you the opportunity to develop your knowledge about the cultural setting you are studying and think in depth about a culturally responsive architectural program and design. Throughout this book you will find detailed descriptions of each stage of the project (look for the boxes titled "Ethnography Project Guidelines") as well as a list of project criteria to help you reflect on and assess your work prior to submitting it to your instructor for grading. You should also refer to Table 2.1 Overview of Ethnographic Design Project for a quick, at-a-glance summary of the major project milestones.

Sample Checklist: *getting started*

- Notebook divided into three sections: personal, emic (inside), etic (outside).
- Read Chapters 1–3 of *Ethnography for Designers.*
- Make plans to visit your proposed site.
- Begin thinking about how you might locate and introduce yourself to an informant.

perhaps even among micro-cultures, may arise; in this case, the architect's job is to come up with solutions that will satisfy the greater number of users or the most important or vulnerable users. For the purpose of the present exercise, most students only have time to conduct one ethnographic study and to describe the culture of one particular user group. Consequently, you only have a partial understanding of the whole social situation when you set to redesign it. Those working in teams and studying different micro-cultures within a single social situation have the advantage of being able to pool all your knowledge to gain understanding of the full situation before proceeding to redesign.

BOX 2.3: LIST OF POTENTIAL STUDY LOCATIONS

AIR TRAFFIC CONTROL TOWER

AMBULANCE SERVICE
- Drivers
- Attendants

ART GALLERY

ATHLETIC TEAMS
- Coaches
- Players
- Assistants
- Spectators

BANK
- Tellers
- President

BAR
- Bartenders
- Waiters/waitresses
- Customers
- Bouncers

BARBERSHOP
- Barbers
- Customers

BEAUTY SHOP
- Hairdressers
- Manicurists
- Customers

BOOKSTORE
- Salespersons
- Customers

BOTANICAL GARDEN
- Gardeners
- Botanists
- Visitors

BOY/GIRL SCOUT TROOP
- Scouts
- Scoutmasters

BUTCHER SHOP
- Butchers
- Customers

BUS/TRAIN STATION
- Drivers/conductors
- Ticket salespersons
- Passengers

CAR SERVICE STATION
- Attendants
- Mechanics
- Customers

CEMETERY
- Grave diggers

CHURCH
- Ministers
- Priests
- Teachers
- Members

COMPUTER STORE

CONVENT
- Nuns
- External workers
- Visitors

COURTS
- Traffic Court
- Criminal Court
- Juvenile Court
- Judges
- Defendants
- Bailiffs

- Clerks
- Attorneys
- Jurors
- Witnesses

FLORIST SHOP
- Florists
- Customers

EMERGENCY ROOM
- Nurses
- Patients

FURNITURE STORE

GUN CLUB
- Members
- Instructors

HEALTH FOOD STORE

HIGHWAY PATROL
- Highway patrol officers
- Violators

HOBBY SHOPS
- Model builders
- Stamp collectors
- Managers

HOSPITAL
- Patients
- Nurses
- Physicians
- Clerks

HUMANE SOCIETY
- Dog catchers

JEWELRY STORE
- Jewelers
- Managers
- Customers

LAW FIRM
- Lawyers
- Secretaries
- Clients

LOCAL GOVERNMENT
- Mayors
- City Council members

LOCKSMITH SHOP
- Locksmiths
- Customers

MARTIAL ARTS CLUB
- Teachers
- Students

MORTUARY
- Morticians
- Embalmers

MUSICAL GROUP
- Musicians
- Agents
- Fans

NEWSPAPER
- Printers
- Reporters
- Copy editors

NURSING HOME
- Nurses
- Patients
- Dietitians

OFFICE SUPPLY STORE/ SUPERMARKET
- Managers
- Cashiers
- Stock boys
- Carry-out boys
- Customers

PARK
- Maintenance
- Administration
- Visitors

PAWNSHOP
- Pawnbrokers
- Customers
- Janitors

PET SHOP
- Managers
- Customers

PIPE SHOP

POLICE DEPARTMENT
- Police officers
- Traffic controllers
- Detectives
- Guards
- Motorcycle officers

PRISON
- Inmates
- Wardens
- Guards
- Cooks

PUBLIC HOUSING
- Children
- Working parents
- Nonworking residents

REAL ESTATE COMPANY
- Real estate brokers
- Real estate salespersons
- Clients

RESTAURANT
- Waiters/waitresses
- Cooks
- Hosts/hostesses
- Customers

RETIREMENT HOME
- Residents
- Counselors
- Cooks
- Managers

SKID ROW MISSION
- Mission staff
- Ministers
- Converts
- Tramps

TELEVISION/VCR REPAIR SHOP
- TV repair persons
- Customers

THRIFT STORE

SCHOOL
- Grade School
- Junior High School
- Schools for the Deaf
- Schools for the Blind
- Teachers
- Kids
- Janitors
- Principals
- Cooks

SHIPYARD

SOUP KITCHEN
- Organizers
- Cooks
- Customers

SPORTING GOODS STORE
- Owners
- Salespersons
- Customers

STOCK BROKER

TATTOO PARLOR
- Tattoo artists
- Customers

ZOO
- Zookeepers
- Visitors

Source: Adapted from Spradley and McCurdy, *The Cultural Experience*, 1972.

2.7 A physical setting is required

As environmental designers, we are interested in cultural knowledge that is related to specific spatial environments, since our professional role is to design or redesign a physical setting to support a particular group of people and their activities. For example, rather than investigating the cultural knowledge of a journeyman carpenter, we would be more likely to study the setting of the union hall—where a variety of "sited micro-cultures" would be in play (the journeyman carpenters, apprentices, union officials, contractors/hirers, etc.). While the former might give us a wealth of data regarding tools, safety considerations, relationships with coworkers, different types of jobs, and so forth, this data would be less immediately relevant to your role as designer of the union hall. The study of the union hall might also include knowledge related to tools: perhaps carpenters discuss the relative merit of tools, trade tools, or sell second-hand tools to each other while waiting around the union hall. If this is the case, the designer could tease out implications for the design of the physical setting; and with clarification and refinement, these implications become your design program. In this case, a comfortable location to "hang out" and talk, with drinking water, perhaps a bulletin board, or a place to store and display a selection of current trade journals or even tools "on consignment" would enhance the "fit" between the setting and its users—depending on what you learn from your informants.

2.8 Accessibility

For your first attempt at ethnography, you should choose a site to study that is unfamiliar. Since you will spend considerable time in your study location, you must choose a place where you can make repeated visits quite easily. This may mean taking into account the hours of operation (which should be compatible with your own class schedule), available transportation (in terms of the amount of time it will take to go there, carry out fieldwork, and return), or even the predictability of the social situation (the location and activities) you intend to study.

Why not choose to study something that could help with other projects? One student selected a senior center because her studio project that same semester was designing housing for seniors, so she used the fieldwork as an opportunity to learn more about the potential users of her studio design project. A Japanese student selected a South American bar that he had never visited, but that was culturally unfamiliar to him and conveniently located in his neighborhood.[6]

One negative example of an inaccessible site should deter you from choosing a place that will be difficult to get to for study: a student chose the micro-culture of a taxi co-op in Oakland. Although the drivers could offer knowledgeable (and insider's) description of the social situation of taxi drivers, the sited micro-culture turned out to be problematic in some ways. She decided to try and hang out at the taxi depot and to find an informant willing to spend time talking to her. But she soon realized that taxi drivers spend most of their time on the road and rarely have time to hang out at the depot. Thus, the group did not use the physical location for their activities. Although taxi drivers do exchange a lot of information, their relationship is rather limited and it remains a solitary occupation. One driver finally agreed to take her in his cab and to talk to her "as long as she got the meter going," which meant that she had to pay for every interview she got with him. She also found it difficult to locate her informant from one interview to the next and she often had to wait a long time at the depot before he showed up. As a result, between such time and monetary costs, and the irregularity of her meetings with her informant, this student was left behind schedule and had difficulty in gathering enough information to support a detailed redesign program.[7]

Another issue regarding access is permission. One does not necessarily need to seek permission to study a sited micro-culture, but you may, depending on the micro-culture you plan to study. You will need the cooperation of one or more informants, but that is a different matter from seeking permission from some authority, which could be the case if you choose to carry out fieldwork in institutions or commercial establishments. A visit to a grade-school classroom will require the permission of the teacher, probably the principal and occasionally the parents. A study of prison inmate culture would require permission from authorities.

While it may be quite possible to obtain permission, you may spend so much time—being directed to successive individuals to explain your project, or waiting for a meeting of the appropriate executing body to consider your request—that your effort may be better expended elsewhere. One student decided to study the AIDS prevention center of a federal high-security prison. Several weeks elapsed before the researcher was granted permission, even though his informant was a caregiver to whom he was personally very close.[8]

For these reasons, we recommend choosing a public or semi-public location for your first ethnographic research project. This doesn't rule out other options, however. If the place you are the most interested in studying is likely to deny you permission to interview users or employees on the job, perhaps you can find an informant willing to meet you after hours. One student decided to pursue her study after school hours and therefore did not have to acquire permission from a school authority. If she had sought permission she might have encountered the same problem another researcher had at a daycare center:

> My first attempt at finding an informant failed miserably. I had hoped to interview some of the children at the . . . daycare center. Whenever I spent time around the play yard, kids would spontaneously come up and talk to me. Not having a middleman to help me find an informant, I decided to make my presence known, to approach the director of the center directly, and to inform her of my intentions. However, I soon found out she was very concerned about "outside influences" affecting the children and parents' fears about kidnapping, and was skeptical of the value of my project. I soon abandoned the prospect of this particular culture, realizing it would be very difficult to work around her.[9]

One easier way to gain access to a location is by using your own connections—students have studied the place where their roommates work, where they themselves have been customers, and where their friends play sports. A personal introduction will usually help to elicit permission where an anonymous request is likely to fail. But remember to select a setting that is not already familiar to you.

2.9 Why you should avoid familiar environments

Many students have wanted to conduct an ethnographic study of their place of employment. You may more naturally be drawn to study a location with which you are already familiar: the situation is less intimidating, you may be curious to discover more about a place you've known superficially, you can more easily locate an informant, you want to save time, and you may already have acquired some of the culture you seek to study. Yet the danger of not learning as an innocent outsider is so strong that studying a familiar place can only be done under special circumstances.

Design students often want to study a location for which they already have "a few ideas" about possible improvements and redesign. The ethnographic process may seem like a good opportunity to address your frustrations or to enhance a place you already like. However, when it comes to ethnography, this is a setup for disappointment. The danger in investigating your place of work, for example, stems directly from your familiarity with the location. You likely already possess a level of knowledge, impressions, and attitudes about a particular social situation and may not be aware of it. Setting these preconceptions aside as you methodically uncover your informant's cultural knowledge may be difficult. You will essentially have a foot in the *etic* (outsider's) view, and one in the *emic* (insider's) view, and as such may inadvertently interpret your informant's comments or fill in the gap in the information—from your own knowledge—which may or may not match that of your informant. Finally, and importantly, such a familiar situation may deprive you of the opportunity to listen deeply to another and thereby identify which seemingly ordinary words have a special meaning in that culture. One student thought it would be difficult to work in an unfamiliar environment, but found that because she "was a newcomer to the space, these words stood out," which made it easier to identify them.[10]

As an ethnographer, your study will proceed as if you were just born into a new society and have to learn its language and all of its rules as a beginner. However, you have to be prepared to go further than simply learning how to get by in a micro-culture! The ethnographer mustn't take anything for granted. Although it is important to discover the insider's perception of what they know, the ethnographer must also discover what their subjects don't know that they know! Therefore, it is very difficult for someone to study a micro-culture of which they are already a part—because you already take for granted the very knowledge you are after. For example, if you have worked in a restaurant, you could likely distinguish between a "two-top" and a "four-top." If you haven't worked in a restaurant, those are the terms used, respectively, for a table that seats two, and a table that seats four. But *why* are they called "two-tops" and "four-tops"? How would you explain these terms and why they are used to someone who has never worked in a restaurant?

We all, of course, interpret what we learn in terms of our own knowledge and experience. However, in a case where the setting is unknown to you, that translation will be more explicit and recognizable, and in turn alert you to the need to verify your own interpretation. Generally, the more that information falls within the realm of what is normally assumed to be shared knowledge—often dealing with mundane aspects of daily life—the more likely that both interviewer and informant will assume an equivalent interpretation. It's easy to see how this type of problem might emerge when a student studies, for example, his own fraternity house, or the café she works in part-time. Again, we do not want you to use your home or job or other familiar site as a setting for study.

A second problem arises from working with informants who already know that you are familiar with their particular micro-culture. Consider the following example. If a student from the English department decided to come and study the micro-culture of your design studio and selected you and your friends as informants, he could ask almost any question. If he asked, "What is a section?" or "How is a Google SketchUp different from AutoCAD?" or "Why do design students stay up all night?" you would not think it strange once you know that he came from another department where they know nothing about your way of life. It would seem appropriate for him to ask such questions. In contrast, if a third-year design-student-turned-ethnographer were to ask these same questions he would appear to be strange, ignorant, even annoying.

Under special circumstances, you might have people at work or even roommates serve as informants for an unfamiliar micro-culture. This is preferable to having them act as informants for a micro-culture with which you are both familiar.

Eventually, after you learn to listen to people in an active way (by listening to their specialized vocabulary and constructing taxonomies of how they order their categories of thought) you will be able to listen to people in your own environment in a new way and be able to see the culture that you now take for granted. But for now, practice how to listen actively by talking with people who can tell you things that you have not heard before.

2.10 Dealing with unfamiliar settings

While this may have seemed counterintuitive at first, we think you can see by now that unfamiliarity is a major advantage in studying social situations. By choosing a setting where you know little about the participants, activities, spaces, and objects used, you enter the situation expecting, even needing, to learn from your informant. This expectation, together with unfamiliar terminology and new categories of information, will help you to be certain to uncover your informant's interpretation of the knowledge being shared, rather than relying on your own. The presence of much that is unfamiliar to you will also make that which appears familiar stand out, and remind you to verify meanings and connections.

Be aware of two potential drawbacks to unfamiliar study locations. A certain setting may be fascinating and entirely appropriate in terms of all the preceding requirements, but if it is literally foreign to you—because a language you do not understand is the only one spoken, for example, or if it is tremendously complex, you may not be able to learn enough of the relevant information within the limits of the time you have to enable you to make appropriate design recommendations. Settings that might have these characteristics include those that are highly technical—a highly specialized factory, for example—or that embody important religious or cultural institutions to which you are a complete outsider. Such settings may be beyond the scope of this ethnographic design project.

The other potential difficulty of unfamiliar study locations relates to social ease, and is, in a way, another question about access. You must be honest with yourself in assessing your ability to carry out your fieldwork, to visit your study location and spend time there, and to identify and establish a relationship with your informant. Even if a truck-stop seems like a great form of vernacular architecture to you, and the long-haul drivers a fascinating micro-culture, you must decide whether or not you will be able to "hang out" there with sufficient personal comfort to carry out the assignment, and if you will be comfortable enough to approach someone who can steer you toward an informant.

This is not to say that you should feel at home—one reason for choosing an unfamiliar setting is to have the chance to get to know a social situation that is definitely not part of your own territory. That is also often what makes the process such a powerful way to learn. Many students have experienced the exhilaration of choosing a place where their internal feeling of shyness or confusion gave way to a glimpse of an entirely new world, new insights into others, and new friendships.

Finally, we want to stress that the most basic characteristic of your study location should be that it *genuinely interests you.* Students who really want to know about the social situations they choose invariably learn a great deal about them, including enough of their informant's worldview to support appropriate design recommendations. A true desire to understand can overcome many of the obstacles discussed here, and conversely, a lack of interest will weaken the outcome of a study of even the most carefully chosen setting. This means that you should not choose an exotic, unknown setting just because you think the novelty will impress everyone or automatically lead to a good study. Nor should you choose the place you worked last summer just because you think it will be easy. No matter what the setting is, you will invest considerable time and energy in it simply to carry out the project, so choose a place that means something to you.

BOX 2.4: SKILL SPOTLIGHT—CONDUCTING BEHAVIORAL OBSERVATIONS

Semantic ethnography, a "process of discovering and describing a culture," employs informant interviews to uncover the ***explicit cultural knowledge*** of a group.[1] Meanwhile, visual means of data collection are ingrained in our culture and, moreover, can uncover ***implicit***—or unspoken—cultural knowledge. Therefore, prior to conducting ***semantic interviews***, you will conduct a casual ***observation*** of your site in order to formulate and record your initial impressions. These initial impressions will help to inform and complement your semantic interviews later in the project.

Behavioral observations are a specific method of data collection, conducted in a natural setting, and used to understand and describe "naturally occurring patterns" of activity and behavior.[2] During such observations, researchers "systematically [watch] people use their environments" and, in so doing, uncover insights about spatial and social relationships within a culture. In other words, through observational methods, you can collect data about what people do and where, and how the environment supports or interferes with behavior.[3]

Conducting Casual Observations

Because this is an early stage in your research, the purpose of your casual observation is to see what you think might need to be redesigned. You are not expected to use systematic observation techniques, such as those famously used by William Whyte in *The Social Life of Small Urban Spaces,* which involve preplanned categories and scoring methods. In contrast, your goal is to "eyeball" your site, use your design training to date to propose a redesign, and gain initial information to complement and inform the other data collection methods you will use in your research.[4] Because observation allows you to obtain information "about behavior opportunities and constraints that environments provide," your initial insights regarding the interconnection of activities, space, and social relationships can help inform your first design. Complementary research methods (and perspectives)—such as observations (***personal perspective***), interviews (***emic***), and ***literature reviews*** (***etic***)—will produce a well substantiated design. However, compiling complementary information also requires that you acknowledge the limits of each type of data you obtain. Though observations are useful in helping you identify the *range of behaviors* that occur in a given site, they cannot convey—or help you uncover—the *meaning* of these activities. Meaning is established in the realm of interviews.[5]

Observations: What to Look For

- **Look for who is doing what, with whom, and where**. Where are activities happening? Is there enough space to accommodate everyone? Make sure to notice what or who is present *as well as* what or who is absent.[6]

- **Pay attention to your initial impressions and reactions.** We recommend you record your impressions of and questions about the site, including points of interest or confusion you want to follow up during your informant interviews. These observations will also inform your initial site redesign.

Recording Your Observations

First and foremost, be clear—both in your notes as well as in your own thinking—about the distinction between your *observations* and your *assessment* of the site. Zeisel recommends dividing your notes into two columns for this purpose: in one column, record only a factual (non-interpretive) description of what you see, and in the other, record any reflections, thoughts, comments, or questions that come to mind.[7] As mentioned in section 2.3, objective observation and analysis requires that you record things *as they really are* rather than how you believe them to be. Separating your factual observations from subjective interpretations in your notes helps to accomplish objectivity. To help you separate the sources of your data, divide your notebook for this project into at least three sections: ***personal***, ***emic***, and ***etic***. The personal observations are in turn divided into factual and assessment.

Second, take notes *during* your observation. Of course, recording notes can be easier and less conspicuous in some contexts and more difficult and obvious in others: think about the difference between taking notes while observing a classroom setting vs. recording your observations of passers-by on a busy sidewalk.[8] Still, you should look for a place to jot down a few notes and even sketch a ***plan*** of your site. If you cannot take notes while conducting your observation, be sure to dedicate time immediately afterward to write down every detail—you don't want to forget anything! In addition to recording a written narrative of your observations, Zeisel offers a number of suggestions to help you take copious, descriptive notes:

- **Annotate floorplans of your site.** If you can access maps, plans, or other images of your site beforehand, you may find it helpful to write your notes on the plans, using arrows to denote locations you reference.
- **Keep a tally and create checklists.** If you want to keep track of the number of people you see, keep a simple tally. Additionally, you might create a list of the activities you see and keep an informal count of the number of people doing each.
- **Record *physical traces*.** Note the relationship of paths and locations to the activities and behaviors you observe. For example: *Is there a common pathway people take from one place to another? Are certain locations more or less populated than others?*[9]

Finally, you should take notes in a *non-obtrusive* manner, meaning that you should situate and comport yourself in a way that does not draw attention or let others know they are being observed. Because your goal is to observe *naturally occurring* behavior, you want to make sure that your actions do not impact or disrupt the people—and their activities—you are attempting to observe.[10]

Remember that even taking a photo, depending on the context, could be more obtrusive than simply sketching a quick drawing (4.10).

A Word of Caution

Zeisel cautions: "*the force of concrete visual impressions can be . . . so great . . . that they dominate a researcher's mind.*"[11] Thus, though observations can provide some data that is helpful to obtaining an initial sense of your site and offer a compelling vision of the people and activities present in your site, remember that the focus of this project is on the words your informant uses to convey her cultural knowledge, *not* the visual evidence you obtain from your personal observation (still, the two sources of information can *and should* complement each other). Recording your notes in separate categories can help you remember and practice this idea.

Notes

1 McCurdy et al., *The Cultural Experience,* 2005, p. 9.
2 Groat and Wang, *Architectural Research Methods,* 2002, p. 206.
3 Zeisel, *Inquiry by Design,* 2006.
4 Groat and Wang, *Architectural Research Methods,* 2002, p. 209; Sommer and Sommer, *A Practical Guide to Behavioral Research,* 2002, p. 49.
5 Pavlides and Cranz, "Ethnographic Methods in Support of Architectural Practice," 2012.
6 Zeisel, *Inquiry by Design,* 2006.
7 Ibid., p. 208.
8 Sommer and Sommer, *A Practical Guide to Behavioral Research,* 2002, p. 52.
9 Zeisel, *Inquiry by Design,* 2006.
10 McCurdy et al., *The Cultural Experience,* 2005.
11 Zeisel, *Inquiry by Design,* 2006, p. 162.

2.11 Initial redesign proposal

Both anthropologists and architects might want to study the culture of the people who share a particular social situation, but design ethnographers are concerned with the role that built form plays in the life of the insider. Concretely, this means that you must be sure to record information about the physical setting within which the culture exists. Moreover, you should record your first impressions of the space and your initial design ideas before you embark upon the ethnographic research. This will help you cultivate awareness of the constraining or enabling capacity of the existing setting for the types of activities its occupants may need to perform. And, later it will provide a benchmark for you to use to assess the effects of your study on your own design ideas.

To record the existing state of the physical setting, use the forms of representation you learned from your design education. These might include plans, sections, sketches, photographs, or physical or virtual models. Then we ask you to propose an initial redesign based on your first impressions of the site, in partial ignorance of the culture you are about to study. This initial design proposal is based on some combination of your previous architectural education, ongoing debates within architecture, and your personal feelings about what would improve the space/place in some way. Drawing upon yourself in this way could be viewed as a form of introspection, which can be a useful approach in that it allows you to become aware of your own preconceived ideas about particular groups of people and about what you consider the best physical setting for them.[11] However, subsequent cultural investigation may demonstrate that your value judgments may not be well founded or that your prejudices have misled you regarding how a particular environment is conceived and used. You might also find that your design was a good match, but would be better explained with different reasons than you first thought.

When recording information about the existing site conditions and expressing initial design ideas, you should go beyond a simple ***floor plan*** in order to articulate the ambience and experience of a place. Sketching, measured drawings, perspective drawings, and photographs can all be used to convey your ideas (see sample site sketches in Figure 2.1(a) and (b)). Some students dread sketching and prefer using a camera to record visual information; both methods are valuable and allow you to record different types of information. Anyone who has spent some time sketching the interior of someone's house will tell you how you become aware of details you would not otherwise have noticed. We encourage you to take the opportunity on one of your first visits to the site to sit discreetly in a corner and sketch the environment. You can put this drawing in your research notebook as a way to get it started. This will allow you to get a real feel for the place and familiarize yourself with it even before talking to an informant. The details you take down and the knowledge they give you will be useful later to understand answers to your questions. If the site is busy enough that you can sketch unnoticed, sketching may be preferable to photographing because cameras are nearly always obtrusive: people pose for a photograph, but they will usually not pose for a sketch. Cameras are especially noticeable if you use a flash, and you may be required to get permission if you are studying a private or semi-private environment. Two examples of sketches from a previous student ethnography are in Figure 2.1(a) and (b).

You should create detailed representations of the site and make several copies. The copies will become useful later in the research process, to be used as base sheets on which to record observations or comments on behavior in space. Plans drawn to scale and photographs can also be used to elicit comments from your informant.

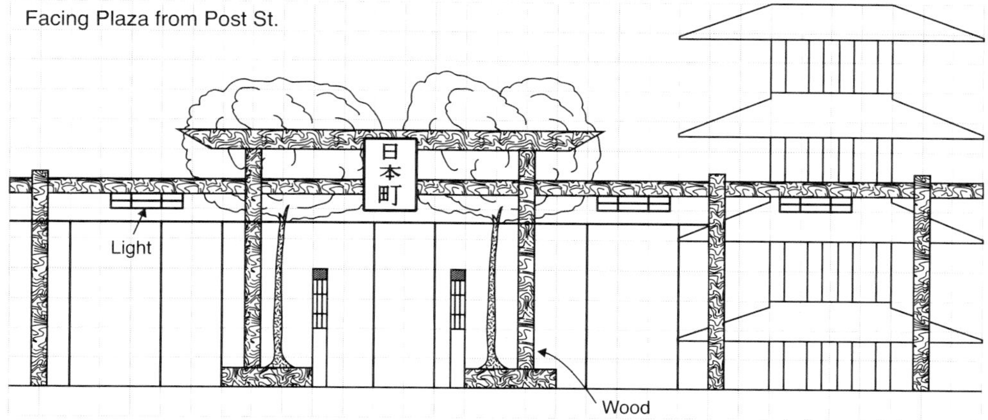

Figure 2.1a Adrienne Ito (2012) sketched a section view of the entryway to the Japantown Peace Plaza

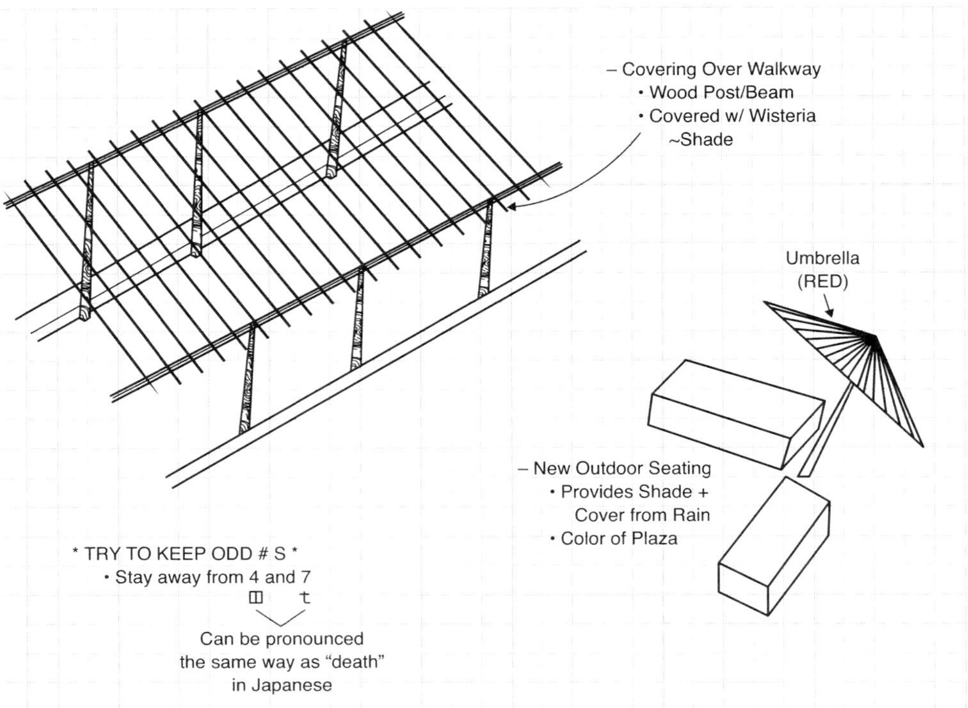

Figure 2.1b Adrienne Ito (2012) sketched various elements of the Japantown Peace Plaza as well as ideas for improvement

2.12 Chapter review: summary of main ideas

- The limits on your time require you to narrow your project to a manageable size (2.2).
- A major component of objective observation and analysis is to write things as they really are, rather than what the ethnographer believes to be happening (2.3).
- Researchers can make up for their lack of objectivity. The first step is to recognize the problems of selective observation and interpretation and to be aware of one's own personal and cultural prejudices by being conscious of what may influence data gathering (2.4).
- Another basis for bias and selective observation is *ethnocentrism*, the deeply ingrained attitude that our own culture is superior to others (2.4).
- Researchers never simply go out to "gather the facts." Rather, researchers take with them an implicit theory of what is important. Having a theory does not guarantee freeing oneself from bias, however. Theories can be used unsystematically, outside of awareness, and include the personal and cultural biases of the investigator that we have discussed (2.4).
- You should acquire some sort of a notebook or journal for use in recording information about the site. You can also use the same notebooks as for lecture notes. You should not pre-edit what you put in the journal: you will never have to show

it to anyone else, so you can always edit or redact its contents later for inclusion in your project report (2.5).

- For your first attempt at ethnography, you should choose a site to study that is unfamiliar. Since you will spend considerable time in your study location, you must choose a place where you can make repeated visits quite easily (2.8–2.9). We recommend choosing a public or semi-public location for your first ethnography project.
- While this may have seemed counterintuitive at first, unfamiliarity is a major advantage in studying social situations. By choosing a setting where you know little about the participants, activities, spaces, and objects used, you enter the situation expecting, even needing, to learn from your informant (2.9–2.10).
- Although it is important to discover the insider's perception of what they know, the ethnographer may also discover what their subjects don't know that they know! (2.9–2.10).
- The most basic characteristic of your study location should be that it genuinely interests you (2.10).
- To record the existing state of the physical setting, use the forms of representation you learned from your design education. These might include plans, sections, sketches, photographs, or physical or virtual 4D models (2.11).

BOX 2.5: ETHNOGRAPHY PROJECT GUIDELINES

Part 1: Research Proposal

Identifying and observing a cultural setting

Research method: observation

Summary of required activities: For this segment of the ethnography project, you will select and visit the site that will be the focus of your research. During your first visit to the site, you will conduct an observation and record what you notice—people, activities, behaviors, built or natural features of the site, etc.—as well as your personal reflections on how the site does or does not accommodate the activities and people you observed. Finally, based on your observations and personal reflections, you will propose an initial redesign of the site. *Looking ahead: though you will not be required to select an informant at this stage of the project, you should begin thinking of how you might locate and introduce yourself to an informant, two primary elements of Part 2 of the ethnography project.*

Summary of research proposal components: Begin your report by identifying the site you have selected to study and, based on your initial observations, describe the physical setting in plan and section and its use. In one or two additional pages, include annotated photos or sketches from your initial visit. Next, draw a set of building plans and sections that describe how you propose to improve the site; explain the changes you would make and provide rationale for each of your proposals. This is your personal point of view as developed by your design education to date.

Grading Criteria for Part 1

Does your project conform to the following criteria?

- Identification of your sited micro-culture: name/title, address, location, map
- Description of your sited micro-culture: its history, members, other relevant details
- Visual documentation of the site: drawings, photos, sketches, plans, sections, diagrams
- Additional, relevant information to understand the site: what you observed, your first impression of the site, why you selected the site and/or micro-culture
- Proposed improvements or changes to the site: drawings, sketches, plans, annotations
- Explanation of and rationale for proposed changes
- At least 2–4 pages in length; well written; legible; high quality.

Notes

1 Kelly and Gibbons, "Marketing Methodologies Ethnography," 2008, 264.
2 Donna Haraway. "Situated Knowledges: The Science Question in Feminism and the Privilege of Partial Perspective," *Feminist Studies* 14, no. 3 (1988): 575–99.
3 Eleftherios Pavlides and Jana E. Hesser. "Vernacular Architecture as an Expression of Its Social Context in Eressos, Greece," *Housing, Culture and Design: A Comparative Perspective* (Philadelphia: University of Pennsylvania Press, 1989): 357–74. See also Eleftherios Pavlides, "Vernacular Architecture in its Social Context: A Case Study of Eressos, Greece," Ph.D. dissertation, University of Pennsylvania, 1985.
4 Students can use the same notebook as for lecture notes.
5 Adapted from Spradley and McCurdy, *The Cultural Experience*, 1972.
6 Shelly Irving, "A North Berkeley Senior Center" (Spring 2001); Nori Nakamura, "A Neighborhood Bar" (Spring 2001).
7 Mazeko Phumzile, "A Taxi Co-op" (Spring 1996).
8 Junge Sutherland, "A Prison AIDS Prevention Center" (Spring 1997).
9 Tu Tuan Nguyen, "The Play-yards at a Campus Day-care Center" (Spring 1997).
10 Sarah Medrano, "Driving Range" (no date).
11 I thank architect Madeline Speer for pointing out the value of documenting this first design; it shows designers that they design differently after doing the research than they would have done before doing it. Otherwise, the temptation would be to think that the final design is "what I would have done anyway." More generally, documenting the first design helps make the relationship between ethnographic fieldwork and suitable, culturally relevant designs more deliberate.

3 Sited micro-cultures

3.1 Defining culture

What is culture? How can understanding this concept help us design human environments? We can start with a definition of the term "culture" and its usage in the social sciences. Culture, as Raymond Williams puts it, "is one of the two or three most complicated words in the English language."[1] Historically, the idea of what "culture" is has varied widely. Originally, the term meant to cultivate or to support natural growth, a sense that can still be seen in the biological sciences.

The social sciences (sociology, anthropology, geography, some approaches to history and the like) have an altogether different definition for the term "culture," and it's that definition which most interests us, as students and thinkers about society and meaning. In the social sciences, "culture" is seen as a whole way of life, the complex sum of the material life, intellectual activity, and language systems of a particular group. It is all the processes of a particular society (or group of societies)—law, religion, material objects and structures, morals, customs, rituals, languages, family and kinship structures, trade systems—everything!

From this broad perspective, most behaviors and exchanges that might occur during the design process would be considered examples of culture. Culture also includes the written and unwritten rules for how the design process must proceed, its spatial and physical aspects including the visual media used to present ideas, where the designer works, and how the designer is dressed. According to this broad definition of culture, vehicles, appliances, food, buildings, and anything else made by members of a group is part of their material culture. The patterns of emotions, social practices, law, art, and the institutions of society are all part of culture. Accordingly, culture influences and in some cases wholly determines all aspects of our lives.

In this workbook, we shall restrict the concept of culture. The concept we are concerned with is the system of meanings shared by a group. Meaning is knowledge that is learned and shared. Take technical drawing as an example. Designers and engineers learn a set of rules for constructing drawings (whether digitally or on paper), using conventional symbols to represent complex sets of information. With this knowledge, one can make sense of different kinds of drawings, including plans, sections, and details. Others with this knowledge can translate this information into spatial relationships, structural details, and technical data. While someone without such knowledge only sees lines and unintelligible symbols, designers can see and imagine with much precision an entire thing that does not yet exist. This shared knowledge is essential for communication with different people in design—drafters, engineers, construction workers, planners, and other designers. Without such knowledge, people are left out of the communication process.

Culture, according to the definition we shall use, is not the behavior that occurs when someone is drafting. It is not the product of that behavior such as architecture, landscape, or material culture, nor is it the tools of the trade like drafting boards or computers. Culture is what one must know in order to read plans, draft, and design; in other words, what knowledge must be shared for communication to occur.

3.2 Culture as knowledge

This cognitive definition of culture as knowledge greatly affects the way we investigate, describe, and design for groups of people sharing cultural knowledge. Semantic ethnography gets to the heart of the examined culture's meaning-making process through direct inquiry. We are trying to discover, understand, and relay the insider's point of view, while not imposing an outsider's way of thinking on the cultural situation we are studying. Anthropologists call this the ***emic*** perspective, or the insider's point of view, versus the ***etic*** perspective, or the outsider's point of view.

The words **etic** and **emic** are drawn from the terminology of linguistics, which uses the word phon**etic** to describe how a word *sounds*, and the word phon**emic** to describe what it *means*. Cell phone text messages often use phonetic spelling (what the word sounds like). The difference between the meaning and the sound of a word is enormous; think of how casually non-English speakers can say a "bad" word without embarrassment. Ask them to tell you the same word in their own language and they might be uncomfortable.

If culture is knowledge that is learned, shared, and coded in language—as defined by McCurdy, Spradley, and Shandy—then the insider's view—the emic perspective—is not merely an objective description of people and their behavior.[2] It is a systematic attempt to discover the knowledge a group of people have learned and are using to organize their behavior in space. This approach can help designers understand the social settings in which they intervene so that they can increase their chances of developing environments that fulfill the needs of their users. Instead of asking, "What do I see these people doing?" we must ask, "What do these people see themselves doing?" To use our own language to describe the scene keeps us on the outside of what is happening and forces us to limit our observations according to our own ideas. The best way to answer the question about a group's self-perception is by using the terminology that the group uses and understanding the ways the group uses these terms. Accordingly, you will find that this method emphasizes learning the vocabulary of the group for whom a design is intended.

In conducting an ethnographic project, you must view your goal not as studying people but as learning from them. You must see other people as experts in understanding their own culture, and ask them to instruct you on the way of life they find meaningful. You might hear a street performer explain how to find a "good spot" or attract the "right crowd." You might listen to a mechanic describe the organization of her garage and explain the various tasks performed in different sections of the repair shop. You might sit patiently with an elderly woman to learn about the rites and rules of a bingo parlor. Whatever you study, you will learn to speak and understand the language of those you study. Unfortunately, too few designers have or take the time to study the cultural environment for which they are designing. Designers, like other people, often assume their personal experience to be a valid basis for making decisions that will affect future users and are not trained to question the assumptions and views they take for granted.[3]

In the long history of world architecture, numerous designs have failed to fulfill their function because of lack of understanding of the needs of future user groups by the architects and because of erroneous projection of the designers' own prejudices about social behavior. Postwar public housing in the United States is a sad example: lack of knowledge about the living requirements of lower income families and the culture of different resident groups has led, at least in part, to the failure of numerous large-scale public housing projects that often turned into unsafe neighborhoods with high crime rates and low levels of maintenance. If prior studies had been conducted—and valued—by policy makers, some of the policy and design flaws could have been avoided. More recently, the Hope VI program renovated old housing and built new housing as part of mixed-income developments. All the housing in the neighborhood appears to be of the same quality, the intention being to make low income people not feel stigmatized by the appearance of the buildings they live in.[4]

Today, design professionals who recognize the diversity of cultures and cultural settings may want to learn how to view the buildings they design from the users' perspective. Some designers still believe in the power of the environment to determine behavior, while others think there can be no relationship at all, having decided that ***environmental determinism*** is naive, arrogant, or at best hit and miss. Even those who do not believe (or do not want to believe) that they can *determine* behavior through their buildings may still want to design buildings that *enhance and facilitate* people's actions in space. The quality of an object or building benefits when the designers have varied sets of people in mind. Designers can and should understand and serve different cultures through design. Ethnography is one way to translate an understanding into the design of a place.

3.3 Understanding sited micro-cultures in our complex society

How do you identify the different cultural groups within a place? Even though culture is a pattern for a whole way of life, our society does not have a uniform culture. Immigrants have brought many different cultures to the United States so that it is not possible to study "American culture." At best we can study "American cultures," and even one subculture is too vast and diverse for most design purposes. Groups overlap and compete in nearly all places today, which makes it difficult to identify a well-defined "community" where everyone shares one culture. Spradley and McCurdy recommend that cultural researchers find coherent and therefore very small sub-sub-subcultures that they once called "scenes" and now call "micro-cultures." As designers conducting ethnographies, our task is slightly different. We are examining the uses and experiences of a particular place, and the interactions of the people within that place. In order to emphasize that our micro-cultures are sited in the physical world, we will use the term ***sited micro-culture*** to refer to these focused, relatively small cultures.[5]

One student studied an adventure playground and observed that "the essence of adventure playgrounds is that they allow creativity and independent actions ... [and] that the kinds of people who go to the park and the activities that they choose to pursue while they are at the park *are the park*" [emphasis in original].[6] Note that the culture of people and activities in this case is completely bound to the physical setting. One could choose to study a bounded local group such as an entire neighborhood. The problem is that such large entities are not homogeneous and may actually share very little cultural knowledge. The case of a downtown soup kitchen may be quite different: although they only spend a limited part of their daily lives in that specific physical setting, both volunteers and customers share an important amount of knowledge about the rules, functioning, and particularities of this environment, in the moments they spend together daily during meal hours. Over the years, sets of implicit and explicit rules have been developed that are clearly understood by regulars but are unclear or invisible to the occasional visitor.

3.4 Sited micro-cultures and social situations

Social situations that occur on a regular basis are especially good places to *begin* the investigation of sited micro-cultures, such as a farmers' market. The knowledge used by the people who are part of that situation, as sellers, customers, or farmers, would be the focus of study of that culture. Designers often use *place*—as in a physical site—as the starting point for a design, but here we want to work through cultural knowledge *first* in order to get to new ways of thinking about place. Sited micro-cultures and social situations are closely linked, but different. Social situations are what can be observed by the outsider, but micro-cultures are the experiences of the situations held by the insider. One way to think of a social situation is like a stage play: there are actors (people), their dialogue (social interactions), the set (a place or site) and props (objects). For example, a farmers' market is a social situation made up of people who are interacting with one another. They are located in a particular place that includes a variety of objects such as tables, awnings, baskets, trucks, and produce.

Social situations are good places to find a micro-culture. For example, the practice sessions of a basketball team, a church service, a Boy/Girl Scout meeting, the checkout desk at a library, service stations, and hospital wards are all recurrent social situations where you will find groups with shared cultural knowledge. Their perspective will offer you insight into the design of a building that serves many different groups, such as a gymnasium, church, clinic, stadium, or community center.

People can define the same social situation in many different ways. In other words, several different micro-cultures may use the same place. We have mentioned the farmers' market as one example. The micro-cultures there are experienced quite differently for the regular vendor with produce to sell, the stall worker interacting with shoppers, the musician entertaining the crowd, or the customers comparing vegetables.[7] Once observed, the social situation becomes a stepping-stone for the researcher to get into what people know. He can ask his informant what kinds of people are present, what they are doing, where they are located, and the identity of objects in the setting. At the beginning of your study you will inevitably observe many events, objects, and people interacting. You should keep your observations recorded separately from your record of the words you hear used in the setting. Further discussion of note taking is in Chapter 4, "Cultural Informants."

3.5 Sharing cultural knowledge, or not

Every person is part of a great number of sited micro-cultures. Many ethnographers have recognized that different subcultures exist in every society and that some people have learned the appropriate cultural information and others have not. Differences in cultural knowledge can be based on gender, ethnicity, membership in secret societies, exclusive religious rituals, or specialized occupations.

Even members within the same micro-culture do not necessarily share all cultural knowledge. Not all the members of a group share *everything* they know with each other. While members of micro-cultures share a perspective and self-perception, not all knowledge is held in common. Thus, one can study what can be called *cultural* or *cognitive non-sharing*.[8] Nonsharing occurs when different people have learned a different definition of the same social situation. This difference, however, does *not* prevent social interaction between people sharing different knowledge. For an example of non-sharing in action, let us return to the farmers' market. Each week, the merchants set up their stalls to sell their produce. They arrange the fruit and vegetables attractively, set up a cash register, and hang a sign. Shoppers browse. They may ask the seller about growing methods, request tips for proper storage, and a few may haggle to reduce the price of some less-than-perfect items. At the end of the day, the farmer goes back to the farm with money, and the customer goes home with fresh produce. Although both the farmer and the customer were involved in the same sited culture, the farmer and customer do not have identical definitions of what has occurred.

The customer has not just purchased vegetables; instead, the customer has come away with a positive feeling from the *experience* of shopping at the farmers' market. By speaking with the person who apparently grew the produce the customer will eat, he will enjoy his purchases more than had he simply purchased them from a pile in a supermarket. Meanwhile, the farmer's back may hurt from lifting and carrying crates of produce. He has an ongoing quarrel with the person who undercuts his prices in the stall next door, he is uncomfortable from too much time spent in the sun, and does not feel like his customers can possibly appreciate the amount of work that goes into the produce he sells.

The customer views his experience at the farmers' market as wholesome and restorative, satisfying in a unique way. The farmer's experience of the market, however, is quite different. Although it represents a portion of his income-generating activity, his presence there is work and he shares more with other farmers selling produce at the market than with his clients. Farmer and customer share the culture of exchange at the stall, but have radically different perceptions of the culture of the farmers' market as a whole.

So whose point of view do you take? How many sited micro-cultures within the social situation should a designer study? This is an important practical question for each practitioner. Here, you will study only one micro-culture, but you might consider joining forces with one or two others to study the same social situation from the points of view of different informants, each representing a different sited micro-culture. This could also be an opportunity to compare and contrast two different American cultures, e.g. Hispanic and Asian. In design practice, a team of designers and researchers can investigate different points of view.

When you design a space, failing to consider all the sited micro-cultures or groups of users can lead to the failure of that space. For example, carefully designed parks or open spaces are sometimes ignored by the intended user groups; social spaces and lobbies in housing for the elderly may be unused; commercial spaces remain empty; and several public housing projects have had to be evacuated, radically remodeled, or even demolished.

One of the more general values of this ethnographic approach goes beyond architectural applications to the understanding of social conflict. When we see how people operate in different sited micro-cultures we can comprehend why they misunderstand each other. Sometimes different cultural views of the same social situation do not seriously affect the social interactions and may even facilitate them. At other times, the diversity of cultural knowledge leads to misunderstanding and underuse, or worse, conflict. As a designer you will witness conflict between members of a couple, among workgroups within an organization, between sponsors and users; sometimes you might be able to use that tension to create special forms. For example, a Bay Area architect came up with an inventive solution to a difference of opinion between a married couple. The woman came from the East Coast and wanted a large front sun porch, while the man liked shade. The architect created a veranda enclosed with diagonal lattice that satisfied both—*and* was considered aesthetically noteworthy enough to be published by his peers.[9]

One student project proposed the use of movable walls—decorated with community-inspired mural paintings—during a weekly brunch event at a Buddhist temple to help create a visual barrier between the temple and neighboring homes. She explained the need for visual and acoustic barriers: "The neighbors are . . . trying to 'shut the temple down' because of the noise, smells, congestion . . . that the busy Sunday brunch causes on a weekly basis." The walls would serve as more than opaque barriers by communicating through the murals the history of the local Thai community for whom the temple has significant meaning. This solution, which the student classified as a "spatial negotiation," responded to the desire of the Thai temple community to preserve their religious site and practice and to the neighbors' desire to ease congestion and noise that result from the weekly brunch event.[10]

Another example of the value of learning to listen actively to multiple groups came to me in the mail recently. The President of the San Francisco Zen Center, Victoria Austin, learned ethnographic interviewing from me when she was an undergraduate in the Department of Architecture at Princeton University. Thirty years later she wrote, "I want you to know that the early training I did with you has given me many gifts that become apparent now. Please check out the web site, at sfzc.org, particularly the vision section, which started with 30 active listening interviews of nine broad constituencies. Being heard is making this community happy and united in its purpose and vision."[11]

3.6 Chapter review: summary of main ideas

- The concept of culture we are concerned with is the system of meanings shared by a group (3.1).
- Culture is the knowledge that must be shared for communication to occur (3.2).
- Anthropologists distinguish between the emic, or the insider's point of view, and the etic, or the outsider's point of view (3.2).
- The emic perspective is a systematic attempt to discover the knowledge a group of people have learned and are using to organize their behavior in space (3.2).
- In conducting an ethnographic project, your goal is not studying people, but rather learning from them (3.2).
- Designers can and should understand and serve different cultures through design. Ethnography is one way to translate an understanding into the design of places (3.2).

- In order to emphasize that our micro-cultures are sited in the physical world, we will use the term "sited micro-culture" to refer to these focused, relatively small cultures (3.3).
- Designers often use place as the starting point for a design, but here we want to work through cultural knowledge *first* in order to get to new ways of thinking about place (3.4).
- In design practice, a team of designers and researchers can investigate different points of view, or "micro-cultures" within the same social situation (3.5).

Notes

1 Raymond Williams, *Keywords: A Vocabulary of Culture and Society* (New York: Oxford University Press, 1976), 87.

2 David W. McCurdy, James P. Spradley, and Dianna J. Shandy, *The Cultural Experience*, Second Edition (Long Grove, IL: Waveland Press, 2005).

3 In *Interviewing Users* (Brooklyn, NY: Rosenfeld Media, 2013), Steve Portigal adds that the practice of "self design"—designing solely based on one's own perspective—not only precludes the possibility of learning from users, but also limits the possibility for design innovation.

4 Sam Davis, *The Architecture of Affordable Housing* (Berkeley: University of California Press, 1995).

5 You will not necessarily study all the people who are associated with a location because it might support more than one culture.

6 Myra Horiuchi, "The Adventure Playground," (no date).

7 During his presidency, the senior George Bush famously marveled at bar codes and the checkout counter of a grocery store because he had never had to go shopping for himself. This was cultural knowledge that he did not have. The decline in cultural knowledge among store clerks may be contributing to shopping by television. In the Martha Stewart Living television program Stewart shared what used to be widespread cultural knowledge about homemaking 50 years ago, but now the importance of housekeeping has been transformed, either neglected or professionalized, by the emergence of the two-paycheck household.

8 Anthony F. C. Wallace, *Culture and Personality*, Second Edition (New York: Random House, 1970), 34.

9 For more on the Allewelt House, see Donald Watson and Kenneth Labs, *Climatic Design: Energy-Efficient Building Principles and Practices* (New York: McGraw Hill, 1983), 16–17; and Kevin Matthews, *The Great Buildings Collection*, CD-ROM (Artifice, 2001).

10 Elizabeth Leah Cohn-Martin, "Community Sustenance: Sunday Brunch at a Thai Buddhist Temple" (Fall 2008).

11 Victoria Austin, personal communication, ca 2005.

4 Cultural informants

I was able to find a resourceful informant who introduced me to the world of the erotic sex shop. (Often, this would be more than I ever wanted to know, but I did it anyway, in the name of academia.)[1]

4.1 The informant

Working with informants is central to ethnographic fieldwork. In other kinds of research about the use of space, one may never even set eyes on the people who responded to questionnaires, and even face-to-face contact with interviewees is limited. In traditional architectural practice, most designers never meet the future users of the environment they design. In contrast, semantic ethnographic research obviously requires talking with people. One might ask, "How many?" Within the limited time available to you as a student or as a practicing professional, conducting a large number of interviews or even a small number in depth can be difficult. Selecting one representative of the cultural group, who will inform you about the cultural knowledge in the sited culture, may be more practical. This representative will become your informant. Having one informant who knows the sited culture really well is not only a practical consideration, but also it is more consistent with the general norms of our social life. We establish trust with others individually, not in groups. If you are conducting a study of many different micro-cultures within one place, other researchers can each work with another informant.

Your relationship with your informant is probably the most important part of fieldwork, and it can be challenging. After all, you are going to a place where you have to establish the legitimacy of your activity, ask strangers for information, and, on top of all that, develop rapport with an informant. This chapter will address the problems of finding an informant, gaining his or her trust, explaining your purpose, and compiling information from the informant.

4.2 Talking to strangers

Many people find it difficult to talk to strangers. Anxiety is a common feeling when meeting unfamiliar people and inquiring into their way of life. Acknowledging how common fear is in such a situation should help you overcome it. Don't let fear undermine your confidence in your own ability. Everyone is comfortable as long as we are with others who share our way of life. Familiarity breeds security and, conversely, unfamiliarity can create anxiety. You have to learn how to get along with and talk to people who are quite different from yourself: this is a skill you can learn, but you must work to develop it.

Students often rationalize their shyness of new situations by saying it is unethical to intrude where they are not wanted. Sometimes, students become frustrated with the project after a painful social encounter, but most students are pleased to find that informants actually like them.[2] In general, people like talking about themselves, and they particularly like it when others seem genuinely interested in what they do. If you have chosen the site of your study carefully, you should be able to communicate this genuineness to the people you meet there.

If you are still feeling anxious, a specific way to deal with anxiety is to admit your fear. Talk it over with a friend. Try to identify what it is that you feel and why. Is it the difficulty of the task? Is it the fear of approaching a stranger? Do you find it difficult to ask questions? As a designer, meeting new people is an essential skill to be learned. Designers cannot wait for clients to come to them, but rather have to be confident and outgoing to convince clients of their abilities and to secure interesting projects.

In the process of paying attention to other people's ideas about how things are you may find yourself shocked to have your own assumptions revealed to you. Spradley and McCurdy note, "As you begin to learn another culture you will become conscious of your own stereotypes and misconceptions."[3] Interaction with those who have different lifestyles, whether they are construction workers, homeless people, retail clerks, or bicycle messengers, makes it hard to continue to think in stereotypes about others. The beliefs and practices that once might have seemed "strange, narrow minded, and bizarre become meaningful when they are seen from the point of view of those studied. When people with another culture become your teachers," you may discover that "'stupid reasons' and 'irrational behavior' are merely labels used by outsiders to explain what they consider strange."[4]

An easy way to deal with anxiety is to select a sited culture that is not psychologically threatening. A local church might be easier for you than a gay bar—or perhaps you'd feel more comfortable in the bar. A sixth-grade boy who is part of the local gymnastics club has a wealth of cultural knowledge and might be easier to interview than the president of a bank. Children make excellent informants, and many students will find them easier to approach than adults; be sensitive to the possible need for parental permission.

Finally, since fear is usually most intense at the beginning of your project, you can cope by recognizing that these feelings will pass. Fear usually gives way to enthusiasm once you have met your informant and started the study.

4.3 Working in teams

Another way to deal with anxiety is to work as a member of a team. Pair up with a friend, classmate, or coworker. Although you should each concentrate on a different micro-culture, you can work with different informants within the same social situation. Also, working in teams may be a good idea for your own safety. If you decide to study bars in some neighborhoods, teaming up with another person might be wise. Teamwork has other advantages: it is easier for two people to observe and record a wider range of events and informant statements. You could take turns helping each other record interviews. After each period of fieldwork, team members can discuss what transpired and thus make their field notes more complete.

But teamwork can have drawbacks. To start, be sure that you are not threatening to your informants. If two investigators intrude into a small situation (for instance, a nail salon) to interview a lone professional and observe what occurs, it might be overwhelming. An informant may be happy to talk to one or two investigators with ease; one additional person may be just enough to make it difficult to gain his confidence and establish rapport. In addition, you must be aware that duplicating all the work and discussing your findings with another researcher will likely take more time than working by yourself. Take all these factors into consideration when designing your research strategy.[5]

4.4 Combining observation, participation, and talking to informants

Culture can be tacit—meaning something about which people have a shared understanding yet cannot articulate in words, such as Hall's concept of *proxemics*—or explicit, wherein meaning is coded in language and thus can be explained in words.[6] Each of these facets of culture requires a different research method to understand: in the case of Hall's study of *proxemics*, observation was required in order to see people's reactions to different physical circumstances. Though Hall's informants were able to articulate why certain social distances were more or less comfortable than others, they did not have words to describe the rules or distances they enacted. However, for parts of culture that are coded in language—think of the short-hand words and phrases used by line cooks at a restaurant—interviews are a better research method because your informant can explain the meanings of terms.

Thus, if you are going to describe the sited micro-culture people have learned and to understand the way they inhabit space, you will want to do more than merely observe their actions. If you had a great many years to spend, you might be able to infer much of what people know and do by observation alone. Without this luxury, you must depend upon informants to help you. You will want to observe them, participate with them, and interview them. When possible we recommend this combined approach. But even when you can only do an interview it will be a better interview than you might have conducted before learning how to listen actively for structure. But in many cases, you may be able to do all three: observe, participate, and then interview.[7] How do you combine these three approaches?

You can start by *observing* from the outside point of view, in contrast to the ideas of people on the inside who know the rules. You might spend one or two or three visits observing what happens before finding an informant who can tell you what insiders think is going on. This underscores the importance of keeping different columns in your notebook for what you observe versus what you are told. You might observe actions taking place in a social situation in one column, and record what people say, the categories they use, and to whom they speak in a second column. In a third column you might note how you are feeling about what you observe and hear.

Strictly speaking, semantic ethnography could be done using only interviews. However, you will get insights if you *observe* that you might have missed by only interviewing. A simple way to do this is, as anthropologists would say, "to get out into the field" and go to the place that you are studying. "Hang out" for a while—bring a sketchpad or journal if you feel that you need something to do. By spending time at the site, you will observe the physical layout of the setting and people's behavior in this social environment. Of course, sometimes you cannot visit the site because it is too far away or because it does not yet exist. In this case, seek out a similar situation where you can observe people. If you are able to observe as well as interview, separate what you observe from what you are told in your study and final report, again using the device of three columns in a notebook. Make note of similarities and differences between what you observe, hear, and feel.[8]

The type of observation we advise you to do is conceptually different from "participant observation," which, as defined by anthropologists, has traditionally required more active participation than you will be able to do. You might better think of yourself as a "friendly witness." But participation remains an important adjunct to your project in that it will allow you to gain an emic point of view and thus help you become a source of information yourself. Typically, we think research must be "scientific" and "objective" without bias from the researcher. In this case, subjectivity actually becomes a key to doing good research. This does not mean you can ignore everyone's impressions but your own. Instead, you should try to cultivate an insider's point of view so that your subjective view comes closer to the members of the culture's own subjective view. Then you could possibly rely on introspection (looking to your own feelings and judgments) as a way to get an idea of what others are likely to favor. The underlying rationale for this is that the designer who can take the point of view of the other is better able to understand and therefore meet the needs and desires of the client.

Steve Portigal adds that interviewing "creates a shared experience"—which he terms *empathy*—that leads to a deeper understanding of an informant's experiences and emotions. This perspective can help designers advocate for users and create designs that support and celebrate an informant's needs; the experience of developing empathy can also increase a designer's—or researcher's—capacity for empathy.[9]

Still, in order to cultivate an emic perspective you can trust, you must invest time hanging out at the setting and interacting with its inhabitants. This is important because we know there can be a great discrepancy between what people say and what they do. Therefore, you may need to go beyond interviews to get a more complete sense of the culture. This is where observation is so valuable; if you notice a discrepancy between what people say and what they do, you can ask about it and learn even more about the nuances of their culture. For example, your informant might *say* that he or she favors public transit in general, but you observe that he or she uses a car for everything. Instead of asking about public transit in general, you might ask if they favor it for each of a specific set of activities, for example shopping, going to work, taking the kids to school, running errands, going to the doctor, etc. You might ask if they intend to use public transit for one of these activities *tomorrow*. Learning why they can or cannot use public transit for each of these activities would tell you a lot about *why* their "green behavior" is different from their "green attitude."[10]

4.5 Number of informants

Because your time will be limited, you may not be able to work this way with very many informants. For your first experience with ethnographic research, we strongly suggest that you limit the number of informants you interview to one. Sometimes people are skeptical of interviewing just one or two or even ten people about views shared by many. They ask, "Is one informant's view a reliable measure of how the group sees the world, or is it merely her personal opinion?" Since most of us have been taught that science involves treating others as "objects" by sampling them, observing them repeatedly, and making statistical correlations, the process of interviewing just one or two people looks unreliable. You can, however, interview only one informant as long as you realize the limitations of this approach, make every attempt to select an informant who is widely respected by the group, and follow the guidelines listed in Table 4.1.

Additionally, because your informant will be explaining to you the cultural knowledge they share with a larger group—rather than their personal opinion—it may be more accurate to think of your sample size not as a single person but as the sum of "all the interactions . . . the important details . . . the cultural information" your informant can share.[11]

4.6. The good informant

Some informants are better than others. Sometimes you may not have any choice—a single informant may be all you can locate for the micro-culture you wish to study. But in most cases, you will have a choice. Table 4.2 shows several things to consider when selecting an informant.

Do not despair if your first choice of informant is a flop. The person who turns out to be a poor informant can still be of great help for your research project: she can act as an intermediary to put you in contact with a more talkative, willing, and nonanalytical informant.

4.7 Locating an informant using an intermediary

As a newcomer to the sited micro-culture that you have chosen to study, you will know very little, if anything, about the way that culture works. The value of an intermediary is that she serves as the link, a kind of translator or representative, between you and the micro-culture, similar to a go-between. For example, an architecture student wanted to do an ethnographic report on an elementary school classroom. She had a friend whose mother was a fifth-grade teacher nearby. The friend introduced her to his mother, making it easier to gain entry into the classroom.

Table 4.1 Ways to increase the reliability of what a single informant tells you

Developing good rapport with an informant will decrease the possibility of lying.
Rather than inquiring about her personal opinions, ask what she thinks others in the group believe or experience. For example, you might ask, "Can you describe *a* typical day at the restaurant" rather than "Can you describe *your* typical day at the restaurant" as a way to refer to the group experience rather than a personal experience.[1]
By asking the same question in different interviews you can learn whether your informant is being consistent. You can even ask him directly to check what you have learned and to see if you got it right. For instance, after learning about the different tools used by a mechanic to perform specific tasks, you might say: "I'd like to go over the tools we talked about last week and see if I got them right." As you read them back to your informant he can correct you or add to the list.
If you have the time, you could check with other informants or even administer a questionnaire later based on what you have learned.

1 McCurdy et al., *The Cultural Experience*, 2005, 27.

Table 4.2 Characteristics of a good informant

A good informant is one who knows the culture well. In contrast, a person could be a newcomer to a social situation who has not yet learned the sited micro-culture others share.

Another characteristic of a good informant is her willingness to talk. Sometimes a person knows a lot, but will not reveal her knowledge for one reason or another. Perhaps she has learned by experience not to trust strangers, or perhaps she never developed her verbal skills. Semantic ethnographer James Spradley found such a person who became an excellent informant only after being encouraged to write a diary of his experience in jail.[1]

Finally, a good informant is one who communicates about his culture naturally, nonanalytically. He accepts his culture as the way things are, and is probably unaware that other people might see things differently. Student Junius Hoffman found the perfect informant: a sales clerk at a second-hand store. Hoffman noticed that even though the people who entered the store rarely bought anything, his informant persisted in calling them customers. Hoffman says:

> Wanting to pursue what I perceived to be an invalid vocabulary in their Store User Taxonomy, I tried to get Mary . . . to develop a Store Function Taxonomy. "Why do people come *here*?" I asked. "To shop." "Why do they shop here?" I then asked. "They're customers," Mary answered a bit uneasily, "they come here to shop." "How does the store itself work?" I tried, taking a different approach. "Do the customers use any particular areas in other ways?" Both questions received blank responses.[2]

Avoid an informant who wants to translate his information into concepts he thinks are more familiar to you. This may be especially problematic after he learns that you are studying design. He may offer a list of problems with design, architecture, structure, or space and even suggestions for solving them before you have been able to develop a comprehensive picture of the culture as a whole. For this reason, introducing yourself as a student might be better than introducing yourself as a designer or architecture student.

1 James P. Spradley and David W. McCurdy, *The Cultural Experience: Ethnography in Complex Society* (Chicago: Science Research Associates, 1972), 47.
2 Junius Hoffman, "A Second-hand Store" (Spring 1977).

A go-between can be almost anyone. Once you have some places in mind, ask people if they know others who are acquainted with those places. Ask everyone you know. If you want to interview a building inspector, you may be surprised how often someone you know casually has a nephew who is married to a woman whose brother was once a building inspector. Besides making initial contact with an informant, working through an intermediary has another important advantage. If you make contact with an informant through an intermediary, you will have an easier time establishing trust and gaining cooperation; if your informant is still suspicious of your intentions, she is probably also suspicious of her friend, your intermediary.

4.8 Other ways of choosing an informant

You do not have to use an intermediary to find an informant. You can approach someone directly, but this may require more persistence than being introduced by an intermediary. You may be turned down by the first person you meet, although most people are pleased to cooperate. You might begin with a casual visit to a place, such as a school playground, a courtroom, or a restaurant. You may be able to attend a public meeting. One student who had a hard time finding an informant began his search by telephone:

> The phrase "to select an informant" is actually quite inaccurate in terms of how I met the person who provided the bridge into the culture group that I studied. I feel strongly that a more accurate description would be "the informant who selected me." After spending an afternoon on the phone contacting various possible sites, I found, quite discouragingly, that very few people were interested in committing the time required to help me with this project. The majority of the possible informants were at most willing to share an hour or slightly more of their schedule. I finally contacted a woman by the name of M_____ , head of the . . . Preschool. She was incredibly gracious and was enthusiastic about engaging the possibility of better understanding her own environment through another person's eyes.[12]

Another student described how her informant found her and not the other way around:

> I simply walked into the base and directed myself towards the person who seemed to be in control . . . the person that everyone was going up to with questions. I introduced myself as an architecture student and was welcomed quite graciously by an older gentleman who turned out to be the Committee Chairman. After two seconds of discussion, I realized I would never get a word in edge-wise as he was quite the "chatterer." The conversation continued for about 20 minutes when I realized that I was never going to get to interject. So, frightened by receiving too much information, I was able to get away to do some sketching. A skipper who was interested in my sketching approached me. I instantly felt at ease talking to him and he seemed to have a lot to say. He is a former member of [the group] and now, at the age of 25, is the skipper of two ships on the base. I opted not to tell him right off what my mission was, and would just let the conversation flow as it may—obviously I reconsidered who my informant would be and after about half an hour of conversation, I filled him in on my purpose and he actually lent himself to the position of informant.[13]

4.9 Explaining ethnographic research

Trust is the first step in creating a good relationship with an informant. And, you need to build trust in a way that is comprehensible to the informant. If you say to a local carpenter: "I am doing ethnographic fieldwork and would like to do a semantic ethnographic study of your particular sited culture within this social situation," you will probably have to find another informant. You must explain your purpose in a way that can be understood.

Always, your explanation must be honest. Do not hide your identity and purpose; otherwise, your informant will not trust you. State plainly that you would like to know about their way of life and that this project is part of your educational requirements. Honesty does not mean you should explain the details of your project and methods of research. An explanation should be as simple as possible. In our complex society, one of the most easily understood roles you have is that of student. Stating that you are a college student puts you in an excellent position to be taught by an informant.

Since the ideal role of the ethnographer in every society is as a novice or student who seeks to learn, adopting the role of student is a good way to begin. Be careful how you present your identity as a designer, however, because respondents might feel they have to give you information they presume relevant to design. As noted above, often all you will get is a list of environmental problems and their possible solutions. A general statement that you are doing a project or assignment for a social science or design research course will usually be an adequate explanation for most people. Emphasize that you are engaged in research *about* design rather than designing.

BOX 4.1: ETHNOGRAPHY PROJECT GUIDELINES

Part 2: Cultural Informant, Interview, and Coding the Interview

Selecting and interviewing an informant

Research method: semantic interviews

Summary of required activities: Your priority for this stage of your project will be to identify and interview a cultural informant. By conducting a series of interviews with your informant, you will obtain a basic understanding of the culture you are studying. Thus, as already mentioned, your informant should be someone who is knowledgeable about the situation you are studying. To encourage your informant to articulate a broad description of the sited micro-culture, you should begin your first interview with a "grand tour" question and then ask for definitions and clarifications of terms as needed.* *Note: You should conduct at least two interviews with your informant for this stage of the project and at least three to five interviews total by the end of the project.*

Summary of research proposal components: Write a summary of how you identified, gained access to, and developed rapport with your informant. Make sure to provide specific examples of your informant's availability and attitude toward you and your study—each of these details will more convincingly describe your relationship than simply saying you have a good rapport with your informant. In less than a page, briefly summarize your first interview with your informant, including the types of questions you asked, the ***cultural terms*** you learned, and anything else you find noteworthy from the encounter. You may also choose to comment on topics you would like to follow up on in future interviews. Finally, transcribe and code your interview notes.

Grading Criteria for Part 2

Does your project conform to the following criteria?

- Identification of your informant**: name, role, description of why your informant will be a good source of cultural information about the site you have selected.

- Description of the process of identifying your informant: how you found and selected your informant and any challenges you faced in the process.
- Assessment of your rapport: describe your relationship, including your informant's availability, demeanor, and his or her attitude to your project.
- Brief (less than one page) summary of your first interview: note the types of questions you asked, what you learned, and anything you found surprising or interesting.
- Transcription and coding (*identification of primary themes, vocabulary words, and basic illustration of terms and connections*) of your interview notes.
- 1–2 pages in length.

Notes

* If your informant approves, you may want to use a tape recorder during your interview.

** Remember that, in order to protect the confidentiality of your informant, you should not use her real name in your report. Instead, invent a pseudonym and note in your paper that you have done so.

You can be honest without volunteering more information than is needed. Some architecture students have found it useful not to reveal their interest in architecture, so as not to influence their informants into thinking they should focus on the physical characteristics of their environment instead of the total cultural setting. Here is one student's experience in finding the right way to frame her research intent:

> After two unsuccessful tries at finding an informant for my subculture of food kiosk workers, I finally met a woman, Mrs . . ., an employee who was willing to become my main informant. For the two unsuccessful contacts, I had introduced myself as a student doing a report on the daily routines and activities that occurred inside a kiosk. They were instantly skeptical and probably thought I was a spy from the Food and Health Administration doing a surprise check-up. After learning from this, I explained my research project as a study of self-reliant environments and its successes and failures to both workers and customers. Mrs . . . and her employers were all very supportive and welcomed me to study their Chinese food kiosk.[14]

Table 4.3 You might use each of the following statements during the first few encounters

First visit	I would like to find out about the Association of Architectural Historians from someone who is a member and knows about it from first-hand experience.
Second visit	Our talk yesterday was very interesting and I want to tell you how much I appreciate your taking time to give me an insider's perspective on the Association of Architectural Historians.
Third visit	I have some more questions to ask you this week and, again, I want to know how members of the Association of Architectural Historians feel about them. I am interested in the members' point of view.
Ensuing visits	I would like to follow up on some of the terms you gave me and make sure that I understand them accurately.

4.10 Recording ethnographic research

Recording information for later analysis is essential. We recommend you take written notes, use a recorder, and you might also document your interviews with photographs or video. (*Note*: You must obtain your informant's permission prior to using either technology.) Even the simple act of jotting down a few written notes can make your informant uncomfortable. Sometimes you can take notes in the presence of an informant, but at other times you may need to remember what is said and done until you can record it, which should be done *immediately* after each field session. Direct note taking is the more accurate way of recording data, but whether or not you can use this method depends on the nature of the relationship. If, when you concentrate on writing, you lose focus on your informant, then you should make notes after the interview. But taking notes, even if you are a slow scribe, can also show your informant how seriously you take his knowledge. If you cannot record a full set of notes on the spot, try jotting down short reference words or phrases immediately after the interview is over and use these later to help you reconstruct as fully as possible what was said.

Record your impressions throughout the study. Keep a journal or a notebook. You should keep your observations recorded separately from your record of the words you hear used in the setting. If you are taking written notes, you can easily do this by enclosing your own thoughts in brackets [like this—and of course it's fine to use another symbol; just keep it consistent]. This way you will not confuse what you wrote with the meaning that it has for your informants. At a later stage in your research you may decide to merge the observation and its interpretation, but it might be important to keep the distinction because you might see a major contradiction between what you observe and what people think it means. We find that often this junction can work as a springboard in thinking about your design proposals.

Since your understanding will grow, you must be willing to reflect upon how your understanding of the sited culture has changed over time. At the same time, the flood of new and sometimes conflicting information can be so overwhelming that you will certainly forget some significant observations if they are not written down and available for review later. Since you will not know what is significant when you first begin, write quickly and without editing. Later, something you initially thought was insignificant may emerge as part of an important pattern.

We also recommend that you use a recorder, because it records what people say verbatim, and such statements are necessary for establishing subtle, but significant, distinctions of meaning in the culture. Transcribing recorded interviews takes a lot of time, but the effort can be worthwhile. Without transcribing the interviews they can still be useful to you because you can listen again and take notes that express the distinctions drawn by your informant. Do not record a conversation without your informant's knowledge. If your informant discovers that you have been recording his words without permission, you may lose the faith he has in you and endanger your whole research project. Furthermore, recording people without their consent is also illegal in many cases.

For designers interested in the way a specific cultural group uses space, visual records may also be essential. Taking photographs or video footage and sketching during demonstrations or explanations are excellent ways of recording what, where, and how things are done.[15] They also require specific skills that as future designers you are expected to acquire. In taking photographs as much as in sketching, you must learn to be quick and as unobtrusive as possible, including people without asking them to pose for you. In some ways, taking pictures is similar to using a recorder in that a camera can make people self-conscious. But most informants quickly forget both recorders and cameras as they concentrate on what they are doing. You must, however, ask for permission *before* starting to take pictures or video, which may not always be given, depending on the site under study.

Yet photographs and video recordings remain precious pieces of information from which a great deal can be learned, even long after you leave the cultural setting. You can later consult them to refresh your mind, and studying them closely may reveal new facets of the culture you had not previously noticed. Furthermore, Pavlides has shown that showing photos to interviewees can elicit information about the site or the social rules of the group.[16]

BOX 4.2: SKILL SPOTLIGHT—QUICK TIP FOR QUICK NOTE TAKING: DIAGRAM YOUR NOTES

Effective note taking can help you understand, organize, and remember information. Whether recording important ideas in meetings or classes, taking and reviewing notes are fundamental skills for college students and professionals alike.

For this ethnographic project in particular, a few simple steps can help you take quick, concise, and accurate notes while interviewing your cultural informant. Here are a few suggestions:

Before the Interview

- Identify areas of interest to you (but be sure that you do not ask leading questions; instead, ask the "grand tour" question) and leave ample room to write follow-up notes.
- In subsequent interviews, write down the terms from the first interview that you would like to know more about.
- If you have photos or floor plans of your site, you can put them in your notebook to make sure they are easily accessible (either to annotate or use as a visual reference) during your interviews.

During the Interview

- As your informant speaks, listen carefully for important ideas—for example, cultural terms, descriptions, spatial issues, etc.—and record key terms as you hear them. You may find it helpful to circle or underline important words or ideas to locate them easily later on.
- Do *not* write down what your informant says word for word. Instead, write down single words, such as cultural terms or descriptions. For example, rather than writing:

  "A conference is a type of event open to members only,"

you could simply write:

> *"conference → event, members only."*

You can also represent this information *diagrammatically*. Diagramming your notes is a way to represent the content of what your informant says and can help show the relationship between terms. Referring to the same example above, you could place the two main terms, *conference* and *member event*, into boxes or circles to begin building a diagram of relationships. For example:

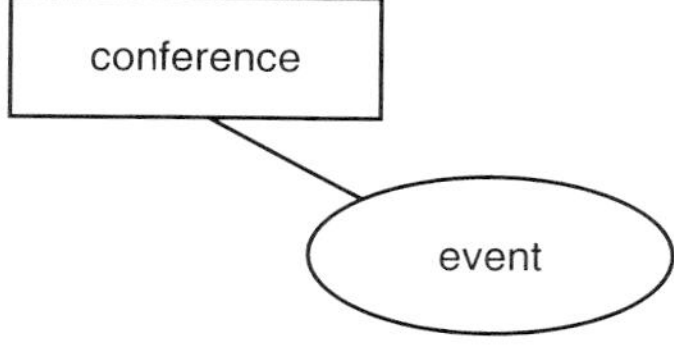

Figure 4.1a

Diagramming your notes in such a way has two benefits: first, it is a quick way to record information and relationships between terms; second, it allows you to identify helpful follow-up questions. For example, once you have identified a *conference* as a type of *event*, you might ask: *What other types of events are there?* You can easily make additions to your diagram:

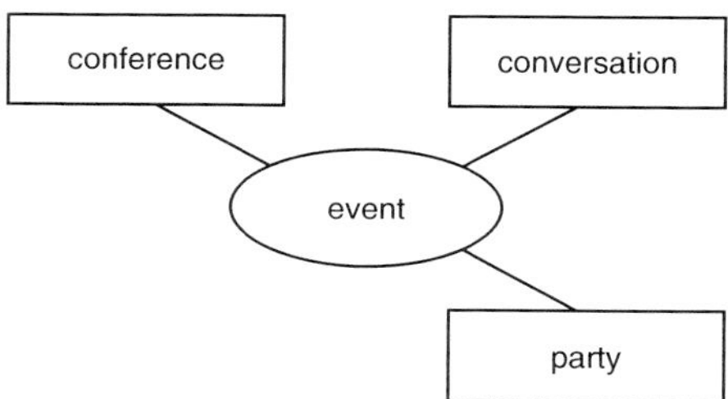

Figure 4.1b Note: In Chapter 5 you will learn about taxonomies; at that time, the above diagram will look familiar. In fact, after completing the ethnography project, one student explained that creating a taxonomy of cultural terms was easy for him because he had diagrammed the notes he took during his interviews

- Another way to take notes quickly is to use abbreviations, symbols, or acronyms rather than whole words or names. You can create your own abbreviations and symbols; just make sure you are consistent and will be able to remember what your symbols mean.
- If you miss something in your notes, leave a noticeable blank and fill it in later, either when asking a follow-up question or listening to a recording of the interview if you choose to record your conversation (for more on recording your interview, see 4.10).

- Some students may find it helpful to annotate photos or floor plans when taking notes. In this case, instead of writing full sentences about what a space is used for, by whom, and when, you could simply record key words on the plan itself.[1]
- Here is an example of notes employing some of the suggestions mentioned above:[2]

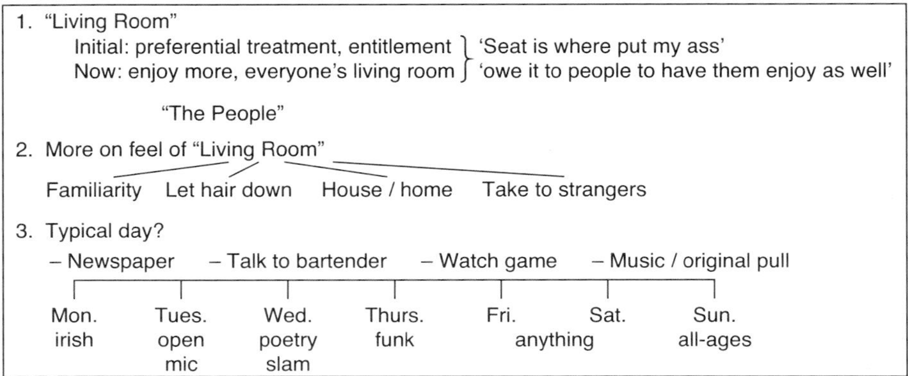

Figure 4.1c Notice how the notes that Selena Feliciano (2014) took during her informant interview take a taxonomic form

After the Interview

- Immediately review your notes and fill in any details you may have missed.
- Listen to your recording (if you have one) and make any necessary additions or changes to your notes.
- List any remaining questions you have and identify places you need to clarify; you can follow up on these items in a subsequent interview.
- When reviewing your notes, you may find it helpful to use different colors (pens, colored pencils, highlighters) to distinguish different categories or concepts (for more on cultural categories and terms, see Chapter 5) or identify questions you have.[3]

Notes

1 For more on annotating floor plans, see Zeisel, *Inquiry by Design*, 2006.
2 Selena Feliciano, "Choosing Informant and Interview Summary" (Fall 2014).
3 For more on note taking, see Princeton University, "Listen Actively and Take Great Notes" (The McGraw Center for Teaching and Learning, www.princeton.edu/mcgraw (last accessed May 21, 2013)).

4.11 Chapter review: summary of main ideas

- Select one representative of the cultural group who can inform you about the cultural knowledge in the sited micro-culture. This representative will become your informant (4.1).
- As you begin to learn another culture you will become conscious of your own stereotypes and misconceptions (4.2).

- If you are able to observe as well as interview, separate what you observe from what you are told in your study and final report, again using the device of three columns in a notebook. Make note of similarities and differences between what you observe, hear, and feel (4.4).
- For this project, you should interview only one informant; however, you should also realize the limitations of this approach and make every attempt to select an informant who is widely respected by the group. Follow the guidelines in Table 4.2 (4.5).
- By asking the same question in different interviews you can learn whether your informant is being consistent (4.1).
- Always, your explanation of ethnographic research must be honest. Do not hide your identity and purpose; otherwise, your informant will not trust you (4.9).
- Be careful how you present your identity as a designer, however, because respondents might feel they have to give you information they presume relevant to design. You can be honest without volunteering more information than is needed. Some architecture students have found it useful not to reveal their interest in architecture, so as not to influence their informants into thinking they should focus on the physical characteristics of their environment instead of the total cultural setting (4.9).
- Record your impressions throughout the study. Keep a journal or a notebook. You should keep your personal observations recorded separately from your record of the words you hear used in the setting (4.10).
- Since you will not know what is significant when you first begin, write your notes quickly and without editing. Later, something you initially thought was insignificant may emerge as part of an important pattern (4.10).
- We also recommend that you use a recorder, because it records what people say verbatim, and such statements are necessary for establishing subtle, but significant, distinctions of meaning in the culture. Do *not* record a conversation without your informant's knowledge or permission (4.10).
- Taking photographs or video footage and sketching during demonstrations or explanations are excellent ways of recording what, where, and how things are done (4.10).

Notes

1 Oracio Burgos, "A Sex Shop" (Spring 1997).
2 John A. Price, "The Field Course in Anthropology." Paper presented at the American Anthropological Association Meetings in New Orleans, November 1969: 7.
3 Spradley and McCurdy, *The Cultural Experience,* 1972, 43.
4 Ibid., 44.
5 For additional information about conducting interviews, see McCurdy et al., *The Cultural Experience*, 2005; and Portigal, *Interviewing Users,* 2013.
6 McCurdy et al., *The Cultural Experience*, 2005, 8; see also Hall, *The Silent Language,* 1959.
7 Observational techniques are helpful in conveying the range of activities and behaviors in a given location but do not, however, explain the *meaning* of any of these aspects. For this reason, it is often helpful to conduct observations in tandem with other research methods such as interviews or surveys (cf. Pavlides and Cranz, "Ethnographic Methods in Support of Architectural Practice," 2012).
8 E. T. Hall on the investigator's feelings: "I think that one of the things that your students will need is the thing they are taught not to do. They should pay very close attention to their

feelings and what is setting them off. You might ask them to talk about what really bugs them. What bugs you in particular? It is very important for people to know how they feel. This is a culture [U.S] that downplays feelings. You are not supposed to feel. Well, that's an Anglo thing. [You may feel that you are] at a terrible disadvantage [if you] have no way of hiding [your] feelings. . . . You use your eyes and your ears and nose and feelings. And as a matter of fact, this is a good thing for people to do anyway. Watch your feelings and see what is ticking them off. But we are told not to do that, not to pay attention. But what we are told is just plain wrong. It is so important to pay attention to your feelings." ("Gifts of Wisdom: An Interview with Dr. Edward T. Hall," interviewed by Kathryn Sorrells, Associate Editor, *The Edge* http://people.umass.edu/~leda/comm494r/The%20Edge%20 Interview%20Hall.htm).

9 Portigal, *Interviewing Users,* 2013, 10.

10 See Alice Jones, "The Psychology of Sustainability: What Planners Can Learn from Attitude Research," *Journal of Planning Education and Research* 16 (1996): 56–65.

11 Kelly and Gibbons, "Marketing Methodologies Ethnography," 2008, 281.

12 Michael Kao, " A Montessori Pre-school" (Spring 1996).

13 Annallee Baldwin, "A Sea Explorer's Base" (Spring 1996).

14 Eva Kwok, "A Chinese Food Kiosk" (Spring 1996).

15 To see examples of notes sketched during the interview, see Portigal, *Interviewing Users,* 2013, 114.

16 Eleftherios Pavlides and Jana E. Hesser, "Vernacular Architecture as an Expression of Its Social Context in Eressos, Greece," in *Housing, Culture and Design: A Comparative Perspective* (Philadelphia: University of Pennsylvania Press, 1989): 357–74.

5 Finding meaning in taxonomies

5.1 Understanding a sited culture

Recall a time when you came upon an informal conversation in which people had been talking about architectural history or a new musical satire. Although you were interested, you found that you could not really understand the conversation because you had not yet taken that course or heard that music. Some of their terms may have been unfamiliar, but even recognizable words did not make sense. It's likely you'd be confused until someone said a particular word, or spoke in a particular way, that let you understand the frame of reference. That moment of insight let you see the meaning behind what was being said. You were even able to understand what other unfamiliar words meant, because now you understood the context of the exchange. You could begin to understand not only what was being said, but also how the speakers organized their knowledge and the way they looked at their world.

Your process of coming to understand a culture may coalesce in a similar flash of insight. Cultural knowledge is organized, but often implicit. This cultural knowledge is like an agreed-upon set of rules for sport that allows participants to synchronize their behavior and share understanding. When you figure out the rules you will suddenly appreciate the game!

In this chapter we shall examine some of the fundamentals of cultural knowledge and how they are organized. You will start by learning how to ask questions that will reveal cultural meaning systems.

5.2 Elements of cultural knowledge

Cultural knowledge is made of several basic elements, and the most important of these for ethnographic fieldwork is the category. Watson and Watson explain: "All knowledge depends on categorization; that is, the classification of objects according to their similarities and differences from other objects."[1] Members of a university bureaucracy and a remote tribal village face the same problem—they must take the jumble of stimuli they experience daily and make it manageable. Humans "do this by treating different objects and events *as if* they were equivalent.[2] This is the essence of categorization. If we could not do this, we would become hopelessly enslaved to the uniqueness of each event." Instead of different categories of people making up a group, each member would be unlike any other. Spradley and McCurdy continue, "Instead of professors, students, administrators, and staff on a college campus there would be thousands of individuals—each different from all the others. Every category of person, place, time, or object *simplifies* our world. Once a person is placed in a category—be it 'student', 'professor', 'shaman,' or 'mother's brother'—it is easier to anticipate [and thus understand] his behavior."[3]

While most members of an academic community share such categories as "first year," "teaching assistant," "professor," and "dean," there are other concepts that only one or two groups on a campus use. For example, architecture school students might categorize other students as "tree huggers," "blobitects," "parametricists," and so forth. These categories make up part of the student culture. These architecture students have developed labels that enable them to identify other students and relate to them in a predictable manner. It seems strange to Americans that some people, like the Chinese, use special terms to distinguish a mother's brother from a father's brother, since Americans call both "uncle." To an outsider, it also seems strange that architecture students from a particular school are classed into dozens of different categories with names such as "junior postmodernist," "senior cad monkey," and "graduate deconstructivist." But the importance of these categories, strange or not to an outsider, is that they facilitate the organization of people's experiences.

Categorization is not a discovery of the natural grouping of objects in the environment. Instead, categories are invented by cultures and perpetuated by use. Anthropologists understand that objects and events do not imply their own meaning. For example, colors are grouped together and named in different ways by different societies. Categories are invented. Our work as design ethnographers is to uncover the specific categories created by members of a sited micro-culture to understand how they organize their knowledge. An insightful designer can use this understanding to capture, amplify, or even challenge the distinctions made by clients.

5.3 Discovering cultural categories

The ethnographer discovers cultural categories first by finding out when someone is considering different objects as equivalent. The ethnographer does not impose her own categories on what she sees. Instead, she looks for a common response to an array of different objects.[4] "If your informant blushes in the presence of some people but not others, you infer that he has at least two categories of people. If his response to different places on a college campus is to name them . . . 'that is a *classroom* and all those rooms and that wing of the building are *classrooms*' . . . then we infer he has a category. Many, but not all, categories of a culture have linguistic labels or names, and so research begins by recording the names people use for categories," such as people, places, activities, and things.[5] For example, an informant might say: "After classes some students drink coffee," thereby providing you with at least three category names: classes (places or times), students (people), and drinking coffee (activity).

Your contact with your informant will be verbal, so you can easily record names for categories. You must take care to record them accurately. Substituting names in the various categories yields different results. For example, if your informant said "have tea" *and* "drink coffee," you might infer that the two activities have different meanings. Further conversation would be necessary to determine how your informant views these different activities. Not only will you have to record your conversations in one way or another, but also you will need to note what categories the informant defines as he or she goes about his or her social activities at the site of study. You may need to ask specific questions about these categories for clarification. The best place to start is a ***grand tour question***.

5.4 The grand tour question

In order to elicit useful information, you must take nothing for granted. Tell your informant that although you may sound ignorant, you will ask all kinds of questions because you want to hear his or her own point of view. Think back to the first time you visited the campus you are currently attending. It's likely you were taken on a tour, shown the main departmental buildings, the administration, special historical sites, social spaces, perhaps some athletic facilities. Your tour guide no doubt explained the general significance and use of these places. This was a *grand tour*. Your investigations should start with such a tour. Your informant should be able to give you such a tour.

There are cues in the grand tour about significance and meaning. Any tour of a sited culture will eventually include information about space, time, people, objects, and activities. However, at the beginning do not ask about place, people, or activities, but rather ask about what the place is like. It is tempting to start out asking about activities, but then you lose the opportunity to find out what is uppermost in your informant's mind.[6] Unfortunately, the investigator who was studying nurses working in a hospital's post-surgery recovery room asked the following grand tour question: "Could you describe the kinds of things nurses in the recovery room do?" The informant carefully explained the official duties of nurses in the recovery room, and then told about a lot of her interesting experiences.[7] The information gleaned was useful, but it came prematurely—before learning if activities, places, or persons (who would have access to the recovery room) was most salient for this informant. There would have been design implications for knowing whether parts of the rooms, social roles, or activities were most salient in this micro-culture.

This conversation actually took place many miles away from the recovery room, but the investigator was guided on a survey of this micro-culture with the help of a detailed plan of the existing premises. This is one of the advantages of this kind of interviewing over the method of participant observation on site.

Sometimes the answers to a grand tour question are quite brief. For example, in a study of the play-yard of a day-care center using a 4-year-old girl as an informant, one student reported:

> I asked her to tell me what happens during the day. She started by talking in very general terms about the day's succession of events: "First we play, then we read stories, then we eat, then we play again, then we take a nap then we play again, then we go home."[8]

Consider the difference between the following two questions one might ask a pawnbroker:

a. Tell me about a typical day in your pawnshop.
b. Could you begin with the start of a typical day, from the moment you open the door and walk into your shop, and describe what you might do, what

> kinds of people might come into your shop, and so forth, from then until you close your door at night and go home?

You will get information from answers to both questions, but the answers to the second question will be much more focused and detailed, and answers to the first question will give you insight into the hierarchy of subjects in the informant's mind.

Grand tour questions work well as introductions to your subject because they give you an idea about how your subject conceptualizes both the space that the sited culture occupies and how people function within it. It also functions as an introduction to the particular ***taxonomy*** (an organization of concepts) of your subject. Your study will start from your understanding of your subject's taxonomies. They will serve as the foundation for your entire study. The grand tour question is the initial road map to your work. Additionally, this type of question can be asked throughout the project, as you learn about new areas, not just at the beginning.

After the grand tour question, asking follow-up ***questions*** yields the next level of information. To the preschool student above, one might ask: "Now, could you describe more about how you go about storytelling and what kinds of games you play?" Another helpful follow-up question is to request a tour of daily activities at a site. When studying a computer lab, one student asked follow-up questions like, "explain the structure of a typical discussion section," "describe the devices that you use in the lab," and "how do you prepare for a class discussion?"[9]

Not only must you learn to elicit the right kind of information by asking different kinds of questions, but also you have to learn to listen to the answers your informant will give you. Good listening is more difficult than any of us care to admit. In terms of ethnography, there are some specific things you want to listen for—the most important being vocabulary. You want to remember the specific words your informant uses to break his world down into categories and concepts. Another important thing to listen for is the relationship between categories. You listen for the structure of what people say. You can also listen for the informant's priorities. For instance, things mentioned earlier, more often, and with more elaboration are generally more important to the speaker than items mentioned later, infrequently, and with little embellishment.

5.5 Taxonomies: the organization of categories

You might be overwhelmed by the wealth of information you are able to gather through observation, participation, and interviewing. At some level, all of it is helpful to your global understanding of the sited micro-culture. But the question students ask most often is: "Out of all this, what part is useful for design?" The response is: "All of it—but some parts more than others." So how do you determine which are the more useful parts?

The first step in deciding what is important, useful, or of a high priority is to structure the information in some way. Writing your field reports and making drawings are two ways to structure information with which you are likely familiar. In semantic ethnography, a new type of structure is introduced: the taxonomy.

As defined in Chapter 1, a culture is a set of practices, an entire way of life, an organized way of looking at the world. Through semantic ethnography, we study the system of organization that informants use. One basic principle of organization is

Table 5.1 All taxonomies should have

Terms or elements: the words your informant uses to label categories
Connections: these connections vary with different people and different subjects

inclusion. To return to an earlier example, kinds of students in a Midwestern school of architecture, one category known as "senior postmodernist" is included in another called "postmodernist." Thus, it is possible to refer to someone by saying either "He is a postmodernist" or "He is a senior postmodernist." "Senior postmodernist" is a subcategory of "postmodernist," and as such is an *inclusion of reference*. An inclusion of reference is so commonplace we hardly ever think about it. It's a very simple concept, and one we use all the time: you make an inclusion of reference when you say things like "a dog is a pet" or "I need to clean the whole house including the kitchen." A taxonomy is a structure used by ethnographers to arrange categories related by inclusion.

Taxonomy is a logical structure of meaning—logical in its own terms, even if unique to that micro-culture. A diagrammatic format allows you to summarize the information provided by your informant in graphic terms. Generally, it is a hierarchical diagram—that is, each term or phrase in the diagram contains as subsets the ones below it—and, conversely, each term or phrase is a subset of the ones above. In ethnographic research, these terms are based on people's speech and reflect the subject's (hence, literally subjective!) particular manner of understanding the world. Thus, the words that comprise a taxonomy are placeholders for an underlying mental order.

What you are attempting to portray in a taxonomy is your informant's subjective category system. This means it will often not fit neatly into an orderly, logical group of exhaustive sets and subsets. Do *not* try to force your version of logic into their system of categories. It is precisely your informant's perception that will provide insight for your understanding of the micro-culture and subsequent design work.

Taxonomies to represent a subject's categories can take many forms including: tree charts, tables, and outlines. Different examples of student taxonomies are shown in Figures 5.1–5.11.

When you interview your informant for the first time, you will probably wonder how you could ever diagram a neat, organized, let alone, logical taxonomy from your notes. People's perceptions of their own micro-cultures are generally quite complex and this means it may take several interviews before the taxonomy seems right and somewhat complete. By trying to diagram your informant's speech into a taxonomy, you will discover the next questions to ask. And remember, it is a good idea to show a draft of the taxonomy diagram to your informant to see if you understood correctly.

Ideally, when asking questions to refine a taxonomy that you have already started to organize, you should ask questions that are open-ended enough that you do not force a particular response from your informant and thereby bias the information. Pay close attention to how your informant is structuring his knowledge, because both the ***content*** (codes, vocabulary) and the ***structure*** (connections) of the taxonomy are emic. After you feel you've done your best at diagramming the things you've been told, once again you can show the diagram to your informant so it can be further refined or amplified.

Ritual	Fun	Work
Sea explorer history	Sailing	Advancing through ranks
Advancement Ceremony	Regattas	Maintenance of ship
Ranks	Competitions	painting
Cabin boy	Knots	new masts
Apprentice	Anchors	controls are operational
Ordinary	Sailing	cleaning the deck
Able	Obstacle courses	cleaning base
Drills	Ski trips	storage areas
Meetings	Picnics/BBQ	maintenance
1st Tuesday	Summer cruise	inventory
every Sat & Sun	Dances	throw out old crap
Aquatic Park	Camping on ship	Sea wall
Needs improvement	Competitions	Coast guard rules
WWII shelter	Water slides	
Uniforms	Socializing	
ugly		
cool		
Teach nautical skills		

Figure 5.1 Table Form Taxonomy (Annallee Baldwin, "A Sea Explorer's Base," 1996)

A few warnings: first, you can inadvertently influence your informant's worldview by concentrating on design too early. Let the first two interviews wander, following your informant's idea of what is important to tell, with only the most general questions from you. Taxonomies that do not focus on space or design can turn out to be essential to your basic understanding of the micro-culture. Second, try to make taxonomic diagrams immediately following the interview. The longer you wait to structure discourse into outline diagrams, the less representative the outlines become. In fact, you can try to construct a mental image of the taxonomy—or sketch one in your notebook—as it might emerge while your informant talks. Finally, ask for clarification even, and especially, when you think it unnecessary. You want to get their exact words into their structure, not something you made up because you missed a word or misunderstood. It helps if you take careful notes while someone is speaking. Put their exact phrases and terms in quotation marks in your notes.

Let us consider briefly a taxonomy of categories from a previous study. One student studied the culture of the Golden Gate Ferry on the San Francisco Bay. His informant, a security worker on the ferry, distinguished between two main kinds of people: commuters and workers, i.e. people who are part of the ferry's staff. But he also had much more specific ways of categorizing people. Commuters and workers were only broad terms within which finer distinctions could be made.[10] When a number of categories are included in a more general one, the general one is called a cover term. It is a name that can be used to refer to, or "cover," many other more specific ones.

The lines of a tree-form taxonomy show a relationship of inclusion that may be expressed as: "X is a kind of Y." An *out-of-town* is a kind of *tourist*—and both are kinds of *commuters*. If you describe a person as a commuter you could mean any of the half dozen different kinds of commuters. If you are an outsider and want to know the meaning of "commuter," you must investigate all the different kinds of commuters. This organization of categories enables a person to refer to oneself or to others at several levels of generality. If you want to call attention to certain general features

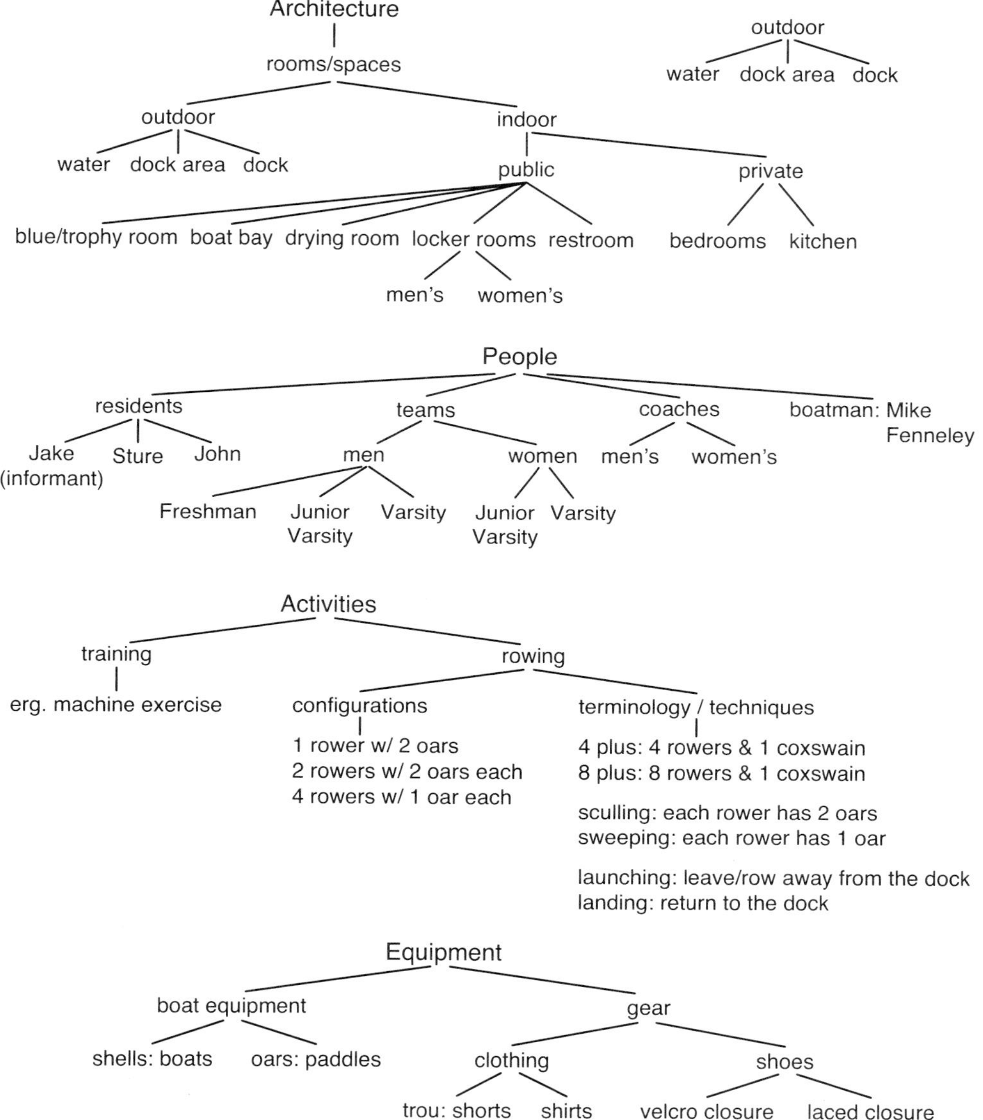

Figure 5.2 A Tree-Form Taxonomy (Vanessa Miller, "Boathouse," 1998)

of this set you can simply say: "Joe is a commuter." Alternatively, you may wish to indicate something more specific and say: "Joe is a tourist from out of town taking the ferry to the city."

Be aware that systems of cultural knowledge exhibit both structure and content. Just as in physical design, structure and content are interrelated and mutually determining. Though we seek the content, we also need to pay attention to the structure

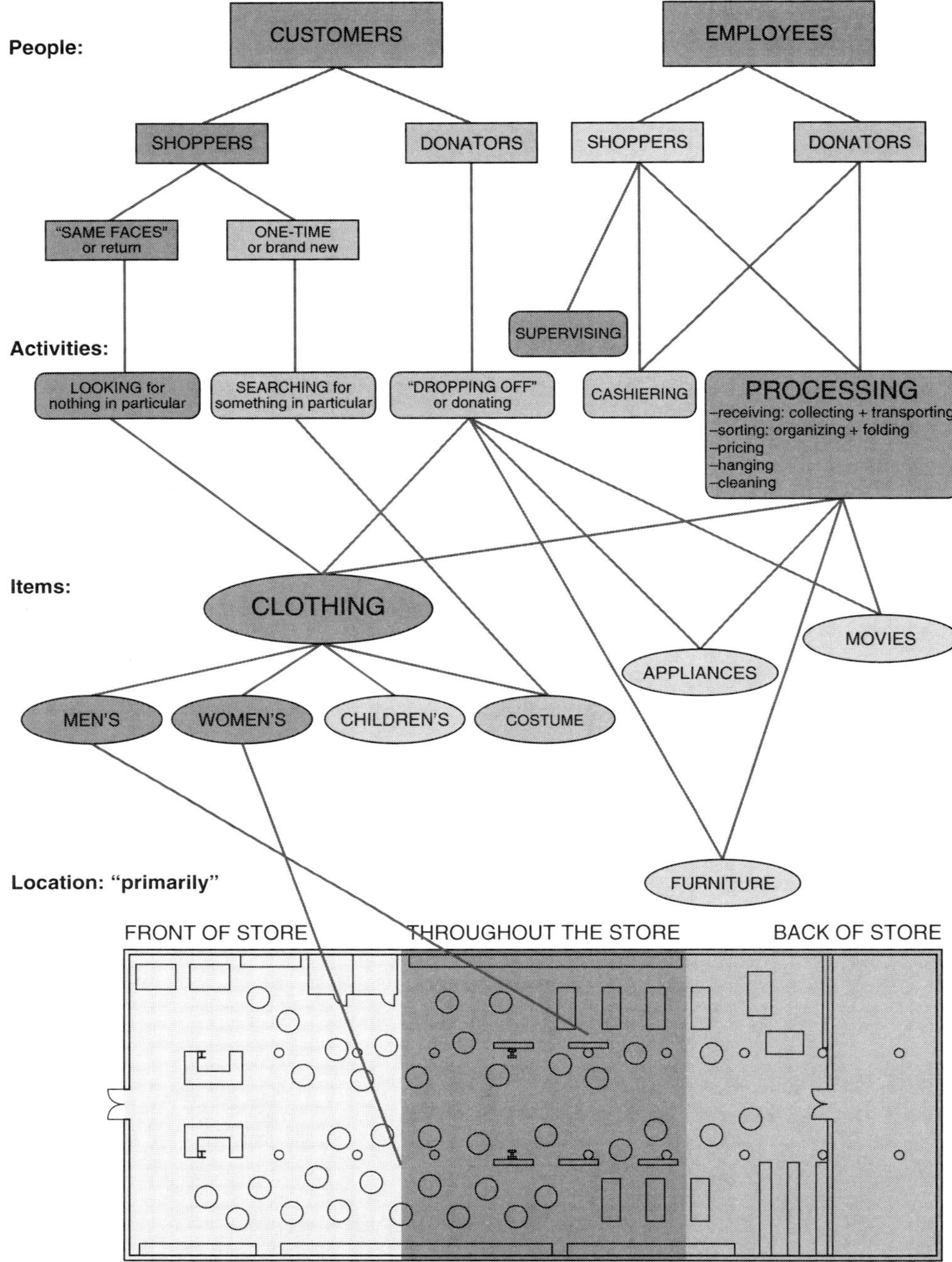

Figure 5.3 Tree-Form Taxonomy with Spatial Relationships (Sam Palfreyman, "Goodwill Taxonomy," 2009)

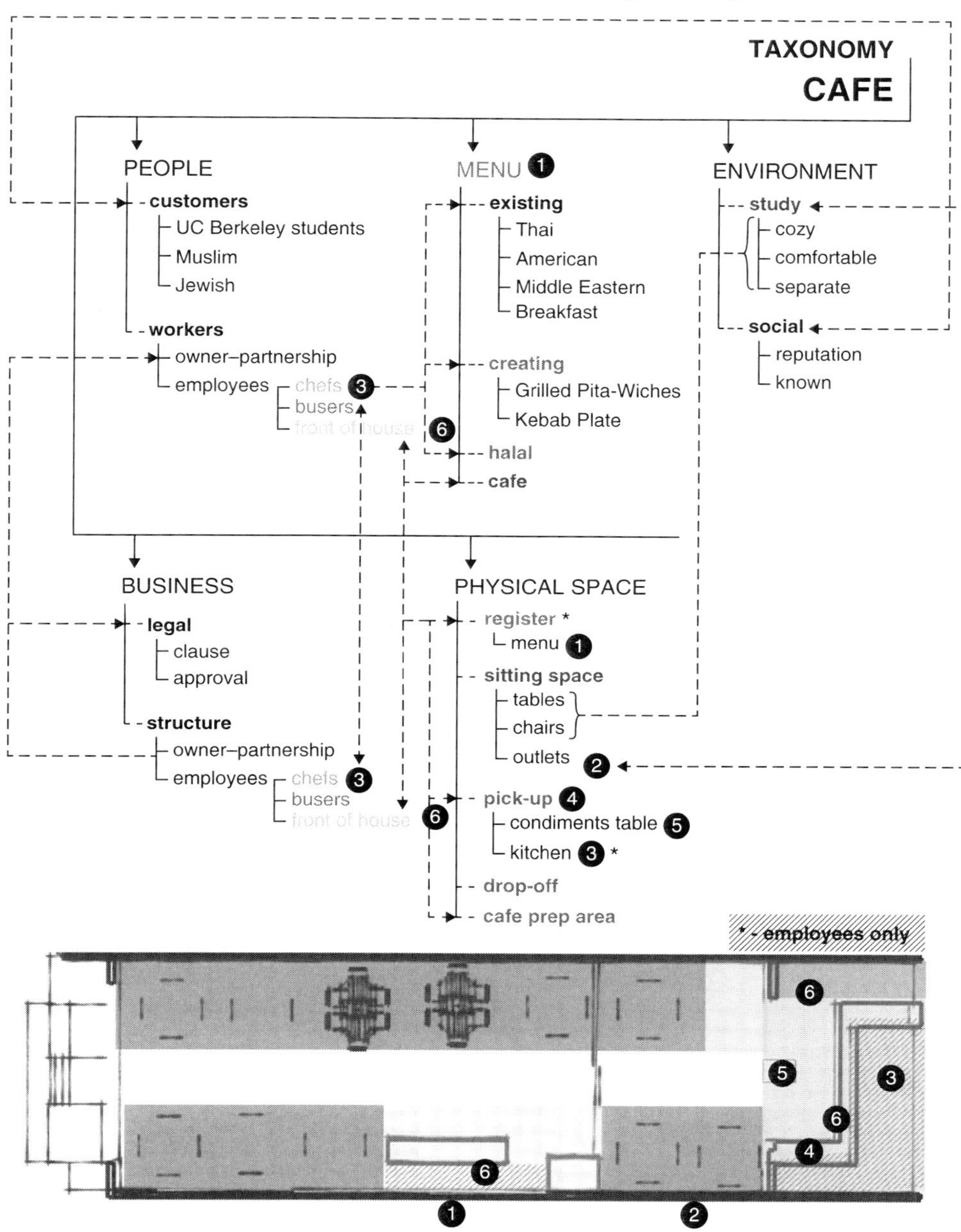

Figure 5.4 Taxonomy with Spatial Relationships (Aline Tanelian, "A Café," 2013)

of that content. The subcategories of particular terms need to be investigated to get a complete picture of the culture. Meaning or content is revealed through structure. Potentially, either the structure, or the content, or both, could inspire a design idea.

A name may be consistent but the meaning of the word changes over time or in different contexts. For example, a walking stick, which can be a simple piece of wood, probably a branch or sapling, used as an extension of the arm and aid in walking,

PRE RUN
Driver check in
Pick up "transfer pouch" and assignments
Inspect coach for defects
Activate coach
Start engine
Build air pressure
Adjust mirrors
Adjust driver's seat
Climate control
Punch transfers

PULL OUT
Deadhead to line terminal
Display head sign

RUN
Board passengers
Operate doors
Operate 'kneeling' floor (if need)
Operate wheelchair lift (if need)
Greet passengers
Answer transit-related questions
Determine fare category
Base fare
Youth fare
Senior fare
Determine transfer/pass validity
Collect fare
Count currency
Issue transfers
Eject fare evaders
Drive bus
Drive defensively
Watch for potential traffic hazards
Maintain schedule adherence
Supervise passenger behavior
Watch for safety hazards
Prevent/monitor
Watch for pranks and drunks
People watching
Watch for potential passengers
Watch/greet friends in route
Drop passengers off
Watch for potential safety hazards
Operate doors

LAYOVER
Clear bus of passengers
Park bus
Change destination signs
Change transfers
Inspect bus (occasionally)
Coffee break
Smoke
Snack
Read
Relax
Use bathroom

PULL IN
Display "not in service" headsign
Deadhead to garage
Park coach
Deactivate coach
Fill out "defect card"

CHECK OUT
Return unused transfers
Sign out

Figure 5.5 An Outline Form of a Typical-Day Taxonomy. (Kenneth Lin, "Bus Driver," 1980)

is still called a stick even when it is manufactured from aluminum tubing. The word "stick" in this context refers to a cane, itself probably once a reference to organic plant material, but now a mechanical extension of the arm used to stabilize or supplement the power of legs for walking.

Designers are usually interested in the spatial relationships within a cultural group. In this case, the taxonomy becomes a useful tool to organize the information collected, recognize physical solutions in cultural taxonomies, and develop design guidelines. In this way, the creation of a taxonomy is the first step in clarifying the

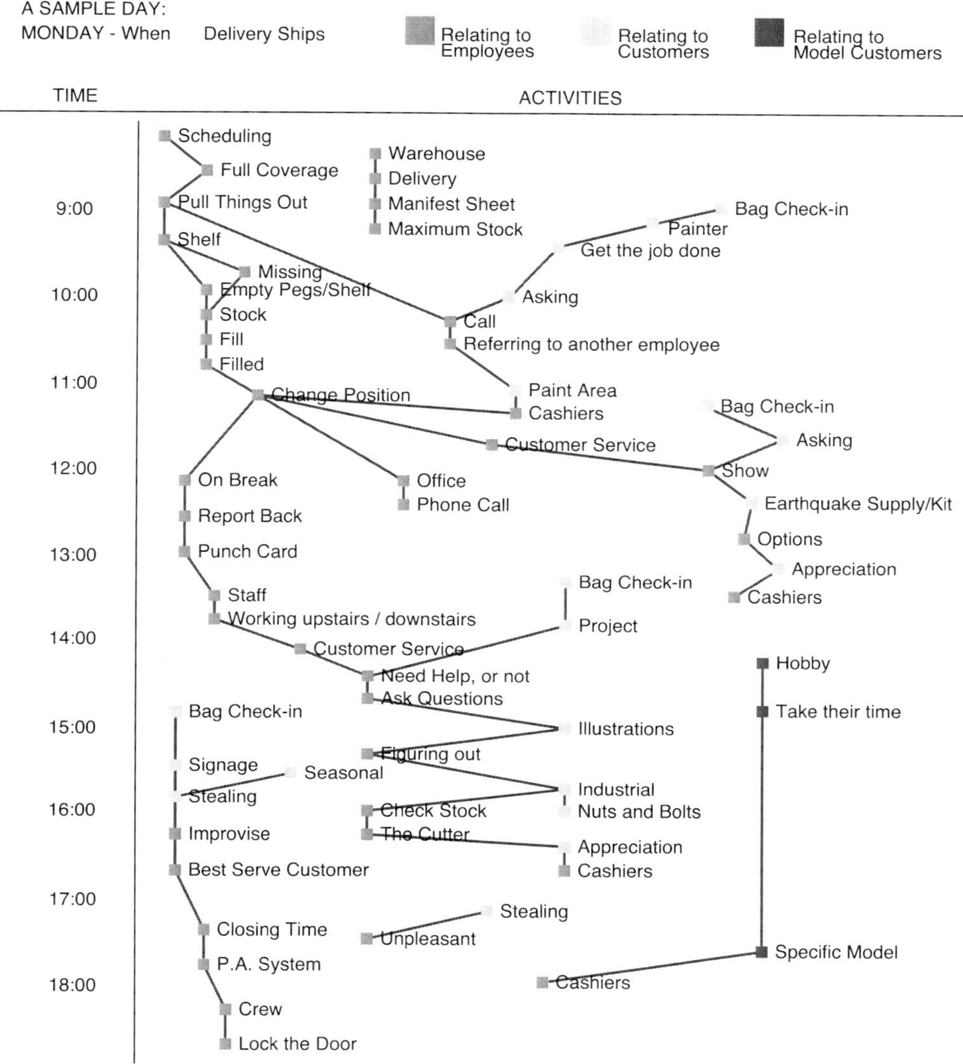

Figure 5.6 Time-based Taxonomy of Activities. (Annie Chen, "A Hardware Store in Berkeley," 2013)

relationship between ethnographic description and physical design: the construction of detailed and well-organized taxonomies, using a tree chart or other organizing method, allows you to visualize relationships between places, things, activities, and people, and to relate them to spatial organization. One can draw taxonomies of people, of activities, or tasks, and of spaces and objects. For example, a student studying a Chinese food kiosk identified five zones devoted to different functions that she discussed with her informant: the selling area, the chopping area, the cooking area, the storage area, and the "exterior" features. For each area she listed the different tasks performed, the people involved in them, the equipment necessary

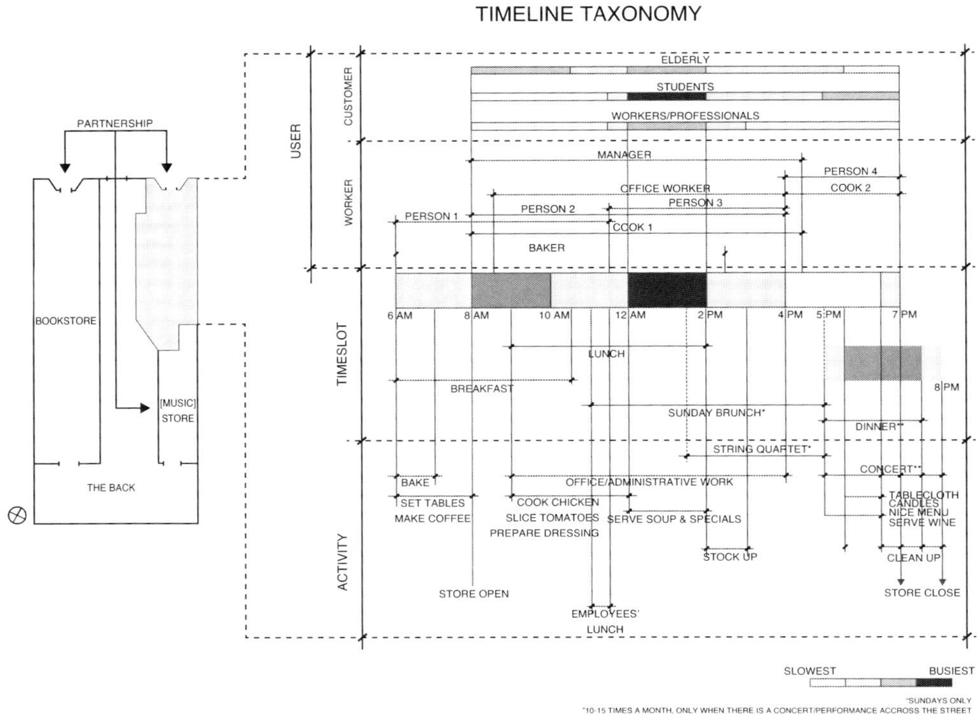

Figure 5.7 Time-Based Taxonomy of Activities with Spatial Relationships. (Grace Witanto, "The Music Store and Café ," 2013)

to perform different tasks, and the spatial requirements for each task. She overlaid information from her taxonomy on an axonometric rendering to help her understand how different categories of people and activities could be separated or regrouped to make the design more efficient.[11]

5.6 The structural question

The structural question is one of the basic tools used in the construction of a taxonomy. Imagine you are asking your informant to name all of the objects in a particular room. While you can easily see the room and ask about its contents, discovering the "cover term" for a category system may be more difficult. In the appendix when reading student projects, you will encounter numerous cover terms such as "activities of the social club," "merchandise," "items on the menu," and "regulars." As you go back over your record of what your informant has told you as a result of grand tour questions you will note terms that might be cover terms. Structural questions can thus be used to obtain information about elements within any kind of category. The terms and questions in Table 5.2 illustrate the formulation of structural questions.

Table 5.2 The structural question

Cover term	*Structural question*
1. Components of concrete	What are the substances that are necessary to make concrete?
2. Trusses	Are there different types of trusses? How would you describe them?

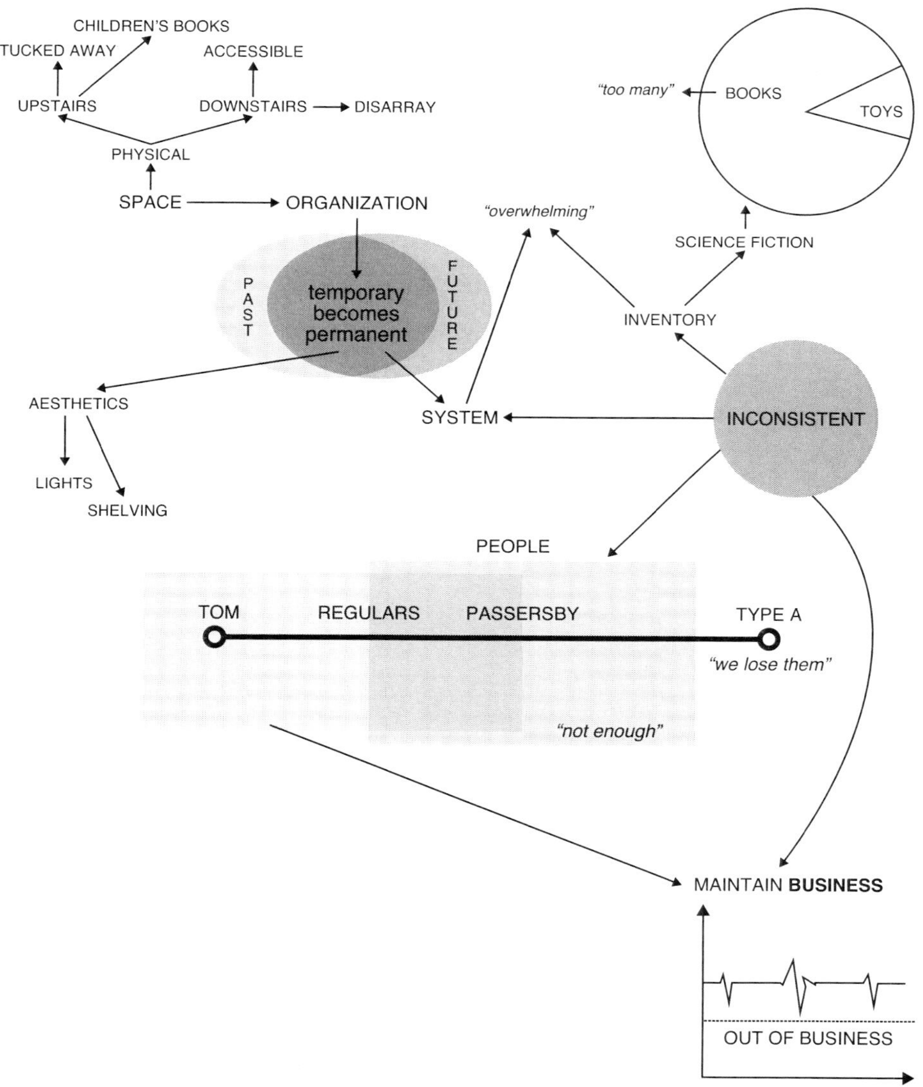

Figure 5.8 Graphic Taxonomy (Megan Landes, "You Are Now Entering a Sci-Fi Bookstore: Getting Lost in the World of Science Fiction & Fantasy," 2014)

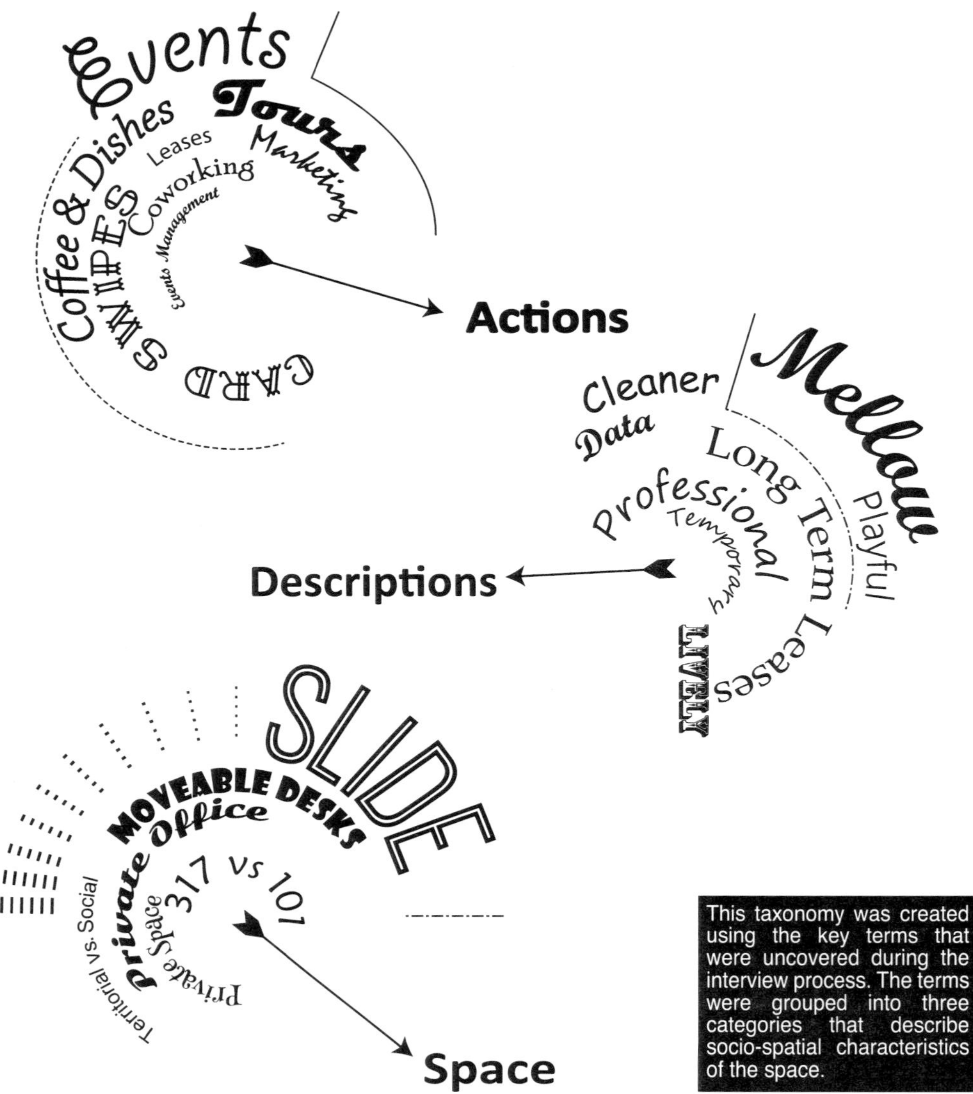

Figure 5.9 Graphic Taxonomy (fonts convey the diversity of work styles and spaces) (Ryan Hunt, "Coworking," 2013)

5.7 Different kinds of *definitions*

There are many different ways to define terms. When doing spatial ethnography, the most useful way to define a term is with respect to its location in a taxonomy. Since this is probably unfamiliar to you, we will compare and contrast it to other modes of defining things.

A ***perceptual definition*** is one of the most basic ways of defining something. When asked to define "commuter," an informant may simply point to another person and say: "Here's one." The category "good smell" can be defined by allowing someone

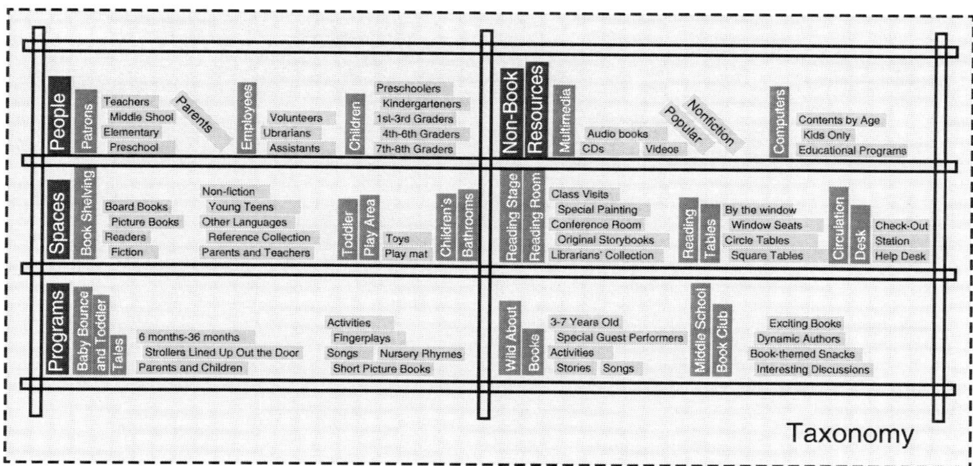

Figure 5.10 Graphic Taxonomy (Inspired by the Form of a Bookshelf) (Emily Russell, "The Children's Library," 2007)

to sniff the roast cooking in the oven. "Beauty" can be defined by pointing to something visually harmonious. Also, definitions imply contrast. You can contrast people with other kinds of people, as well as with books, trees, oceans, presidents, and any number of other things in the universe. Even conceptual categories such as "community," "spirit of place," and "soul" may still be defined perceptually by pointing to conditions that are believed to result from them or indicate their existence.

Another way is definition-by-naming, or ***nominal definition***. An object or condition is associated with a linguistic label. In this method, an object is presented and you ask its name. This object may be a practice, person, object, event, or any sort of thing that can be labeled or named. You point to something and ask: *What do you call that?*

A ***dictionary definition*** is another method of determining meaning. For example, earlier we defined a commuter as a person who uses the ferry to cross the bay. Your grand tour questions will elicit many such descriptive statements. You should use this type of definition to define the vocabulary terms you will list as a lexicon in your report. However, this is only a first step because these three modes of defining terms—perceptual, nominal, and dictionary—provide relatively little information. Each tends to contrast the category with everything else in the universe.

A ***taxonomic definition***, however, "defines a term by indicating those categories with which it is in more restricted contrast."[12] The differences between "word processor" and "the Virgin Mary" (high contrast) are not nearly as significant for their meaning as the differences among such terms as "drafting paper," "film," "vellum," and "Mylar," (limited contrast) are for theirs. These are all related by inclusion in the term "drawing material" and an understanding of any one is dependent on how it is distinguished from the others (such as thickness, translucence, use). While a dictionary would define a garage as a shelter or storage place for an automobile, a taxonomic definition would read something like this: *A garage is one kind of building. Other buildings are churches, houses, barns, sheds, schools, office buildings, apartments, libraries, and so forth. There are different kinds of garages, including attached*

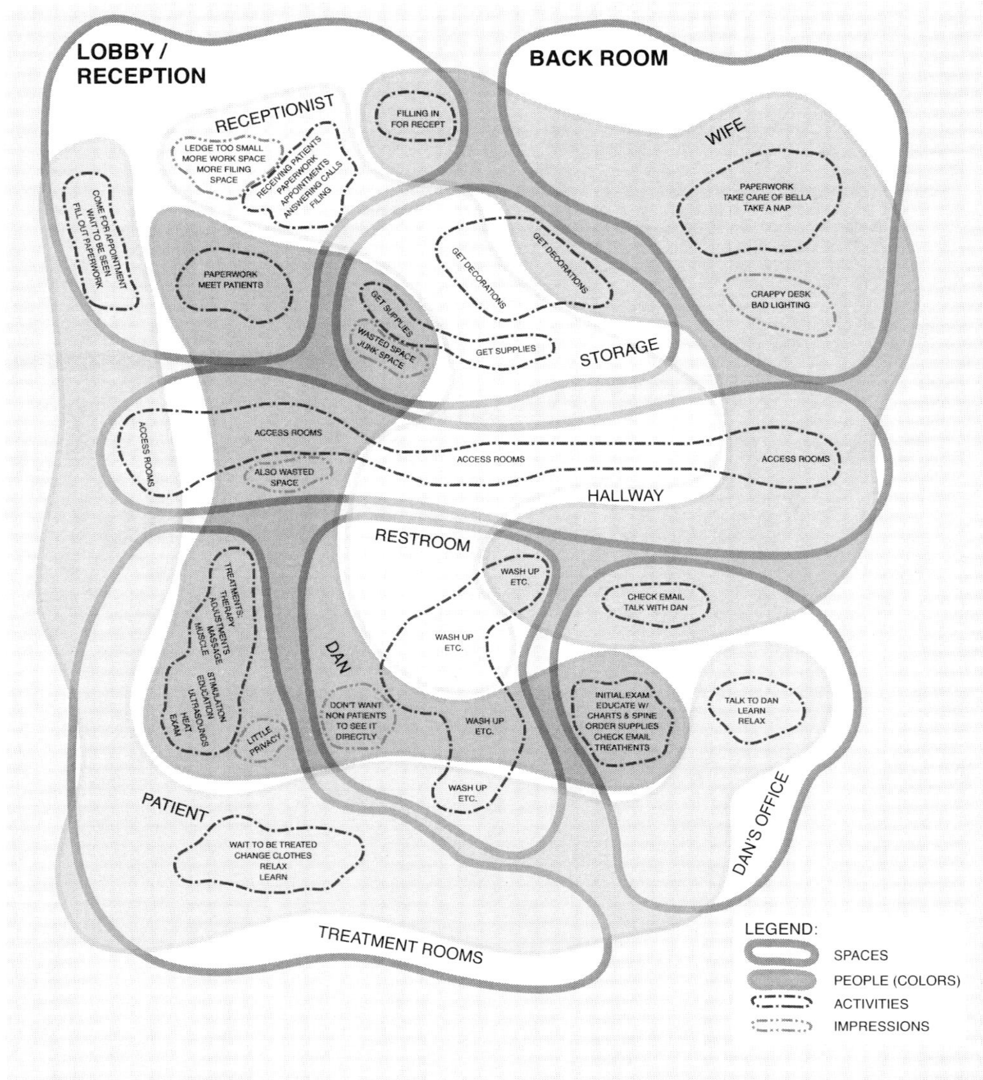

Figure 5.11 Graphic Taxonomy (shapes reminiscent of spinal vertebrae) (Mark Mattson, "Chiropractor's Office," 2008)

garages, free-standing garages, two-car garages, integrated garages, service station garages, multistory parking garages, and so forth.[13]

Lastly, you will sometimes be interested in componential definitions. Each *cultural category* is composed of many bits of data. They constitute the meaning of the category. For example, if your informant says that Steven is outside, then you can infer that there is almost certainly a male outside, because the name "Steven" is almost always used only for men. The cultural rule of naming according to gender tells us so. Other terms or names, such as "daughter," "sister," or "Rebecca" denote "female," while "sibling" (or "designer") could refer to either gender. If one could enumerate all of the characteristics implicit in a cultural category, you would have a complete *componential definition* of that category. Each characteristic would be one part of a category's total meaning.

A taxonomic definition reveals the categories that are in restricted contrast, and a componential definition tells us how those categories are different. What attributes do you use, for example, to distinguish between a garage and a house? Size? Purpose? Construction costs? Gender? Spirit? Color? Relation to the outdoors? Any of those things *could* be employed in distinguishing between garages and houses. Always when someone says that two things are similar or different he or she is choosing certain attributes for making judgment. Each culture creates linguistic categories for things; some things fit together and others do not. This knowledge is learned by understanding the attributes for each category. Your job as an ethnographer is to discover the categories and their attributes. If you want to describe a culture as the locals see it, you cannot impose your own categories and attributes.

5.8 The attribute question

Structural questions are useful for discovering similarities, while attribute questions are useful to discover *differences*. The pieces of information locals use to distinguish one thing from another are called *attributes*. If you were to study a carpenter shop, you would want to ask both types of questions for the domain "kinds of wood." The example in Table 5.3 reveals the difference between them.

Note that the structural question and the attribute question are equated graphically in Table 5.3. This may seem misleading insofar as the structural question is more important than the attribute question. Structure comes first, then the attributes. Nevertheless, one cannot exist without the other. Houses are a different *category* than tents, but in the end we only know this because the *attributes* (permanence, amount of protection from the outdoors, construction) are different.

Eventually, repeated use of attribute questions leads to a *componential definition*. If an investigator asked carpenters to contrast every kind of wood with every other kind, she would, ideally, arrive at a componential definition of kinds of wood. The cluster of attributes carpenters attach to each kind of wood enables them to choose which tools to use and to select wood for different purposes. One would probably have to observe carefully as well as ask questions in order to discover all the attributes carpenters employ to distinguish the various types of wood. Because people often take differences among categories for granted, you will want to learn to ask attribute questions, so that your informant will be prompted to express such differences. For example,

Table 5.3 Structural vs. attribute questions

Kind of question	*Question*	*Answer*
Structural question	What are some kinds of wood?	Softwood, hardwood, reconstituted wood, tropical wood, etc.
Attribute question	What is the difference between hardwood and softwood?	Hardwood is dense and nonporous. Softwood is fibrous and sappy.

instead of asking for the differences between only *two* categories, you can ask an informant to make distinctions among three categories. The ethnographer presents his informant with three familiar terms such as *customers*, *sales clerks*, and *owner*, which are members of the same set. Rather than asking for the differences among all three, you could start out by asking a two-part question: of these three terms, which are alike, and which is different from the other two? Sometimes a series of questions can help illustrate taxonomies and structures of meaning. To uncover attributes, you can also use a method similar to the game called Twenty Questions.[14] To do this, ask your informant to ask you questions. For example, in a study of carpenters, an investigator told his informant that he was thinking about a tool. To guess what tool it was, the informant asked questions such as: "Is it a tool used to cut wood?" "Is it a hand tool?" "Is it a power tool?" "Is it a tool used for finishing?" With each answer, the informant revealed attributes of the terms.

A last way to elicit attributes is by sorting cards with category terms written on them. If you were studying ecological building techniques and discovered that there were many different kinds of techniques, each would be written on a card. You could then request your informant to divide the cards according to similarities or differences. You could then ask him the reasons for the particular divisions. After recording the results, you could ask him to do the same, this time using different criteria. This can be done several times, until you understand each category fully.[15]

5.9 Identifying themes

Once you have a set of detailed notes or a transcript of your informant interviews, you can begin the process of *content analysis* in which you will identify—or, better yet, *discover*—the primary themes and sub-themes articulated by your informant. Ryan and Bernard describe this process as "winnowing themes to a manageable few."[16] As we mentioned above, though all of the information your informant shares is important, some of it is more important—and useful to your goal of redesigning the site—than other information. Identifying themes (also called *coding* in other forms of qualitative research) is a way of both identifying and establishing the relative importance of terms and themes articulated by your informant; likely, you can see how building hierarchies of themes relates to the task of creating taxonomies of key words. Though some of this type of analysis may occur at the time of note taking as you listen for main ideas, categories, themes, names, and attributes, it is more likely that you will engage in an in-depth analysis of interview notes and transcripts at a later point in your study to identify themes.[17]

Because the ethnographic method you are using is a process of discovery, you will be looking for *inductive themes*, meaning themes that come from your data (rather than *a priori* themes you may identify in a literature review). Ryan and Bernard suggest a number of techniques for identifying themes in qualitative data, including semantic interviews:[18]

- Repetition: look for the use of a word many times; the repetition of a concept implies a greater likelihood that it can be construed as a theme.
- Similarity and difference: similar to the structural and componential questions you asked in your interviews, you can review transcripts to try to find pairs of expressions that convey either the similarity or difference between terms.

- Cutting and sorting: this technique, relating more to the processing of data than examples of what to look for, "involves identifying quotes or expressions that seem somehow important and then arranging the quotes/expressions into piles that seem to go together."[19]
- Indigenous typologies: look for the use of unique vocabulary or a novel usage of vocabulary with which you are familiar.[20] A student studying a skateboarding shop noted two terms that are particularly rich examples of indigenous typologies: *bros* are a subset of skateboarders from Southern California who are thought to hold a "surf culture" attitude and are not held in high regard by local skaters; while *loques* or *locals* are people from the neighborhood who are somehow connected to skating culture.[21]
- Linguistic connections: semantic statements of comparison (X is like Y, X is a type of Y, etc.) are similar to our ideas of taxonomic definitions and can be helpful in identifying both terms and connections between terms.

Once you have read through your notes and identified a series of themes and subthemes, the next step will be to transfer the terms embedded in the narrative to a list. Using the examples from student projects in Figures 5.12–5.14, you can see how you can progress from identifying themes to creating lists to translating words into taxonomic structure.

As you begin to make your own taxonomy, look again at the samples in the figures we provided in this chapter. As you review the sample taxonomies, notice both the variety in their style—tables, tree-form, and graphic styles are all useful ways of organizing key terms or themes into a taxonomic structure—as well as the way in which they are sequenced.

The first taxonomy (Figure 5.1), a table, is a basic structure that might serve as an example of how to begin making your taxonomy. Then, the second taxonomy (Figure 5.2), a basic tree-form, is essentially conveying a similar grouping of themes and hierarchies of terms therein; yet does so in a more graphic (visual) manner. The following two examples (Figures 5.3 and 5.4) expand on the basic tree structure to connect terms and elements of the taxonomy to the physical space of the site being studied.

Whereas the first few taxonomies follow a thematic logic—wherein primary themes, such as work, rituals, architecture, people, or activities provide the principal organizing logic for the taxonomy—the next examples (Figures 5.5–5.7) use time as an organizing factor (based, of course, on the significance of time in each of the informants' respective micro-cultures). Again, taxonomies are sequenced from a basic list to a more complex representation of space and time.

Finally, the last few examples (Figures 5.8–5.11) show how fonts, layout, and graphics can be used to help convey cultural or symbolic aspects of the sited micro-culture in visual form. Thus, not only do the cultural terms themselves express meaning, but also the way in which they are organized and graphically conveyed enhances their expression.

5.10 Distorting your informant's knowledge

One perplexing problem faced by ethnographers is how to not distort what your informant knows. Some distortion is likely, even inevitable. It may be that you simply cannot make sense of everything your informant is telling you. The information may interview summary

Q: who uses the bart station?
A: people who live around the area mostly.
El Cerrito / Kensignton / Richmond / Albany / some of Berkeley
Q: like?
A: kids, students, "older folks", commuters, biciclests people wearing suit / dont sit / clean.
- el cerrito / kensignton / albany / richmond
Q: what kind of students?
A: high school / middle/college -> cal/comm. colleges
Q: what kind of commuters?
bart riders / bus / cabs / bike
Q: What do they do in the bart station?
A: they either just take transportion or hang out
Q: what do you mean by hang out?
A:"fool" around / have lunch / dance / fight/ drugs
(group competitions)-->often get in fights
Q: for how long do they hang out?

data analysis

"older folks": harji site serves the LOCAL refers to non-high **community** (serves nearby school / teenage cities)
people: seniors / parents / adults / people on suit (- assumption of professional jobs, therefore a higher level of maturity.
Students: -2 High schools near by / Albany and Richmond - middle school

two categories:
younger crowd long term (time): from 2-3 hours -(students category)
older crowd short term (time): 1 - 30 minutes -(Commuters)

people (studens,bart commuters: commuters,bikeriders) approach the site through two main intersections.
SouthEast - intersection: richmond st / fairmount ave

commuters:
-pedestriants
-bikers
-shoppers
-joggers
-dogwalkers

vocabulary

older folks
local community

younger crowd
older crowd

long term users
short term users

commuters
pedestrians
bikers
shoppers
joggers
dog walkers

"watch and laugh"
audience

Figure 5.12 Theme Identification (Coding) from Interview Transcript. (Daniel Malagon, "BART station ethnography," 2009)

C: The teachers have to pay membership too, or the teachers are members? **AF:** Well, teachers are members C: It sounds like a lot of different groups that use this place. Lots of different age groups. How do the different people interact with the Alliance? **AF:** We don't offer **classes** to children, because, actually, this space doesn't work that well for children or even for sometimes, we've had a few adolescent classes in the past but it didn't work out. So it's adults. So different levels of **French language** learning are offered . . . **a theatre group** has used the space **C:** Oh, cool. **AF:** There's also one of the, um, requirements is that it has something to do with the **French** culture and language. So this group is actually in **French**, the **French theatre** group.	Now we are talking about more **People** at the schiool, namely, the **members**. The different categories of members pay different fee levels. • Vocab: **members, teacher, student** These categories of **People (members)** all interact with the school in slightly different ways; **programming** is more available to adults than children and adolescents. Also, the AFB is more of a language school, so the primary programs offered are French classes. • Vocab: **theatre group, French language learning, classes**

Figure 5.13 Theme Identification. (Caitlin DeClercq, "L'École Française: Education, Ethnography, and the French Language and Culture," 2012)

be contradictory or incomplete, and you as an ethnographer will have to make a choice about what you perceive to be the correct significance and organization. You can no more be entirely accurate than you can be entirely objective.

A way to think about this problem is to simplify your data. Divide it into two large groups: names and attributes. You might also think of this as the difference between nouns and adjectives. Although this may seem an oversimplification, this distinction is very useful for the beginning ethnographer. Names are a good place to start. They act as place markers or easily identifiable labels for objects or conditions. It helps you relate things to one another.

However, occasionally your informant might refer to the same thing in different ways, or use the same name for different things. Take the case of a Macintosh laptop computer. An informant may say, "I use a Macintosh." Alternatively, he might also say he uses a Mac, a PC, a laptop, or an iBook. If you ask, "Are there different kinds of computers?" you might get all these answers—some from one informant, some from others. Can all of these names refer to the same thing? How can you decide which name is most appropriate to use?

In answer, any category contains a large amount of information. The label we search for in order to get a handle on the category is *the one our informant uses most frequently in casual conversation*. If you are unable to record category labels during ordinary conversation, it is useful to use hypothetical questions to test whether you have the name or some attribute of a category. You might pose a question for your informant like, "If you were buying a printer and the clerk asked what kind of computer you had, would you say, 'I have a PC?'" Your informant could then respond,

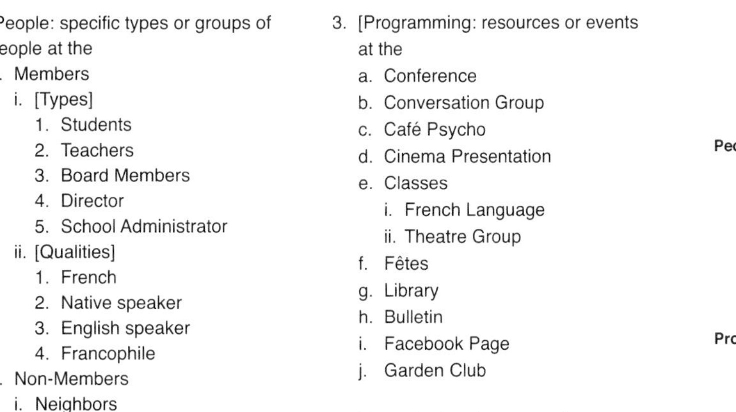

Textual Taxonomy of Vocabulary Words

Note: items in [brackets] are my convention and have been added for organizational purposes; colors correspond to Relational Taxonomy (right).

1. [People: specific types or groups of people at the
    a. Members
        i. [Types]
            1. Students
            2. Teachers
            3. Board Members
            4. Director
            5. School Administrator
        ii. [Qualities]
            1. French
            2. Native speaker
            3. English speaker
            4. Francophile
    b. Non-Members
        i. Neighbors
        ii. Les Amis de la Culture Francaise
2. [Physical Space: specific features of the physical environment or that dictate use of/access to the space]
    a. House
        i. Dining Room
    b. Garden
    c. Fence
    d. Special Use Permit
        i. Parking
        ii. Zoning
3. [Programming: resources or events at the
    a. Conference
    b. Conversation Group
    c. Café Psycho
    d. Cinema Presentation
    e. Classes
        i. French Language
        ii. Theatre Group
    f. Fêtes
    g. Library
    h. Bulletin
    i. Facebook Page
    j. Garden Club
4. [Organization: bureaucratic or operational elements of the AF and AFB]
    a.
        i. Chart de Qualité
        ii. National Meeting
        iii. Regional Alliances
        iv. French Ministry of Culture
    b.
        i. Board Meetings
        ii. East Bay French Alliance
    c. Dues

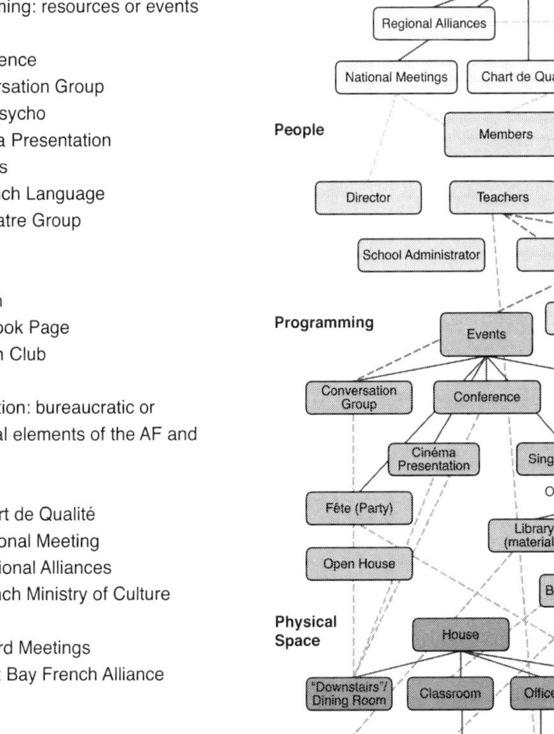

Figure 5.14 Taxonomies of Vocabulary Words. Notice how the vocabulary words identified in Example 2 are organized into a hierarchical list (textual taxonomy) and then translated into a graphical taxonomy below. (DeClercq, "L'École Française," 2012)

BOX 5.1: ETHNOGRAPHY PROJECT GUIDELINES

Part 3: Taxonomy

Creating and organizing vocabulary lists into a taxonomic structure

Research methods: analysis and visual presentation of semantic data

Summary of required activities: Your work for this stage of the project will focus on a careful analysis of the cultural terms used by your informant during your interview; ultimately, you will organize and express this cultural data in a visual—or taxonomic—form. Remember that taxonomies can take many forms—table, chart, list—so we encourage you to be creative and graphic with your taxonomy. Before submitting your work, you should check your taxonomy against your vocabulary list to ensure you have incorporated every term into the structures of meaning; additionally, you can show your taxonomy to your informant to make sure your understanding is correct. Finally, be sure to record any observations or thoughts that come to mind regarding the structure of the behavior, setting, and culture; however, make sure to keep your personal reflections separate from what your informant says for later contrast and comparison. You can record your personal thoughts in the "Personal Reflections" portion of your notebook and/or annotate copies of site plans with your ideas.

Summary of research proposal components: Begin by making a list of the terms your informant used to describe the setting (site, people, and activities) and assemble the terms into a comprehensive vocabulary list including definitions. Based on the major categories your informant used, organize the cultural terms into a visual format by constructing a taxonomy of terms. Next, begin to organize your vocabulary list into a taxonomic format that reflects the (structured) cultural knowledge of your informant. To do so, you should sort terms by content (vocabulary and meaning) and structure (cover terms and categories). Your major categories should include at least site-specific categories such as cultural characteristics, users, uses and activities, and spatial qualities, though you may also use other categories such as time, process, history, vision, and objectives. Be creative in creating your final taxonomies: they should be visually appealing and easy to understand and can be more graphically interesting than a simple chart. You can use plans, photos, and drawings to help create visual juxtapositions between categories.

Grading Criteria for Part 3

Does your project conform to the following criteria?

- Vocabulary list: list all cultural terms that carry particular meaning and significance for the sited micro-culture *in alphabetical order.*
- Definition of terms: define all terms based on what you learned from your informant.

- Taxonomies: create taxonomies that graphically correspond to your informant's logic, clearly define the content and structure of your informant's cultural knowledge, and boast good graphic (visual) quality.
- Additional, relevant information to understand the vocabulary and taxonomies.
- 3–5 pages in length, depending on the information you obtain from your informant.

"Oh no, I would say, 'a Mac.'" In some situations, she may call it a laptop, but in very restricted contexts.

However, you cannot eliminate all ambiguity. Nevertheless, you still need to create order out of what you discover. Accordingly, your final goal is to be able to describe your informant's cognitive map for your sited micro-culture and try to minimize subjectivity and distortion.

5.11 Chapter review: summary of main ideas

- Cultural knowledge is made of several basic elements, and the most important of these for ethnographic fieldwork is the category. Watson and Watson have noted that: "All knowledge depends on categorization; that is, the classification of objects according to their similarities and differences from other objects."[22] (5.2)
- Categories are invented by cultures and perpetuated by use. Our work as ethnographic designers is to uncover the specific categories created by members of a sited culture to understand how they organize their knowledge (5.2).
- Many, but not all, categories of a culture have linguistic labels or names, and so research begins by recording the names people use for categories, such as people, places, activities, and things. Not only will you have to record your conversations in one way or another, but also you will need to note what categories the informant defines as he or she goes about his or her social activities at the site of study (5.3).
- You should start with some very general questions because you don't want to direct your informant's responses, but rather have him talk about what he thinks is important, interesting, unique, and ordinary. Assure them that although you are a student of design, this is a "different" kind of course and that you are interested in all aspects of people and their activities, not just their physical environment (5.4). In the end you will want to discover who, does what, where, when, and how.
- Be determined to ask the grand tour question first before moving on to follow-up with more focused questions. In terms of ethnography, there are some specific things you want to listen for—the most important being vocabulary. You want to remember the specific words your informant uses to break her world down into categories and concepts. The other important thing to listen for is the relationship between categories. You listen for the structure of what people say (5.4).
- The first step in deciding what is important, useful, or of a high priority is to structure the information in some way. Writing your field reports and making drawings are two ways to structure information with which you are somewhat familiar. In semantic ethnography, a new type of structure is introduced: the taxonomy (5.5).

- Taxonomy is a logical structure of meaning—logical in its own terms, even if unique to that sited micro-culture. A diagrammatic format allows you to summarize the information provided by your informant in graphic terms. What you are attempting to portray in a taxonomy is your informant's subjective category system. Taxonomies to represent a subject's categories can take many forms including: tree charts, tables, and outlines (5.5).
- It is a good idea to show a draft of your taxonomy diagram to your informant to see if you understood correctly. Ideally, when asking questions to refine a taxonomy that you have already started to organize, you should ask questions that are open-ended enough that you do not force or invite a particular response from your informant and thereby bias the information (5.5).
- A few warnings: first, you can inadvertently influence your informant's worldview by concentrating on design too early. Second, try to make taxonomic diagrams immediately following the interview. Finally, ask for clarification even, and especially, when you think it unnecessary (5.5).
- The construction of detailed and well-organized taxonomies, using a tree chart or other organizing method, allows you to visualize relationships between places, things, activities, and people, and to relate them to spatial organization (5.5).
- As you go back over your record of what your informant has told you as a result of grand tour questions you will note terms that might be cover terms (5.6).
- Your job as an ethnographer is to discover categories of thought and their attributes. If you want to describe a culture as the locals see it, you cannot impose your own categories and attributes. (5.7).
- Structural questions are useful for discovering similarities, while attribute questions are useful to discover *differences* (5.8).
- One perplexing problem faced by ethnographers is how to not distort what your informant knows. A way to think about this problem is to simplify your data. Divide it into two large groups: names and attributes. You might also think of this as the difference between nouns and adjectives. Although this may seem an oversimplification, this distinction is very useful for the beginning ethnographer. Names are a good place to start. They act as place markers or easily identifiable labels for objects or conditions. It helps you relate things to one another (5.9).

Notes

1 Richard Watson and Patty Jo Watson, *Man and Nature: An Anthropological Essay in Human Ecology* (New York: Harcourt Brace Jovanovich, 1969), quoted in Spradley and McCurdy, *The Cultural Experience*, 1972, 60.
2 Similarly, McCurdy et al. define categories as "groups of things that people classify together and treat as if they were the same," in McCurdy et al., *The Cultural Experience,* 2005, 36, and Spradley and McCurdy, *The Cultural Experience,* 1972, 60.
3 Spradley and McCurdy, *The Cultural Experience,* 1972, 60.
4 Jerome Bruner, Jacqueline J. Goodnow, and George A. Austin. *A Study of Thinking* (New York: Wiley, 1956), quoted in Spradley and McCurdy, *The Cultural Experience,* 1972, 61.
5 Spradley and McCurdy, *The Cultural Experience,* 1972, 61.
6 You similarly want to avoid leading questions—those which limit a respondent's possible answers by circumscribing the topic or preferencing a certain response due to how the question is phrased—because they impose the worldview of the person asking questions onto

the informant and thus devalue and misrepresent the informant's point of view.

7 Nissa Stuckett, "A Recovery Room" (Spring 1997).
8 Tu Tuan Nguyen, "The Play-yards at a Campus Day-care Center" (Spring 1997).
9 William Tressler, "A University Computer Lab" (no date).
10 Thi thi Thongbenjamas, "Commuters on the Ferry" (1996).
11 Eva Kwok, "A Chinese Food Kiosk" (Spring 1996).
12 Harold C. Conklin, "Lexicographical Treatment of Folk Taxonomies," in *Problems in Lexicography,* F. W. Householder and S. Saporta, Eds. Indiana University Research Center in Anthropology, Folklore and Linguistics Publication, 21: 119–141, 1962.
13 Based on Spradley and McCurdy, *The Cultural Experience,* 1972, 70.
14 Spradley and McCurdy, *The Cultural Experience,* 1972, 75.
15 Ibid.
16 For an excellent introduction to coding and content analysis, see Gery W. Ryan and H. Russell Bernard, "Techniques to Identify Themes," *Field Methods* 15, no. 1 (February 2003).
17 See Steve Portigal, *Interviewing Users,* 2013, for more on sketching notes to identify important themes during interviews.
18 Ryan and Bernard, "Techniques to Identify Themes," 2003, 89–92; 102.
19 Ibid., 94.
20 This is also called "in vivo coding" or "local terminology"; see Ryan and Bernard, "Techniques to Identify Themes," 2003; and Strauss and Corbin, "Grounded Theory Methodology," 1994.
21 Pablo Traverso, "Skateboarding" (Fall 2007).
22 Watson and Watson, *Man and Nature*, 1969, quoted in Spradley and McCurdy, *The Cultural Experience*, 1972, 60.

6 Literature review

What do others say?

6.1 The basics of a literature review

At this point in the project, you will learn what others have written about the behavioral setting and cultural group you are studying. A review of the literature is a way to understand the outsider's, or etic, point of view. This process can also help you understand the differences and similarities between the insider's point of view and others' analyses.

Even if no one has studied the same setting you will be able to make meaningful comparisons. For example, the study of a Jamaican grocery store could be compared to published research on neighborhood grocery stores, specialty grocery stores, Jamaican restaurants, or Caribbean cultural centers. Wei-hsiang Wang explained her search for literature to help her understand a pizza restaurant in Berkeley:

> The process of research began on a larger scope, as I intended to involve bigger ideas and comparisons because I knew from the start how different the structure and organization of people and ideas were at this collective business. A few articles described the franchise food service industry, and through contrast helped me identify certain things that appeared natural but are actually unique to the cooperative team. More subtle moments and relationships between workers, as well as workers and customer, reveal themselves after seeing how differently the franchise pizza businesses are run. The differences in conflicts in both kinds of structures also reveal themselves and also in the approaches to business survival. Surprisingly, I learned how much information is revealed to the public. I appreciate what I have seen and learned within the group as part of the team, but at the same time I am intrigued by the amount of information published that reveal[s] the inner workings and personalities of the collective. These articles help give me a clearer understanding of the mission, processes, and growth over time behind collectives in general, as well as the [restaurant], specifically.[1]

After you find sources for your research, you will write an ***annotated bibliography*** to convey the content and relevance of the materials you have found.

BOX 6.1: SKILL SPOTLIGHT—CONDUCTING AND WRITING A LITERATURE REVIEW

Sommer and Sommer describe science as an "accumulative enterprise" wherein "each researcher builds on what has been done before."[1] Similarly, in researching your sited ***micro-culture*** from an ***etic*** perspective, your task will be to learn about what others have concluded about similar topics. To do so, you will conduct a ***literature review***.

What is a Literature Review?

As a student in architecture—or any other subject—you likely have conducted literature reviews in the form of design inquiry (e.g. finding previous examples of buildings designed for children with autism) or research inquiry (e.g. looking for books and articles about the history of Central Park in New York City). Investigating previously published work on a subject is referred to, in academic terms, as *conducting a review of the literature*.[2] If ***literature*** refers to a "body of information, existing in a wide variety of stored formats that has conceptual relevance for a particular topic of inquiry,"[3] then a review of the literature is, quite simply, a structured, focused survey and analysis of a range of previously published sources. In Part 4 of your ethnography project, you will produce an ***annotated bibliography***—a common milestone of the literature review process—in which you will list, summarize, and assess each source you reference in your paper. Additionally, you will write a narrative summary (*review*) of your findings (from the *literature*); in other words, a *literature review*. Together, these assignments will comprise your investigation of the etic (outsider) perspective of your site. For additional details, see 6.1–6.4.

In fact, the term *literature review* is used to describe a number of activities, from searching for sources on a specific topic to writing a summary situating your findings in a broader intellectual context. Literature review, an essential aspect of academic scholarship, serves a number of purposes for researchers. Once you learn the mechanics of conducting a thorough literature review, you can use the practice to find inspiration and/or refine a potential topic of study, learn about what others have said about a particular topic, or test and refine your ideas by comparing them to others' findings.[4]

Where Do I Go From Here? The Nuts and Bolts of a Literature Review

Inspired by Sommer and Sommer, we compiled the following checklist with step-by-step instructions to help you with the literature review process in Part 4 of your ethnography project:

- **Compile a list of subjects or concepts you want to research.** The topics you choose to investigate should relate to what you learned from your informant, the cultural group or setting you are studying, or any topic from the field of person–environment studies that is relevant to your site. For example, to supplement her ethnographic study of an Irish bar in San Francisco, Flávia Carvalho researched Irish immigration patterns, Irish architecture, the architecture of bars and clubs, and the social significance of the Irish pub.[5] Leslie Becker, who studied first time mothers in San Francisco, used literature regarding child-centered designs (places and products), psychological development theories, public health policies relating to children, and even product manufacturers' marketing materials to inform her design proposal.[6] In these examples, students were creative in thinking about a variety of themes relating to the historical, cultural, social, and built environment contexts of their sited micro-culture.

- **Organize your list of concepts into major and minor keywords.** Just as you created taxonomies to represent the structured knowledge of your informant, in order to help structure your literature review, Sommer and Sommer recommend that you organize your concepts into categories of key terms. Returning to the example of Carvalho's study of the Irish pub, we might structure the terms like this:

  Irish immigrants
  - History and demographics
  - Experience of immigration

  Architecture
  - Irish (vernacular)
  - Bars and pubs

  Social significance of the pub
  - Irish/in Ireland
  - Irish-American/in America.

  Organizing your list of subjects (and refining as needed once you begin your research) will help you identify the areas of literature that pertain to your topics of interest.[7]
- **Conduct a search using the keywords you identified.** Search for books on your school's library website, and search for articles by using a variety of databases (e.g. JSTOR, Google Scholar, ProQuest). As you search each database, take detailed notes about the sources you find so that you can track your progress and retrace your steps if you want to refer back to sources later in your research. In particular, we recommend you make note of the following *for each source you find*:

  - Books: author name, book title, date of publication, call number (you may note that the books you find are clustered around a common call number, which means that spending a few minutes browsing that section of the library might be a fruitful complement to your online research).
  - Articles: author name, article title, journal name, volume and issue number, and any keywords cited in articles you find of particular interest (these keywords might help illuminate adjacent topics to inform your work).

- **Go to the library to locate the books you found online.** If you haven't done so already, browse the areas near the books you locate to see if any other titles sound relevant. For each book, you should begin by skimming the *Table of Contents* to get a sense of the scope and organization of the book and then skim any chapters that seem particularly relevant. This first step will help you narrow down your list of possible references to those that will be most relevant to your work. For any articles you download, read the *Abstract* and *Keywords* sections and then skim the *Discussion* and/or *Conclusion* sections to assess the relevance of the article and obtain a sense of the author's argument. With any source you find, you should skim the list of references cited and make note of any author names that continually appear (a sign that you may want to look into their work) and additional topics or concepts that are relevant to your area(s) of inquiry.
- **Assess where you are.** Ask yourself: *Which resources—books, articles, and other resources—are most relevant to your work? Which are not? What authors and keywords have you discovered that need to be further researched? Are there any areas you are having difficulty researching?* Read in greater depth the books (or chapters) and articles most relevant to your work, and if you are having trouble locating books or articles on a given topic, you should consult a reference librarian, who can help you locate article databases and brainstorm similar topics. See 6.3 for more information on working with reference librarians.
- **How do you know when you're done?** Technically, a literature review is never done; yet Groat and Wang offer a helpful way to assess your progress: once the names and concepts you encounter begin looking familiar, you have conducted a thorough review of the literature.[8] More pragmatically, you should aim for *at least* two or three high-quality sources for each topic you research. See 6.4 for more information on evaluating the pertinence and trustworthiness of sources.

Writing a Literature Review

In addition to the above activities relating to searching for and assessing publication, the term *literature review* also refers to a genre of writing that summarizes the main sources, findings, and limitations of work that has already been published about a given subject. In the context of your ethnography project, the literature review is an exploration of the ***etic*** perspective, or what others *external to your sited micro-culture* have said about your topic. The goal of your written literature review is to provide a concise summary of what you discovered in your research and the pertinence of your findings to your project. In particular, you should address the following questions:[9]

- What are the main concepts you researched? What have others concluded about them?
- Are there any areas of overlap between sources you read?
- Are there any questions left unanswered?
- How does what you found in your etic research relate to your ethnography project? How are you making sense of your review of the

literature? *Note that in Part 4 of the ethnography project you will be asked to comment on the similarities and differences between the emic, etic, and personal perspectives you have researched.*

- Are there any significant limitations you noticed in the studies you read?
- How does this earlier research impact how you think about and plan to redesign a space for the sited micro-culture you are studying?

At a minimum, you should address the above questions for each topic or concept you researched. Your annotated bibliography (see 6.1 and 6.2 for more information) might help you get started on this task.

Citing Your Work

As you write your literature review, be diligent in citing others' work by using both in-text ***citations*** (parenthetical references or footnotes) and a full bibliography at the end of your paper. Keep track of and communicate to readers where you found the information (facts, arguments) you reference in your paper;[10] doing so will lend your paper credibility and assist readers in locating the sources you used in your work. Remember that every fact or argument you mention in your literature review *other than your own* must be cited so that anyone who reads your paper will know where to find more information should they be inspired to do so. If you use more than five words in a row from someone else's text, those words must be put in quotation marks and cited. It is fine to quote someone else's work as long as you cite the original author and work; even if you paraphrase an argument or idea, you still must cite the original work you reference. Failure to do so is plagiarism, a serious offence against the norms of scholarship that can even be grounds for dismissal from the university. Sometimes students from other countries do not understand how seriously US universities take plagiarism.

Regarding the *formatting* of your citations, you have a bit more flexibility: you can select from among several citation styles (see 6.2 for more information about APA, Chicago, and MLA styles); just be consistent with the one you choose. Though the specifics of each style vary, they share the convention of noting citations both in-text (through parenthetical references, footnotes, or end notes) and at the end of the paper. This dual citation system sets up the same helpful framework in your paper that you used in conducting your literature review: readers can skim the full list of sources at the back of your paper to ascertain the types and authors of texts you used *and* link specific arguments or data in the body of your literature review to specific sources.

Tips, Tricks, and Helpful Hints

- When conducting a search for books and articles, some students may find it helpful to conduct a general search on Google Scholar, make note of sources that seem interesting, and then locate specific books or articles at their home institution (e.g. the UC Berkeley Library).

- If you choose to use Google Scholar, make sure to adjust your *settings* so that you can see the articles and books that your home institution has access to (instructions: go to Settings → Library Links, then search for your institution).
- Remember that all online databases have their limitations, even Google Scholar. Therefore, you should expect to search a variety of databases, particularly when looking for articles. If you're feeling overwhelmed by this task, a quick visit with a reference librarian can help you get going.
- Many scholarly search engines (e.g. Google Scholar, ProQuest, JSTOR) offer links such as "articles citing this" or "cited by" to help you locate related sources.
- The Online Writing Lab at Purdue University is a helpful source of examples and explanations for references and citations as well as other mechanics of academic writing. Visit http://owl.english.purdue.edu for more information.

Notes

1 Robert Sommer and Barbara Sommer, *A Practical Guide to Behavioral Research: Tools and Techniques*, Fifth Edition (New York: Oxford University Press, 2002), 23.
2 Ibid. For more on design precedent and literature reviews, see Linda Groat and David Wang, *Architectural Research Methods* (New York: John Wiley, 2002).
3 Groat and Wang, *Architectural Research Methods*, 2002, 46.
4 Sommer and Sommer, *A Practical Guide to Behavioral Research*, 2002.
5 Flávia Carvalho, "An Irish Pub" (Fall 2004).
6 Leslie Becker, "First Time Mothers and Babies" (Spring 2004).
7 Groat and Wang, *Architectural Research Methods*, 2002, 52.
8 Ibid., 23.
9 Sommer and Sommer, *A Practical Guide to Behavioral Research*, 2002.
10 Ibid.

6.2 The format of an annotated bibliography

An annotated bibliography is similar to other bibliographies that you have written, except that, after each citation of a source, you will write one or two sentences about the information in the source and your evaluation of its relevance. Make sure to note the page numbers of the information you cite from the source, so that you or anyone else wanting to verify or read your citations can find them easily later.

A minimal annotated bibliography will include at least ten sources and notations. In your annotated bibliography and your final report, we recommend that you follow one of the three main formats for citing sources: the MLA style, the APA style, or the Chicago style. Table 6.2 lists some information about the MLA, APA, and Chicago styles.

6.3 How to find sources

Allow plenty of time to find sources. While you will likely be able to find the bulk of your sources using online searches, key material may only be available in physical form, and may need to be sent to your library via inter-library loan. This process can take weeks. Cultivating a friendly relationship with a reference librarian, much like developing rapport with an informant, also takes time. Librarians like helping people

Table 6.1 The format of an annotated bibliography

Example entries from a student's annotated bibliography in a project about an Indian fast food restaurant:1
Sethi, Sunit. "Tables and Chairs" *Tandoori Magazine*. "How and why it is important, in Indian restaurants, like other low-end or fast food restaurants, to have chairs that are not too comfortable because the owner is aiming for quick turnover."
Brandtzg, Brita. *Women, Food, and Technology: a study of an Indian city*. Universitet I Oslo: Oslo. 1982. "The author analyzes the connections between women and food in India. The regulations and expectations surrounding women and the preparation of food as duty is very common in India. These issues bring to light my informant's opinions about the women who work at his restaurant."

Notes
1 Ami Mehta, "Indian Restaurant" (Spring 2001).

Table 6.2 Citation style and usage

Citation style	*Books*
MLA The Modern Language Association recommends parenthetical notes, but also offers guidelines for footnotes or endnotes.	*MLA Handbook for Writers of Research Papers*
APA The American Psychological Association recommends parenthetical notes. The APA sets the style for psychology and the other social sciences.	*Mastering APA Style: Student's Workbook and Training Guide*
Chicago The Chicago style, also known as "humanities style," places bibliographic citations at the bottom of a page or at the end of a paper.	*The Chicago Manual of Style: The Essential Guide for Writers, Editors, and Publishers*

find information, and they tend to be especially helpful if you show that you are appreciative of their efforts to help you. Spending time in the library lets you get the most from the librarians by asking specific questions of them. A reference librarian can also help you structure and direct online searches so that you can find the most relevant hits quickly.

If you have trouble finding sources, make an appointment to meet with a reference librarian. They are available in most libraries, but those that might be most helpful for the ethnographic project are university libraries focused on anthropology, sociology, environmental design, and American culture.

Table 6.3 Questions to ask yourself when evaluating the relevance and validity of a source

- Has the author formulated a problem, topic, or issue?
- What theoretical framework (e.g., psychological, anthropological, Marxist, feminist or combination) does the author employ?
- Has the author evaluated other literature relevant to the topic? Does the author discuss literature that argues positions she or he does not agree with?
- If the source is a research study, how good are the basic components of the study design? How reliable and valid are the measurements? Does the author show sensitivity to any methodological shortcomings of his or her own study? Are the conclusions based upon the data and analysis?
- Is material written for a popular readership? Does the author use emotional appeals, one-sided examples, or rhetorically charged language? Is there an objective basis to the reasoning or is the author merely "proving" what he or she already believes?
- How does the author structure the argument? Can you "deconstruct" the flow of the argument to see whether or where it breaks down logically?
- In what ways does this source contribute to the understanding of the problem? In what ways is it useful for practice?
- How does this book or article relate to the specific thesis or question I am developing?

6.4 How to evaluate sources

As the name indicates, an annotated bibliography includes a discussion about how relevant each source is to the topic of your ethnography project. You will also want to evaluate how trustworthy they are. Your goal is to find the most useful and authoritative published research. Many ethnography projects will call for a wide range of research sources, which includes not only articles and books, but also Internet sources, government reports, and interviews with experts. Mention in writing any concerns you have over the legitimacy of sources in your annotated bibliography. Of course, if you are concerned about the legitimacy of a large portion of your sources, you should gradually widen your search until you find more established sources. Internet sources are generally considered less trustworthy than print sources because Internet sources often do not have editorial oversight.

6.5 A list of useful online resources for architectural ethnographies

Archnet
—especially useful for Muslim cultural/architectural references.
http://archnet.org/library/documents/

Architecture Week's culture section
—topics change every week, archives available.
www.architectureweek.com/culture.html

The Australian Broadcasting Corporation's Gateways to Arts and Culture
—good for Australian and Southeast Asian cultural information.
www.abc.net.au/arts/design/default.htm

Google Scholar

JSTOR

6.6 A note of caution on Internet research

Internet research has many advantages: it's fast, it can be done from home or in the library, and the plethora of information available allows students to find sources on almost any possible topic. For instance, in 2001 information about an Ultimate Frisbee league came almost exclusively from Internet websites because it was a relatively new sport. A decade earlier one would have had to make inferences from sources about other sports leagues or the science of Frisbee throwing.

But Internet research needs to be viewed with scrutiny. When you get references from the library to get books or journal articles, a librarian has already established that those materials have some academic legitimacy. This is not true of all sources, even those that look legitimate, on the Internet. For a further discussion about how to evaluate Internet sources, as well as how to cite them in a paper, ask a reference librarian for guidance, or see the UC Berkeley library's website at: www.lib.berkeley.edu/TeachingLib/Guides/Internet/FindInfo.html.

6.7 Comparing the etic and emic points of view

Armed with knowledge from your initial experiences in the field, the results of your ethnographic interviews, and your literature review, you will now go back to your cultural setting to re-examine the setting and to clarify questions from the personal, emic, and etic points of view. In writing, reflect on the differences and similarities among the three points of view, and report and summarize any additional insights from this site visit. Was the etic point of view different from the emic? In what ways? Why might the two perspectives not be the same? If the points of view are different, did the new point of view prompt you to query your informant again for confirmation of their point of view?

For example, one student showed her informant a list of terms she'd found in a book published in 1976. She asked her informant about them, and found that "he was familiar with many of them and about one third of them would still be used frequently in his tennis team. Other expressions, however, have either changed their meanings, got lost through time, or are considered out of fashion. Here, we have a slight disagreement between the etic and the emic, which is due to change of language usage through time."[2]

Comparing the emic and etic thematically will help articulate implications for design. For example, in a study of an Indian restaurant, you might include a paragraph on the culture of food preparation in which you compare what you observed in the kitchen of the restaurant, what your informant told you about food preparation, and what you read about the culture of preparing Indian food. The next paragraph might compare the three points of view in the arrangement of the kitchen and its relationship to other rooms or facilities within the restaurant.

6.8 Chapter review: summary of main ideas

- A literature review is a way to understand the outsider's, or etic, point of view. This process can also help you understand the differences and similarities between the insider's point of view and others' analyses (6.1).

BOX 6.2: ETHNOGRAPHY PROJECT GUIDELINES

Part 4: Literature Review

Researching the etic perspective and linking findings to your project: how the insider's (emic), outsider's (etic), and personal perspectives compare and contrast

Research method: literature review

Summary of required activities: At this point in the project you will learn what others have written about the behavioral setting and cultural group you are studying. To do so, use library resources to research and write a review of the literature relevant to your study. Remember that even if no one else has studied your exact setting you can still make meaningful comparisons: for example, the study of a Vietnamese grocery store could be compared to published research on neighborhood grocery stores, specialty grocery stores, Vietnamese cultural centers, or Vietnamese restaurants. Once you have located and reviewed all of the sources you will use for your research, create an annotated bibliography and then synthesize your findings into a written review of the literature and comparison of the three perspectives you have researched (personal, emic, etic). *Note: For this part of the ethnography project, you will make another visit to your site to help inform your comparison of the three perspectives.*

Summary of research proposal components: Define the topics you want to research for your literature review, search for a range of books, articles, and other sources about each topic, and scan each to assess its relevance and trustworthiness. Produce an annotated bibliography of at least ten articles or books, making sure to properly format your bibliographic citations (for example, APA, MLA, or Chicago style). Be sure to include equivalent numbers of sources regarding both the design of the type of place you are studying *and* the subculture of similar or different settings. Your annotations should assess the content, relevance, and trustworthiness of the source; importantly, you should summarize how others' research compares and contrasts with yours. Armed with knowledge from your initial experiences in the field and your literature review, return to your cultural setting *physically and mentally* to re-examine the setting and to clarify questions from personal, insider (emic), and outsider (etic) points of view. Finally, in two or three pages, comment on how others' research compares and contrasts with your findings, making sure to note the differences between the emic, etic, and personal perspectives you have researched. Summarize each perspective separately, and then analyze the differences and similarities among the three points of view. Conclude with any additional insights from your recent site visit.

Grading Criteria for Part 4

Does your project conform to the following criteria?

- Ten sources for bibliography*: also include reference to the topics you researched.

- Annotations: write one or two sentences for each entry, noting the relevance of each source to your topic area.
- Bibliographic style: consistently format your bibliographic entries according to APA, MLA, or Chicago style.
- Etic point of view: describe outsider's point of view by summarizing the main findings of your literature review.
- Emic point of view: describe insider's point of view based on your semantic interviews.
- Personal point of view: describe your observations and personal reflections.
- Compare and contrast: explicitly discuss how these three points of view—emic, etic, and personal—compare and contrast; include additional insights as needed.

Notes
* A minimum of eight of the required ten sources should be either books or peer-reviewed journal articles.

- To create an annotated bibliography you will write one or two sentences about the information in the source and your assessment of its relevance (6.2).
- Additionally, an annotated bibliography includes a discussion about how relevant each source is to the topic of your ethnography project. You will also want to evaluate how trustworthy they are (6.4).
- Internet research needs to be viewed with scrutiny. When you get references from the library to get books or journal articles, a librarian has already established that those materials have some academic legitimacy. This is not true of all sources, even those that look legitimate, on the Internet (6.6).
- When you are ready to begin writing your comparison of etic and emic perspectives, in writing, reflect on the differences and similarities among the three points of view and report and summarize any additional insights from a final site visit (6.7).
- Comparing the emic and etic thematically will help articulate implications for design (6.7).

Notes

1 Wei-hsiang Wang, "The Pizza Collective" (no date).
2 Christin To, "Developing a Program for Design: A University Tennis Complex" (2005), 18.

7 Translating into physical design

7.1 Serving society through design

Every human action is place-based (that is, geographically located), and conversely every built space plays an important part in human activities as either a facilitator or restraint. Therefore, designers will want to be conscious of the range of activities that may take place in a room and how they are related conceptually, rather than only technical characteristics like required square footage.

Empathy, or a deep understanding of and interest in another's sociocultural context, can foster social change. A recent article by the Public Policy Lab explains that "when humans move beyond themselves to truly see, feel, and comprehend others' realities and/or participate in the telling of others' stories, the results can be revelatory" and transformative on a social scale.[1] Ethnographic research is one way for designers to gain such awareness.

In particular, ethnographic research allows the designer-researcher to:

(1) understand why the current environment is organized the way it is, even though some arrangements may have at first sight appeared irrational, messy, or in poor taste to the uninitiated observer; and
(2) conceive how the existing space could be *reorganized* to accommodate the specific needs of this particular group.

One must be attentive when engaging in this last phase of the project. Many students have struggled to make the connection between their study of a sited micro-culture and the translation of their findings into redesign. The goal of the exercise is to redesign the physical environment of a sited micro-culture based on the specific way of life or worldview of your informant. As a designer—or future designer—you probably have a better command of space than most people and have been trained to find ingenious solutions to all sorts of design problems. But to redesign the physical setting for this culture solely according to your own dictates defies one of the purposes of design—to accommodate and celebrate various ways of living. We encourage you to embrace this charge as an opportunity to seek innovative design solutions.

Admittedly, several forces other than cultural description may legitimately influence your design. For example, the constraints imposed by working within an existing setting reduce the range of possibilities. Nevertheless, you have the opportunity to start fresh; imagine that your informant is a client who gives you the opportunity to design a new environment for her sited culture on the same site. Perhaps the building burned down and you have to decide if the new space should reproduce the conditions of the old space because it so perfectly reflects the micro-culture, or, more likely, if you should make changes to the space to support the micro-culture—including the sum of activities and meanings articulated by your informant—more completely.

Cultural information can inform your design proposals in a couple of ways. First, the results of your cultural investigation must guide your design, not your personal preferences and desires to express originality and inventiveness. In this exercise, we ask you to put your talents at the service of the micro-culture you have chosen to study. Some of you may go so far as to redefine your role from an autonomous "creator" to a socially conscious environmental "facilitator," a designer at the service of society. Second, working with informants may influence your proposals if you chose to test preliminary designs with different informants and see how they react to your ideas.

7.2 *Conventional programming* versus *deep programming*

We emphasize the difference between the narrowly defined program of a building (the technical description of the main functions of this building) and the conceptual as well as physical use of a building by its occupants.[2] In other words, we see the ideal space as one that transcends the technical functionality of a space and considers as well the ways in which form helps to express and create meaning and facilitate social interaction. For example, consider the difference between two descriptions of a staff lounge: (1) 45 sq. ft., with microwave, sink, storage space, cupboard to fit each employee's mug, refrigerator, dining table, seating for ten, radio and sofa, versus (2) a setting for a staff surprise-party (that you attend) for a retiring employee, including 20 staff members, the "Big Bosses," a cake, presents, decorations, whistles and hats, and music from the 1970s. At other times the program might involve quiet time for someone who needs time alone or privacy with another to discuss a sensitive topic. Architects, interior designers, and landscape architects best view space not only as what is created by formal devices, but also as a setting for human activity, closely related to social relationships in everyday life.

Creating an ideal space can also mean removing constraints in the environment simply by rearranging components. For example, Danielle Borden proposed a redesign for a restaurant based on information from her informant, a waitress there who pointed out the frustrating and dangerous circulation by the hostess stand. Without changing the required programming—a hostess stand, an entrance, customer waiting, a coffee bar, tables for dining—she changed the relationships of each to the other, and eliminated the circulation problem.[3]

7.3 Moving from description to design

Moving from ethnographic description to physical design is not just a matter of "adding"—everyone thinks you need "more space"—but rather rethinking existing space. You may be able to fulfill dreams as well as needs—or at least provide the option to do so—so that users are not stuck with activities and patterns governed by the current situation. As a designer, you are the expert at spatial resolution, so don't feel guilty if you don't use your informant's solution literally. If you get to the "deep structure" of their solution (the logic behind the structure of their taxonomy), you may be able to find a more appropriate way to structure their space.

Remember the example of the fireplace (from the Preface): how "deep structure" can help you identify a design solution that honors the underlying—rather than surface—expression of the user's values. The fireplace might be a location for family togetherness, a source of heat, or the visual centerpiece of a home.

Imagine for example that you have been commissioned to design a new tourist hotel, which must accommodate a whole variety of people. You decide to conduct ethnographic research on the micro-culture of visitors to this particular town, within the setting of one of the already existing hotels, in order to establish their preference in types of accommodation and activities. After your study of the visitors and their preference, you come up with a list of categories:

- the businessperson, who wants to find the comfort of home and the practicality of his office in this foreign setting;
- the adventurous tourist in search of authentic exoticism;
- the retired couple, seeking tranquility, sun, and comfort at a reasonable price;
- the nouveau riche holidaymaker who seeks high-quality service, luxury and glamour.

For the businessperson, you envision an air-conditioned room with easy accessibility, free Wi-Fi and other communication facilities, decorated in a homey and comfortable way, with a view over a lawn. For the adventurous type, you imagine a detached cabin in the hotel's garden, very rustic with thatched roof, hammock, outdoor shower, and palm trees. For the retired couple, you design a room with a view of the sea, decorated in an exotic style, and equipped with all modern comforts. Such variety of ideas may never have occurred to you if you had not at first investigated the different types of people coming on holiday. You would have probably designed a single room type targeted for a hypothetical hotel user whose preferences closely match your own. Instead, you might propose that the plan include different room shapes and amenities, or if only one room type were economical you would carefully evaluate the room design for how it would work for each of these kinds of guests. The result of designing based on your ethnographic study of the different types of hotel users is an interesting, well-informed hotel design for your client, the hotel owner. Similar research could be done to understand the cultures of other groups within the hotel, such as staff members, management, cooks, and activity organizers.

A similar example comes from Michael Kao, whose ethnography project focused on the culture of young children in a Montessori preschool. In this project, Kao identified certain categories of activities in which the children engaged; these activities in turn defined social groups: artists, the gymnasts, the horticulturists, the architects, the musicians, and the racers (on tricycles). In his proposal for the redesign of the school's play yard, Kao provided a series of integrated, but differentiated, areas for each of the different kinds of play. Every child could thus find a different environment suited to his or her own interests.[4]

Another student proposed the redesign of a record store such that the space would "allow people to engage with music in ways that they never have before." To accomplish this goal, Talon Smith designed a series of listening rooms, each of which supported a different way of experiencing music:

- Music as therapy: to enhance the emotional, spiritual, and meditative aspects of music, this listening room features soft cushions, ambient lighting, and incense.
- Music as spatial experience: so that listeners can experience music visually, floorboards move up and down according to the frequency of music.
- Music as community: to convey the goal of not only listening to but discussing music as well, couches arranged in a sociopetal fashion.
- Music as an island of interest: to invite any number of personal styles to be expressed in the experience of music, from dancing to singing to sitting quietly; movable furniture in this room.
- Music as a study catalyst: music as a source of inspiration offers study carrels to invite students to read and write in an environment that welcomes.[5]

Of particular importance to this design is its focus on the latent function of the site—the experience of music, rather than just the mere sale of records—as well as the sensory aspects of experience.[6]

Another student proposed the use of music inside a Japantown hardware store in order to "drown out the irritating buzzing noise from the store's fluorescent lights" and to create a more tranquil atmosphere for customers and staff alike.[7]

Social research design projects are not always this straightforward. In fact, Sanjoy Mazumdar acknowledges that the "conversion of social and behavioral information into spatial relationships is difficult."[8] Yet, the examples included in this text illustrate the way ethnographic research can be a useful tool in design. Without having spent some time studying the type of people who may inhabit the future hotel, or the kind of children using the play yard, these students may never have come up with such clearly defined solutions.

One place to begin is to think metaphorically about the place you are designing. Ask yourself: *Is this place most like a theater? A mountain retreat? A school? A home away from home? A machine for entertainment?* Each of these not only conveys specific design implications, but also can inspire you to think creatively about and consider the deeper programmatic potential of your site. You also should think about the cultural values and meanings you want to express through your design. Consider the influential work of Franklin Becker, Edward T. Hall, and Oscar Newman, and how their findings about environmental messages, privacy, communication, and territoriality might inform your design.[9]

Sometimes, a verbal element from your ethnographic research will be symbolically translated into the redesign. Consider the following example of architect Maya Lin's description of her work on the Civil Rights Memorial in Montgomery, Alabama:

> I studied and reviewed much of the material sent to me by the center before I visited Montgomery. I spent months researching films, literature, and news clips about the time period so that I could get background on the civil rights movement . . . It was on this first visit to Montgomery that I came across a quote from Dr. Martin Luther King in his "I have a dream" speech: "We are not satisfied and we will not be satisfied until justice rolls down like waters and righteousness like a mighty stream." Immediately I knew that the memorial would be about water and that these words would connect the past with the future.[10]

Indeed, the final design incorporated water as a symbolic reference to King's speech. Water may have been a theme in King's thinking, but maybe Lin was inspired by an important but atypical quote. The ethnographic question would be, "Do the people who visit the Law Center use water as a category in their conceptualization of social change, the civil rights movement, or the Southern Poverty Law Center?" Ideally, the etic point of view would match the emic point of view. You could draw a concept or idea either from your literature review or your informants' taxonomies to influence your redesign in the same way that Lin drew inspiration from King's quote. Here, too, it would be ideal if the two points of view were compatible.

One student, studying a café popular with Muslim students, proposed the addition of a prayer room with both functional and symbolic elements. The addition of the prayer room in the back of the café would create a formal yet private place for prayer in a space already used by students for that purpose, and wooden floor panels in the room would be oriented in the direction of prayer to convey the practice symbolically.[11] Another student who studied a café in a gentrifying part of Oakland observed that the bulletproof glass window in front of the café's cash register, coupled with the metal security grates covering all exterior windows, conveyed a different message to users and passers-by alike—one of "alienation, fear, and segregation"—than the welcoming, positive attitude the café's owner expressed in interviews. To address the issue of security without sending unintended messages, the student proposed treating the exterior grates more aesthetically: rather than using ubiquitous, industrial window guards, screens could be made from scrap metal purchased from local scrap yards, fashioned into a sculptural object, and integrated aesthetically into the building's façade.[12] Ultimately, this design would communicate a much different message than that expressed by the building's current security bars.

In this same way, your design should be both utilitarian and symbolic: your site should work for your informant's micro-culture—for example, accommodating everyday activities of all user groups—and also be used symbolically to express the cultural meanings and/or identity of users.[13]

BOX 7.1: SKILL SPOTLIGHT—CONCEPTS: OPERATIONAL DEFINITIONS AND TRANSLATION INTO DESIGN

A recent article in *Education Week* proclaimed that open and flexible classroom designs could foster a sense of community among students.[1] Though this idea sounds wonderful, it requires a bit more scrutiny: What, exactly, is an *open and flexible* classroom? Is it a room without a roof or walls? Is it one in which all furniture is lightweight and movable? Or is it something other than a traditional room, such as an outdoor space or a small corner of a large multi-purpose room?

The concept of *community* raises similar questions: How do the authors of the article about classroom design—or the students who learn in those settings—define community? Is it the same idea that comes to my mind? And how do we know that students' sense of community has improved? Finally, if I wanted to design a classroom that fosters community, how would I do so?

As we explained in 1.3, ethnographic methods can inform two aspects of the design of places: the ***evaluation*** of how well a building meets the intentions of its designers and needs of its users and the ***programming*** or planning of a building's purposes and functions. We see programming and evaluation as two necessary components of design, and indeed in the course of this project you engage both: your initial observation, semantic interviews, and review of pertinent literature (all part of your *evaluation* of the site) inform your final design proposal (and *program* for your site).

As a thoughtful student of ethnography and design, you may have noticed that translating cultural knowledge into design is not obvious. How, then, might you create and assess a space that celebrates and supports the needs of the micro-culture you are studying? Let's use the above example of building community in classroom settings; after all, *community* is a common person–environment concept in student ethnography projects.

Evaluating the Existing Site

Is the building doing what it is supposed to do? How well does it meet user needs? Here are a couple of ways to get started with your site evaluation:

Operationalize the concept. *Operationalization* is a term used in social science research that means *the definition of a concept in measurable terms*. Thus, to operationalize a concept is to make it definable and empirically measurable and observable. Operational definitions of *community* (in the case of school classrooms) may be any—or none—of the following:

- The number of friendships formed.
- The percentage of students who engage in discussion with others in class.
- A feeling of belonging.

How do you know which definition is correct? For the purposes of your ethnography project, you should begin by reflecting on what your informant said during your interviews to identify the definition that most closely aligns with what you learned from your informant.

Select the best *data collection* method.

- Depending on the type of information you want to obtain to evaluate the existing site, you will rely on different data collection techniques. For example:
- If you want to count the number of friendships formed, you may administer a *survey* or conduct an *interview* since the idea of friendship may be difficult to observe.
- If you are interested in the percentage (number) of students who engage in discussion with other students in class, you can conduct a simple *observation*.
- If you want to explore students' feelings of belonging—something that cannot reliably be observed—*surveys* or *interviews* can help you obtain the insights you need.

Designing and Programming a New Site

How can you translate complex cultural concepts into design? How can you design a space that accommodates and celebrates the needs of users? The following ideas can help you get started:

Brainstorm different designs that match your operational definition. The above definitions of community have different implications for design. Once you have a clear idea about how a concept is defined by the micro-culture you study, you can begin to think of ways to design a space that best reflects that idea. *Note: To practice this skill, try to think of different design ideas for each of the above definitions of community and then see how the different designs compare to and contrast with each other.*

Research design precedents. Remember that research is an accumulative endeavor, meaning that research projects build on previous research.[2] Similarly, you can look at previous designs to see (a) how others have used design to promote community and (b) the extent to which various designs have had the desired impact. *Note: This is where* ***post-occupancy evaluation*** *becomes especially important: to assess the outcome of the design.*

Identify the primary design intervention you want to make in your space. Articulate your rationale and create visual images to convey your ideas. *Note: You should also think about how you might assess the efficacy or impact of your design; though this is not explicitly required for the ethnography project, thinking about how you might do so can help you self-assess and anticipate the ways in which your designs might be perceived, used, etc.*

Ask yourself: Would my design meet the needs of my informant? Reflect on the definition of community—and other information about the members and activities that comprise your sited micro-culture—articulated by your informant. Would your design meet the needs of the **emic** perspective? How and why? *Note: This reflection will inform one aspect of Part 5 of your ethnography project.*

The Bigger Picture: Exploring Other Environment–Behavior Concepts

Though *community* is a common environment–behavior concept, it is not the only one that you are likely to encounter in your work. Try to listen—both in your ethnography project as well as your later work as a designer and researcher—for the deeper issues that people experience in and express about their environment. Common environment–behavior terms include (but are not limited to): community, privacy, surveillance, wayfinding, identity, territoriality, stress, and density.

Though each of these concepts may manifest differently in different cultural contexts, we encourage you to make use of the bodies of literature on these concepts when evaluating or designing a space. Always begin by clearly defining—or *operationalizing*—the concept you wish to research and try to notice how concepts are operationalized (or not!) in the books and articles you read. For example:

- In *The Great Good Place*, Oldenburg's definition of a good *third place*—a vague term that describes places other than home and work—includes quantifiable measures such as the quantity of conversations that occur within a space.[3]
- Evaluating the *soft classroom*, a "softer, warmer, more intimate" instructional space they created at the University of California, Davis, Sommer and Olsen defined a key measure of the room's success in increasing student participation as the number of (observed) voluntary comments to the teacher or to another student.[4]
- Finally, Edward T. Hall's theory of personal space (proxemics) was operationalized into four primary zones: intimate, personal, social, and public, each with different implications for design (regarding size, spacing, orientation).[5]

Notes

1 Jaclyn Zubrzycki, "Building toward a Positive School Climate," *Education Week* 32, no. 16 (January 10, 2013).
2 Sommer and Sommer, *A Practical Guide to Behavioral Research*, 2002.
3 Ray Oldenburg, *The Great Good Place* (Cambridge, MA: Da Capo Press, 1989).
4 Robert Sommer and Helge Olsen, "The Soft Classroom," *Environment and Behavior* 12, no. 1 (1980): 3–16.
5 Hall, *The Silent Language*, 1959.

7.4 Translating ethnography into physical design

As ethnographers of sited micro-cultures, you will discover a tremendous variety of activities and actions performed at a particular site. Such a wealth of raw data can seem overwhelming to any researcher, especially when parts of what you learn contradict one another. To make sense of the situation, you do not have to consider every last shred of activity and meaning. Rather, you focus on the *shared* activities that people refer to in order to make meaning that is shared with others.

One student described the change in attitude she experienced after completing the ethnography this way:

> In looking back at my first redesign proposal, I became aware that I had "stereotyped" [the hardware store]. Since the store is located in Japantown, I assumed that many tourists frequented the store. Thus, my original redesign included changing the design of the front façade of the store to a more Japanese style, in order to catch the eye of the tourists. However, Mr. K told me that tourists do not make up a large percentage of his customers.[14]

Your main purpose in your redesign is to remove the constraints that the existing setting explicitly or implicitly imposes upon its users. As we suggested at the beginning of the chapter, imagine if the building had burned down (heaven forbid), then your question would be, do you replace it exactly as it was because it works so perfectly for the micro-culture, or would you take this opportunity to make some changes that better supported that culture? Do the taxonomies translate into distinctive buildings, rooms, or parts of rooms? The best way to start thinking about redesign is by exploring some of the design techniques you already know:

(1) **Relational diagrams and adjacency studies**
Think about adjacencies, scale, and atmosphere qualities (such as, soft, quiet, or active zones). Explore these issues using bubble diagrams or section drawings to test different arrangements of programs and users. You can also test the relative scale of different spaces using simple diagrams.

(2) **Sketch perspectives**
Go beyond floor plans: you can use *perspective drawings* to identify the atmospheric qualities of your spaces. Exterior perspectives can be used to test different identities for the building in relation to its city or neighborhood and interior perspectives allow you to try out ideas about tectonics, materials, lighting, and interior spaces.

The actual structure of your taxonomy can be a starting point in developing sketches of possible spatial arrangements. Try defining zones based on combinations of your different taxonomies, bringing them together in diagrams of spatial relationships. Keep your thinking schematic to try out ideas. Doing so is much less constraining and can yield more inventive solutions than immediately jumping to the actual plan. Make photocopies of your different taxonomies and draw upon them using color codes, bubbles, and arrows to underline possible relationships. Often, this type of diagramming can help you see patterns emerge.

Ethnographic description need not always translate literally into design implications. The method allows many different kinds of design responses, alone or in combination. The designer may choose to fix problems that the culture itself defines and recognizes, to celebrate social groups and their practices, to call attention to contradictions and conflicts within a culture, to expose and express deep habits of thought. Ethnography is not a constraint, but rather a stimulus to creativity in design. It allows the designer to unite his or her voice with the voices of others to make a harmonious, resonant design.

One example of a highly abstracted pattern in a built project is in Steven Holl's Bellevue Art Museum. Holl and his associates interviewed the staff of the art museum, and found that one consistent response was that the employees viewed the museum as having three roles to fulfill: to provide experiences to see, explore, and make art. They also saw the museum as lying at the intersection of art, science, and technology. Holl took this theme of "three" and developed it into a spatial plan for the building with three separate galleries and three levels.[15] Here the deep structure of the taxonomy (three) was more important than the specific content of the terms within it.

Sometimes directly solving the problems spelled out by the informant may be the best way to solve difficult situations where the need for change is not widely shared and must be legitimated. Sticking close to what people themselves had identified as problems could make introducing architectural change and the social changes that go with it comparatively easy.

How extensive can your recommendations be? If the chief problem in an organization is the need for economic survival and a business plan, the task of creating the business plan is bigger than design, although design is included in it. For example, a feminist bookstore in Berkeley needed a café on the street in order to increase business, or, alternatively, it needed a nonprofit foundation with dues and membership to pay for the owner's informal consulting services. The design implications of the café are obvious because locating the café, planning, and designing it would involve site planning, circulation, storage, signage, symbolism, and atmosphere. Less obviously, the foundation alternative requires a place for collecting dues, holding collective events, and providing privacy for one-on-one counseling.[16] Sometimes a policy implication of your study might be to share space rather than create a new one. That too is a valuable design conclusion.

Policy changes were as important as physical changes in another study of a hotel in San Francisco. The student researching the site discovered that about 20 percent of the guests, usually families with children, were not happy with the amount of noise generated in the evening by the party atmosphere at the bar, but the other 80 percent, mostly singles, not only liked it, they made it! As a designer the author wondered if she should intensify the social life of the bar since it served the needs of so many, and simply ignore the reported complaints of the minority. Instead, she recommended changing the room assignment policy, so that the guests are offered the option of being on the quieter side, which could be called the "cool down and relax" option as opposed to the "music lovers" option.[17]

One way to make sure your design works on several levels is to make sure that you do not limit yourself to only one design solution. After working on an idea for a while, it is tempting to become committed to it and stop exploring other ideas. Try to come up with at least three or four design solutions, and then go back to the taxonomies to evaluate each one in terms of how it responds to the particular worldview of your informant. How would "Joe", "Diane," or "Mrs. Martin" use this new environment? Would it support the different tasks they need to perform each day and provide meaningful exchanges with those who also use this place? Does it reflect the distinctions or the groupings in meaning? Your final design will likely be a combination of ideas from more than one of such preliminary designs.

The required drawings for your redesign are ***floor plan(s)***, ***section(s)***, and a portrayal of the desired atmosphere, using either photographs or perspective drawings (or both). You should also provide a written comparison of your initial and final design proposals. This is important because it will help both you and your readers understand how the cultural investigation changed your consciousness. A particularly effective way to make this comparison after you have completed your final design is to go back to the initial redesign and write up a brief analysis of how you think this design would have failed or succeeded in serving its user group. This short exercise will convince you of the usefulness of going through ethnographic programming before designing for a cultural group you do not know.

Will you be able to translate every piece of cultural knowledge into design? Probably not. Some subsets of cultural knowledge may not have obvious connections to design issues. For example, in a study of a Japanese acupuncture clinic in San Francisco's Japantown, not every category in Japanese acupuncture had design implications. Most of you will end up knowing more than "necessary," but who's to say what is necessary? We can't know in advance what will turn out to be relevant to redesigning the physical environment of the clinic. Therefore, the designer has to know as much as possible about the micro-culture as a whole.

Three general guidelines may help in the process of teasing out the physical implications of sociocultural knowledge.

(1) Solve the problems presented by your informant. Because your informant spends a lot of time in the setting and knows it well his or her list of problems in the

space is a good starting point. Of course, your solutions might be more inventive, efficient, or daring than their imagined solutions, but you want to start thinking about the problems they perceive. When informants learn that you are a design student they may err on the side of telling you about their problems with the space, but that is a good starting point as long as you do not get stuck there.

(2) You should make sure there is a place for all of the social roles and activities in this sited culture. Check to see who might have been left out, unwittingly or perhaps on purpose.

Sometimes one space can accommodate several different activities, especially taking time of day into account. A space can work as a place for mothers with toddlers in the morning, an afterschool hangout in the late afternoon, and a music center in the evening as long as the walls, windows, furniture, or landscaping can be used in different ways. An office can be a place to meet people, or to be alone to think, read, write, or have a nap in solitude, and use as an archive and storage unit.

(3) Look for deeper meanings and patterns that can be expressed practically in plan or symbolically in ***elevation*** or decoration. Imagine, for example, that most categories had three attributes. You could take advantage of this latent pattern to introduce a mural in three parts, a triptych. It would fit into the culture in a quiet way, creating a sense of harmony even if below conscious awareness. We note that architect Steven Holl did exactly this.

Sometimes a latent contradiction that only appeared to you after you constructed a taxonomy could become the basis for an exciting design that expresses the split in thinking in some way—perhaps as two different materials in the flooring, or a twist in the plan.

7.5 Responding to conflicts (and ethical challenges) in design

Because the focus of your ethnographic study is the cultural information that your informant conveys to you through interviews, some of what you learn will inevitably be more indicative of their personal role and/or bias than the shared meanings of the micro-culture of which they are a part. This is not unusual to our study, but rather, as described above, an inherent challenge in conducting qualitative and ethnographic research.

What if you—or others in the site you are studying—disagree with your informant's perspective? [18]

Sholeh Mazgub studied a movie theater as a teenage hangout, and uncovered a tension about planning for teens. The author felt that there should be a place for teenagers to hang out, but learned that they want to act independently of adult planning and supervision.[19] Would it be a contradiction for adults to design a place for them? Or should adults, including the police, simply allow teenagers to appropriate some space informally—as they did in the streets immediately adjacent to the movie house on Friday nights? What would you design? Would you propose a civic center with distinctive parts, so that *different* groups could appropriate different sections as informally theirs? Or would you follow the recommendations in William H. Whyte's *The Social Life of Small Urban Spaces* for movable seats, street orientation, water, food, and triangulation that taken together invite many kinds of users? Or would you design a space *with* teenagers, for teenagers? How would you symbolize the desire for a place and the desire for autonomy?

Or say, for example, you were studying a beach club and your informant talked about how surfers wanted to "watch girls all day." Even if you disagree with (or find offensive) your informant's perspective, you can't ignore it. Rather, you should think about how you can use design to find a solution: perhaps your redesign would offer women a choice of walking in view or out of sight.

Occasionally, students will select a site for their ethnographic study because, through their research, they personally want to be able to give a positive review to a shop or increase a store's customer base. Though well intended, such an explicit aim is only tangentially related to the goals of design ethnography and possibly biases the study from the start. Of course, depending on the type of site you study—including restaurants, community centers, and stores—your informant may very well want to increase clientele. How might you use design to respond to this need?

You could use objects symbolically to make a less-visible community within the shop more visible to passers-by. Annie Chen, studying a hardware store, learned that the DIY (or "do-it-yourself") community comprised a large part of the store's customer base, yet there was little visual evidence of the community in the store itself (outside of the small room often used by DIY-ers for projects). So, she decided to feature projects from and tools relevant to the DIY community in the store windows as a way of appealing to that segment of the store's user base. This solution has the combined strength of enhancing an existing practice—displaying products—and rewarding the store owner for doing a good job.[20]

BOX 7.2: ETHNOGRAPHY PROJECT GUIDELINES

Part 5: Program Development and Site Redesign

Programming and redesigning space to reflect cultural knowledge

Design method: evidence-based design

Summary of required activities: By now you have obtained enough cultural knowledge from your informant and acquired sufficient information from your literature review, the general concerns of person–environment studies, and your personal observations to develop a proposed program and design for your site. For this part of your ethnography project you will focus on developing an architectural program and initial design concepts for the behavioral settings you have been studying. You will design a new space (or redesign the existing site) and use a variety of drawings, images, and written descriptions to describe and provide a rationale for your ideas. At the end, you will be asked to reflect on how your final design compares to, contrasts with, or supports your initial redesign, the information you acquired from your literature review, and the needs of your informant's cultural group.

Summary of research proposal components: Typically, a building matrix consists of a matrix of room names and square footages; for this project, we are asking you to develop a new standard for architectural programming that goes beyond this traditional format and gives more information about each space, and articulates the richness of and rationale for the project. To do so, develop a new design for your site and convey your ideas using a combination of words and images to describe the desired activities, separations, adjacencies, moods, and any other details you want to articulate about the spatial characteristics of your proposal. Translate the program you have created into physical consequences: use architectural drawings, sketches, or modifications of photographs to provide visual descriptions of your site; annotate your drawings with written commentary to show how your ideas reflect and celebrate the sited microculture you studied. Finally, comment in written form on your vision for the new site, your rationale for any proposed changes, and the similarities and differences between your current proposal and your initial redesign in Part 1. *For example, in your initial redesign, had you brought an outsider's point of view that missed the insider's needs or perspective? Would the emic perspective have been satisfied by your initial vision? Is it satisfied with your final redesign proposal? Why or why not, and how?*

Grading Criteria for Part 5

Does your project conform to the following criteria?

- Revised program: describe your program for a final redesign using a combination of words and images and reflecting the knowledge obtained from your semantic interviews, literature review, and personal observations.
- Plans, sections, and perspectives: translate your ideas into plans, concepts, and other visual images and annotate your documents to describe the purpose of and rationale for your design and to compare it with the existing space and your initial redesign.
- Comment on similarities and differences: in written form, reflect on the differences between the existing site, your initial proposal (Part 1), and your final redesign. Be explicit in addressing to what extent your initial proposal would have satisfied the insider's perspective: why or why not, and how? Also make sure to reflect on how your final proposal supports and celebrates the needs of the micro-culture you studied.
- 3–5+/– pages in length.

7.6 Chapter review: summary of main ideas

- Ethnographic research allows the designer-researcher to:
  - Understand why the current environment is organized the way it is even though some arrangement may have at first sight appeared irrational, messy, or in poor taste by the uninitiated observer
  - Conceive how the existing space could be reorganized to accommodate the specific needs of this particular group (7.1).
- The goal of the exercise is to redesign the physical environment of a sited micro-culture based on the specific way of life or worldview of your informant. Thus, to redesign the physical setting occupied by this culture solely according to your own dictates defies one of the purposes of design—to accommodate and celebrate ways of living (7.1).

- Cultural information can inform your design proposals in a couple of ways. First, the results of your cultural investigation must guide your design, not your personal preferences and desire to express originality and inventiveness. Second, working with informants may influence your proposals if you choose to test preliminary designs with different informants and see how they react to your ideas (7.1).
- Pay attention to the difference between the narrowly defined program of a building (the technical description of the main functions of this building) and the conceptual as well as physical use of a building by its occupants (7.2).
- Moving from ethnographic description to physical design is not just a matter of "adding"—everyone thinks you need "more space"—but rather rethinking existing space. As a designer, you are the expert at spatial resolution, so don't feel guilty if you don't use your informant's solution literally. If you get to the "deep structure" of their solution (the logic behind the structure of their taxonomy), you may be able to find a more appropriate way of structuring their space (7.3).
- Your main purpose in your redesign is to remove the constraints that the existing setting explicitly or implicitly imposes upon the micro-culture. Sometimes, a verbal element from your ethnographic research will be symbolically translated into the redesign (7.3).
- The actual structure of your taxonomy can be a starting point in developing sketches of possible spatial arrangements. Try defining zones based on combinations of your different taxonomies, bringing them together in diagrams of spatial relationships. Keep your thinking schematic to try out ideas. Sometimes, a verbal element from your ethnographic research will be symbolically translated into the redesign (7.4).
- Ethnographic descriptions need not always translate literally into design implications. The method allows many different kinds of design responses, alone or in combination. The designer may choose to fix problems that the culture itself defines and recognizes, to celebrate social groups and their practices, to call attention to contradictions and conflicts within a culture, to expose and express deep habits of thought. Ethnography is not a constraint, but rather a stimulus to creativity in design. It allows the designer to unite his or her voice with the voices of others to make a harmonious, resonant design (7.4).
- One way to make sure your design works on several levels is to make sure that you do not limit yourself to only one design solution; instead, try to come up with at least three or four design solutions then go back to the taxonomies and evaluate each one in terms of how it responds to the particular worldview of your informant. Ask: *Would the design support the different tasks group members need to perform each day and provide meaningful exchanges with those who also use this place? Does it reflect the distinctions or the groupings in meaning* (7.4)*?*
- The required drawings for your redesign are floor plan(s), section(s), and a portrayal of the desired atmosphere, using photographs or perspective drawings. You should also provide a written comparison of your initial and final design proposals. A particularly effective way to make this comparison after you have completed your final design is to go back to the initial redesign and write up a brief analysis of how you think this design would have failed or succeeded in serving its user group (7.4).

Notes

1 Lina Dragoman, "An Empathetic Lens" (Public Policy Lab: Policy X Design Blog, 2012). Retrieved from http://publicpolicylab.org/2013/03/an-empathetic-lens/.
2 See Sanjoy Mazumdar, "How Programming Can Become Counterproductive," 1992.
3 Danielle Borden, "A Mediterranean Restaurant" (Fall 2006).
4 Michael Kao, "A Montessori Pre-school" (Spring 1996).
5 Talon Smith, "Bring the Beat In: An Iconic Music Store" (Fall 2013).
6 Often sensory elements—other than vision—are neglected in design.
7 Karen Okazaki, "A Japantown Hardware Store" (Spring 1982).
8 Mazumdar, "How Programming Can Become Counterproductive," 1992, 22.
9 Territoriality—including visual and auditory means of demarcating space, expressing self, and the idea of defensible space—often comes up in students' ethnographies.
10 Maya Ying Lin, *Boundaries* (New York: Simon and Schuster, 2000).
11 Aline Tanelian, "A Café" (Fall 2013).
12 Malin Rönnerfalk, "The Small Café on 12th and Oak" (Fall 2013).
13 This comes from Magda Saura, former Graduate Student Instructor for Architecture 110AC, currently Professor of Architecture in Barcelona (no date).
14 Karen Okazaki, "A Japantown Hardware Store" (Spring 1982).
15 Steven Holl, *Tripleness* (Bellevue, WA: Bellevue Art Museum, 2001).
16 Eunah Cha, "A Feminist Bookstore: Books, Gifts, Events, and More for Women" (Spring 2004).
17 Pam Treetipbut, "A San Francisco Hotel" (2004).
18 Conflicting viewpoints between various micro-cultures within a larger site (or even between different members of the same micro-culture) may not always be readily apparent. However, sometimes the conflict may be more acute: think about the difference in perspective between a prisoner and a prison guard, for example. To the extent it is possible, you should try to select your informant with the possibility for this type of conflict in mind: whose perspective do you want to represent?
19 Sholeh Mazgub, "Movie Theater" (2005).
20 Annie Chen, "A Hardware Store in Berkeley" (Fall 2013).

Part 2

Report-writing and sample reports

8 Preparing the final report

A final report is much more than just a collection of everything you have done before. Preparing a final draft of any project takes care in selecting only the most relevant information and revising what you have written before to be clear, coherent, concise, and engaging. While the material you generated for previous projects will comprise the majority of what goes into your final report, the format of the final report is more standardized and formal than what has been expected for Parts 1–5.

There are a number of components essential to a final report.

8.1 Introduction

One approach to an introduction is to draw readers in with a story:

> Everyday I rush to school where I slave away for hours working on design models and attending class. As an architecture student, my classes are located mostly in one area of the UC Berkeley campus, Wurster Hall. When I walk to class in the morning, my stomach grumbles. Waking up ten minutes before class makes time for breakfast unrealistic. But as I step on campus, I grab a bagel and juice from Rio, a little food cart that sells breakfast and lunch. Thank goodness. I have something to tide me over until lunch . . . The other food cart in the area, Chinese Kitchen, serves a quick, hot and hearty lunch. People are sitting, relaxing, eating, and taking a break around the food cart's perimeter. Deciding to do the same, I realize how nice it is to eat here.[1]

Another approach to take is to introduce ethnography first, explaining why it is an important process to designers:

> To design a successful space for any constituency requires broad cultural competence and specific knowledge about the cultural group for whom a building is; therefore, architects are concerned with and seek to understand the systems of knowledge and cultural practices of the people who will or could reside in the buildings they design. . . . In this project, I used a specific type of ethnographic methodology, semantic ethnography, to learn about the culture—the activities, language, values, and spatial context—of the École Française community.[2]

8.2 Site description

Introduce readers to your site, using words and images to convey its spatial *and* social characteristics. Include a range of visual sources, including as-built drawings and plans, photographs of existing space and usage, and a map of location.

8.3 Methods

Describe your data collection methods—observation, interview, and literature review—in detail. Imagine that your reader is unfamiliar with the purpose and limitations of each method. Include details such as the number of visits, who your informant is, the questions you asked her, and where you were when you spoke. Also be sure to comment on your own observations and perceptions of the site, as well as the extent to which they changed over time. The more story-like your writing, the more you will engage your reader's interest.

8.4 Findings

The data section is where you present your findings, meaning everything you learned about a sited culture. Data includes your personal observations, key vocabulary and insights you learned through informant interviews, and findings from your literature review. In this project, taxonomies, lists of functions, schedules, selections from your project journal, selected quotes from your informant or publications, or anything else that has helped you redesign the site can count as data. Be sure to present your findings in an organized, meaningful fashion. For example, you might organize this section first by the method type (e.g. findings from your personal observation) and then by theme (e.g., people, behaviors, places). Headings and subheadings can visually help delineate to your reader the primary themes you explore in this section.

Graphic presentation is important here because graphics give you an opportunity to reinforce your findings visually. For example, in regard to your taxonomy, terms at the same level in a branch diagram should be the same size and at the same level spatially. Additionally, tables and diagrams, font size and style, and photo placement all offer ways to convey the structure of meaning in the culture you have studied.

8.5 Redesign and discussion

Explicitly justify each element of your proposed redesign, drawing on knowledge you gained either from your informant or from the literature review, or from your own opinion. You also might choose to comment on aspects of the site that you chose not to change, and also justify your decisions using data obtained through your various research methods. When and if the sources disagreed, discuss why you chose to design based on one source over another.

8.6 Conclusion

You might choose to add a conclusion; in so doing, you might reiterate the deeper implications of your study and/or articulate what you learned in the process of conducting ethnographic work.

8.7 Your bibliography

Your report should have a bibliography of the studies you used in your review of literature relevant to your topic. You also should include reference to any informant interviews you conducted (be sure to invent a pseudonym for each informant in order to maintain her privacy). The bibliography used in creating this workbook is an example of a bibliography using Chicago Style for formatting the entries. Yours might be annotated, but this one is not.

8.8 Sample reports

In Box 8.1 we outline project guidelines for the final report, and in Chapter 10 you will find 12 sample reports.

BOX 8.1: ETHNOGRAPHY PROJECT GUIDELINES

Final Report
Compiling and editing a final report of the entire research process and conclusions

Research methods: presenting findings and writing about a systematic research project

Summary of required activities: The final report is a comprehensive, edited version of all previous parts of the ethnography project (Parts 1–5). However, not simply a collection of previous work, this part of the project requires substantial new writing and organization: some new elements will need to be composed and old elements heavily edited to make this a comprehensive report of your research process and outcomes. You may add images, visuals, and/or narrative descriptions, and improve the style, grammar, and punctuation of your previous assignments as you wish (or as recommended by your instructor).

Summary of research proposal components: Begin by compiling Parts 1–6 and making any necessary edits based on feedback you received from your instructor, classmates or colleagues. Next, review the grading criteria and make note of the starred (*) items below, which denote new elements required in your final project (in other words, additional sections to write beyond what you have already produced in Parts 1–5). Once you have compiled, added new content, and edited your report, collate all sections—including any photos, drawings, and images previously used and a reduced-size image of your poster—into a single 8.5 × 11-inch document.

Grading Criteria for the Final Report

Does your project conform to the following criteria?

- * Cover page
- * Table of contents

- Improvement to Parts 1–5, based on feedback received
- Introduction
  - * Introduction to the entire ethnography project (1 paragraph)
  - Description of the site you selected, why you wanted to study it, the existing space, and your initial observations (see Part 1)
- Methods (observation, interview, literature review are all your methods)
  - * Sequential narrative of the process of data collection (1 paragraph): How did you conduct your research? *Note: Think about how you might explain your process to someone unfamiliar with this project*
  - Include information about your informant, how you met, etc. (see Part 2)
- Findings
  - Summary of the emic (insider) point of view (e.g. taxonomies from Part 3)
  - Summary of the etic (outsider) perspective (e.g. literature review from Part 4)
  - Summary of your own observations and reflections (see Parts 1 and 4)
  - Comparison of the three perspectives: emic, etic, personal (see Part 4)
- Final Redesign
  - Initial and final redesigns, conveyed in words and images (Parts 1 and 4)
  - Comparison of the designs: *How did your design change, and why*? (Part 5)
- Conclusion
  - (If relevant) Reference the poster and presentation you made (also include image of poster in a reduced size)
  - * Reflect on the contribution of your own case study to existing literature and ***future implications*** of research and design of similar buildings
  - * Comment and reflect on if and how this assignment influences your approach to designing new buildings, your own process of research, and method for design
- Bibliography
  - Include you annotated bibliography (see Part 4)
  - Include proper citations for all sources including informant interviews.

Notes

1 Janet Cheng, "Rio, A Food Cart "(1998, p. 2).
2 Caitlin DeClercq, "L'École Française" (2012).

9 The design board

9.1 Purpose of design boards

Design boards (posters) are commonly used to succinctly present findings and/or proposed solutions to a public audience. If you create a design board (as described in this chapter), you should use this opportunity to show how your findings influenced your design decisions. For example, one column might list your key findings and the next spell out the design implications (see Figure 9.2). Or a plan could be annotated with each of the findings that led to each physical feature (see Figure 9.3).

9.2 Tips for effective poster-making

Creating a design board (poster) is an exercise in condensing a lot of information into a visual form in order to describe your project and plan to a "public" audience (meaning a group of people who are not familiar with the details of your project, site, or proposal). Here are a few simple guidelines to help ensure that your poster is engaging and easy to read and understand:

- *Use minimal text.* You should aim to represent the majority of your project *visually*. You can use photos, floor plans, sections, elevations, and other graphics to convey the sited micro-culture, your informant's cultural knowledge, and your proposed ideas. By using a variety of visual forms, your need for written text will be minimal; however, you should make sure that you clearly label all sections of your poster as well as any graphics used. It is especially important to clearly distinguish between *current* and *proposed* floor plans.
- *Use bullet points.* Doing so will help you:
    - Succinctly list key ideas
    - Make text easy to skim.

  Organize text into columns. Have you noticed that newspapers and magazines divide text into narrow columns? The reason they do so is to help readers quickly skim or read articles. Similarly, you should format the text on your design board into columns that are no more than 3–4 inches wide. The posters in Figures 9.1–9.3 offer good *and bad* examples of this principle.
- *Make your poster legible from several feet away.* Be as concise as possible with any text you use and be sure to use *at least* size 16 font (larger fonts are preferable for headings). You can use bolding, colors, and/or different sizes of text to

BOX 9.1: ETHNOGRAPHY PROJECT GUIDELINES

Visual Presentation

Creating poster or video to communicate project, findings, and proposal to a public audience

Research method: visual presentation of information

Summary of required activities: Imagine that you need to communicate to a community group how you came up with your architectural program and design proposal: What would you say, and how would you convey your ideas in a concise and compelling manner? For this stage of your ethnography project, you will create a poster (or video) to present your process, your project, and your proposal to a wider audience.* This part of your project provides an opportunity to obtain feedback about your work from your classmates and others besides your instructor. The purpose of a poster (or video) is to communicate to others what you have done and to give you tangible experience in conveying complex information to clients and community groups in visual form.

Summary of research proposal components: On one 24 × 36 inch display board, summarize your research process, proposed program, and design. Your poster should include the cultural knowledge (perhaps your taxonomies) that helped you develop your architectural program as well as any other visual media—drawings, photographs, sketches, etc.—that help to convey the vision and rationale for your project. Use at least size 16 font (with larger fonts for headings), minimal text, and lines of text no wider than 3–4 inches for easy reading. Videos are an acceptable alternative to the poster, though they should be limited to 90 seconds and must include the same information described above. *Note: You will present your poster (or video) to your classmates at the end of the semester, so think carefully about what you want to say in your visual presentation (poster, video) as well as your verbal presentation.*

Grading Criteria for the Poster Board

Does your project conform to the following criteria?

- Inclusion of cultural knowledge: make reference to the most important cultural terms and knowledge (e.g. taxonomies) that inspired your design.
- Summary narrative of program and design: succinctly describe the project, site, and your proposed design.
- Emphasize visual drawings and photos: use the drawings, photos, and images you have produced to emphasize the important stages of your research (e.g. analysis of current, initial, and proposed site plans).
- Coherent, communicative, creative presentation of the ethnography project in primarily visual format; attractive; easily legible from a distance.

Note

* Remember to review the sample posters (Figures 9.1–9.3).

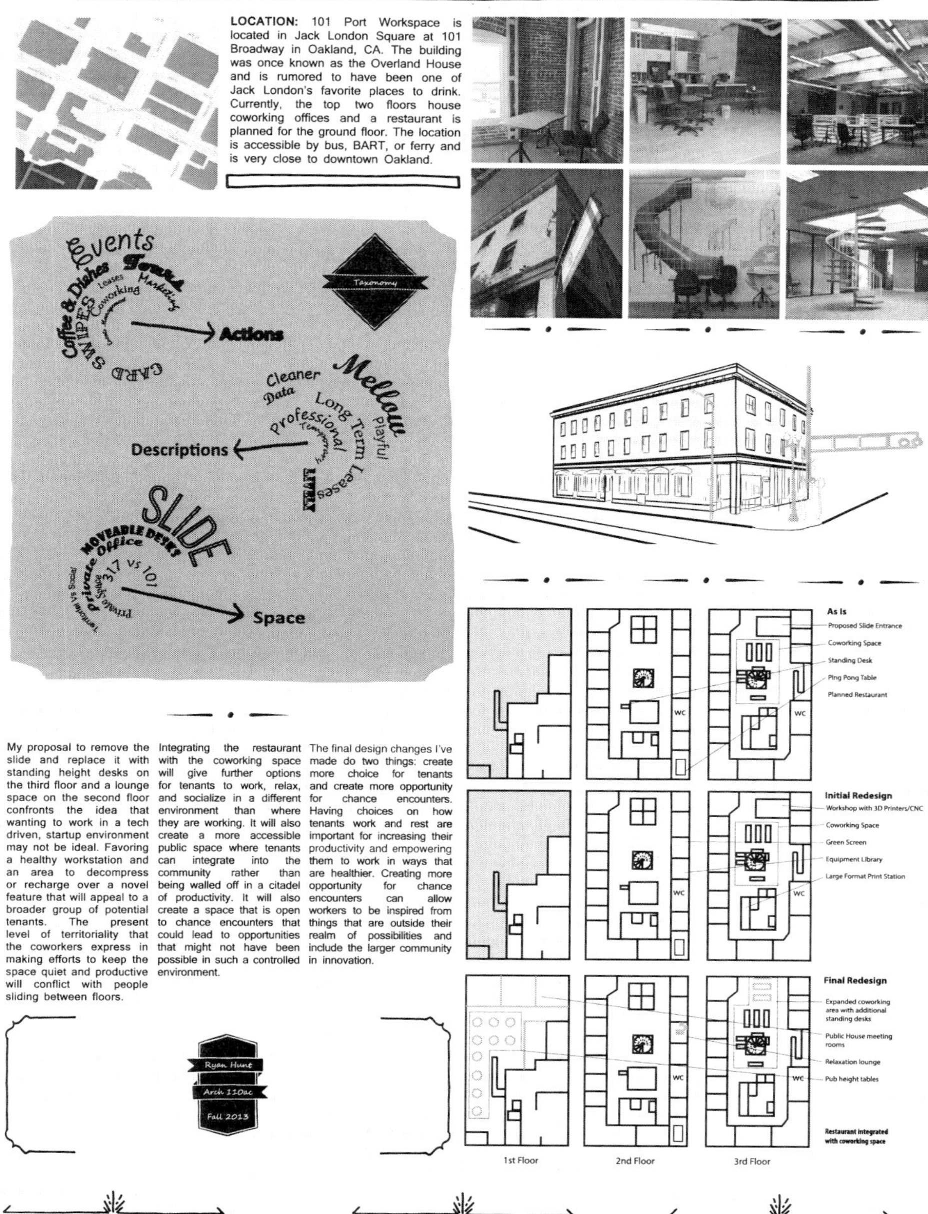

Figure 9.1 Ryan Hunt, "Coworking," 2013

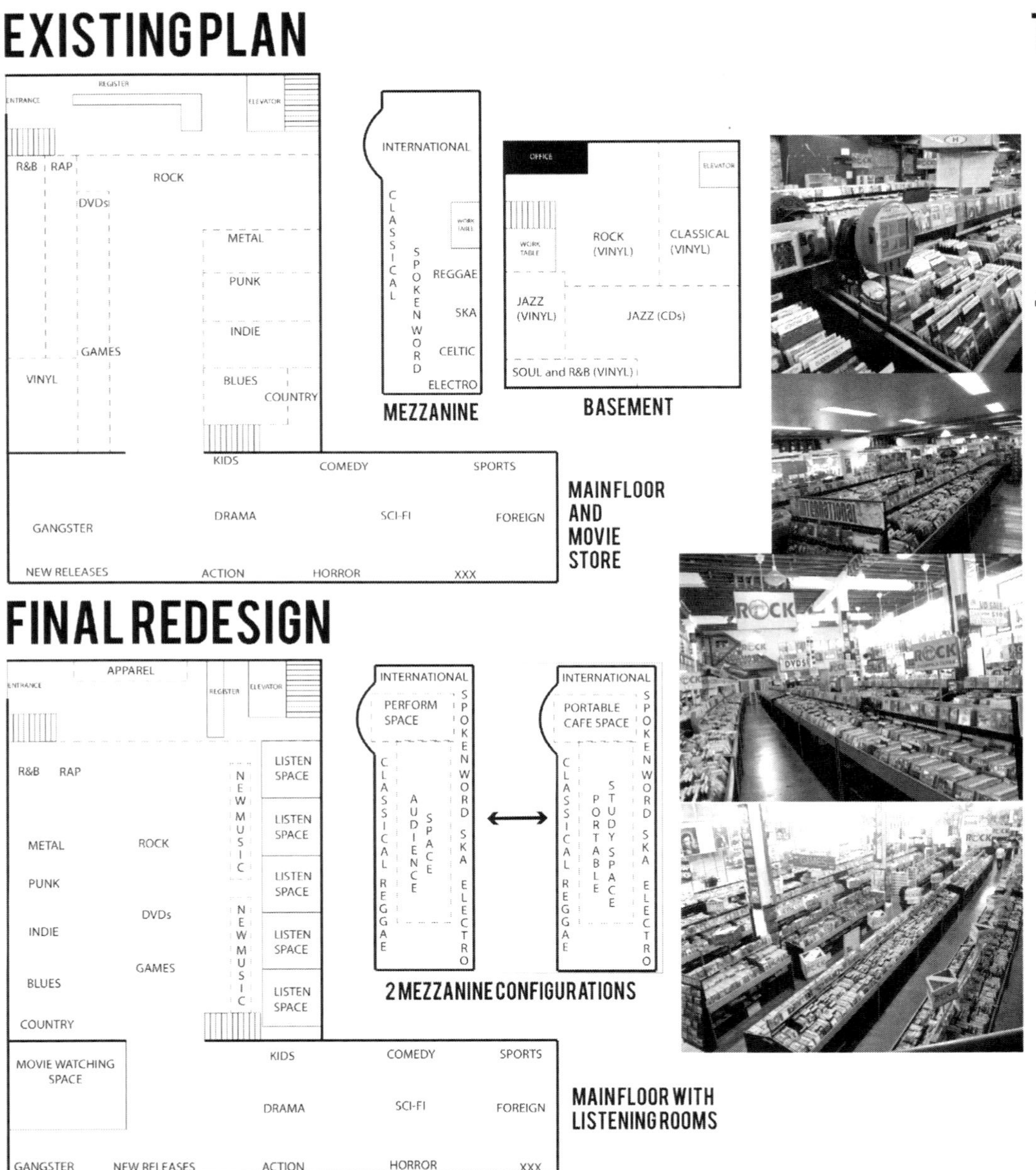

Figure 9.2 Talon Smith, "Bring the Beat; An Iconic Record Store," 2013

LISTENINGROOMPROGRAMS

1. Music as Therapy
A room with cushions, ambient lighting, and incense to allow the listener to engage with music on an emotional, spritual, or psychological level in a meditative state.

2. Music as a Spatial Experience
A room constructed with internal rods in the floor that rise and fall based on a particular audio frequency allows the listener to experience a spatial change as well as an auditory change when music plays.

3. Music as Community
A room with simple couches to engage groups of people to discuss and experience new music. This allows the listeners to listen intently and to form opinions about music.

4. Music as an Island of Interest
A room with movable seating and a rug for sitting or dancing to allow groups of people to engage with their favorite music by dancing, singing along, or simply enjoying the music.

5. Music as a Study Catalyst
A room with long desks and chairs to study allows listeners to use the stimulating, focusing power of music to study for tests and do other work.

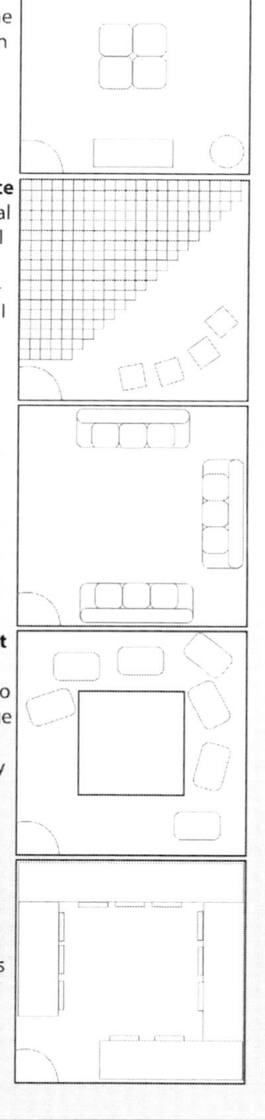

ONOMY

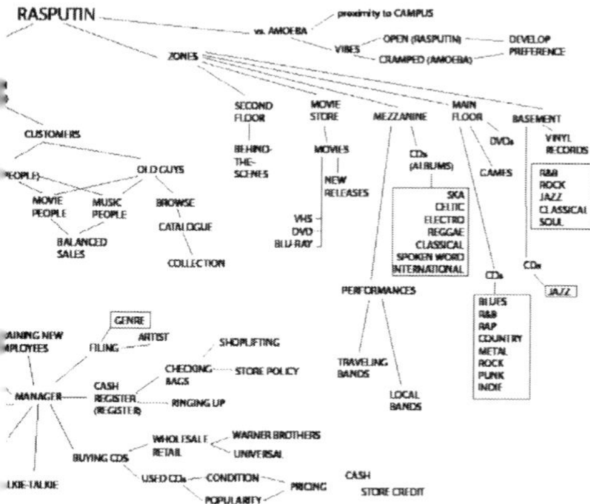

INMUSIC is a place where people of all ages, ethnicities, ss levels come to engage in the music culture. In a time hysical music purchases are on the decline, it is a breath air to come into a record store such as Rasputin Music, th an astounding collection of old and new, popular scure, and traditional and experimental.
r, this space meant to engage music-lovers to fall more with music is not fulfilling its purpose. Although its n is impressive, the current programmatic function of e is nothing less than storage of music with an option of ing it. Of course, the store also provides a movie n, small performances, and the ability of patrons to sell the store, but these are all peripheral functions.
n needs a redesign which allows people to engage with ways that they never have before.

posed redesign calls for the construction of five g rooms' on the main floor, which allow listeners ways to immerse themselves into the music, either with of by themself (see listening room prgrams on the nother proposed change would be to keep the mu- e mezzanine along the perimeter and use the central ther for performances and audiences or for a study and ce. When performances were not occurring, the mez- would be filled with portable chairs, tables, coffee, and iendly music.

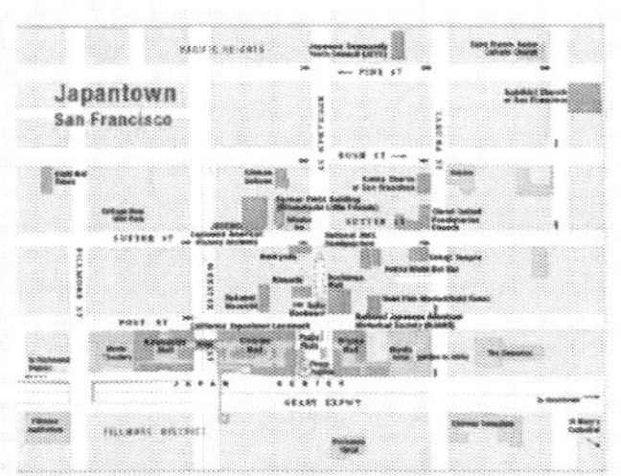

JAPA

~preserving an

The oldest and one of only three nationally recognized Japantowns left in the entire United States, the San Francisco Japantown is home to the Japantown Peace Plaza, an open public space that acts as a walkway between the Miyako (East) Mall and Kintetsu (West) Mall and connects to the Buchanan Mall across Post Street. The Peace Plaza is also used as a concourse for performances, events, and other festivities hosted by Japantown and/or the Japanese American organizations within the area. The main elements of the plaza include the 100-foot Peace Pagoda in the southwestern corner, the *sakura* (Japanese cherry blossom) trees that line the western side of the plaza, and a climbable water element along the wall of *sakura* trees. The plaza itself is a hardscape made mostly with a combination of stone and concrete elements with small planters scattered around the area and is raised above Geary Boulevard to the south, making the southern end of the plaza more private in comparison to the northern side which has more pedestrian traffic from the street and walkway between the malls.

a combination of wood and concrete elements in this planter/bench are used to bring the sense of nature and greenery to the hardscape of the plaza.

POST ST.

Kintetsu (West) Mall

Miyako (East) Mall

Pagoda

GEARY BLVD.

round and freeform concrete planters add some color to the plaza while providing some scattered seating, but little to no protection from the weather

rows of *sakura* trees line planted by the Peace Pagoda provide shade and some sitting and exceptional views during spring when the flowers bloom.

REDESIGN

As my informants, 'Preserving Califo
Jill Shiraki and San Francisco State s
satisfied with the design of the site,
focuses on adding more green spac
the plaza open for events, much of
The changes are instead on the per
outdoor kiosk would attract people
visitors with food and drinks. New s
plaza give users various places to sit
gather here instead of move into th
street access to Geary Blvd. and ope
Lastly, more greenery, which includ
maples, Japanese pine, etc., is place
bring more color and energy to the
currently not running, would also b
nature.

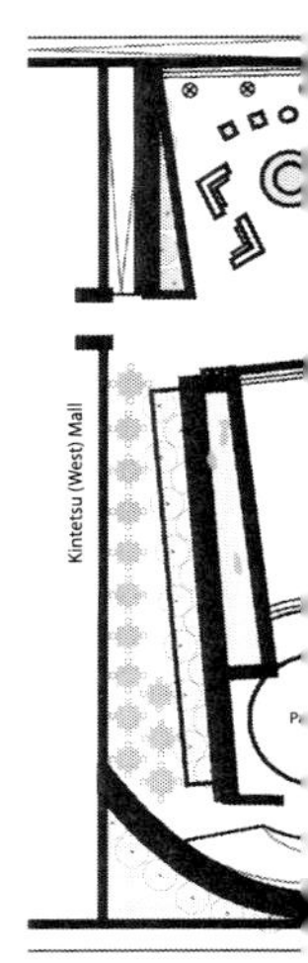

Methods and Findings

Initial observations of the site indicated that the plaza wasn't used by many people and most were just walking between the two malls. Howev
when the Peace Plaza is crowded with people. This dramatic contrast and the fact that, unless a major event, like the annual Cherry Blossom Fe
that the plaza belongs to a certain ethnic group encouraged research and understanding of the rich history of Japantown and Japanese Ameri
(Japanese Americans) about Japantown and from case studies about Los Angeles' Little Tokyo, another surviving Japantown, and Sacramento's
American communities that has disappeared over time, it was found that much of Japanese American history is tied directly to the history of S
that, but Japantown itself has changed and evolved as its people struggled through each major time period of American history. Interviews wi
American) Jill Shiraki and *yonsei* (4th generation Japanese American) Heather Ito also gave interesting insights to the past and present use of t
perspective on how different generations of the same ethnic community view and use the same space.

Adrienne Ito | ARCH 110AC | Section 103 | Stathis | Fall 12

Figure 9.3 Adrienne Ito, "Japantown Peace Plaza: Preserving an Ethnic Community and Cultural Identity," 2012

NTOWN PEACE PLAZA
San Francisco, California

thnic community and cultural identity~

San Francisco Japantown
1610 Geary Boulevard
San Francisco, CA 94115

Japantowns' Project Manager
at Heather Ito, were both quite
edesign of the Peace Plaza
sitting areas. In order to keep
iddle area has been left alone.
r. First, the addition of an
he street while also providing
g areas on either side of the
rest and encourages people to
ls. Stairs also provide direct
plaza more to the public.
re *sakura* trees, Japanese
ng with the new sitting areas to
. The water element, which is
on for more connection to

an outdoor kiosk with drinks and snack items would provide a place for people to gather as well as bring in revenue and give street pedestrians a taste of Japanese cultural foods.

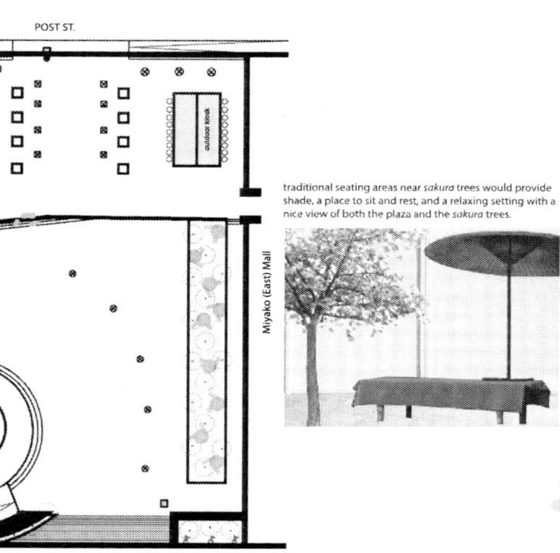

traditional seating areas near *sakura* trees would provide shade, a place to sit and rest, and a relaxing setting with a nice view of both the plaza and the *sakura* trees.

tables and chairs give another seating option for people to sit and rest and could provide an outdoor sitting option for an indoor cafe or grocery store while giving the user amazing views of the *sakura and pagoda*.

n past visits, there are times
is in progress, people can't tell
Using books written by *Nikkeis*
town, one of many Japanese
ncisco's Japantown. Not only
sei (3rd generation Japanese
a in addition to offering a

TAXONOMY

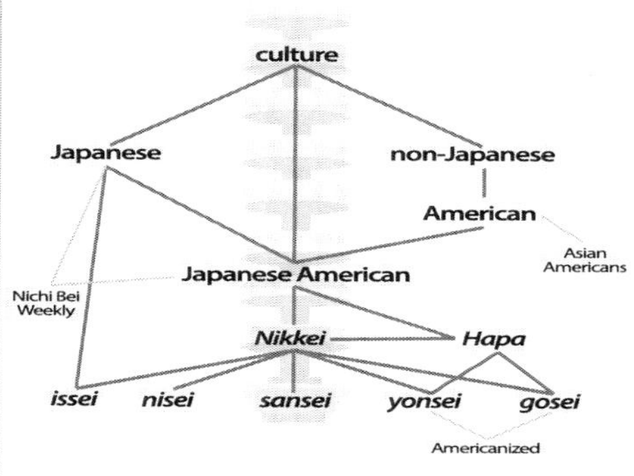

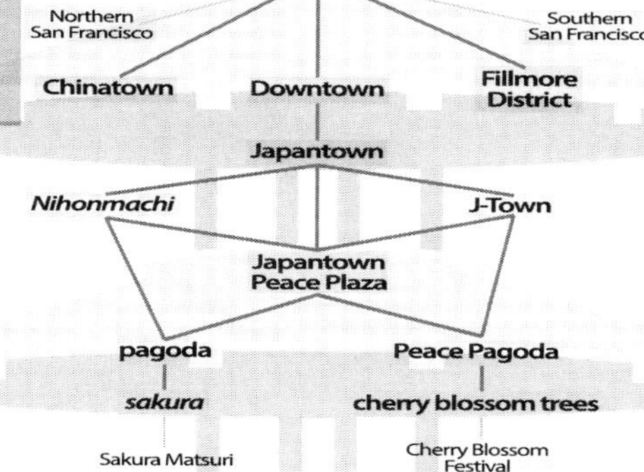

social cultural geographical

distinguish titles, headers, or key concepts. Organize information in a hierarchy of size.

- *Use fonts that symbolize the character of the micro-culture.*

9.3 Sample design boards

Figures 9.1–9.3 are posters from student ethnography projects. Because the goal of these posters is for you to present your design proposal to a public audience, we recommend you review these posters with an eye to their efficacy in achieving the following:

- Legibility: is the use of text (amount of text, color, size, etc.) sufficiently legible from a distance? Are the most general terms in the largest font, sub-categories in mid-size font, and details in the smallest (but still a least 16 point)?
- Quality of visual communication: does the layout, use of images, and sizing of words and pictures support or detract from the communicativeness of the poster? Do you lead the viewer in?
- Visual appeal: which is the most appealing design? Why? Is one orientation (portrait or landscape) preferable to the other? Was the choice of color, images, or fonts more effective in some and less so in others?
- Efficacy: which poster presented the most convincing argument to you? Why?

10 Sample ethnographic reports

10.1 Introduction to sample projects

Below, we have selected 12 ethnographic design projects from previous years for you to review. Each report has been edited for content and length; thus, not all facets of the ethnographic design project are highlighted to the same extent in each report. In the introductory paragraphs below, we **bolded** elements of Parts 1–5 (for example taxonomies, vocabulary lists, redesign plans) that are emphasized in each report. Though each report has strengths and weaknesses, together they show what an ideal project could be. Place and informant names have been changed to maintain confidentiality.

10.2 List of ethnographic design projects

Alter, Emily. "Fast, Slow Food: A Gourmet Fast Food Restaurant," Fall 2008.

Emily's study of a restaurant in Berkeley, California is well written and conveys a genuine interest in and concern for the issues raised through her research of the gourmet food culture, industry, and local Bay Area food scene. Pay attention to how Emily's use of emic (interview) and etic (literature) data gives compelling substance to her study. Emily's study also contains high-quality plans and analytic diagrams of the existing site plan as well as those corresponding to her proposed improvements.

Becker, Leslie. "First Time Mothers and Babies," Spring 2004.

Leslie conducted an impressive number of site visits and interviews in her study of new mothers and their babies. Often observing several moms and babies at a time, Leslie had to be creative and flexible with her methods. She also employed a range of sources to obtain information from an etic perspective: child development literature, studies of recreational spaces, and reviews of children's furniture all informed her astute, thoughtful ethnography of first-time mothers in a San Francisco neighborhood. Leslie's report contains a good example of a **taxonomy** of key terms.

Carvalho, Flávia. "An Irish Pub," Fall 2004.

Flávia's ethnography of an Irish pub in San Francisco is a model for integrating personal, emic, and etic perspectives into the final report and design proposal. Pay particular attention to her literature review, notable for its exploration of both the pub as a building type and cultural institution, as well as its attention to the Irish culture and immigrant experience. Flávia's inclusion of a **verbatim transcript** create a strong narrative and justification for her proposed design changes.

Chen, Justin. "An Assisted Living and Alzheimer's Community," Fall 2004.

Justin's paper is well written and makes expert use of **professional-quality graphics,** both of which make his study of an assisted living community all the more compelling. Pay attention to the ways in which Justin's proposed redesign changed between the first and last iterations. Clearly, the data he obtained through the semantic interviews and literature review he conducted were thoughtfully integrated into his final design proposal. See Justin's **annotated bibliography** to learn more about how he related emic findings to the site he studied.

Chong, Kevin. "Recipe for an Engaging Farmers' Market," 2014.

Kevin's thoughtful study of a farmers' market held at a historic urban site engaged the tensions between the original purpose of the site as a means to commemorate a historic event, its contemporary use as an event space, and its success and challenges in accommodating and integrating a diverse range of users. Kevin's report offers excellent examples of how to **code informant interviews to identify key terms** as well as **high-quality visual images to convey his proposed designs.**

Cohn-Martin, Elizabeth Leah. "Community Sustenance: Sunday Brunch at a Thai Buddhist Temple," Fall 2008.

Elizabeth deftly balances two (often competing) community perspectives of a weekly brunch event hosted by a Thai Buddhist Temple. Additionally, her proposed design interventions are thoughtfully inspired and clearly justified by information gained from the observations, semantic interviews, and literature review she conducted. Elizabeth's report includes a partial **vocabulary list and definitions.**

DeClercq, Caitlin. "L'École Française: Education, Engagement, and the French Language and Culture," Fall 2012.

Note how Caitlin used the personal and emic data she collected through observations and interviews to guide her literature review. Also, as a self-proclaimed "new [student] to the field of architecture," Caitlin looked for **ways to express her design vision beyond architectural drawing**: she used images of existing designs, superimposed on her floor plans, to convey the desired design and feeling of her proposal for the École Française.

Hunt, Ryan. "Coworking," Fall 2013.

Ryan conducted a thorough literature review, situating the coworking space he studied in a much broader cultural and economic context. See Ryan's extensive **bibliography** for evidence of the depth of his literature review. Despite this broad focus,

Ryan does not lose touch with the specifics of the site and its users: in fact, in his final redesign proposal, Ryan advocates for a greater integration of the physical site with the members of the surrounding community.

Landes, Megan. "You Are Now Entering a Sci-Fi Bookstore: Getting Lost in the World of Science Fiction & Fantasy." Fall 2014.

Megan's study is a beautiful, heartfelt celebration of the quirks of a special place: a science-fiction bookstore—with some of the most original and culturally appropriate design proposals like arched bookshelves to create a portal into another world. Pay attention to how Megan deftly integrates her informant's words—through quotes, a **word cloud**, and a **taxonomy**—into her final report. The result is a vivid introduction to the world of science fiction and the people who love it.

Look, Douglas. "A Martial Arts School," Fall 1990.

Douglas chose a compelling site—a martial arts school—and his inclusion of **taxonomies** and **detailed visual images** (from a variety of perspectives) help to convey both the subtleties and complexities of the site and his proposed redesign. This ethnographic report therefore serves as a model for the power of images to convey the ambience of a space and provide a complement to the written word.

Moore, Marianne. "For Whom the Booth Tolls," In Concrete, *5(3), February 20, 1979.*

Marianne chose a fascinating, yet often overlooked site for her study: toll booths on a local bridge. In a concise yet compelling report on her findings, Marianne offers a critical glimpse into the social life—and isolation—of this space and **proposes a redesign** of the booths to promote improved health and interpersonal activities for operators. Ultimately, Marianne argues that proposed changes should both include and transcend design. You might consider this question as you read: What might a similar study look like from the perspective of the driver?

Okazaki, Karen. "A Japantown Hardware Store," Spring 1982.

In recommending the addition of music to the hardware store, Karen pays attention to something often overlooked: the sensory environment. She recommends adding music as a way to quell the ambient noise of equipment and also appeal to customers and employees alike. Karen also takes into consideration cultural context in which her site is located; though, importantly, she offers an example of how her initial perception of the cultural space differed from that held by her informant, the shop owner. Karen's report offers a thoughtful **comparison of her initial and final design proposals**, both described using visual and verbal media.

EMILY ALTER, "FAST, SLOW FOOD: A GOURMET FAST FOOD RESTAURANT," 2008

Introduction

The culture of the design world emphasizes the end product; architecture school may emphasize the process, but in the real world designers and architects are concerned mainly with the final product of their work: the building. They see the cutting of the ribbon as a moment, a culmination of all their work and a cutting loose of their responsibility to the project. Research is rarely performed after the fact to ensure that it was a *successful* culmination and to reconfigure anything that fell short, but the ethnographic study I performed at a small restaurant in North Berkeley addressed this shortcoming. It was an attempt to understand and suit the needs of the clients by recognizing that architects are not hired to build moments but rather to build spaces. The project consisted of semester-long research on the restaurant via interview, personal observation and a detailed literature review. It helped illustrate that spaces are not simply created but are continuously being reworked and reconfigured, and it is important that designers remain involved in and understand this process; they must observe and interact with the built environment to create effective and responsible spaces. By studying buildings one can understand how places are not only shaped by interactions, but also help shape interactions.

Existing space

This restaurant, located in North Berkeley's Gourmet Ghetto, specializes in gourmet food made exclusively from organic and locally grown products. Both their lunch and dinner menus change monthly to ensure that all recipes include only the freshest ingredients. Due to the size of the restaurant—no more than 250 square feet—and its location less than a half block from a busy street, the restaurant attracts takeout orders almost exclusively. Customers range from college students to families—all in search of the same thing: the unique experience of eating gourmet entrees from small octagonal cardboard boxes with plastic cutlery. The restaurant manages to provide exceptional food with a laidback attitude; the limited seating and space work to create an atmosphere of leisure and community as numerous parties will often sit at the same table or on the same bench to wait for their food. This space also allows for chance encounters. For example, on my first visit, a couple was sitting at one of the outside tables drinking a bottle of wine from plastic cups when one of their friends came running by on an evening jog; he stopped to chat with them for a while, enjoyed a potato puff, and then continued on. It is this space of unpredictability that initially attracted me to the site; I was also intrigued by the thriving business that had taken root in this small shack on the sidewalk.

Despite its simplistic design, the elegance of the restaurant places it among some of Berkeley's top restaurants. Due to its relatively higher prices and its distance from campus it has not become a regular eating spot for the college population; instead, it attracts a steady flow of customers from throughout the city and surrounding area, who wander in and out enjoying all North Berkeley has to offer. A small kitchen built into the bottom of a house, the restaurant forgoes expansive space for gourmet excellence. The space is highly efficient and the employees are friendly and welcoming, while also highly capable. They provide quality products to happy customers who understand that occasionally sacrifices must be made in order to achieve real value.

Unfortunately, in the case of this restaurant, that sacrifice is made in its building, where minimal space is accepted to allow for high-quality, organic food. The exterior is relatively plain, decorated only by a large sign announcing the restaurant. The interior has no ornamentation, only three bar stools and limited counter space. As illustrated in Figure 1, there is a clear delineation between customer and employee spaces that allows for, but doesn't enhance interaction between the two; additionally, there are also clearly assigned spaces for each subcategory of employee. A small cubby next to the door holds monthly menus and a fridge next to the front counter displays beverage options; the space is nominal and provides very limited information about the restaurant, its business model, or the ideals upon which it was founded. A customer walking by is left to discern what the space entails, usually taking most of their cues from the cardboard to-go boxes stacked on the front tables.

Methods

It is from this viewpoint of customer that I began my research at this site. As with any ethnography one must be careful to approach the site or subject from all angles to avoid biases, so my study included personal observation, some participation, interviews, and a detailed literature review. Initially I visited the site as an uninformed customer to get a feel for my role in the space and the general layout of the restaurant, but I needed an emic point of view, so I chose an informant who was employed by the restaurant. I performed an initial interview to be sure that he would provide a cohesive and informative point of views of the workings of the business and the space. After choosing Matt, a new cook at the restaurant, I conducted two additional interviews to get a fuller understanding of Matt's role within the business. We steered away from discussions of the space, though his comments intrinsically raised a number of concerns to be addressed. From these interviews I created a taxonomy to map my informant's observations and get a better sense of the layout and the hierarchy of the spaces. With this information I performed additional observations to verify and expand upon this information. I then performed a literature review of fourteen books and articles related to the rise of fast food restaurants, the slow food movement and Berkeley's unique culture. The literature review provided an etic point of view that helped translate my observations and interviews into tangible evidence for my design. It was the final step in the ethnography process from which I could begin to incorporate my findings into a redesign justified by the demands of my informant and the details from my literature review.

Informant

Matt is a new cook at the restaurant who also understands the restaurant from an exterior perspective: he used to be a frequent customer. As a cook, Matt shares the kitchen space with the chef, a sous chef, and a cashier. After initial inquiry, he was quick to share information and offered a unique perspective as user, consumer, and learner. This kitchen space is more or less new to him, but he's worked as a chef for several years throughout the Bay Area. Now he's a new cook in a unique restaurant, learning "the ropes" from some of Berkeley's most notable chefs.[1] It was on one of my second or third visits to the restaurant that I was introduced to Matt. I stopped in for an order of the famous potato puffs and started to talk to the cashier. She was energetic and enthusiastic about the restaurant and its customers. I wanted to test the waters for an informant, so I began to ask her questions about what it was like working there, how the kitchen and restaurant were run, what sorts of customers came in most often. She had numerous anecdotes, but we were close in age and I seemed to be getting more social responses to my questions than I hoped for. I asked if there was a manager I could talk to or someone who knew the lay of the land. As she went to the back to find the manager, Matt interjected that there were no managers of the restaurant. There are chefs, sous chefs and cooks, he explained, as well as those who run the counter and ring up customers.[2] Because Matt took the liberty to interject this information and as he seemed to be very comfortable in his surroundings—he talked as he stirred, flipped, fried and grilled—I decided to question him further about the restaurant as a whole. Mid-sentence he pulled a spoon out of his rolled up chef jacket and tasted one of his dishes. Matt and I continued to talk for a few more minutes and I realized that he could provide valuable insight to the space. He was freshly trained so he could present the space as its owners hoped to present it, while adding additional commentary from his own personal experiences both as customer and employee, as well as valuable insight as a seasoned chef; thus I chose Matt as my informant. I performed two additional interviews with him over the span of a month and each interview provided supplementary layers of information to incorporate into my ethnography.

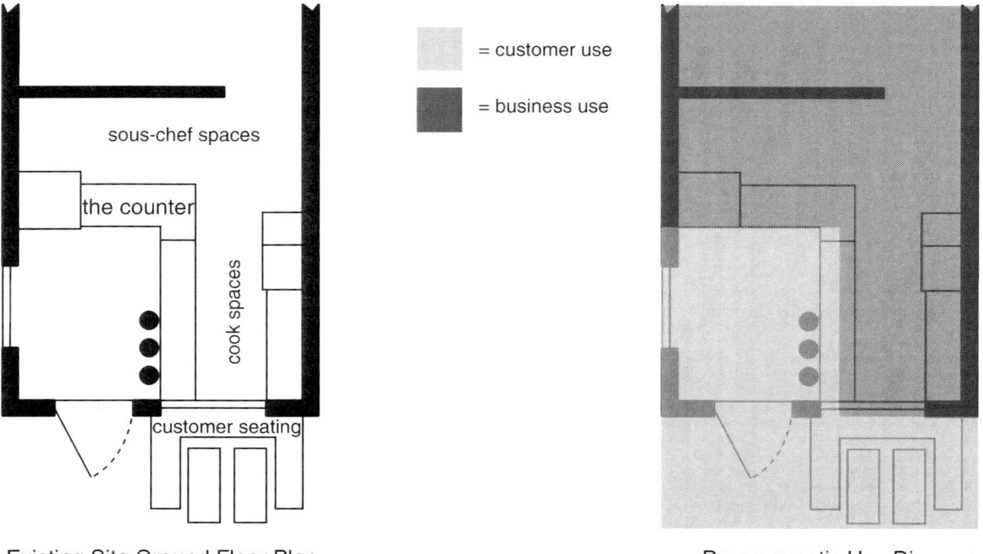

Figure 1 Existing site conditions and program

Findings

Emic perspective

Matt saw the restaurant as a popular place with an interesting spatial layout that creates an intimate and unique relationship between employee and customer. Beginning with the "back of the house" he presented me with a hierarchy starting with the most closed-off places and working towards the street-spaces where most interaction takes place.

Matt viewed the culture as a diverse one united by their desire for delicious gourmet food; his understanding of the site as a takeout restaurant was a positive one where the novelty of the presentation—steak in a distinctive hexagonal cardboard to-go box for $15—attracts customers instead of turning them away. The detail that is put into the preparation and planning of each item overcomes the spatial limitations of the restaurant. To Matt, no one comes to the restaurant for the atmosphere, only the food. This led him to stress the importance of the employees, but also to categorize and impose a specific hierarchy over the group. The business plan is integral to the working of the site, in that every member must work together to define and create the restaurant's delicious food. Produce providers are equally important to the restaurant as the head chef.

Resting on the ideals of Slow Food and organic, gourmet cuisine, this restaurant places itself in the larger context of Berkeley's Gourmet Ghetto. This is a fact that Matt was quick to emphasize. The uniqueness of the establishment, paired with the quality of its products, places it among Chez Panisse, Cheeseboard and other notable restaurants in the area, as I had observed on my initial visit. These aspects of the food: local, organic, carefully prepared, seasonal, are the "selling points" to customers.[3]

Etic perspective

In performing a literature review, finding information pertinent to the specific sited culture being studied is important; according to my informant and my personal observation, the restaurant I studied is representative of a hybrid space that fuses principles of both fast food and the Slow Food movement in a way that is unique to Berkeley. The Fast Food Industry has come under scrutiny in recent years by books such as Eric Schlosser's *Fast Food Nation* and the documentary "Super Size Me." These critiques are not based on the concept of "fast food," but instead dwell on the quality of food and the social equality of these spaces. The site I study, however, counteracts such arguments by implementing the principles of the Slow Food movement. The rise of this movement since the 1980s is based not only on a desire for healthy living, but also on the ideals of the sustainable practice of consuming locally grown, organic foods. Restaurants based on these Slow Food principles tend to be high-end and inaccessible to the general population. The cuisine is limited to "regional cooking" as examined by Adrian Peace, "The Representation and Rhetoric of Slow Food's Regional Cooking." The restaurant I studied incorporates the efficiency of "fast food," the sustainable and the gourmet dishes of Slow Food restaurants, with a changing menu of unique items. This micro-culture is distinctive for its integration of a range of motivations and expectations on the part of the consumer: quick food, gourmet food, a unique experience, a specifically Berkeley restaurant.

Personal perspective

A design student learns to analyze the built environment such that sizing up facades and studying spatial orientations becomes second nature. When I visited this site for the first time this past summer, however, I knew that it wasn't my "architectural tendencies" that noted the peculiar layout of the restaurant. The small space was efficient, vibrating with sensory stimuli, and the place clearly worked. The continuous stream of people in and out the front door was indication enough that there was some draw to this place that was clearly not architectural extravagance. As I began to watch the chefs and the customers interact—I saw one chef peer out the window, a sous chef pass cardboard boxes over heads, customers greet the cook behind the grill—I realized that this was an integral aspect of the employee's day. This interaction was not, perhaps, the main draw for customers, but it was a positive to the chefs; I began to understand how the small kitchen was made possible by this open atmosphere. No barrier exists between the consumer and the producer, which distracts the chef from their 3 ft. by 3 ft. workspace (see Figure 1).

This point about small size has continued to interest me throughout my month of observation: if the restaurant were transformed into a sit-down restaurant, would it be the same restaurant? In talking to Matt and in reading literature dealing with either end of the spectrum—fast and slow food—it is apparent to me that it is the unique, fast-gourmet experience that continues to draw people in. Everyone I know who frequents the site is eager to grab some potato puffs and go to the Rose Garden or pick up a sandwich on the way home to watch a movie. Occasionally, my friends and I like to sit on the benches and watch Berkeley life go by, but there again, it is the context (the quaint neighborhood, the outdoor seating) and not the interior of the restaurant that attracts people to eat there.

Comparison

Differences exist between my opinions and those of my informant: to him, the spatial relations enhance the customer–employee interactions, yet I initially saw them as detrimental. The interactions that could take place while customers sit and wait for their food are not accommodated in the current design; thus, while we agree on the social aspects of the space, I see architectural barriers to this goal. Further, the chefs and cooks are busy, so while they enjoy the personal interaction that the space allows, more interaction may, in fact, hinder their ability to perform their tasks efficiently. Customer interaction is a positive when there is a lull in orders, but customers who want to sit and chat while one cook is preparing four meals might be more of a burden.

Additionally, the communication of sustainable ideals through architecture, as I studied in my literature, was not touched upon by my informant. Matt emphasized the importance of the restaurant's involvement in the sustainable, Slow Food movement but at no point voiced hope that it would also be involved in the green building trend of recent years. While there are numerous elements of the building that make it sustainable—its small size, its southern-orientation, its recyclable cardboard boxes—these built forms are not emphasized in the same way that the restaurant's food is.

It is this complicated space where the demands of the client, the information of the experts, and the opinion of the designer must come together to create an effective space that meets the needs of the client via lessons learned from previous examples with the opinion of the architect interjected. The social space of the restaurant can be enhanced to accommodate the desires of my informant, meanwhile incorporating the sustainable practices from my literature review, which in turn would communicate to and enhance the experience of the customer.

Site redesign

Initial redesign

In my initial redesign I kept two key elements in mind: the original intent of the restaurant and its current atmosphere. The owner opened this small restaurant in 2002 hoping to produce a one-of-a-kind restaurant: delicious, gourmet food to go. The two, almost contradictory ideas of organic food in takeout boxes function well in the existing space, but in my redesign I looked to push these ideas even further. I proposed to eliminate the interior customer space, reorient the kitchen to face the street, and open up the entire facade for ordering and viewing. I also proposed adding additional seating on either side of the front window to accommodate more people. By eliminating an interior space for customers, the feeling of a grab-and-go eatery would be enhanced; however, the placement of additional seating, as well as the opening up of the entire front would encourage people to stay and watch the food being prepared.

Final redesign

After performing the research described above, I realized that my initial redesign fell short on several key elements. First, this is a small restaurant with limited space and no room to expand. Yet the size of the space is not inherently problematic: it does not look like a restaurant, because it does not want to be a restaurant. In fact, the mission of this restaurant is clear and its ideals coherent. The restaurant is part of a larger Berkeley gourmet food movement and their restaurant is prosperous and busy. Besides the people streaming in and out, however, there is limited indication of their identity, success, or complex social setting. I propose that a design that better reflects the goals of the restaurant would increase the legibility of the space to enhance and infuse its culture. For this reason I propose to open up the space to improve employee–customer interaction and to implement various green technologies to add to their sustainable, slow food practices.

Figure 2 reflects a number of priorities that guided my redesign of the space. Matt repeatedly cited customer–employee interaction as one of his favorite aspects of the restaurant, so I wanted to remove the barrier between the employees and the outside world.[4] I sought to increase interaction by opening up the front and reorienting employees to face to the front of the building. Whereas the current interior provides only space to stand and order, requiring that customers move outside to wait for their order, in my redesign I sought to attract more customers into the open interior

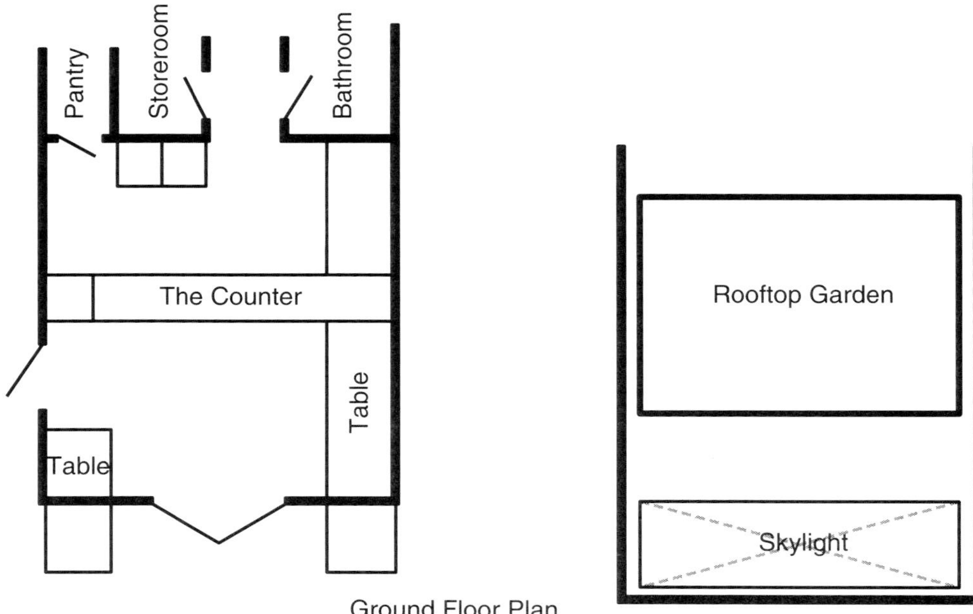

Figure 2 Site redesign (left), including new rooftop garden (right)

by providing space for them to linger, including interior seating and more open floor space. Though I do not think that the restaurant should be converted into a conventional sit-down space, Matt indicated that there was a considerable number of "lingerers," so my redesign aims to better accommodate this portion of the customers.[5] In doing so, however, I had to avoid blending the employee space too much, as the internal hierarchy of the business—a condition that Matt pointed out repeatedly—appears integral to its success, so I maintained nodes of productivity by keeping the various tasks isolated. I pulled the chef spaces forward by reorienting the backrooms to open into the public space. This also worked to enhance the privacy of the house access through the back hallway.

The implementation of green building practices is not only an attempt to infuse the building with the ideals of the business, but also to aesthetically represent to the passersby and customers what it is that the restaurant stands for: a small, organic, gourmet restaurant that upholds the principles of the Slow Food movement.

Comparison

My initial redesign was informed by my outsider's point of view as a customer. I emphasized additional seating space for the customer in my initial redesign and ignored the overarching principles of the space, as well as the opinions of the employees who are the daily users. The moveable and flexible interior would not have worked for the business. Moving the customers away from the window would have cut them off from the interior and the employees. In contrast, the emic and etic perspectives together provided new insights. This layering of information led to a far more complex redesign that considered a range of needs. In this way, the final redesign reflects multiple points of view. The mindset of my first redesign is most often associated with architects in that their designs are not the result of detailed research, but instead are a manifestation of their personal, professional opinions.

Conclusion

This detailed ethnography is not the first I have performed; yet through this project I learned much more about my own process and the site itself. Ethnographic methods are not traditional in architectural education and thus imply a serious reworking of design traditions. The possibilities and challenges that such an approach presents ensure that the designwork will represent the needs and desires of the clients or users of a given space far more than is typical in design. This does not mean that architectural taste and opinion are no longer relevant; design is still important to any space, but as architects, our job is to incorporate style and detailing into a building that suits the needs of future and present users.

Architectural ethnographies do not limit findings to present buildings or contexts, but similar to anthropological ethnographies, broader implications or understandings can be taken away from any given project and applied to sites in the future. Just as we performed literature reviews to enhance our understandings of the current space, we can add our information to the given body of knowledge to be applied to similar cases in the future.

In this study, I realized the importance of communication through architecture. If a building or business has a clear and coherent mission statement or business plan then designers must use the building to communicate it to the general public; in the instance of this restaurant, it was the implementation of green architecture via a living roof and compost piles. How this communication is manifested is a fluid and adaptable process that is at the will of the designer. I believe that buildings associated with the Slow Food movement or other ecologically-minded movements should represent and uphold their values in their architecture.

Bibliography

Anonymous. "Visual Vegetarian." *The Architectural Review* 210 (2001): 84.

Castillo, Encarna, ed. *Cool Restaurants Paris*. Boston: TeNeues, 2004.

Cook, Peter. "The architecture of fast food kiosks gives specific identity to streets and cities." *The Architectural Review*, 219 (2006): 42.

Hurley, Amanda. "Shaking up the storefront." *Architecture Magazine* 63rd ser. 96 (2007).

Jakle, John A., and Keith A. Sculle. *Fast Food: Roadside Restaurants in the Automobile Age*. Baltimore, MD: The Johns Hopkins UP, 1999.

Kunz, Martin N., and Katharina Feuer, eds. *Cool Restaurants San Francisco*. Boston: TeNeues, 2005.

Laurier, Eric, Angus Whyte, and Kathy Buckner. "An Ethnography of a Neighborhood Cafe." *Journal of Mundane Behavior* 2 (2001): 195–232.

Leitch, Alison. "The Social Life of Lardo: Slow Food in Fast Times." *The Asia Pacific Journal of Anthropology* 1 (2000): 103–18.

Matt. Personal interview. 29 Sept.–3 Nov. 2008.

McPherson, Edward. "Counter culture: fast-food restaurants are flirting with high design—would you like some corrugated steel with that order?" *ID* 63rd ser. 54 (2007): 48–53.

Peace, Adrian. "The Representation and Rhetoric of Slow Food's Regional Cooking." *Gastronomica* 6 (2006): 51–59.

Rival, Pierre. *Paris Gourmet: Belles et bonnes tables de la ville*. Paris: Flammarion, 2005.

Schlosser, Eric. *Fast Food Nation: The Dark Side of the All-American Meal*. New York: HarperCollins, 2005.

Steen, Karen. "Organic barn raising: for a Slow Food restaurant in San Francisco, Cass Calder Smith deploys recycled materials for durability with popular appeal." *Metropolis Magazine* 26 (2007): 70.

Weise, Ellen, and Kiran Singh. *Berkeley: The Life and Spirit of a Remarkable Town*. London: Frog Limited, 2004.

Notes

1 Matt. Personal interview. 29 Sept.–3 Nov. 2008.
2 Ibid.
3 Ibid.
4 Ibid.
5 Ibid.

LESLIE BECKER, "FIRST TIME MOTHERS AND BABIES," 2004

Introduction

I chose to observe a group of middle-class mothers who know each other as a result of having been pregnant with their first child at the same time. Through this study I interviewed and observed a number of women, all of whom are connected through a complex web of partially overlapping mutual friendships and shared places. Each of my informants in this study is a first-time mother and committed to thoughtful, responsible mothering and child-rearing practices. These women meet at each other's homes, local parks, swim classes, music classes, organized get-togethers, birthday parties, and yoga classes. Through these social connections, the mothers share with each other an ever-increasing and extensive knowledge of the various aspects of rearing a new baby. Ultimately, I focused my re-design of just one site frequented by the mothers I interviewed and observed—the changing room for mothers and babies to use before swim classes—yet my proposal was informed by a broad understanding achieved by studying my informants (and their children) in a range of settings.

The micro-culture

The core group of first-time mothers met each other at a local childbirth preparation class. Many of the women were joined in these classes by their partners, the fathers-to-be. The women continue to get together occasionally and in smaller groups. Additionally, other new mothers in the neighborhood who are friends of the mothers from the original birth class have become part of this larger, informal network of new mothers.

This group of women is in constant flux and continually re-constitutes itself for a variety of reasons. Some of the mothers have gone back to work part time and thus do not have as much time to dedicate to the group; one is expecting another baby in a couple of months. Pre-arranged get-togethers are often postponed or not attended by group members due to grandparents visiting, babies having colds, or mothers being sick. Thus, get-togethers have become more infrequent and spontaneous. The mothers who live within walking distance of each other seem to have remained in closer contact, sharing information about child-related resources, such as the reliability of certain brands, enrolling in preschools, and infant swim classes.

Sited micro-culture

The micro-culture I studied, new mothers, was not tied to a single site; rather, members moved from house to house, house to park, or house to class. My initial interest was in how knowledge possessed by these women materialized in domestic spaces and thus I initially focused my observation on mothers' child-rearing practices and consumption of child-related products. I attempted to determine what—if any—effect group knowledge has on individual adults who are part of the original group of women. However, needing to narrow the scope of my inquiry to fit the limits of a semester, I later attached my study to a particular site, the swim class center attended by some of the group members. Swim class—and its constituent spaces—seemed like a logical choice because it meets on a reliable, predictable schedule in a consistent location.

Selecting my informant (Leah)

I am fortunate to have a family member who both inspired my study topic and is a perfect informant. Leah is twenty-nine years old and, at the time of our initial discussion regarding this project, a first-time mother of a ten-month-old baby girl. Since her profession is in a branch of environmental science, Leah tends to be community-focused and stays well-informed about a variety of environment-related topics. She has a circle of friends and acquaintances whom she met at a prenatal class in her San Francisco neighborhood. She stays in touch with several members of this group and has met friends of the original group members to form a network of new mothers in her neighborhood.

Leah is a particularly good informant because she is well-connected to her peer-group of mothers and proactive about arranging shared activities. One of her ongoing relationships is with another mother and child with whom she shares a nanny. Leah currently works three days per week outside the home and does additional work at home. She is extremely bright and articulate.

Meeting with my informant

I spent a couple of hours with my informant in her neighborhood in San Francisco. We went into a local café, with Leah's baby, and while there Leah began to talk to another mother who was sitting at an adjacent table and holding a baby who appeared to be about the same age as her own baby. The mothers discovered that the two children were weeks apart in age. She learned that the woman and her baby attend the same music class as Leah and her child. The two women also noticed that they had the same stroller and then proceeded to discuss and exchange ideas for finger food, other classes (e.g., swimming), and balancing work and childcare. Finally, the two women exchanged contact information and Leah was invited (with her husband and baby) to a first-Sunday-of-every-month family picnic in a park that the other woman has attended routinely since having her baby.

The fact that this encounter resulted in an actual get-together reflects what appears to be a need among first-time mothers to share these new baby-related experiences as they attempt to gain a level of mastery over their new caregiver roles. All of the women in the group are well-educated and apparently have an expectation for a reasonably high level of competence in their child-rearing practices; this desire is manifested in the women's information exchanges, online research, and reading of child-rearing books.

Assorted methods and findings

Conducting research in the presence of babies is often difficult: conversations with parents are frequently interrupted by the needs of the babies. Also, the noise level achieved by a group of babies in an enclosed space makes it almost impossible to hear what is going on. In such instances, tape recordings are useless. For these reasons, early on in my study I realized the need for flexibility in my data collection methods.

I also found it difficult to record everything that is said and done by mothers and babies. Thus, I had to make on-the-spot decisions about what might be the best method to gather information at any given time: note-taking, tape recording, photographing, questioning (to clarify or elicit more information), or sketching. Sometimes I used a combination of these methods in a single encounter. Ultimately, I realized that I collected limited—but hopefully representative—information.

I also understood that the variety of interviews and observations I conducted would open up the world of shared knowledge among this group of mothers and provided me the necessary information to create a taxonomy of their world (see Table 1). This process relied on a mix of one-on-one interviews in homes as well as observations in group and class settings. Interviewing mothers one-on-one and observing smaller get-togethers yielded more information about child-rearing attitudes and focused on more detailed kinds of knowledge about child products, types, medical concerns, and foods.

I used a combination of these methods and found that in the venue of the swim center, the most useful information affecting spatial decisions would come from listening to conversations between mothers and watching the relative ease or difficulty of navigating the changing spaces. Yet my understanding of the changing area at the swim center was also informed by my observations of and interviews with this group of mothers in a range of settings.

Personal observations

The commercial area near Leah's home is known to be a place full of people with babies and small children. Many of the shops have small areas set aside for babies to play in while parents shop; some have infant and toddler toys for use by customers. The neighborhood, therefore, is characterized by an incredible tolerance for small children in restaurants, coffee shops, and other stores.

On one visit to a cheese shop in the area, I mentioned to the owner that I have a new grandchild that lives in the area and she asked that I bring the baby in so she could meet her. This interaction is illustrative of the neighborhood's child-friendly climate.

Interview with Sandra at her flat

Sandra and her husband were part of the original pre-natal class with Leah. I visited Sandra and her baby, Noah, at their home. During my visit, Sandra's husband was working in a small home office at the front of the flat, and Sandra explained that he works from home three days a week and in Silicon Valley the other two days. Noah is eleven months old and for the entire time Sandra and I talked, he played quietly and crawled around the living room where we sat. He never left the room, though no physical barriers prevented him from doing so.

During the interview, I observed that Noah preferred to play with a cat toy rather than his own toys and also had a clear preference to stay physically close to his mother. Regarding the latter, Sandra commented on her belief in "Attachment Parenting" in which the parent tries to be as physically close to the child as possible. Sandra said she recently purchased a sling in which to carry Noah; this emphasis on physical proximity was also evident in the sleeping arrangment I observed, in which Noah's crib was in Sandra and her husband's bedroom.

After the interview, we toured Sandra's flat. Sandra was happy to show me around but apologetic about the mess at the back of their house. I had no trouble discerning the spaces that were used by the baby: the kitchen and bedroom floors were covered with toys, blankets, and baby-related gear. The living room was orderly, with only one corner dedicated to toys and baby books, neatly arranged on shelves. When we were in the bedroom, Sandra commented that one of their methods for child-proofing was to move everything up high. She also said that Noah is a loud crawler so she can hear when he begins to move around.

Sarah's house

The following people were present during my visit to Sarah's house: Sarah (hostess) and her fourteen-month-old baby girl; Leah and her baby girl; Victoria and her one-year-old-baby girl; and Marina and her ten-month-old baby boy. Sarah's baby was still napping when I arrived. Sarah showed us around her house, which she explained had been completely redone since moving in a few years ago and was thankful to have all of the renovations finished, since she was expecting a second baby in just a few months. The living and dining rooms were clean and offered little evidence of a baby in the house, except for a high chair on a mat next to the table. Once everyone arrived, we went into Sarah's baby's room—a large, bright room with windows on three sides—at the back of the house. The room can only be accessed *through* one of two rooms, either the home office or the parent's room.

The group was very hospitable toward me. I told them I would just be observing and initially stay on the floor on the side of the room. This gave me a full view of all of the action in the room. Due to the extreme noise and bustle of activity (with four moms and four babies moving around), I decided to observe and take notes rather than use a tape recorder. I also moved around to be able to hear in better detail various, overlapping conversations. Interestingly, I observed that if one mother left the room, the other mothers—generally those closest to the child—immediately and without any discussion would take over.

Leah's baby's first birthday party

At this gathering, every child in the group was in attendance, in most cases with both parents. At this age, children tend to cling to the parents and do not move around too much, though most of them are at least crawling. Although several of these families initially met in childbirth classes, it is obviously the women who are in close contact with each other and are fully comfortable with each other's children. The men/partners seem to know each other more superficially and, with the exception of two couples in the group who are particularly close, the mothers are the ones who readily take over for each other.

The choices of foods at the party were divided into baby and adult foods, with the exception of the birthday cake (homemade carrot cake). The baby "buffet" included bananas, Cheerios, homemade baby muffins, and string cheese. The food selections for parents and children revealed careful attention to healthy foods. One of the babies rejected the carrot cake in favor of roasted beets!

Also notable was the type of gift given: a disproportionate number of musical instruments—particularly wooden ones—and books and puzzles were gifted by the mothers' group. The other family members who were present at the party or who had sent gifts tended to give large, plastic toys that talk or light up. I was intrigued to observe this difference in the type of gifts given and how consistently it differed according to membership in the mothers' group.

Music class

The music class meets in a large, airy room in the basement of a neighborhood church. An area rug serves to define the class space in this large room. Several overstuffed chairs and sofas with low tables provide a place for mothers to sit, watch their babies, and chat with other mothers before and after the class. Leah, along with Sandra, Marina, and Victoria—all of whom are regular class attendees—chatted after the class about a range of parenting issues including a serious health scare brought up by a mutual friend, Jamie. Jamie explained that a swim center owned by the same people who own the center used by this mothers' group was closed the previous week due to the discovery of a waterborne genital wart virus. This created a serious concern and Leah said she would check into the health conditions of the pool that she and her friends went to with their children. The mothers also discussed colds and possible remedies, including echinacea. One of the mothers said she gave echinacea to her child, but another expressed concern that the remedy was not good for babies. The first mother explained that her pediatrician said echinacea was fine, as long as it was not used for a long period of time. This brief exchange illustrates the ways in which mothers share and expand their knowledge.

The swim center

I chose the mother/child changing room at the swim center as the site for my redesign because it is a fixed site frequented by the parents and babies mentioned above. I attended a swim session three times and photographed the second and third visits. Note: it was not possible in the changing room because both mothers and babies use the room as a changing room and thus taking photographs would have raised privacy concerns.

The swim center is located in the middle of a commercial street in the downtown area of a San Francisco suburb. Leah commented that this is a well-known swim center for babies, frequented by middle- and upper-middle-class parents in the Bay Area. Classes, she explained, are fairly expensive.

Site description

Upon entering the swim center from the street, visitors see the following: a fairly underused play space to the right and a sign-in desk and office to the left. Straight ahead, a glass wall and door provide a direct view into the pool. Just past the desk on the left is a three-level gallery with benches for people to observe the pool area. The mother/baby changing room is accessible through a door behind the play area. Relatively few fathers or other male family members bring babies to class, and the male/baby changing room is located behind the pool and accessible only through the pool deck itself.

During the course of three visits to the swim center, I observed two different classes in which Leah and other mothers from the original pre-natal group participated. Classes for young children are only thirty minutes in length. Parents appear to know the routines, including songs, group games, and the ways in which a variety of pool toys and equipment are used. Four classes may be going on at the same time, each with five or six children.

The changing room

Observing and listening to the discussions between mothers inside the changing room resulted in the most useful information to inform my proposal. Because the space accommodates both mothers (and babies) changing into swim suits in preparation for classes about to start *and* mothers and babies leaving after other classes have ended, the changing room is a crowded and chaotic scene. Mothers voice concerns about the meeting times of classes with respect to baby nap times, to babies being cold and wet, and to babies being hungry. Several of the mothers nurse their babies before or after class. The wall-mounted changing tables, when down, block access to the benches below them, but this is precisely where many mothers leave their diaper bags and clothing. The problem with this practice is that, while the changing tables are down, others can neither access their own clothing nor sit on the benches below the changing tables. In this crowded space, typical questions I heard included: *Can I get through there? Can you keep an eye on my baby while I go to the bathroom? Can I get to my bag there? Can you hand me that?*

Up to twelve pairs of mothers and babies are in the changing room at a time. In one corner of the room sits a "Pack-and-Play" (a small, portable playpen) in which mothers put their babies while they are trying to change. This small playpen holds no more than three babies at once. One potential danger identified by mothers is that in such a crowded space, an older child eating raisins (or another snack food) could drop them in the playpen where they could be picked up by younger babies still at risk of choking on raisins and other small foods.

Emic perspective

My informant, Leah, and other mothers using the swim center obviously share an implicit understanding of the value of having their babies in the water from a young age. I did not observe any evidence of discomfort in the water of mothers or babies; thus, I assume that everyone in the class, once in the pool, had a good time.

The changing room itself is a social setting and place for the exchange of information among mothers. Topics discussed included whether babies were still napping twice a day and whether they were beginning to stand or walk. Although I did not hear the mothers complain to each other about the design of the changing room, it was clear to me from my observations that the space was tolerated as a necessary, if unpleasant, part of going to swim class.

Etic perspective (literature review)

Despite the plethora of literature on child development, only a small portion explores spatial considerations. Additionally, literature on pools and recreation centers tends not to focus on babies as users. Thus, my literature review

Table 1 Taxonomy of key terms

Primary	Secondary	Tertiary
Classes	Childbirth Pre-natal yoga Post-natal yoga (*mothers only*) Mother/infant yoga Music for infants **Swimming**	**(At the swim center):** Storage Baby is cold Ease of changing Safety
Gear	Strollers Mats and rugs **Sippy cups** **Toys** High chairs **Diapers** **Bed (crib) furnishings**	**(Sippy cups)** Spilling Difficulty in drinking **(Toys)** Unusual stuffed toys France Japan US **(Diapers)** Cloth vs. disposable **(Bed furnishings)** Spreads
Foods	**Finger foods** **Spoon feeding**	**(Finger foods)** Beans Cooked carrots Cheerios—original only Raisins (*choking hazard—wait until molars come in*) Dried fruits—apricots and pears Sautéed spinach **(Spoon feeding)** Preference for baby foods over finger foods
Nursing	Frequency When to wean Nursing bras	
Health	Pediatrician Virus in pool Safety of echinacea for babies **Ear infections** **Allergies** Diaper rash Teething Iron deficiency and diet **Physical development** **Activity readiness** **Interaction with others**	**(Ear infections)** Homeopathic Antibiotic use **(Allergies)** Berries and citrus **(Physical development)** Height Weight **(Activity readiness)** Standing Walking Climbing on furniture Going up stairs **(Interaction with others)** Age appropriateness Site of

spanned a range of topics—early child development, recreational facility design, health and safety issues—to better understand how the changing room might be improved. Surprisingly, some of the more helpful resources I found were publications by product manufacturers that described pragmatic issues of installation, maintenance, and cleanliness. Diaper changing tables are potential breeding grounds for bacteria, so important design considerations are hygiene and ease of maintenance.

Babyscapes.com, the website for a retail company that produces videos to encourage children's development, describes recent research regarding child development; for example, I learned that, in the first couple of months of life, babies react more to objects that come into their view from the right side. This has important design implications.[1]

The literature on the Diaper Depot changing station emphasizes safety advice for users of the equipment: users are reminded to never leave children unattended, to only use changing tables for children under 50 pounds or 3.5 years of age, to keep one hand on the child at all times, and to always use the restraint system provided with the product.[2] Though most changing stations are equipped with these restraint devices (belts), I did not see anyone use them in the changing room at the swim center. Mothers were typically in a hurry and these restraints slowed down the changing process. To me, this discrepancy indicates the need for simple, attractive signage in the space to remind mothers about the safety function of restraints as well as the provision of restraints that are easier and faster to use.

Building for Sure Start: A Design Guide is a complete design guide for planning, space development, and furnishing of early childhood centers. This guide emphasizes the design of attractive centers that are safe, accessible for and inclusive of a variety of children's needs, secure, and appropriate for the kinds of activities that occur within them. The authors advocate the importance of planning for play areas, storage areas (including for children's clothing and bags), eating spaces, and toilets and articulate specific recommendations for privacy while changing and disposing of soiled diapers. Additionally, the design guide stresses the importance of wall materials that are easy to clean, floor materials that are accommodating of strollers, and daily cleaning of any carpeted areas.[3] The changing room at the swim center makes few affordances for privacy; thus, this is a primary area for improvement.

One facet of the literature I read on children's cognitive development pertained to how babies learn language. Manuela Viezzer investigated the role of a baby's *physical* environment in facilitating language acquisition;[4] her insights made me reflect more deeply on the changing area at the swim center: what if the space was perceived not as a peripheral, necessary-but-evil "holding pen" but rather a place that provides another opportunity to foster child development and social interaction among mothers?

Through my literature review, I realized that children's concerns span a number of genres; nevertheless, it is precisely this range of sources that illuminated the possibility for the changing room to be re-thought as a more productive space for children and caregivers alike.

Translating findings into design

The most relevant information derived from an ethnographic study is that which allows the designer to question *a priori* design assumptions. Doing so allows spaces to be re-thought through the lens of the needs and actions of the users of a space. This process requires humility on the part of the designer to give credit to the users of a space and allow them to reveal, through the ethnographic process, what it is they need from their environment.

Domestic spaces

I learned from my informants that domestic spaces are not static, but ever-changing. Because child and parent needs change so rapidly, domestic spaces present particular design challenges with respect to demands for flexibility (due to changes in motor development, cognitive development, and changing privacy needs). First-time parents are often short-sighted with respect to storage and play areas and tend to react to current needs such as child-proofing (covering electrical outlets, adhesive foam edging strips, child locks on kitchen and bathroom cabinets) and thus often stay barely one step ahead of a child's present state of ability and mobility. To respond to the changing needs of children and parents—and their implication for the flexible design of domestic spaces—requires its own, more extensive ethnographic study. For now, I simply raise the observation of the disjunction between a fixed architecture and the changing needs of parents and children alike.

The changing room at the swim center

My initial perception of the changing room as a marginal space meant that I did not immediately recognize it as a space in need of attention. However, my observations of the space revealed the need for dedicated attention to the many functions of the space. Thus, my design proposal includes the following priorities:

- Create two center islands that include changing stations for babies and overhead bins for the storage of personal items; the islands should have space for 6 changing stations to accommodate 12 mothers and babies total.
- Arrange changing stations in two clusters to allow women to talk to each other while changing their babies.
- Create private dressing room and bathroom areas for mothers to increase the opportunity for privacy.
- Allow additional storage areas by adding hooks to perimeter wall spaces.
- Create a larger, gated play space for children, enclosed by half-height walls to aid with easy surveillance; position this play space in the center of the room so that mothers can be in close proximity to their babies and collectively monitor the play space from changing stations.

A sketch of my proposal is below (see Figure 1).

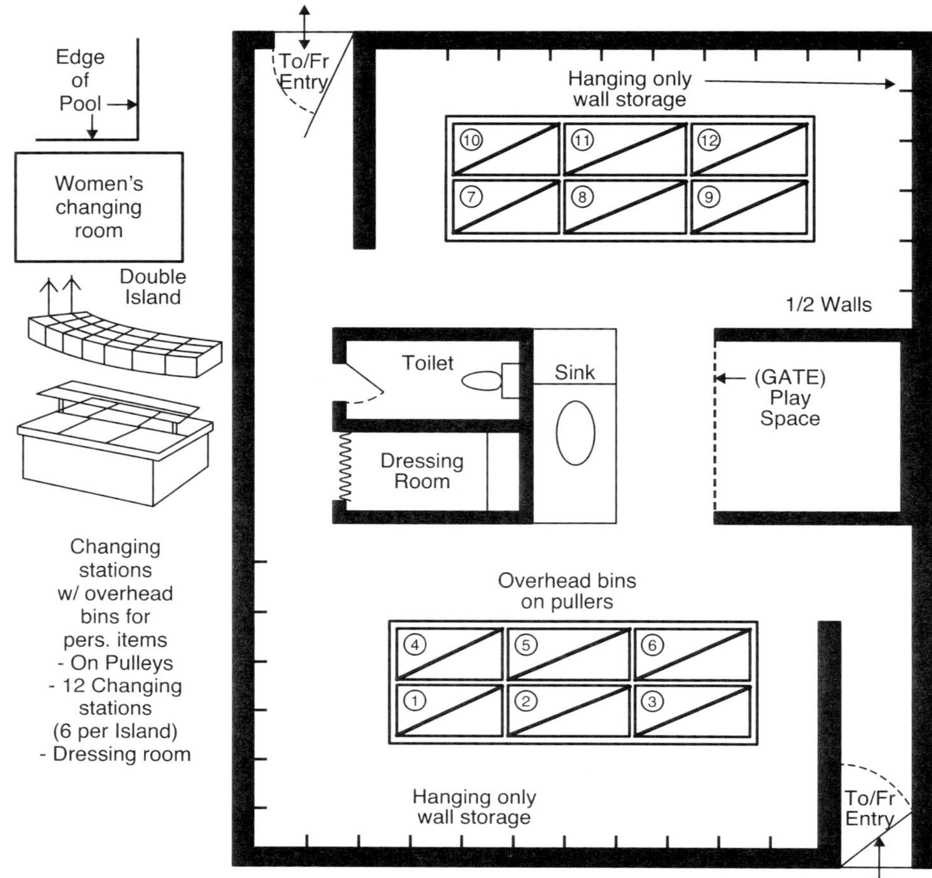

Figure 1 Redesign proposal for the mother/child changing area at the swim center

References

Babyscapes. Website accessed online at www.Babyscapes.com.

Diaper Depot. "Diaper-Depot Oval Changing Station." Accessed from www.diaperdepot.com.

Greenman, Jim. *Caring Space, Learning Places: Children's Environments That Work*. Redmond, WA: Exchange Press, Inc., 1988.

Viezzer, Manuela. "Theory and Implementation of Early Conceptual Development." *DECISLab*, January 30, 2004.

Watson, Lucy. *Building for Sure Start: A Design Guide. Integrated Provision for Under-Fives*. Nottinghamshire, UK: Schools Building and Design Unit, March 2004.

Notes

1 For more, see the Babyscapes website at www.babyscapes.com.
2 Information about this diaper changing station is at www.diaperdepot.com.
3 Lucy Watson, *Building for Sure Start: A Design Guide*, Nottinghamshire UK: Schools Building & Design Unit, 2004.
4 Manuela Viezzer, "Theory and Implementation of Early Conceptual Development," *DECISLab*, 2004.

FLÁVIA CARVALHO, "AN IRISH PUB," 2004

Introduction to site: the Irish pub

Irish pubs exist in almost every major city around the world. Famous for their traditional cozy atmosphere, the pub has become a place not only for drinking alone but also socializing. I chose to study an Irish pub because I think the design of pubs typically takes the customers into consideration more than the merchandise (alcoholic beverages) they sell. Unlike restaurants needing kitchen space, the bar is a sociable place that only needs space for the bar counter, with the rest of the space dedicated to other user-centered activities. Further, my interest in the Irish pub rather than any other bar comes from my interest in the Irish culture itself.

The Dublin Pub

The site I have chosen to study, the Dublin Pub, is a typical Irish pub visited mostly by immigrant Irish men. Women in the Dublin Pub are a rare find, yet when a woman is present, she is neither an outcast nor a distraction. I chose this particular pub because it appears to be an authentically Irish domain, visited by Irish customers and staffed by Irish workers.

The physical setting

The Dublin Pub sits on a street dominated by Asian restaurants. During the day and into the early evening, many people walk up and down Clement Street to visit pubs and restaurants. However, once restaurants close, Clement Street becomes quiet, except for a handful of people who walk in and out of the neighborhood's many bars. Compared to other Irish pubs close by, the Dublin Pub usually contains the most people on a typical Sunday night.

The only window of the pub looks out onto the sidewalk and is used to display merchandise like t-shirts and hats; thus, the only way to look into the pub's interior is by walking through its double-doors, one of which (on the left side) is smaller than the other and always remains closed. The pub's interior is dark and a narrow walking space leads customers from the bar to the booths and dance floor. Three booths extend approximately from the middle to the back of the pub. Two of the booths face a small square area against the back wall where a DJ plays music. The third booth sits at the very back of the pub, facing the restroom, and is seldom used.

My first impression of the physical layout of the pub is that it offers few gathering spaces. The bar counter is lined with tall, round stools, creating a linear arrangement in which conversation with more than two people is difficult. If more than two or three people want to converse, they move to the back of the pub where the two booths are located, fitting approximately 10 people each.

Observing the behavioral setting. If at the site during the day, observers of the Dublin Pub might find it to be a quiet place to drink alone: older men sit at the bar and talk to the bartender, typically a woman, while drinking a Guinness. However, at night, men gather at the pub before or after work, during soccer games, after soccer matches, and throughout the day Saturdays and Sundays. Early in the night, the bar counter fills up quickly, each customer taking a stool, until more and more people begin to gather around the bar and eventually move back to the booths and, later, the dance floor. The dance floor is typically used in the later evening hours, when almost everyone is intoxicated. The Dublin Pub is not only a bar to go to at night to drink, but also a place to gather, socialize, and spend time with friends.

Initial thoughts on redesign

Because I found the Dublin Pub to be a hub of social activity, the primary aspect I would change is the bar counter, where the current arrangement makes it difficult to converse as a group. Instead, I would add more booths, reduce the bar's size, and add more lighting so that the ambience is not so starkly dark and gloomy. However, I wonder if it is precisely these quirky characteristics of the space that appeal to the patrons of the Dublin Pub and, in turn, help the pub to serve as a social space for the Irish community.

Informant interviews

Gaining access to the Dublin Pub was not problematic since anyone (over the age of twenty-one) can walk into a pub. However, knowing the pub's reputation as a place frequented by primarily Irish men and women, I asked an Irish friend to introduce me to the site and help me locate an informant.

In selecting an informant, I made sure that he attended the pub frequently enough to know its layout and to be able to reflect on which parts of the space he uses the most, why he goes there, and who he usually goes with. The reason I chose to interview a male patron rather than a female is simply because the Dublin Pub is mostly attended by males. However, I do hope to find out how women who visit this pub are perceived and why bartenders are typically female.

The first informant I selected was Patrick, an Irish-born male who has been living in the United States for approximately two years. Although I had never met Patrick prior to our conversation, his willingness to speak with me about the Dublin Pub as well as his love for Ireland and its culture made it easy to establish rapport with him.

During our first interview, themes such as the music and space of the Dublin Pub dominated our conversation. During our second interview, I decided to investigate further his love for the music played at the pub and learn more about what the place means to him and his peers. Below is a partial transcript of our interview:

Flávia (F): You said the Dublin Pub played good music and mentioned traditional Irish songs as good music. Why?

Patrick (P): Well, those songs speak to us. They say that the Irish can travel around the world but will always find a place to gather; that's what the Dublin Pub means to me. The songs express sorrow and having to leave.

(F): How do you know these traditional songs are county songs?

(P): Each county has their own song in Ireland and each county knows each other's songs so that when your rival county in football [soccer] has their song on and you have friends in that county, you have a slagging match.

(F): What is a slagging match?

(P): You insult each other in a nice way—it's Irish humor, slightly different. We abuse each other.
(F): Do you do anything else when traditional Irish songs are playing?
(P): Oh we dance and sing.
(F): What do you do when the rock songs come on?
(P): The same, dance and sing.
(F): What do you do when you first walk into the Dublin Pub?
(P): You get a drink, stroll down to the back, and see who's there.
(F): Why do you walk to the back?
(P): Because it's so busy and everyone is at the bar and that area is so narrow so you can't see who's at the back, so you go to the back to see who's there. Plus there's a jukebox in the back.
(F): If it's not busy what do you do?
(P): Then you stay and sit at the bar. But people standing at the bar are in the way, standing around in a circle with their stools. I put an elbow on the bar, in Ireland they do that, Americans don't put elbows on the bar counter. You shouldn't put seats on around the bar because it's hard to pass through.
(F): What do you do in the back? Where are you located?
(P): I stand around with my friends at the edge of the dance floor so when a good song comes on you can come in and out.

Reflection on informant interview

My conclusion, after talking to Patrick, was that I have more to learn about the Dublin Pub, its culture, and the people who frequent it. I noticed that my informant did mention seating issues and spaces that are hard to get through, and he also seemed to have an emotional attachment toward the pub due to the music it plays. I decided to investigate further his ideas about what he would do to change the space (if anything), since it seemed like it really bothered him that he had to navigate around other people standing around the bar in order to get to the back of the pub. I wondered if all participants would prefer sitting at the bar, and whether that would drastically change the environment the Dublin Pub now produces with its dance floor.

Two additional informants

Based on these questions, I hoped to interview Patrick a third time, but when I attempted to contact him again, I found out that he returned to Ireland for two weeks. Thus, I decided to obtain another informant in order to learn more about the space. Mark is an Irish immigrant who regularly visits the Dublin Pub. During my interview with Mark, I noticed many similarities between his and Patrick's perspectives. Still, Mark focused on different aspects of the space: Mark emphasized the people and atmosphere of the pub, whereas Patrick focused more on the music and the various activities in which he engages.

While I was interviewing Mark, his friend Sullivan chimed in; it was clear to me that he was excited to talk about the pub and wanted to participate in the conversation. Ultimately I was grateful for the opportunity to interview three informants, all close friends, who share a loving attachment to their Sunday night pub.

Each of my informants had stories to tell about the craziness they have witnessed at the pub, and as they recounted these stories to me, they would laugh and appear to be having fun remembering good times.

Personal reflection

To me, the Dublin Pub seems like a great place for men to gather and converse with each other. Whether drunk or sober, patrons appreciate the ambience of the pub and enjoy listening and dancing along to the music. All three informants knew the owner of the pub and spoke highly of him. My three informants seemed to share both pride in and affection for the Dublin Pub: they consider the place their own pub, a place to go when drunk or sober, to meet friends, get rowdy, and have a good time.

Literature review

To learn more about the site, I conducted a literature review, using the following concepts to structure my search: Irish immigration patterns, Irish architecture, the architecture of bars and clubs, and the social significance of the Irish pub. These themes came from both the issues that arose in my initial observation and interviews as well as my desire to find inspiration for possible design changes. The sources I used to guide my literature review are included in the Bibliography below.

Comparing the personal, emic, and etic perspectives

I investigated the Dublin Pub through three different perspectives: my personal observations and perceptions, my informants' inside or *emic* points of view, and the outside or *etic* perspective provided by my literature review. Below, I will compare these perspectives thematically, using the four primary themes that arose in my informant interviews—physical spaces, people, atmosphere, and music—as a guide.

Assimilation in a dominant society: Irish immigrants and their culture

In a study of Irish immigration, Norman R. Yetman argues that "the nature of an ethnic group's adjustment to the dominant society is contingent upon . . . distinct factors" including the organizations and social institutions formed by the minority group in response to the dominant society.[1] Yetman defines these social institutions as the religious, the educational, and the political, none of which (according to his definitions) includes the public house or pub. Furthermore, Yetman argues that the American Irish no longer consider the three social institutions as an ethnic tie. With the fall of constant participation in religious, educational, and political social institutions, Irish immigrants had nowhere else to gather and relate to their own roots, and, in turn, become Irish Americans. However, as more Irish immigrants arrived and settled in the United States and realized that they had no place to relate to, the Irish pubs became their new common ground: a place to retreat, gather, and catch up on news back home.

This new wave of Irish immigrants, the New Irish, came in the 1980s and "removed themselves not only from their American peers, but from the Irish American community as well."[2] Linda D. Almeida explains that "sixty-five percent of the New Irish spent their leisure time in a bar;" thus, the Irish pub became the singular social outlet for this population. According to Elizabeth Malcolm, "one of the principal centres of popular culture in Ireland today is the public house."[3]

Irish and pub architecture

In comparing both the Irish pub's architecture in Ireland with that of the Dublin Pub, the clearest distinction is the ornate and elegant façade associated with the former and the simple and refined façade of the latter. Unlike the traditional pubs of Ireland whose facades "are often among the best buildings on the street," the Dublin Pub could fit under the description of small village shops that "have simple but dignified expressions that usually [contain] an entire façade picked out in a strong colour."[4] My informants seem to agree with Shaffrey and Shaffrey's categorization of the interior of the traditional Irish pub as warm and cozy,[5] unlike the muggy, crowded environment of the Dublin Pub.

If the Dublin Pub seems so much the opposite of the traditional Irish pub, what attracts the local Irish community to it? Perhaps it has to do with the public house history and its lack of aesthetic sophistication. In the 1830s when public houses were becoming more popular, nothing prohibited Irish drinkers from acting rowdy and getting drunk. However, once the authorities restricted "drinking to a clearly designated and controlled space [they] succeeded in disciplining it."[6] Therefore, though both the emic and etic points of view agree that the traditional Irish pub is an aesthetically pleasing, cozy space and therefore the complete opposite of the Dublin Pub, my view is that the social function of the Dublin Pub shares similarities with the very first Irish pubs.

People

In going to the Dublin Pub, I noticed more men than women present and my informants confirmed that this was usually the case. In learning the etic point of view I also found that "the Irish pub was until recent times a space largely reserved for males."[7] Lyam Ryan points out that the Irish "are basically a well-integrated, cohesive society with no great divisions of creed, class, colour, or race," but what about gender?[8] With no mention of gender by either my informants or the sources I read for my literature review, women appear to be cast out almost entirely from this social space. Perhaps the reason why women's place in pubs is obscured is because the bar began as a place for men to go in order to get away from their home and families. Further, pubs have been characterized as "female substitutes . . . offering 'plentitude, availability, warmth, food, and companionship, a servicing of male needs.'"[9]

As for the male participants of the pub, my informants told me about the "crazy drunk" people on Sunday nights, and I once saw them for myself. Though my informants at the Dublin Pub did not make any reference to alcoholism, my observations align with those of Linda Almeida, who claimed that "community studies expressed concern about alcohol abuse" in pubs frequented by the New Irish immigrants.[10]

According to my informants, the rowdy presence of these drunken men are what makes the Dublin Pub a special pub to which Irish men retreat after a long game or when needing to catch up and have fun with "the guys." Without this drunkenness, the social atmosphere of the pub may not be the same.

Atmosphere

As all three of my informants pointed out, the Dublin Pub is a dark, hot, stuffy, smoky, and crowded place lacking windows. However, these uncomfortable physical attributes do not prevent patrons from dancing, singing, laughing, and staying for long periods of time and returning again and again. What keeps the Irish going back to the Dublin Pub? In fact, the disorder of the space might be its primary draw: Elizabeth Malcolm explains that, from time to time, men like going to pubs in which they can be rowdy.[11] Though my informants seemed to love the rowdy ambience of the Dublin Pub, my literature review revealed differing points of view.

From a designer's (etic) perspective, "the dark, smoky pub simply can't hold a candle to the competition" anymore.[12] Today, patrons prefer stylish, aesthetically pleasing bars and pub spaces and the Dublin Pub lacks both qualities. Moreover, according to Bethan Ryder, in today's bars, "style takes precedence over function," and the pub is a place where people "meet, drink, and gossip."[13] In my personal view, I agree that bars tend to take on a more refined appearance, while pubs feel more home-like. One of my informants, Patrick, also noted that even in Ireland, today's bars are very modern and hip; still, the quaint pub atmosphere persists: author Pete McCarthy described a pub he visited in Ireland: "mercifully, there's no TV, no jukebox [no music], just the gentle hum of about twenty people talking to each other."[14]

In comparing the emic and etic points of view regarding the atmosphere of the Dublin Pub, I now see that it is neither a typical bar nor pub, whether in Ireland or the U.S. My informants shared this view: the Dublin Pub exhibits many of the historic social characteristics of an Irish pub, yet is distinct in its interior and exterior design.

Music

Just as Patrick pointed out, traditional Irish music evokes feelings of home, and people often sing along to these songs. Gerry Smyth explains that "music . . . is capable of creating imaginary landscapes. . . . Music is a map . . . with a point of departure which functions as an image of home."[15] However, Patrick also pointed out that pop music played at the Dublin Pub also has the same effect: patrons sing and dance to Irish and pop music alike. When I asked Patrick to describe the pop music he preferred, he mentioned U2, an Irish rock-pop band. Linda Almeida's study of Irish immigrants, shows that Irish pubs in New York would alternate between two different kinds of music and she also mentions U2 as symbolic of the New Irish immigrants' relationship with America. Not surprisingly, U2 is one of the bands most often heard at the Dublin Pub.

Concluding thoughts

As far as I know, no other studies have been conducted at (or written about) the Dublin Pub. Thus, looking for published sources to help inform my study of the site was both a challenging and fascinating endeavor. I was particularly interested in the intersections between the broad idea of a pub and the specific characteristics of the Dublin Pub. Though I had trouble locating information about Irish immigrants in San Francisco, I found many parallels between the New Irish immigrants in New York and what I learned from my informants. For example, Almeida states that the New Irish of New York no longer try to assimilate themselves into American culture, and my informants, who live in San Francisco, affirmed this perspective, having formed a community amongst themselves.

Program development and final redesign

In my initial redesign of the Dublin Pub, I proposed reducing the length of the bar counter, adding more booths to create more space for small group conversations, and increasing the lighting to make the atmosphere less dark and gloomy. However, upon learning more from my informants and the literature I reviewed, I realized how faulty my initial redesign was. Thus, in my final redesign proposal, I came up with new ideas that prioritize the emic (inside) perspective, as represented by my informants. My final redesign emphasizes function more than aesthetics. Below, I discuss my proposal and the rationale for the main issues I prioritized.

The façade

Although I thought about changing the façade in order to conform to the style of an Irish pub—with brick walls and Georgian windows—in my final redesign I propose leaving the façade alone. If the Dublin Pub changed its façade, it might attract a different crowd and thus might cease to be a welcoming place for Irish men to go to drink and socialize. Furthermore, my informants did not have any complaints about the façade, and in fact, after further reflection, I now see that the prominent Irish flag, red walls, and black trim make the façade distinctive.

Doors/entry/bar counter

In contrast to my initial suggestion to shorten the bar counter, I now see that the bar is an essential part of a pub's design, and reducing the length of the bar counter would prove detrimental to the Dublin Pub. Instead, I propose changing the bar from an L-shape to a U-shape, thereby reducing the seating along its length, and increasing seating on its sides. With this new change, I can add two additional stools and create more space between the door and the left wall to allow more room along the linear entryway for gathering and circulation.

Booths and dance/DJ areas

Although I was correct in my initial assumption that the Dublin Pub needed more space for gathering and socializing, I was wrong in assuming that adding more booths would solve the problem. I now know that standing near the bar or dancing are the most common activities in the pub; thus, adding booth space is no longer a priority. In fact, in my final design, I propose eliminating the back booth altogether (since it is rarely used), tear down the wall that separates it from the front booths, raise the ceiling height in that area, and move all seating to the left side of the pub. With these changes, the middle and right sides of the pub will be more spacious for the DJ and dance area.

Since music is such a big part of the Dublin Pub, I think that the DJ should have more room and his own space at the same level as the dancers so that both parties can interact with each other. Using the knowledge I gained from my informants about the

DJ and his star role at the Dublin Pub, I also propose moving the DJ area to the back wall so that he can better see and be seen.

Bathrooms

One of the main complaints from my informants is the long lines that form outside of the bathrooms: often, lines extend onto the dance floor, causing disruption and crowding. In my literature review, I noticed that bathrooms are almost always located at the back of bars and pubs or in a space that prevents the overflow of restroom lines onto the dance floor. In my final redesign I propose to close off the bathroom

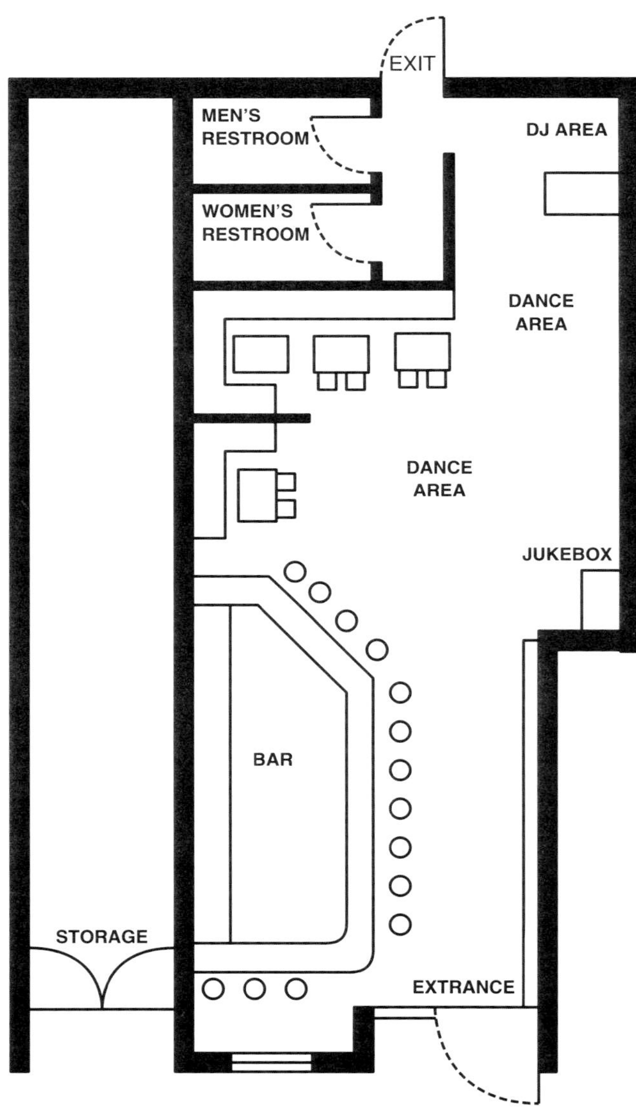

Figure 1 Final redesign proposal

area with a wall; doing so better defines the corridor and, with the addition of a large mirror against the new wall facing the bathrooms, people will be drawn into the space. Both of these interventions serve to minimize the chance of bathroom lines extending to the dance floor. Additionally, the line's proximity to the DJ allows those waiting for the bathroom to converse with the DJ while they wait.

These changes are reflected in Figure 1.

Bibliography

Almeida, Linda Dowling. *Irish Immigrants in New York City, 1945-1995*. Bloomington, IN: Indiana University Press, 2001.

Casamassima, Cristy. *Bar Excellence: Designs for Pubs and Clubs*. New York, NY: Rizzoli International Publications, Inc., 1999.

Fogarty, Michael, et al. *Irish Values and Attitudes*. Dublin, Ireland: Dominican Publications, 1984.

Irish Architecture . . . A Future for Our Heritage. . . . Dublin, Ireland: National Committee for European Architectural Heritage Year, 1975.

Malcolm, Elizabeth. "The Rise of the Pub." In *Irish Popular Culture 1650–1850*. Ed. James S. Donnelly, Jr. and Kerby A. Miller. Dublin, Ireland: Irish Academic Press, 1998, 50–77.

McCarthy, Pete. "McCarthy's Bar: A Journey of Discovery in Ireland." In *The Tourist's Gaze: Travellers to Ireland 1800–2000*. Ed. Glenn Hooper. Cork, Ireland: Cork University Press, 2001, 246–248.

Ryder, Bethan. *Bar and Club Design*. New York, NY: Abbeville Press, 2002.

Shaffrey, Patrick, and Maura Shaffrey. *Buildings of Irish Towns: Treasures of Everyday Architecture*. Dublin, Ireland: O'Brien Press Ltd., 1983.

Smyth, Gerry. *Space and the Irish Cultural Imagination*. Chippenham, Wiltshire: Antony Rowe, Ltd., 2001.

Yetman, Norman R. "The Irish Experience in America." In *Irish History and Culture*. Ed. Harold Orel. Kansas: The University Press of Kansas, 1976, 347–376.

Notes

1 Norman R. Yetman, "The Irish Experience in America," In *Irish History and Culture*, Ed. Harold Orel. (Kansas: The University Press of Kansas, 1976), 347–376.

2 Linda Dowling Almeida, *Irish Immigrants in New York City, 1945–1995*, (Bloomington, IN: Indiana University Press, 2001).

3 Elizabeth Malcolm, "The Rise of the Pub," In *Irish Popular Culture 1650–1850*. Ed. James S. Donnelly, Jr. and Kerby A. Miller, (Dublin, Ireland: Irish Academic Press, 1998), 50–77.

4 Patrick Shaffrey and Maura Shaffrey, *Buildings of Irish Towns: Treasures of Everyday Architecture*, (Dublin, Ireland: O'Brien Press Ltd., 1983).

5 Ibid.

6 Ibid.

7 Elizabeth Malcolm, "The Rise of the Pub," 1998.

8 As quoted in Malcolm, "The Rise of the Pub," 1998.

9 Ibid.

10 Linda Dowling Almeida,. *Irish Immigrants in New York City, 1945–1995*, 2001.

11 Elizabeth Malcolm, "The Rise of the Pub," 1998.

12 Cristy Casamassima, *Bar Excellence: Designs for Pubs and Clubs*, (New York, NY: Rizzoli International Publications, Inc., 1999).

13 Bethan Ryder, *Bar and Club Design*, (New York, NY: Abbeville Press, 2002).

14 Pete McCarthy, "McCarthy's Bar: A Journey of Discovery in Ireland," In *The Tourist's*

Gaze: Travellers to Ireland 1800–2000, Ed. Glenn Hooper, (Cork, Ireland: Cork University Press, 2001), 246–248.

15 Gerry Smyth, *Space and the Irish Cultural Imagination*, (Chippenham, Wiltshire: Antony Rowe, Ltd., 2001).

JUSTIN CHEN, "AN ASSISTED LIVING AND ALZHEIMER'S COMMUNITY," 2004

Introduction

The Hanover Retirement Center is an assisted living community located on a busy street in a residential neighborhood in the Bay Area of California. I encountered the site after taking a walking tour of the area. At first, the only indication of the retirement community I could readily discern was a handicap-accessible shuttle, parked near the front of the building, that had a decal on its side door with the name of the community. Signs announcing the site are visible, but blended into the environment with a green background. The entrance to the building is welcoming and pleasant, more similar to a person's home than a hotel lobby. This residential feeling was similarly conveyed by a porch-style entrance: a few stairs lead to the main doors, which are flanked by two curving ramps that extend approximately 30 feet to both sides of the stairs. The edge of the facility is carefully landscaped and delineated by a wrought iron fence that is partially obscured by bushes, hedges, and small trees. Additionally, a sidewalk that loops around the site perimeter is buffered from the street by a greenbelt of tall trees. This dense use of landscaping stands in contrast to other nearby properties, around which no such buffer is evident.

Initial impression and initial redesign

Given the beautiful greens, pleasant residential feel, the apparently well-maintained site conveyed, my initial impression was that nothing needed to be fixed at this site.

Still, the current site design may not serve the actual needs of residents. For example, the well-maintained and carefully landscaped grounds might be improved by allowing residents to enjoy the exterior landscaping without leaving the protective security of the center. The exterior of the Hanover gives some clues to the intent of the facility. The wrought iron fence is used to help keep outsiders and residents separated, and a buffer of bushes and hedges obscures the view in both directions. However, the area between the balconies of residences on the lower floors of the complex and the fence appears to be largely unused; this interstitial space presents an opportunity for improvement. The distance from the outer edge of the fence to the building wall is enough to create some sort of "park" which could include a small path to be used for walking, sitting, and visiting. Such an addition can be made rather easily; for example by moving the row of bushes and hedges closer to the fence.

Informant

My second visit to the Hanover was dedicated to the task of meeting someone who could help me with this project. I assumed that I would have a difficult time making an appointment because the site is a place of business, and thus staff might be too busy to take time away from work. This was not the case. As soon as I introduced myself—and my project—to the receptionist, she called over the director, Amelia, who was happy to give me a tour of the building. Amelia explained that she would lead me on a tour of the building as if I had a grandfather or grandmother who was in search of a place to live because he or she could not live independently; thus, I obtained a glimpse into how she typically interacts with—and presents the property to—prospective residents.

Amelia was friendly to me, and I could tell she enjoyed her job. She would often greet residents as if they were long-time friends, exchanging pleasantries in a happy tone of voice. I guessed that Amelia was trying to create a caring yet exciting atmosphere for all residents. Before her present position as Assistant Living Director at the Hanover, a position she has held for the last 4 years, Amelia worked the evening shift as a nurse at a local medical center for 13 years. During our tour, Amelia elaborated on why she takes pleasure in her current line of work: because everyone becomes old at some point, we need to take good care of the elderly.

Amelia then explained that, while the Hanover is a nice place to live, its small size limits the availability of on-site amenities, as compared to other retirement communities in wealthier areas. In her opinion, the Hanover doesn't have enough amenities nearby (in walking distance) for residents to use, such as parks or shopping centers, which I guessed might be due to its location in a residential area.

The grand tour

Though I had only asked for a brief tour of the site to get an overall sense of its constituent areas and services, Amelia ended up giving me an hour-long tour that was highly detailed and informative. First, I learned that the facility is more of an "assisted living community" rather than a senior center or nursing home; this distinction has implications for the types of services and autonomy of residents on site.

Amelia began the tour by talking about meals. Food is served "restaurant style" at the Hanover, which means that residents order from a limited selection menu. This style of food service gives residents the feeling of being able to exercise choice.

Many events take place at the Hanover; perhaps most notably, Christmas and New Year's celebrations are held in the living room, which Amelia noted was too small for such gatherings. The lack of space is also problematic for other events such as weekly exercise classes. Occasionally, the Hanover hosts movie nights, at which a popcorn machine is wheeled out to the living room to give a taste of a theater. Adjacent to the living room are two courtyards, which are also used for events and informal gatherings. In one of the courtyards, a woman named Grace kept a little garden, the only personal garden in the otherwise professionally landscaped courtyards. I asked Amelia why Grace was the only one with a garden, and she said that most residents did not have the time or energy to maintain one.

The next area that Amelia showed me was the "Country Store," a small area with hardwood flooring, mailboxes, a square table, several chairs, and a counter from which a variety of small snacks are sold for 25 to 50 cents. The store is open from 3:00–4:30pm during the week and from 10:00–11:30am on the weekends. Additionally, every Sunday the management provides coffee and doughnuts at the Country Store, a perk enjoyed by many residents. In fact, one weekend, managers forgot to purchase coffee and doughnuts, causing endless complaints about the mishap. Reflecting on this experience, Amelia commented on the importance of maintaining a schedule at the Hanover, especially regarding food.

Around the corner is the library, which in Amelia's opinion is not really a library at all: the entire collection consists of two small bookshelves holding a handful of books, with a small table intended for reading. Though the room is lit by a skylight, the overall lighting quality does not seem sufficient for aged eyes, even at midday. The area, perhaps not surprisingly, appeared unused.

Another amenity at the Hanover is a computer center, where staff hold weekly classes to teach residents how to use email and the internet. In contrast to the library, the computer lab boasts plenty of natural light, which is provided through a large window. Yet, this amount of light might be problematic since it creates a great deal of glare when viewing a computer screen. Still, I observed at least one person checking her email.

Behind the computer lab is a large elevator that accommodates wheelchair access.

Next, Amelia showed me a "model room," which was a studio apartment furnished with a bed and a set of wicker furniture. The carpeting appeared untouched, and I could see traces of vacuum tracks, making me wonder if anyone had visited this room in recent days. Despite the welcome counterpoint that fake flower arrangements provided to the bare white walls, the model room did not feel very inviting. I wondered how prospective residents perceived this space.

From there, Amelia showed me the residence of a woman who had recently departed for a cruise to Alaska with her family. Amelia explained that residents in assisted living communities enjoy the freedom to leave at will. Some residents have cars; others take the community's shuttle wherever they need to go. In contrast to the model unit, this residence was decorated with reproductions of famous paintings and photographs as well as pictures of family and friends. Amelia explained that it is common for a family to decorate a resident's room with memories of home, because many residents have to make the painful transition from a large home to a tiny room. Personalizing the space helps to ease this transition.

We proceeded next to the dining hall, which was filled with people. The room holds several communal tables, all round and decorated with elegant table settings—flowers, napkins, glasses, teacups—which are evocative of a restaurant-style dining room. Along one edge of the room is a set of sliding glass doors; yet I suspected these doors are rarely—if ever—opened because they open onto an iron fence that is vaguely camouflaged by bushes. Everyone appeared to be enjoying themselves and their company.

Reflections

One section of the Hanover is devoted to care for patients with Alzheimer's disease and dementia. This section is called "Reflections." The example that Amelia used to explain the name was this:

> One day, a man [with Alzheimer's] was waiting for his wife (who had died several years earlier). He kept wondering when she would visit. Instead of saying to him, "She died," I asked him to tell me about his wife. "Tell me about the time you met her. Tell me about your wedding." In that way, I could help him relive some of his forgotten memories.

The Reflections section of Hanover is kept separate from the rest of the facility by two locked doors that can only be opened with a security code or by leaning on the door for 15 seconds. A park scene is painted on the Reflections side of these double-doors, and various plants, arm chairs, and park-style benches dot the hallways nearby. The pride of Reflections, and presumably the entire facility, is the small courtyard located at the end of one hallway. Amelia was excited to show me the courtyard because it had originally been covered in mulch, "like a playground." The courtyard had recently been transformed entirely by residents into a beautiful garden, complete with a birdbath and park bench.

As we headed back inside, Amelia informed me that the hallways of Alzheimer's care facilities are typically designed as a loop. However, at the Hanover, the hallways are orthogonal, like two perpendicular legs of a rectangle. She continued:

> Not far from here is a community for people with Alzheimer's where the road around the facility is a complete circle. Around the circle are a number of themed houses, like what one might find in Europe. You get the sense that you are in a different world, or at least travelling.

The park scene mural I had seen earlier was intended to disguise the end of the hallway. At the Hanover, Amelia would like to see more murals painted on bare walls to create a stimulating environment for residents. Amelia explained that Alzheimer's and dementia patients like to walk around, and this was evident in the number of people I saw in the hallways.

Comparing points of view

My informant, Amelia, believes that caregiving is the most important part of her work, since many of her residents have been upset by their move from their previous home to the assisted living community. Still, some residents make the transition smoothly; Amelia believes that these residents have realized that they can no longer care for themselves, and thus require assistance in cooking, taking medication, and visiting the doctor. Nevertheless, Amelia knows that the transition from home to "a home" is a difficult process since it represents the relinquishment of some degree of privacy and self-sufficiency.

Informant's perspective

Amelia performs screening interviews for prospective residents in order to better understand their needs; ultimately the person and their family decide whether or not to live at the Hanover. She explained that prior to the arrival of a new resident, the staff is informed of the person's needs such as medication requirements or medical conditions. Once the resident arrives, Amelia always tries to think of ways to make the resident feel more comfortable, such as taking their food suggestions to the cook. In a sense, Amelia wants to make the Hanover community feel like a new family.

The main concern Amelia had about the Hanover was that she did not know "what the person who designed the Reflections area was thinking." This area, arranged around a hallway that dead-ends in two places, causes frustration among residents who have Alzheimer's or dementia. Another challenge is space: the building was constructed a long time ago and designed to accommodate fewer residents. An increase in residents over the years has placed further constraints on space. Nevertheless, Amelia is proud of the residents who helped out in converting the Reflections outdoor space into a garden.

Personal perspective

When I first visited Hanover and observed the building from the exterior, I felt that the front porch and entryway appeared home-like. My second visit confirmed this feeling, since the lobby and living room were furnished in a residential style, with a set of couches, a coffee table, and a television. During the tour, I noticed that all of the hallways are painted white and decorated with a few framed photographs or posters, all with pleasing "nostalgic" images such as sailboats, flowers, and landscapes. The hallways were also slightly labyrinthine, due to the lack of differentiating markers such as views to the outside or variations in lighting and color. I suppose that once a resident becomes acquainted with the building, wayfinding is not a problem. Further, staff are always present in the hallways and can assist residents as needed.

Residents enjoy a variety of daily activities at the Hanover: during my last visit, I observed a group of wheelchair-bound residents enjoying a Sunday concert in the living room. These kinds of activities, including an exercise class and guest speakers from the nearby university, are organized according to the specific needs and interests of residents and appeared to be well-attended. Still, I wondered what residents did when they did not feel like participating in these scheduled events, especially since many are repeated once or twice during the week.

Literature review

I conducted a literature review on assisted living and Alzheimer's care facilities, and almost all of the articles I read proposed some sort of improvement to how caregiving can best be performed. I was pleased to find a number of articles written about housing for the elderly. I researched several types of facilities including life care communities, nursing homes, rest homes, and retirement homes. Each of these provides different services for its residents. I focused my research on assisted living and other living situations similar to the community-style living I observed at the Hanover. An annotated bibliography of selected articles is included in the Appendix.

The general consensus is that living environments are crucial to the well-being of occupants. Additionally, people who reside away from home—whether in a nursing home or assisted living facility—often feel uncomfortable due to their dislocation from familiar people and places. Alzheimer's residents in particular depend on special environmental cues to ease the confusion, disorientation, and memory loss associated with the disease.

Zeisel has described a clear outline of how Alzheimer's units should be planned, though his general suggestions could be modified when translated to specific contexts such as the Hanover. In my opinion, the following are aspects that could apply specifically to Reflections; in a few cases, these ideas are already being implemented.

- **Control exit/entry:** The doors of Reflections are locked so that Assisted Living residents cannot enter the Reflections area, and vice versa. However, for fire safety considerations, doors can be unlocked by leaning on them for 15 seconds.

- **Design wandering paths to allow residents to circulate and move around:** The hallways of Reflections appear to be the most actively used circulation space, since residents are not permitted to leave the building without a staff escort. Yet, the dead-end of the hallway, as currently designed, prevents effective circulation. A loop or figure-8 would be better.
- **Plan a social space to be used by all residents in the special-care unit:** While the Assisted Living unit has a Country Store, living room, activity room, and courtyards, the communal spaces in the Reflections are limited to a small activity space at one end of the hallway and a small garden at the other. The most used space in the hallway was the bench area.
- **Create outdoor healing gardens:** The facility boasts an outside garden, but entry to this space is blocked by a hanging screen that is probably used to keep out insects. Facilitating easier access would better enable residents to benefit from this space.
- **Allow for sensory comprehensibility such as acoustic, visual, thermal, and kinesthetic:** Aside from the mural used to disguise the doors to the Assisted

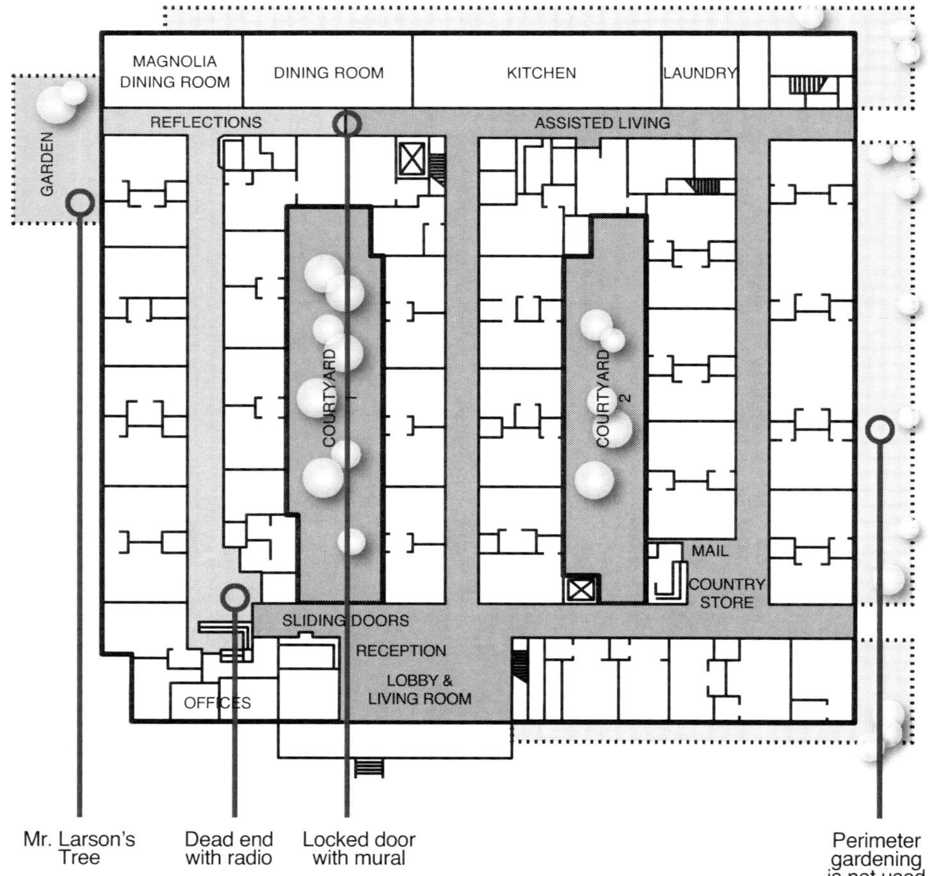

Figure 1 Site plan as-is

The decoration in the hallways of Reflections mirrored that of the Assisted Living section: a few pictures hung on white walls. A radio, placed at one end of the hallway, provided some acoustic interest, but overall the space seemed deprived of sensorial stimulation. Several skylights in hallways brought in natural light, but small planters located in these skylights affected the quality of the lighting. These features demonstrate the need for improvement.

Design improvement proposal

I began this project assuming the need for few changes. My only initial suggestion was to create a pathway in the perimeter gardens. Yet, for my final design proposal

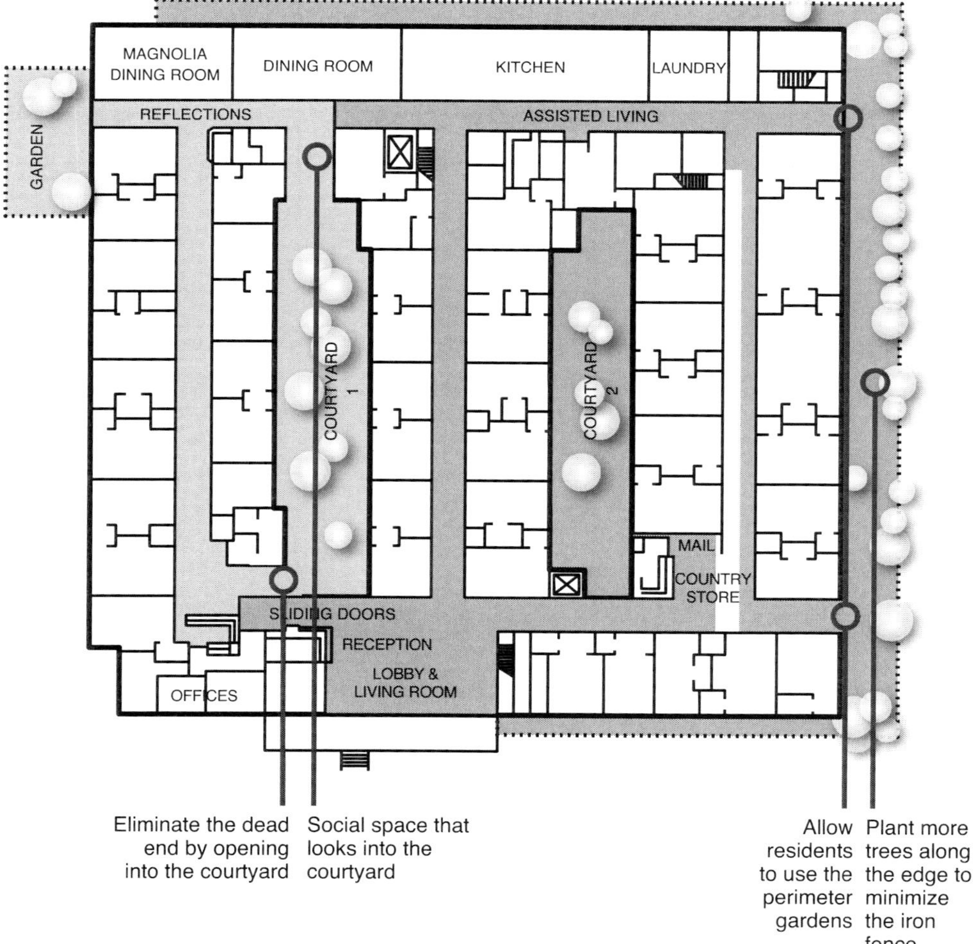

Figure 2 Proposed site redesign

I focused on the hallways of the Reflections area as a primary area for improvement. This focus was partly informed by my curiosity about how residents keep themselves occupied, and partly by my research into the value of circular hallways to better aid wayfinding. I also realized a need to connect—both spatially and visually—inside and outside environments. Figure 1 shows the challenges and opportunities I identified with the current design of Hanover. In particular, evident in the plan is the division of the site into two units: Assisted Living and Reflections (Alzheimer's care).

The perimeter garden is currently not used by residents. Entry and exit to Reflections is controlled by locked doors, while Assisted Living residents are free to wander the site. The circulation of the Assisted Living building is circular, while that of the Reflections area is linear.

My proposed redesign for the Hanover is depicted in Figure 2. I propose connecting the indoor and outdoor areas of the Reflections unit with both a modification of the building plan (to facilitate a circular path and both visual and physical access to the courtyard) and with murals and projections on walls (to create a more interesting visual environment inside). Opening the courtyard to Reflections residents serves to create a social space, which can be opened to residents in the Assisted Living area (or not) through the use of sliding glass doors. In this redesign, I also propose making the perimeter gardens more usable spaces, as spaces to wander or even set up personal gardens.

Appendix: annotated bibliography (selected articles)

Brent, Ruth and Benyamin Schwartz. "The Architectural Metamorphosis of Long-Term Care Settings." *Journal of Architectural and Planning Research*. Vol. 18 No. 3. (Autumn 2001), P. 255–269.

This article explores the changing architecture of buildings for elderly housing. The authors begin by presenting the American nursing home and analyze how they have changed. This article compares nursing home architecture to assisted living architecture, with the latter having a greater appeal to tenants and their families. Assisted living buildings have "captivating architecture and interior design" in contrast to the too-often sterile nursing home environment of a "patient-care floor in a general hospital" which might have fluorescent lighting and vinyl floors.

Bressi, Todd W. and Robert A. Gonzales. "Alzheimer's Special Care Units." *Places*. Cambridge, Mass. Vol 2 No 1 (Fall 1998), P. 38–41.

The authors of this article performed a research project of 30 Alzheimer's Special Care Units in New England to determine how the (architectural) environment affects Alzheimer's patients. The results of the study informed the articulation of design recommendations for an Alzheimer's facility, including: exit control, wandering paths, individual spaces, common spaces, outdoor freedom, residential character, autonomy support and sensory comprehension.

Briller, Sherylyn H., Margaret P. Calkins, and John P. Marsden. "Educating LTC Staff About Therapeutic Environments." *Journal of Architectural and Planning Research*. Vol 2 No. 1 (Spring 2003), P. 68–74.

This article discusses a product called the REMODEL (Resource for Evaluation and Modification of Dementia Environments for Living), which is a cost-effective way for staff to improve the physical and social environments of long-term-care (LTC) facilities. The three components of REMODEL are: an assessment protocol completed by caregiving staff and resulting environmental recommendations; training resources for supervisory staff; training videos for direct-care staff.

Grant, Roy E. "Housing Comparison of Different Methods for Eliciting Exercise-to-Music for Clients with Alzheimer's Disease." *The Journal of Music Therapy*. Vol. 40 No. 1 (Spring 2003), P. 41–56.

This article discusses how exercise and environmental stimuli (visual, auditory, tactile) can assuage a range of problems associated with Alzheimer's disease. Adding music to exercise routines is one way to include both elements. The author sought to investigate which types of music are most conducive to participation in exercise, and found that instrumental music was better than vocal music.

Gullbring, Leo. "The 'Swedish Model' Rehabilitates Community Utopia." *L'Architecture d'Aujourd'Hui*. No. 341 (July/August 2002), P. 58–63.

In the past decade, Sweden has gained recognition around the world for its high-quality care for senior citizens. This article discusses two types of housing, one with a range of age groups (along the lines of co-housing) and another dedicated to the elderly.

Kampfe, Charlene M. "Older Adults' Perceptions of Residential Relocation." *Journal of Humanistic Counseling, Education and Development*. Vol. 41 No. 1 (2002), P. 103–113.

This article describes a study of the psychological effects on elderly residents who have moved from an independent living situation into a specialized housing facility. The author administered surveys to rate residents' perceived level of comfort. Residents' perceived comfort correlated with the amount of control the residents had over their actions and environment.

Zeisel, John. "Marketing Therapeutic Environments for Alzheimer's Care." *Journal of Architectural and Planning Research*. Vol. 20 No. 1 (Spring 2003), P. 75–86.

Zeisel presents a case study of one company that markets "therapeutically designed environments" used in treating Alzheimer's disease. One of the main beliefs of this company, Hearthstone Alzheimer Care, Ltd., is that environment plays a critical role in the health of residents. The company has developed a particular strategy of environmental design that is treatment-oriented, focusing on creating therapeutic environments.

KEVIN CHONG, "RECIPE FOR AN ENGAGING FARMERS' MARKET," 2014

Introduction

Held on the historic United Nations Plaza (hereafter U.N. Plaza) in San Francisco, the City Beat Farmers' Market is a vibrant scene rich with social interactions. Yet the site itself, though located in the symbolic and physical city center, appears to be underused when not hosting events. Intrigued by this juxtaposition between the vibrant Farmers' Market and the plaza in which it is held, I chose the City Beat event as the site of my ethnographic study.

Background of City Beat

According to its website, the City Beat Farmers' Market was founded more than 30 years ago, inspired by a vision to "create a healthy heart of the city" by providing its surrounding communities access to fresh produce in an area that the movement itself has described as a "food desert." The Farmers' Market distinguishes itself by featuring small-scale local growers, offering affordable produce, and donating food to low-income neighborhoods nearby. Currently, more than 50 farmers participate in the event, which operates on Wednesdays and Sundays.

The U.N. Plaza

The U.N. Plaza is a triangular public space located off Hyde Street and Market Street, the main arterial through San Francisco. The red-bricked, three-acre plaza was designed and built in 1975 by landscape architect Lawrence Halprin. Originally built to celebrate the historical heritage of the signing of the United Nations Charter, the plaza now serves as an entryway to the City Hall, and is also a hub for various

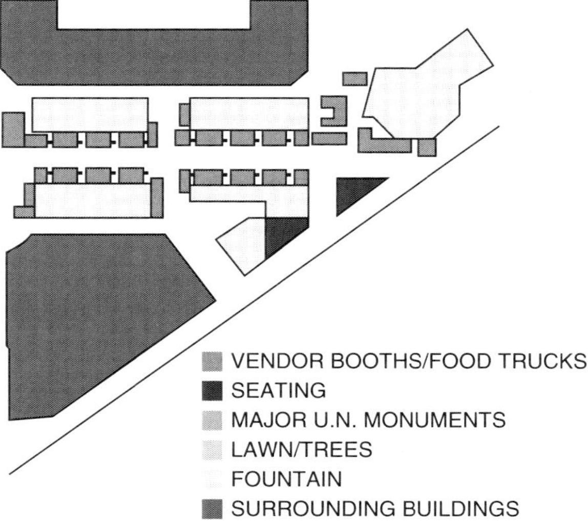

Figure 1 Plan of City Beat Farmers' Market (on U.N. Plaza)

modes of San Francisco's public transportation system. The plaza is adjacent to three universities, including the University of California, Hastings College of the Law, the San Francisco Public Library, as well as the Tenderloin and SOMA neighborhoods.

Initial observations

Three buildings—10 United Nations Plaza, the Federal Office Building, and another mixed use building—surround the U.N. Plaza and create two open spaces used by the market (see Figure 1). Trees line the walkways, monuments dot the landscape, and a fountain punctuates the center of the plaza. The City Beat event space closely aligns with these primary axes and features of the plaza: this intersection of spaces and uses produces an interesting juxtaposition between the monuments and plaques dedicated to the historic U.N. Charter and the ephemeral structures erected for the biweekly event.

When the City Beat Farmers' Market is not in operation, the public space is largely empty. During the market event, I observed a number of collisions of and inefficiencies in function and use. For example, I noticed that the main avenue of the Farmers' Market is rather narrow and often feels crowded during the event. Yet nearby spaces of the plaza receive little pedestrian flow. Additionally, the U.N. monuments and plaques are used as props for Farmers' Market tents, which seemed to me negligent—though practical—use.

Methods

To inform my proposed redesign, I employed three research methods to collect information about the current use of the site and potential user needs: observation, semantic interview, and literature review.

Personal observation

Through this method, I sought to observe and record site-specific conditions. Although I attempted to provide an objective account of the site, I also paid attention to my own perception of the site, in particular the crowding and unexpected use of monuments.

Interviews

In order to better understand the inside—or *emic*—perspective of the Farmers' Market, I located and interviewed a cultural informant: a frequent shopper at the market. My informant, Sarah, is a reliable informant as she has regularly visited the market to purchase fresh produce for over two years. Sarah has developed good rapport with several vendors over her many visits, and was happy to share with me her experiences and observations.

I put a great deal of thought into selecting an informant. As I walked around the market, I noticed a customer who was engaging in a casual conversation with one of the vendors. Her body language conveyed to me a sense of familiarity, which led me to believe that it was not the customer's first visit to the market. I decided this person might make a good informant, so I walked to the booth, joined the conversation, and Sarah (the customer) was very nice and willing to share her knowledge on the culture of City Beat.

Because I am an introvert, the prospect of approaching and interviewing a stranger gave me some hesitation. However, Sarah seemed genuinely interested in my project and was not in a hurry to leave; this put me at ease and provided me with the confidence to proceed with the interview. In our initial conversation I learned that Sarah attends the Farmers' Market at least once a week. Since I knew she was a frequent visitor of the event, I asked her permission to contact her for additional interviews; she gladly complied, and I conducted three additional interviews with Sarah over the following weeks. I transcribed and coded my interview notes to obtain a comprehensive understanding of Sarah's points of view (see Appendix).

Literature review

My goal in conducting a literature review was to obtain information from published resources regarding my site and similar sites. This research formed the outside, or *etic*, perspective of my project and thus served as a helpful complement to the information I learned from Sarah. The primary themes that emerged from this stage of my research included the demographics and cultures of farmers' market customers and vendors, as well as those on the preservation and use of historically significant sites. Each of these ideas helped inform my final redesign proposal.

Findings: comparing emic, etic, and personal perspectives

In our first interview, I asked a series of "grand tour" and other open-ended questions in order to obtain Sarah's general impressions of the market. I learned that Sarah has regularly shopped at City Beat Farmers' Market for two years. She appreciates the market's vision, accessibility, diversity, and the sense of community it displays. In subsequent interviews, I followed up on themes mentioned in previous interviews and also talked about the site itself. I was particularly interested to learn how shoppers like Sarah navigate the market space and to what extent—if any—Sarah had considered the juxtaposition of this event with the historic significance of the plaza itself.

Through our conversations, I identified two primary themes: **site-specific information** included issues of accessibility, programming, and users and **impression-related information** included Sarah's qualitative assessments of the market experience and the products she purchased. Ultimately, I learned—from Sarah's perspective—the strengths and challenges posed by this site and the event itself.

Strengths of City Beat

According to Sarah, City Beat's mission to provide low-cost and sustainable groceries to surrounding neighborhoods is well-reflected in its operations. The Farmers' Market includes more than 50 local farmers and a wide array of fresh produce options. The location of City Beat in the center of San Francisco means that it is "in and of the city," and welcomes a diverse range of customers and vendors. Sarah appreciates the atmosphere of the market and refers to the event as being comprised of a "community" of shoppers; she especially enjoys being able to speak to vendors directly about the produce and occasionally making new friends who share her passion for fresh produce. Because the U.N. Plaza is a node for many modes of public transportation, the event is easily and broadly accessible.

Challenges

Although the site grants City Beat a number of advantages, the challenges the event faces are also site-specific. In particular, Sarah described the problems of the site housing a large homeless population and being a hotbed for drug-dealing, which inevitably affects the ambience of the farmers' market. In addition, the monuments on the U.N. Plaza are seen by customers as a barrier to flow rather than objects that serve educational and historical purposes. Therefore, Sarah would like to see a better way of coexistence of the monuments and the market's facilities.

Emic and Etic point of view

Based on my initial observations and subsequent interviews with Sarah, I identified two main factors affecting the performance of the City Beat Farmers' Market: (1) what differentiates a Farmers' Market from other sources of groceries and (2) the principles of successful public space design, with a focus on reinforcing "identity" and the treatment of monuments. These themes guided my research.

Differentiating factors for vendors

One of the distinguishing factors of farmers' markets is the opportunity they offer for vendors to directly communicate with their customers; this direct interaction between customers and vendors is crucial to their success. Economist Tim Payne defines this exchange as "direct marketing," which means the elimination of middlemen and a direct selling of goods.[1] Farmers' markets offer an important space in which small farmers have direct access to customers and therefore increase their businesses' profitability through direct marketing and a streamlined process of selling. Closely related to this idea is another, described by agricultural policy analyst Alan Hunt, that vendors should be able to closely interact with customers. These interactions are both economic and social, with products purchased in "the context of community."[2]

Differentiating factors for customers

Like vendors, customers enjoy the social interactions farmers' markets facilitate; in fact, multiple studies have found that customers rank social interactions as one of the top reasons to visit a farmers' market.[3] Environmental Psychologist Robert Sommer explains that the popularity of farmers' markets is largely attributed to the "social atmosphere;" this atmosphere is enjoyed by both vendors and customers.[4] The ability for customers to "meet friends, talk politics, and know each other by name" makes farmers' markets a dynamic place that people enjoy going for more purposes than just grocery shopping.

Confirming Sarah's descriptions of City Beat as a diverse community, studies have shown that farmers' market consumers are no different in age, education level, or race than those who purchase produce elsewhere.[5] Instead, what differentiates these consumers is their common interest in healthy food and concern with "food quality and variety", as well as "health and wellness."[6] The shared values of market-goers form an important "cultural identity" for the community.

Principles of successful public space design

Previous ethnographic studies of farmers' markets have suggested that both "physical and psychological" dimensions impact the mode of consumption in farmers' markets. For example, a customer's decision to shop at a farmers' market is dependent on his perceptions of the site. Additionally, successful farmers' markets attempt to "[bring] the outside in."[7] I wonder: how might these ideas translate to the specific site of the City Beat market?

With regard to public spaces with historic significance, Setha Low argues that the "preservation and interpretation of historic values" should take priority in management of public spaces, and recreational activities that take place on the site should be secondary to these concerns.[8] San Francisco's U.N. Plaza—the site of the City Beat market—was built to educate the visitors about the significance of the United Nations Charter. Therefore, extrapolating from Low's study, while the space is home to "recreational activities", such as the farmers' market program, the "preservation of historic values" of the monuments on the plaza should be the top priority of the site.

Significance of monuments

Geographer Nuala C. Johnson discusses the significance of monuments to a place's cultural identity; this identity, in turn, affects users' "memories" of the space.[9] Connecting this theory to the previous discussion about the preservation of historic values, I propose that the monuments on the U.N. Plaza are a primary vehicle through which information about the United Nations Charter is communicated to the public and therefore should be well-maintained.

Personal perspectives

During my first visit to City Beat Farmers' Market, I was intrigued by the energy and sense of community I felt at the market. The direct interactions I observed between the customers and the vendors were starkly different from the atmosphere to which I am accustomed in supermarkets. I also noted a diverse mix of users of the U.N. Plaza in terms of ethnicity, age, and gender.

Still, several aspects of the physical design of the plaza stood out to me as potential areas of improvement. First, I noticed inefficiency in the use of the space of the U.N. Plaza: the main avenue of the Farmers' Market is too narrow to comfortably accommodate the large crowd the market attracts, yet other passageways nearby saw minimal pedestrian flow. Second, since the U.N. Plaza carries significant historical values, and I was struck by an apparent disconnect between the Farmers' Market and the site's historic significance. For example, monumental objects designed to educate the public about the U.N. Charter were experienced, during the hours of the Farmers' Market, as obstacles: the location of vendors' tents seemed to be determined by the location of the monuments (rather than optimal marketing or pedestrian flow), and some vendors treated memorial plaques as a post against which to fix the tents.

Comparing the three points of view

These perspectives intersect in three aspects: first, social interactions are a significant advantage of farmers' markets; second, accessibility to the City Beat Farmers' Market is a particular asset of the event; and third, the U.N. Plaza could be better used and integrated into recreational functions such as farmers' markets. Both my own observations and Sarah's description of the City Beat Farmers' Market conveyed a sense of community at the market. This idea was confirmed in my literature review, where I learned that the social interactions that characterize farmers' markets not only act as positive factors for customers but also are beneficial for vendors. Regarding accessibility, Sarah suspects that the accessibility of the site—connected to a range of public transportation options and located in the heart of Downtown San Francisco—is among the primary reasons for the market's popularity. Sarah suspects that very few people feel educated by the plaques and monuments that punctuate U.N. Plaza, and both my personal observations and literature review revealed the need to better emphasize the historic value of the site and, in particular, better manage on-site monuments.

Final redesign proposal

Based on the knowledge obtained from my semantic interviews, literature review, and personal observations, I identified the following priorities for my proposed site redesign:

- **Spaces for social interaction.** Social interactions are beneficial to vendors because they allow vendors to directly introduce and sell their produce to consumers. Consumers also appreciate being able to interact with each other because it reinforces a sense of "community" and "cultural identity." The farmers' market should therefore be designed in a way that fosters social interactions both between consumers and between consumers and vendors.
- **Monuments as opportunities, not constraints.** My observation of the use (or lack of use) of monuments by market vendors and users demonstrated to me that the monuments on the U.N. Plaza are seen simply as objects around which the plan of the farmers' market is configured. Some monuments are even treated as rigid posts to support the farmers' booths. I propose an alternative: booths and monuments should *coexist* in a configuration that both benefits the farmers' market and serves the original intent of commemorating the signing of the United Nations Charter.

To achieve the goals set forth above, I adopted the following strategies in my final redesign:

- **Encourage circulation and visual connection to on-site monuments.** I created a program diagram chart to inform the visual and physical adjacencies necessary to improve circulation through and maintain the memorial function of the U.N. Plaza site (see Figure 2). Based on this diagram, in my final redesign proposal, vendor booths and food trucks are both easily accessible from seating spaces, but kept physically distinct (separated) from monuments. Instead, visual connections

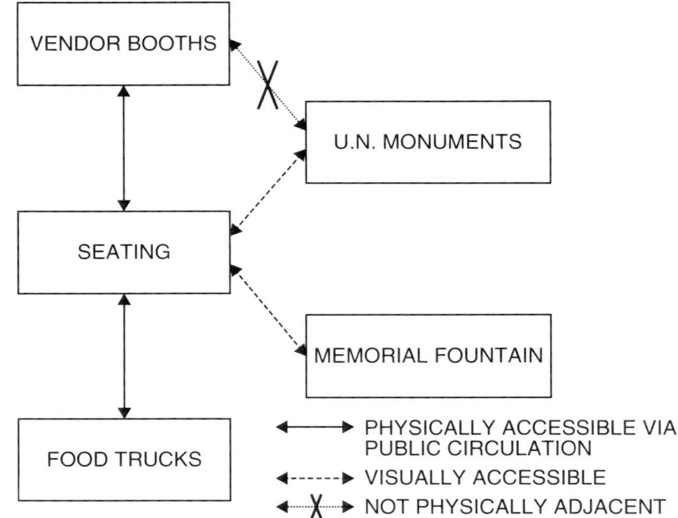

Figure 2 Program adjacency diagram

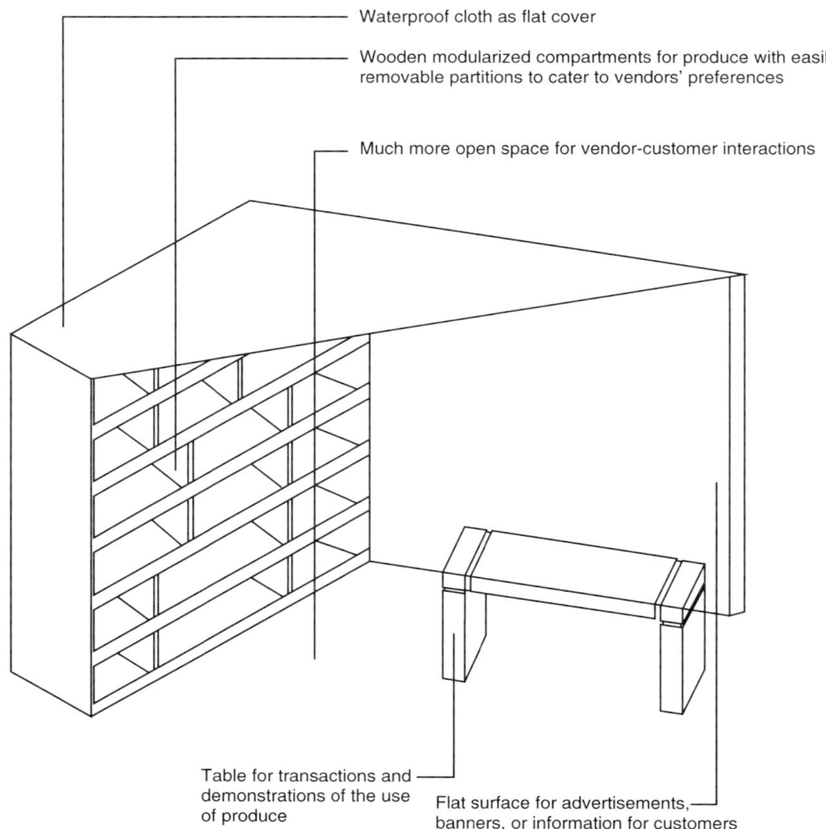

Figure 3 Axonometric drawing of the redesign of the booth

between seating spaces and on-site monuments are created through the introduction of "social bulbs." These "social bulbs" are designed to be spaces that welcome social interaction among a range of visitors (see Figure 4).

- **Reconsider the booth.** I propose a new design for vendor booths. The new design (see Figure 3) opens up the booth and invites the customer to enter and interact with the vendor. This arrangement also allows for a better display of the vendor's produce.

These ideas are visually presented in Figure 4.

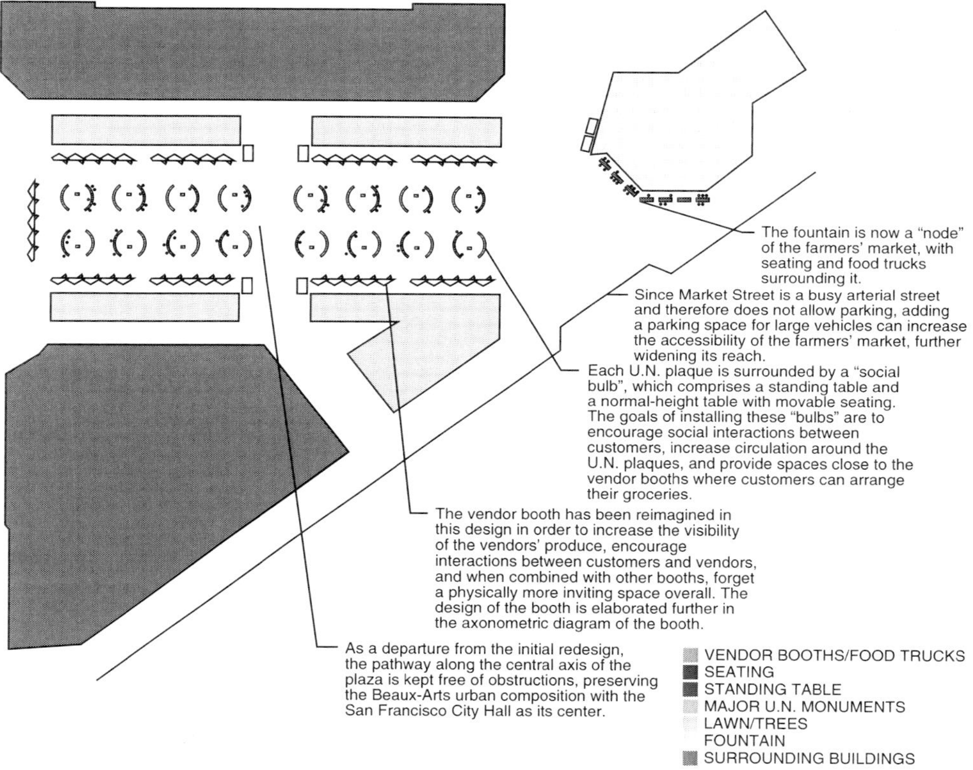

The fountain is now a "node" of the farmers' market, with seating and food trucks surrounding it.
Since Market Street is a busy arterial street and therefore does not allow parking, adding a parking space for large vehicles can increase the accessibility of the farmers' market, further widening its reach.
Each U.N. plaque is surrounded by a "social bulb", which comprises a standing table and a normal-height table with movable seating. The goals of installing these "bulbs" are to encourage social interactions between customers, increase circulation around the U.N. plaques, and provide spaces close to the vendor booths where customers can arrange their groceries.
The vendor booth has been reimagined in this design in order to increase the visibility of the vendors' produce, encourage interactions between customers and vendors, and when combined with other booths, forget a physically more inviting space overall. The design of the booth is elaborated further in the axonometric diagram of the booth.
As a departure from the initial redesign, the pathway along the central axis of the plaza is kept free of obstructions, preserving the Beaux-Arts urban composition with the San Francisco City Hall as its center.
VENDOR BOOTHS/FOOD TRUCKS
SEATING
STANDING TABLE
MAJOR U.N. MONUMENTS
LAWN/TREES
FOUNTAIN
SURROUNDING BUILDINGS

Figure 4 Annotated plan of the final redesign of the site

Conclusion

My case study investigates the intersection between the effectiveness of a space in accommodating its users and in reinforcing the identity of the site. Though I found a number of published sources that address each of these topics, few focused on how to design spaces that achieve both objectives. In many ways, this study is an attempt to reconcile the discrepancies that often exist between the inherent identity of a site and events that take place within its borders. My research indicates the potential of farmers' markets to participate in conversations about the accessibility of healthy foods and the design of successful public spaces that accommodate historic and contemporary uses and meanings.

References

Corburn, Jason. *Toward the Healthy City : People, Places, and the Politics of Urban Planning.* Cambridge: MIT Press, 2009.

Hunt, Alan R. "Consumer interactions and influences on farmers' market vendors." *Renewable Agriculture and Food Systems*, 22, no. 1 (2006): 54–66.

Johnson, Nuala C. "Mapping monuments: the shaping of public space and cultural identities." *Visual Communication* 1, no. 3 (2002): 293–298.

Low, Setha M. *Rethinking Urban Parks: Public Space and Cultural Diversity.* Austin: University of Texas Press, 2005.

McGrath, Mary Ann, John F. Sherry, and Deborah D. Heisley. "An ethnographic study of an urban periodic marketplace: Lessons from the Midville farmers' market." *Journal of Retailing* 69, no. 3 (1993): 280–319.

Payne, Tim. *US Farmers Markets, 2000: A Study of Emerging Trends.* US Department of Agriculture, Marketing and Regulatory Programs, Agricultural Marketing Service, Transportation and Marketing Programs, Marketing Services Branch, 2002.

Sommer, Robert. *Farmers Markets of America.* Santa Barbara: Capra Press, 1980.

Wolf, Marianne M., Arianne Spittler, and James Ahern. "A profile of farmers' market consumers and the perceived advantages of produce sold at farmers' markets." *Journal of Food Distribution Research* 36, no. 1 (2005): 192–201.

Zepeda, Lydia. "Which little piggy goes to market? Characteristics of US farmers' market shoppers." *International Journal of Consumer Studies* 33, no. 3 (2009): 250–257.

Appendix: transcription and coding of interview (partial)

Table 1 Coding of informant interview

Transcript of interview	*Coding and vocabulary*
Kevin (K): Sarah, thank you again for your time. Could you tell me a bit about City Beat? Sarah (S): What do you want me to talk about? K: A general description of the place based on your experience would be great.	Time The farmers' market has operated for a while, and Sarah has visited it for more than two years.
S: Sure . . . so City Beat as you know is a farmers' market that has been around for **quite some while.** I have shopped around here for **more than two years** now since I moved to the city. It's a really great place for the community as there **aren't that many options** for fresh produce around the area. There are quite some vendors around here . . . I think most of the farmers here **local**, and they sell their stuff cheap . . . supports **sustainable agriculture. Very ethical, very San Francisco.**	Mission of City Beat The farmers' market is known to be **local, sustainable, ethical,** and provide **fresh** and **cheap** food.
K: Ah okay . . . so there aren't many options for produce here? S: No, not at all . . . well, actually there are some other places. But the ones here are much **fresher and cheaper** that it would not make	

(Continued)

Table 1 continued

Transcript of interview	*Coding and vocabulary*
sense to go to, like, the supermarket . . . [laughs] it is terrible. They have everything I need here—you want fish, veggies, meat, they've got it all. You're tired from all the walking . . . they have food trucks . . . and everyone here is nice, none of that corporate attitude when you're here, it's all for the community.	
K: Which community are you talking about?	
S: **San Francisco!** But more specifically I would say that this market serves its **surrounding neighborhoods**. . . . There's also a **BART station** right there, a **MUNI station** there, and a **bike sharing** thing—what do you call those? K: Bike sharing sounds about right.	<u>Access</u> Heart of the City is strategically placed within **walking distances** from several neighborhoods, and can also be accessed by public transportation such as BART, MUNI, and bike-sharing facilities.

Notes

1 Tim Payne, *US Farmers Markets, 2000: A Study of Emerging Trends*, US Department of Agriculture, Marketing and Regulatory Programs, Agricultural Marketing Service, Transportation and Marketing Programs, Marketing Services Branch, 2002.
2 Alan R. Hunt, "Consumer interactions and influences on farmers' market vendors," *Renewable Agriculture and Food Systems* 22, no. 1 (2006): 54–66.
3 Ibid.
4 Robert Sommer, *Farmer's Markets of America*, Santa Barbara: Capra Press, 1980.
5 Marianne M. Wolf, Arianne Spittler, and James Ahern, "A profile of farmers' market consumers and the perceived advantages of produce sold at farmers' markets," *Journal of Food Distribution Research* 36, no. 1 (2005): 192–201.
6 Lydia Zepeda, "Which little piggy goes to market? Characteristics of US farmers' market shoppers," *International Journal of Consumer Studies* 33, no. 3 (2009): 250–257.
7 Mary Ann McGrath, John F. Sherry, and Deborah D. Heisley, "An ethnographic study of an urban periodic marketplace: Lessons from the Midville farmers' market," *Journal of Retailing* 69, no. 3 (1993): 280–319.
8 Setha M. Low, *Rethinking Urban Parks: Public Space and Cultural Diversity*, Austin: University of Texas Press, 2005.
9 Nuala C. Johnson, "Mapping monuments: the shaping of public space and cultural identities," *Visual Communication* 1, no. 3 (2002): 293–298.

ELIZABETH LEAH COHN-MARTIN, "COMMUNITY SUSTENANCE: SUNDAY BRUNCH AT A THAI BUDDHIST TEMPLE," 2008

Introduction

Every Sunday for over 30 years Thai brunch has been served at the Thai Buddhist Temple. The temple brunch has significant history, attracts a diverse group of people, and is currently a cause of neighborhood complaint. Nine neighboring homes that surround the site are attempting to "shut the temple down" because of noise, smells, and congestion that the event causes. This ethnographic study, through cultural research both on and off the site, outlines the current debate around the role of Sunday brunch within the local community, explores the meaning of the activity from the point of view of participants, and considers its effects on the surrounding environment. Ultimately, I propose design changes—informed by this research—that could alleviate neighbor complaints and allow the brunch to continue.

Although this cultural hub is a recent discovery for me, many people have been attending the brunch for years. During my first visit there one man asked me why I'm taking pictures, possibly suspecting I'm from the city, and then informed me that he has been going to Thai brunch with his wife since they moved to Berkeley years ago. He insisted that the Thai Temple brunch has been an area of safety, cultural identity, and community in both of their lives. This strikes me as interesting, because he is a Caucasian, middle-aged, white male. In fact, tables, located behind the main temple building, are filled with hungry Sunday brunch goers of mixed ethnicities and cultural identities. The Buddhist, bohemian environment of the weekly Thai brunch attracts people of all cultural backgrounds.

Current site conditions

The site includes multiple small buildings, a tented food serving counter, tables with seats, a garden, and an area for car parking. The entrance to the main temple is decorated with traditional Buddhist Thai colors. Two smaller buildings on the site are related to the temple and a third building is a Thai community center where music and dance are taught. Although most of the space of the site is full with people, tables, buildings, or food, one portion of the site remains empty and unused, offering ample space for design innovation. Any change in design should allow the site to function more efficiently as a food service and community gathering space, meanwhile addressing complaints that the neighbors have voiced.

Methods

I combined multiple methods of data collection in this ethnographic study. Findings from personal observations, library research, and informant interviews informed my proposed redesign of the site.

Observation

My initial research took the form of quiet observation. During my first visit to the Temple, I watched, listened, and drew. I also took pictures to capture the essence of the site and remind myself, after I had left, what the layout of the site was, how many people were there, what kind of people were there, etc. While on the site, I tried to be aware of how I felt within it, and "fit" within it. Yet I also conversed with people about the current neighborhood issues after being asked if I was from the Berkeley City Council or Zoning Board. In fact, my role—initially an outside observer—changed as I spent more time there after numerous visits; I discuss this transition below.

Literature review

My literature review began as a hunt for literary sources on Thai history, temples, language, and culture. I refined my search to focus on the Buddhist religion within urban environments. In addition, I looked for sources on community gardens, Thai mural art, high-tech plastics and other soundproofing materials, and food service. I researched community gardens and food service to obtain a greater understanding about how this site functions and to think about ways to enhance these functions in my proposed redesign. My research on Thai mural making and soundproofing materials inspired (and justify) my proposal for movable, erectable walls to be used during the brunch hours.

Interviews

My informant, an older man named Steven, was an essential resource. At the time of our interviews—I conducted two in-depth interviews in total—he had been coming to the Thai Temple and brunch for over 27 years. Steven was a good source of information because of how long he had been a part of the Thai Temple community. As a volunteer for more than two decades and a crusader for the preservation of the Thai brunch, Steven was able to give both historical data as well as current information on a situation involving the Thai Temple and its nine surrounding neighbors. Steven was very accessible because of his routine attendance: he attends the Thai brunch every Sunday and recently has been tabling for signatures on a petition to save the brunch. Because Steven's table is located at the only entrance to the site, he was the first person to whom I spoke at the brunch event; thus, finding my informant was a relatively simple process.

The conversations that took place between Steven and me were clear, coherent, and thoughtful. My informant's enjoyment of our dialogue was evident and, I believe, resulted from his own passion for the place and preserving the brunch festivities. Steven was happy to provide additional information about his relationship to the Thai Temple. He also informed me about the current issues between the temple and its nine surrounding neighbors.

Findings

Interviews

My interviews with Steven were both informative and inspiring. He provided me with information about the space that the temple community uses and creates. He also made it clear that the brunch needs to be preserved for the financial future of the Thai Temple and its community in Berkeley. Steven was not alone in voicing these desires. Many community members know the benefits that the brunch brings both economically as well as to the community through weekly group interaction. The women working at the token counter asked me if I had signed the petition to "save Thai brunch" multiple times. Long-term attendees like Steven, as well as relatively new additions to the Thai brunch community, simply want their brunch to remain.

Main findings from my interview with Steven are as follows:

- The temple has been running since 1980. Steven has been a part of the temple community for almost the entire time that it has been functioning. His connection to the Thai Buddhist faith is through his wife who is Thai. They both want to see the temple thrive.
- A new building for the temple is being proposed. This new building is called the Buddha Sanctuary and was designed by a Thai architect. It is 40 feet tall at its highest point including stilts and steeple. Thailand is prone to flooding so many structures built in this country are up on stilts. The neighbors want the height of this new building lowered because they are afraid that it will cast shadows on their lots.
- Many different nationalities are represented at the brunch: Chinese, Japanese, Thai, Pakistani, and African American.
- The money made from the brunch goes to pay taxes for the temple including sewer, trash, mortgage, and utilities.
- The site contains four permanent built structures. These include a main temple building, a building for music and dance, and a building for the teachers. The monks live in the upper floors of the temple.
- Nine neighbors surrounding the temple want the brunch to be shut down. Complaints include having to smell the food, hear the sounds of cooking and people, and deal with the traffic congestion caused by community members attending the brunch.

I analyzed the vocabulary Steven used to describe topics such as the functions of the temple, its different buildings, and the people who use the site; my vocabulary list is as follows:

Kinship To Steven, kinship was a term that denoted company and a communal feeling. Kinship often refers to family and it seems to me that Steven was trying to explain, through the word kinship, how close one feels with those who are around when going to the Thai Temple brunch.

Food court The food court was a key term that Steven used multiple times. This term is used to refer to the area directly behind the temple buildings where food is served and people sit, eat and enjoy the scenery. *Note: The food court is right next to many single-family homes. These are the people who are trying to close the Thai Temple down.*

Volunteers To Steven, "volunteers" are the people who continually work within the Thai Temple. These people do a wide variety of tasks, from selling tokens and serving food at the brunch, to tabling—what Steven has been doing when I have visited the site.

Temple The word "temple" refers to the collection of all of the buildings on this site. The word temple can also be used in reference to the building in which worship takes place and in which the monks live. This word has two meanings: one of larger scale, encompassing all of the buildings on this site, and one of smaller scale, just referring to the building within which worship occurs.

Nationality To Steven, nationality, where a person comes from, was a key signifier of diversity within the site. Some examples that he referenced were Chinese, Japanese, and Pakistani.

Communal Group action within which a number of people are involved, i.e. something is "communal" if a number of people are working together. Steven specifically referenced Monks and volunteers working together overseas in other Thai Temples.

Dance The word "dance" was used to refer to Thai dancing techniques that young children were being taught at the Temple.

The interviews with Steven took place in the environment in which he works and socializes. Consequently, our interviews were often interrupted by people walking by. Every time someone new walked by Steven asked them to sign a petition and explained the current dispute with neighbors. This caused our conversation to ebb and flow. Still, I gained substantial insight. Our conversation was influenced by Steven's desire for me to understand why the temple brunch is so important and why it should be allowed to remain within the community. Ultimately, the brunch is the only source of income for the temple, so the brunch is viewed as the key to the future of the entire temple. The dynamic between the Thai Temple and its surrounding neighbors, as well as the needs and desires of both parties, have helped to shape the final redesign of this site.

Literature review

Books, articles, newspaper clippings, and movies can all be very helpful when understanding the cultural environment being studied. I am not Thai. For me, the range of sources increased my understanding, even if they are not directly related to the purpose, community life, or design of the Thai Temple. Sources exploring the merging of urbanism and religion, the Thai language, Thai mural making, community gardens, and food service have allowed me to view this site and relate to it in ways that I could not before.

I now understand how the temple acts as a node, meeting place, community gathering space, and (at times) a safe haven, for members of the Thai and Buddhist communities. Within crowded, urban environments, community meeting spaces are becoming harder to come by as land continues to become more expensive. Much more than eating and mingling takes place here: community growth is visible and evident. Sources such as Richard O'Connor's *Urbanism and Religion: Community,*

Hierarchy, and Sanctity in the Urban Thai Buddhist Temples explain the role of "community builder" that Thai temples take on within the larger urban context that they are in.[1] At the Thai Temple brunch, a strong religious appeal draws people to the site; yet additionally, a strong sense of community and the promise of delicious food attract a diverse, loyal crowd.

Other sources on the Thai language and culture have helped me comprehend the environment of the Thai brunch by understanding words, symbols, and colors that can be seen in the space. For example, I thought that the colors used on the decoration of the main entrance were inviting and vibrant, but I did not realize that they were colors corresponding to the Seven Days of Thai Buddhism. Each day correlates to a specific color.

I also looked at sources on Thai mural making and soundproofing materials because I would like to incorporate movable, erectable walls—decorated with culturally relevant murals—into my final design proposal. These walls would serve the dual purpose of being surfaces for artistic expression as well as noise barriers that would alleviate some of the sounds created by the brunch. From my research, I learned that Thai mural making has extensive historical roots and has been a way for cultural and religious history to be passed on from generation to generation. At the Thai temple, these objects could capture current history in the making and bring the Thai brunch community together through art. My research on soundproofing materials has helped inform my choice for wall materials: thus far, this research has shown that double layer acrylic panels would both create good sound barriers and allow views to remain relatively undisturbed.[2]

Personal observations

This site is vivid. It is full of smells, colors, tastes, feelings, people, actions, and energy. The food smells absolutely delicious and *is* delicious! Gold, red, green, and blue colors are prominent as you come into the space. This space is fascinating to me because it is created through the merging of all different groups of people. The community is strong and incredibly diverse: a large number of Thai people, as well as people of different ethnicities, backgrounds, ages, and genders all participate in the Thai brunch. After coming to this site so many times, I feel like I am now a member of this community. I recognize individuals and groups of people when I come here. I not only feel involved, but also have come to believe that the site needs to be preserved within the urban landscape. This site is special within the city and Thai brunch needs to be recognized as an important multi-cultural event that Berkeley community members love to partake in.

Comparison

My three strands of research each resulted in very different findings. My personal observations resulted in information on how the site feels, appears to function, and is physically set up. I was also able to see who uses the site on a weekly basis. My library research helped me procure cultural and historical information, as well as some current material and art formation studies. Informant interviews illuminated community desires for the future use of the site as well as information about how the site economically sustains itself, the use of each of the permanent structures, and the people who use the space. When comparing these sources, I see that the informant's desires and opinions about the site were the driving factors in my redesign. Other research perspectives helped me meet the needs of both the Thai Temple community and neighbors.

Proposed redesign

My initial redesign did not call for any drastic renovations to the site. In this proposal I allocated a portion of the unused space on the site to bike parking, a new seating area, and a token counter. Additionally, I proposed that the unused space within the site be opened up to the road (rather than fenced in), thus allowing for a second entrance to the site. Creating a second entrance, I reasoned, would aid circulation within the site and advertise the brunch to passers-by. Currently, the single entrance to the brunch is often congested as people waiting in line for food block the entrance. In addition to adding a second entrance, my proposed redesign included a reorganization of seating areas and food lines.

Final redesign

Very little of my initial redesign was modified in the final redesign; rather, I further elaborated my ideas based on subsequent research. In my final proposal, I proposed that the program elements of the site stay the same, with some movement and reprioritization. My final proposal emphasized changes to the food lines and circulatin system including the areas designated for sitting and eating. I also proposed adding new bicycle parking and creating an additional entrance. To expand on my initial proposal, in my final redesign, I proposed the use of temporary barriers to block the brunch off from its surrounding neighbors. Together these changes would help the Thai Temple brunch community streamline its functioning and reduce the noise and traffic that result from the gathering. Additional details are as follows:

- **Better placement of food lines and tables.** Often, community members will get into a line, not knowing which line it is, and then turn to their neighbor to find out. There are seven lines: tokens, drinks, vegetarian entrees, meat entrees, soup, appetizers, and mango sticky rice. Most of the time, these are not well designated and confusion about which line to join creates general congestion throughout the site. Finally, once these people have received their food they need to push through a crowd of people to get to seating. In my redesign, designated spaces for line formation as well as better placement of food and token counters will allow for less congestion and streamline movement throughout the site.
- **Additional seating.** Currently, many seating areas block circulation paths. I propose making use of empty space within the site to add two types of seating: more tables and chairs as well as a grassy area where people can spread out blankets for "picnicking." Regarding the latter, many people currently choose to sit on the lawn area near the street. Expanding this seating area and moving it away from the street will support the existing sitting behavior, simultaneously reducing neighbor complaints of street noise, litter, and general congestion.
- **Bike racks.** The three bike racks on the street near the temple fill up quickly, and many weekends, I have seen multiple bikes locked to trees, light poles, and car

meters. I suspect this kind of "over-use" of space is what is bothering the neighbors who want to end Thai brunch. To resolve this problem and to help reduce car traffic and parking issues, I have included new bike racks at the secondary entrance to the site. These bike racks will offer a safe place for bicycle parking and using them will de-clutter the surrounding streets and sidewalks.

- **Movable walls.** These walls, with the ability to double as mural space and community communication/notification space, fundamentally act as barriers when erected. Although my new redesign is surprisingly similar to my initial design for the site, the movable walls will be a noticeable and enjoyable new addition for both brunch goers and neighbors. In my new redesign the edges of the site will function, when they need to, as physical barriers keeping some, probably not all, of the sounds and smells of the brunch out of the neighboring spaces. Importantly, the walls will not simply act as opaque barriers; rather, they will be made of a translucent material such as acrylic. The translucent material would allow some visual connection to the street, yet help to contain noise. Further, the surface of these walls could be used to display notifications, menus, prices, and even murals. Traditional Thai Buddhist Temple spaces often incorporate colorful murals and other art forms such as sculpture that invoke the history of Buddhism within Thailand.[3] These murals were used to record and pass on cultural and religious history, stories and mythology. Today this art form could be used to display current "history" and events of the Thai Temple community in Berkeley. The act of creating something together, such as a mural, could create and reinforce a sense of community and identity among this very diverse group of people. Additionally, the benefit of using erectable, temporary walls is simply that: they are not permanent. These walls can be and, if desired, will be taken down after the brunch and stored within one of the permanent structures on the site, already being used for storage.

Implications for informant and community needs

The addition of erectable, temporary walls, new bike racks, an additional entrance, and modification of and addition to seating, tables, counters, and food lines was not directly "asked for" by my informant. My experience with this community and interviews with Steven have shown me that there is a strong desire from all of the members of this community to preserve the Thai Temple brunch environment and site. To me, this essentially means ensuring that the space functions as a food serving, gathering place on Sunday mornings while simultaneously addressing the needs and complaints coming from the neighboring homes. Moving walls that do not block views permanently is one example coming from my redesign that meets the needs and demands of both parties. The Thai Temple community can still hold their brunch and the neighbors gain more privacy and reduction in noise and smells that result from the event. Similarly, better circulation flows, enhanced by new placement of food lines as well as additional bike parking and a new entrance, will help diminish issues of congestion and noise caused by people and automobiles. These design measures can please the neighbors and simultaneously allow Sunday brunch to continue.

Conclusion

This project was different from all of my other studio projects, and it allowed me to see a different side of my "designer-self." I have never been asked to design a space for a group of people who are currently coming under attack from their surrounding neighbors. My own, personal process is usually one in which I am constantly crafting with my hands and intermittently doing research. For this real-life site, that process drastically changed. This project gave me the opportunity to work with a "client," otherwise known as my informant, Steven, and actually start to understand the role that an architect can play in the day-to-day process of design. Not only are we designers, but we are also ethnographers, material scientists, historians, and in this case, mediators.

A substantial amount of information was gathered from this study, but I believe that the most important thing that I learned is that current urban landscapes are the sites of our unfolding human relationships as individuals and as groups, constantly fought over and contested. Architecture, as a human creation, reflects the dynamics that we live in (our environment), the dynamics within the self (feelings, emotions, desires, and wishes), and then goes on to show how we communicate both our understanding of the internal and the external outwards. What we, as human beings, value is reflected in the nature of what we build, design, and create every day. At the Thai Temple, any proposed design changes needed to address the conflict at hand from the perspectives of both parties involved. As an architect, I couldn't just design something beautiful to be put on the site. I had to understand the environment deeply, both physically and socially. I learned that most current architecture is not designed to meet the needs of just one client, but in reality, the needs of many clients, even if those "clients," like the neighbors, might not physically be in the space being designed.

Bibliography

Cate, Sandra. *Making Merit, Making Art: A Thai Temple in Wimbledon*. Honolulu: University of Hawaii Press, 2003.

Crouch, David and Richard Wiltshire. *Sustaining the Plot: Communities, Gardens, and Land Use*. London: Town and Country Planning Association, 2001.

Feldt, Barbara H. *Garden Your City*. Lanham: Taylor Trade Publishing, 2005.

"Food Studies Resources." Harlan Hatcher Graduate Library. University of Michigan. www.lib.umich.edu/grad/collections/foodstudies/

Hunchamlong, Yuphaphan. *Thai Language and Culture for Beginners*. Manoa: University of Hawaii, 2007.

International Buddhism Centre. www.fivethousandyears.org/mos/

Matics, K. I. *Introduction to the Thai Temple*. Bankok: White Lotus, 1992.

Numrich, Paul David. *Old Wisdom in the New World: Americanization in Two Immigrant Theravada Buddhist Temples*. Knoxville: University of Tennessee Press, 1996.

O'Connor, Richard A. *Urbanism and Religion: Community, Hierarchy, and Sanctity in Urban Thai Buddhist Temples*. Ann Arbor: University Microfilms International, 1978.

Ringis, Rita. *Thai Temples and Temple Murals*. New York: Oxford University Press, 1990.

Steven. Thai Buddhist Temple volunteer. Interviews: September 28, 2008 and October 5, 2008.

Super Soundproofing Company. http://shop3.mailordercentral.com/supersoundproofing/

Notes

1 Richard A. O'Connor, *Urbanism and Religion: Community, Hierarchy, and Sanctity in Urban Thai Buddhist Temples* (Ann Arbor: University Microfilms International, 1978).
2 See the Super Soundproofing Company: http://shop3.mailordercentral.com/supersoundproofing/
3 Rita Ringis. *Thai Temples and Temple Murals* (New York: Oxford University Press, 1990).

CAITLIN DECLERCQ, "L'ÉCOLE FRANÇAISE: EDUCATION, ENGAGEMENT, AND THE FRENCH LANGUAGE AND CULTURE," 2012

Introduction

To design a successful space for any constituency requires broad cultural competence and specific knowledge about the cultural group for whom a building is designed; therefore, architects must be concerned with and seek to understand the systems of knowledge and cultural practices of the people who will or could reside in the buildings they design. Undoubtedly, this is a challenging proposition for professional architectural practice. First, though meanings, beliefs, and actions are shared among cultural group members, the transmission of this knowledge is tacit—unspoken—and therefore requires a specific and thoughtful methodology on the part of researchers or architects. Second, many ethnographic techniques—which are instrumental in eliciting cultural knowledge—may be too costly or time-consuming for designers to employ. In response to these challenges and limitations, the method I used in this project, semantic ethnography, can enable designers to obtain valuable insights about a sited culture through a series of informant interviews, meanwhile resolving the constraints of time and professional practice mentioned above.

Introduction to project

In this project, I used a specific type of ethnographic methodology, semantic ethnography, to learn about the culture—the activities, language, values, and spatial context—of the École Française community. This research technique—and indeed, any ethnographic methodology—requires a researcher to engage in the interpretive act of translating an informant's words, actions, and/or stated beliefs into textual form;[1] therefore, throughout my research I attempted to acknowledge my own subjectivity and perspective in order to make my own interpretive process more transparent. To that end, in addition to the data I collected through observations and ethnographic interviews I conducted to learn about the sited culture of the École Française, I have also included my personal reflections in this paper. Ultimately, the goal of this research project was to design a space that would better "accommodate and celebrate the ways of living" expressed by my informant; therefore, to obtain a more robust understanding of related research and design precedents, I conducted a literature review (to be summarized further below in the Methods section) to supplement the emic and personal perspectives that emerged in the first stages of my work.[2]

Introduction to the École Française

The École Française (EF) is a non-profit, member-based organization committed to promoting the study of the French language and culture, cultivating a community of people in the local area who share these interests, and offering a multifaceted curriculum of resources and events for a multilingual audience. I chose the EF as the site for my ethnography project because it offered me the opportunity to explore my personal interest in the French language and focus on an organization dedicated to learning and collaborative practice, two themes relevant to my interest in educational environments.

Methods

Though my primary methodological focus was the practice of semantic ethnography, in this project, I integrated a variety of methods into my study: observation, interviews, and a literature review.

Observations

Though direct observations are typically conducted on site (as was my initial observation of the EF), prior to my first site visit, I had already made a few observations about the role and use of space at the École Française as a result of researching the EF online: first, the bright yellow, Victorian façade of the EF building has a prominent position on the EF's website and Facebook page, both in visual form as well as in descriptions of the organization. The ubiquity of this image led me to infer that the physical site of the EF—the yellow house it inhabits—is an important part of the Alliance's cultural identity. However, equally conspicuous on the website was the message that all visits must be arranged by appointment, in advance, which seemed to pose a contradictory assessment of the accessibility of the EF space. I was struck by this contradiction and, in hindsight, I wonder how my initial research about the site conducted online may have colored my perceptions of the space during my initial visit.

Data collection

To begin my observation, I first had to gain access to the École Française site. Thus, I made an appointment—with the goal of asking permission to study the space—and arrived at my scheduled time. I began my visit by meeting with the director of the EF to inquire about the organization and ask for permission to study the space for my research project. Based on my findings from this initial observation, I proposed a preliminary redesign of the space (see Appendix 1). As part of this proposal, I attempted to translate the concepts and principles of way-finding and "sittable space" into tangible design interventions.[3] More information about the specific design interventions included in my initial redesign is below in the Design Proposals section.

Interviews

Once I obtained permission to study the École Française for this project, the director offered herself and another administrator, Claire, as resources to answer my questions. Grateful for the support offered by the director, I anticipated that finding an informant would not be difficult. Instead, the challenged I faced was in deciding on a particular micro-culture of this site to study. French classes are offered several times a day at the École Française—indeed, Claire described the EF as primarily a language school—so I assumed it would be easy to locate a student informant for my study; however, because I identify with a student culture, I decided to focus on a different micro-culture at the EF in order to minimize the potential of my own experiences influencing or biasing my work. Ultimately, I decided to interview an administrator (staff member) for two reasons: first, both staff members are easily accessible via email and appointment; second, administrators are unique in their continuous presence at the EF, meaning they could speak to changes in the use of space (by event or group) over the course of a day, week, or month.

Introduction to my informant

Once I decided on the administrator (staff) micro-culture, I emailed the École Française to request an appointment for an interview, and the person available on the day I was able to visit was Claire, the school administrator at the EF. Thus, Claire became my primary informant for this project. Though I had briefly met Claire during my first visit to the EF and talked to her on the phone to make my first appointment, I had not engaged with her at length prior to our interview. Therefore, I tried to develop rapport with her by offering a description of the project and my personal interests, thanking her throughout our interview for her time and insights, and—using a technique I learned as a health educator—matching her tone and body language to make her feel more comfortable. It is worth noting that the default language spoken at the EF, by which I mean the language used for all salutations and that which is assumed in conversation until English is spoken or requested, is French. Therefore, in this appointment (and in all of my other interactions with the EF, in person or otherwise) I attempted to converse first in French and then, inevitably, in English. I made this concerted effort to speak French in order to challenge myself personally and also demonstrate respect; ultimately, I believe my actions also helped to develop rapport with Claire.

In our second interview, I decided to initiate our conversation by inviting Claire to ask me any questions she had, which led to an interesting discussion about the need for children's educational facilities at the EF to meet local demand. I also suspect that by inviting Claire's questions, I helped her obtain greater clarity on my goals for our collaboration and—I hope—helped her to feel more engaged with the project. I believe the sum of my efforts to develop rapport had a positive impact: Claire was incredibly kind during our conversations, sharing with me several resources she had in her office, offering to take me on a tour of the backyard, and making a couple of jokes during our initial interview.

Literature review

I used Claire's emic description of the cultural activities and current challenges that define the EF as primary points of departure for my etic (outside) investigation. The goal of my literature review, then, was to obtain additional information from other published sources and establish a point of comparison with the emic perspective I obtained from Claire. Based on the primary themes that emerged from my interviews with Claire, I identified four areas of study to guide my research: educational environments, student engagement, language learning, and cultural centers. Ultimately, I selected eighteen books and articles to inform my investigation of the EF from an etic perspective.

Design concepts and proposals

Another important methodological milestone of this project was the translation of cultural concepts (and/or research findings) into built form in two instances: the initial and final proposed redesign of the space. Though the process of design may not be categorized as a specific type of research methodology, I do feel that it is important to discuss the methods I used to create my design proposals. Because I do not possess a background in design, I had to carefully consider how to represent my conceptual knowledge into visual media. The resources I utilized to do so include: hand-drawn floor plans, spatial concepts, and existing images of design elements similar to those I envisioned in my final EF redesign.

Floor plans

For my initial and final redesign proposals of the space, I used my gridded notepad to assist in sketching basic floor plans for each level. These floor plans contained spatial information about room functions, adjacencies, and relative size, as well as existing and/or proposed furniture. Though my floor plans were not drawn exactly to scale, I did attempt to convey the relative size of rooms to reflect (with some accuracy) the distribution of space—and types of space, such as classrooms—at the EF. I used some symbolic conventions in my drawings I had seen in other floor plans, such as the symbol for door openings, but ultimately had to create many of my own, such as symbols to connote stairways, large furniture, windows, and sliding doors.

Conceptual tools

While planning my final redesign, I faced the challenge of deciding if and how to rearrange the floor plans of the École Française. The criteria I developed to assess the need for and outcome of such changes included: location (was the location of a room or furniture item supportive of its function?) adjacencies (were rooms and associated functions located in close proximity to facilitate easy access?); materials (could the use of different materials better serve the function of spaces?); and amenities (are there smaller design interventions, such as the use of furniture or wall décor, that can contribute meaningfully to the space?).

Findings

Personal observation

During my initial visit to the École Française, I was surprised to find the space less welcoming than the organization's website—and indeed, the façade of the house—suggested. To enter the EF house, I had to go through a gate, walk up a few stairs, ring the doorbell, and open the front door; once inside, I noticed a staircase directly ahead of me and a closed door (a classroom, I was later informed) to my right. Because the EF is situated in a converted house, I initially felt like I was walking into someone's home, which made me reluctant to wander too far inside—or upstairs—without permission to do so. In that circumstance, I felt a conflict between the cues I received about how to inhabit and navigate the space as a house and as an organizational building.

An electronic beep signaled my entry into the EF, and, shortly thereafter, the director of the École appeared at the top of the stairs and invited me to her office on the second floor. Though I engaged in a genial and informative conversation with the director, I did notice that during our conversation she had to monitor the front door, an activity that required her to stand and walk to the top of the stairs since the front door is not visible from the upstairs office. Additionally, when another visitor arrived, there was no place for a third person to sit in the office. The design of the entryway and the lack of sitting options upstairs made the EF building seem, to me, informal and reserved for purposeful meetings, rather than a casual visit or engagement with classroom or library resources as I would have expected (particularly since some of the EF's library materials are stored in that office area). Nevertheless, the office was cozy: I appreciated its colorful walls and the small, circular table in the center of the room.

Once I finished my conversation with the director, I went downstairs to finish packing up my bag (in order to more quickly vacate the room for the next visitor), but had difficulty locating a space where I could rest my backpack, rearrange its contents, and sit down for a few minutes to record my initial impressions. Because the classroom doors were closed, the only option I saw was a long table, lined with chairs, in the main room. At the head of the table was an easel with flipchart paper, so I assumed this space was a classroom. Not wanting to seem like I was meddling, I didn't investigate the other downstairs rooms any further (as it turns out, I should have spent more time wandering around, because on a later visit to the EF I saw that there was a couch in the room I assumed to be a classroom, and learned that the room was, in fact, a living room); instead, I headed outside to write my notes. On my way back to my car, I noticed a woman sitting in her vehicle, reading a French textbook, making me wonder if she was waiting there for her class to begin because there wasn't anywhere to sit inside.

Proposed changes

After my initial visit, I proposed three changes to the layout of the École, primarily based on my own perceptions of the space and observation of others in the house. First, in response to my own uncertainty about how to navigate and occupy the EF space due to what I perceived as the blurring of cues the space communicated as both a house and non-profit organization, I proposed the use of signage to welcome and orient visitors. Second, I noted the need for—and potential benefits of—informal seating options, both outside of the main office on the second floor (where the second visitor was unable to sit while she waited for my appointment to finish) as well as in the main entryway downstairs. Adding additional seating would not only make visitors more comfortable, I reasoned, but would also create a more casual, inviting space. Finally, I noticed that each time the front door opened (signaled by a beep from an intercom system), the director had to stand up, walk to the top of the stairs, and monitor who was entering/exiting the building. To me, this seemed like an excessive amount of work to have to do simply to greet, intercept, and/or assist each visitor, so I proposed the relocation of the office to the first floor, where a direct line of sight to/from the front door would enable easier surveillance of the entryway and also help to orient first-time visitors. Floor plans that depict my initial proposal are in the Appendix.

Change in perception

On subsequent visits to the EF, I was surprised to notice so many more details of the space that I had overlooked during my first visit: a couch in the living room, tables full of French magazines, and bulletin boards decorated with posters and postcards from France. These details—precisely what I was looking and hoping for during my first visit—speak to the desire of the EF to create a welcoming and inspiring space. I also noticed that students did, in fact, seem to linger after class to chat with each other, but did so on the front porch, rather than socializing inside as I would have expected. When I mentioned this to Claire, she reiterated that the École strives to develop a sense of community and expressed her disappointment that the students didn't use the indoor spaces for studying or social purposes. Claire conjectured that members may not want to sit inside to chat out of fear that associated noise would disturb classes being held in adjacent rooms.

Emic perspective: ethnographic interviews

During our interviews, Claire offered thorough descriptions of the history, organizational structure, and programming of the École Française; additionally, she articulated challenges regarding member engagement and limitations imposed by the built environment. Claire also described the successes of the EF: the establishment of the École as a language school, the creation of a full schedule of French language classes for adults, and the development of a robust community around the two primary monthly events offered, the *conference* (a topical lecture delivered in French) and the *conversation* (an informal potluck and opportunity for people to converse in French). Claire mentioned that she is constantly surprised at how well attended the conversation events are each month. Given the number of students involved in classes, conferences, and conversation events, the majority of space at the EF is currently dedicated to these three programs.

After our interview, I reflected on my initial impressions of the space and wondered to what extent some of these challenges are manifested in—or reinforced by—the physical site of the École Française. To that end, Claire helped illuminate several important spatial issues:

Need for flexible spaces

The spaces downstairs, especially the library and dining room, require a great deal of flexibility in order to accommodate classes, board meetings, conversation (potluck) events, and conference events. Each of these activities requires a different configuration of space: for classes, the library is closed off from the dining room by a sliding door; for conversations, the doors are retracted to create a large, open space; and for conferences, the large table typically in the center of the dining room is either moved or placed into storage to accommodate anywhere from 15 to 30 people.

A successful "teacher space"

The EF recently converted a room upstairs to a "teacher space," including a copy machine, a closet full of educational materials, and a private bathroom. Claire said that the teachers appreciate having their own space and proceeded to describe how teachers have invested that space with meaning and developed a sense of ownership of the room; her comments made me reflect upon the concept of territoriality.

Challenge for visitors

Finally, I asked Claire about the number, type, and primary concerns of visitors to the École Française. Though the EF typically welcomes about 1–2 new visitors each week, Claire predicted that October would be a busier month: many French families take advantage of a 2-week vacation in the academic calendar and use the time for travel. Frequently, French families visiting the area see that there is a local École Française and stop by in the hope of getting information about local tourist activities. Unfortunately, because the EF is primarily a language school, there are not many resources that it can offer visiting families. Though this insight does not speak directly to the physical space of the EF, it does provide an important reminder that the façade, name, and online presence of the École can communicate a range of potential functions to visitors, not all of which may be accurate. Additionally, I think this is another example of how the creation of a more informal space to welcome visitors may be beneficial to the École.

Etic perspective: literature review

Based on the themes that emerged from my observations and interviews, I organized my literature review into four distinct yet interrelated areas of inquiry: educational design, student engagement, cultural center design, and bilingualism/language learning. Below, I have summarized the primary findings from each area, particularly relating to the mission of the École Française and the challenges it currently faces.

Education design

Educational scholars confront the difficulty of proving causality in environmental interventions regarding classroom behavior and student outcomes, but describe the ways in which the student experience is shaped by spatial and built environment characteristics.[4] Most notably, lighting and color are "basic physical variables" that affect learning, cooperative behavior, and productivity, though other elements in the built environment similarly impact student—and teacher—experiences in other dimensions: attainment, engagement, affect, attendance, well-being, and participation.[5]

One theme that continues to emerge in educational design literature is the need for *flexible* spaces. Daniel Kenney and colleagues frame flexibility as a method of meeting ever-changing user needs in both the short and long term.[6] However, environmental psychologist Robert Sommer cautions that "one drawback of flexibility is that it precludes the use of specific design features intended to optimize particular functions,"[7] an insight that is particularly important to the EF: though certain spaces need to accommodate a range of activities, others need to be designed specifically for the French classes (6–8 students) that are offered daily.

Student engagement

Writing about engaging architectural spaces, Himanshu Burte defines engagement as "a relation of involvement (as towards some people) that often springs up between us and specific places." Meanwhile, in the context of higher education, George Kuh offers a more quantitative measurement of student engagement, defined as the sum of: "[b]oth the time and energy students devote to academic activities, and how students perceive different facets of the institutional environment."[8] Both definitions of engagement are relevant to the École Française's mission: Burte's emphasis on place-making emphasizes the sensory and memory experiences that are often invoked by the EF's role as a cultural center and community of Francophiles, while Kuh speaks to how the organization of activities and space shape students' perception of and involvement within an environment and community.

Cultural centers

My research regarding the design and organization of cultural centers focused less on the particularities of cultural activities and artifacts and more on the need for cultural centers to integrate a variety of functions, accommodate a variety of users (diverse in age, interest, background, and needs), and engage with the public.[9]

Bilingualism and language learning

I was curious to learn about theories of language learning and concepts pertaining to bilingualism in order to build the unique needs of the multilingual EF community and programming into its design. Practicing bilingualism—an activity that requires the brain to engage with and make sense of two language systems—builds the brain's cognitive capacities, in particular the "executive function," that enable bilingual speakers to perform better on tasks such as planning and problem-solving. Therefore, the confrontation of two languages is like "a workout [for the brain] that strengthens its cognitive muscles." [10] In order to build multilingual competency in students, teachers should treat all languages in a learner's repertoire simultaneously and employ a multimodal pedagogy that includes all parts of communication and semiotic symbolism beyond and including language, such as "gesture, sound . . . images, diagrams, pictures, icons, and color."[11]

Analysis

Based on the areas of improvement I identified in my initial observation, as well as those articulated by Claire, I conducted my literature review with the hope of identifying environmental interventions that could: help solve current challenges with member engagement and organizational change; find ways to make the École Française more accommodating of children and visitors as well as enable casual uses of the space; and support the dual mission of the EF regarding education and community-building. Through this etic analysis, I saw the need for considering the entire property of the EF as instrumental in facilitating its mission and communicating its values. For example, the backyard and other informal spaces can be utilized for classes and community events; and the walls of the EF can be used to display student work and/or made transparent to create better visibility of student and member communities at work. The colorful walls and natural lighting that the EF currently boasts play an important role in education design.

What is clear from my literature review is that many of the design functions that promote student learning also engage students, create legible spaces, and facilitate a feeling of ownership; therefore, a small investment in the physical environment at the EF can have a significant impact.

Site redesign

In my initial redesign of the École Française, which I created in response to my experiences and observations during my first visit, I proposed the addition of informal seating options to make the space feel more welcoming; the relocation of the EF office to the first floor to assist with monitoring and greeting visitors; and the creation and usage of signage to facilitate way-finding. Additionally, knowing that the EF is a non-profit organization, I proposed my initial redesign under the assumption of the same floor plan in order to minimize costs. After collecting both etic (literature review) and emic (ethnographic interviews with informants) perspectives, and visiting the EF several more times, in my final redesign of the site (see Appendix 2) I proposed a more profound renovation of the existing space in order to better respond to current challenges and support the teaching and community-building goals of the EF. Still, to maintain the same spirit of the more budget-conscious change I adopted in my initial design, as part of my final proposal, I extrapolated my primary design interventions and compiled a list of alternative, less invasive changes that could be implemented for a greatly reduced cost (see Figure 1 on page 197).

Final design proposal

Based on the observational, emic, and etic data I collected, I compiled a list of design priorities to guide my final design process. Though I addressed many of the same themes from my initial design—way-finding, visibility, "sittable space"—in my second redesign of the École, my final proposal ultimately responded more profoundly to the strengths and challenges the EF faces in its current configuration.

Accommodating all social roles

During our interviews, Claire mentioned two groups of people the EF is currently unable to accommodate: children (there is not currently a space in the EF that meets requirements for elementary education, for example, the availability of bathroom facilities sized for children) and visiting French families (who often come looking for information about local activities while on vacation in the United States). In my proposed redesign, both groups are accommodated and welcomed: First, I added a room on the first floor to be dedicated to children's classes. This room features a bathroom specific to this population (part of the aforementioned requirement), colorful walls, a mural, flexible furniture arrangements featuring small tables and chairs, and large glass doors that overlook the outdoors. Second, the seating areas by the front door and in the dining room are designed to be accessible, visible, and comfortable for a variety of people. I imagine that a family visiting the EF looking for information on local events may be grateful for a cozy place to rest while speaking to staff.

Embracing and enhancing existing spaces

The EF—in its current configuration—boasts colorful walls, a nice backyard (sometimes used for events), a home-like *feel*, and many library resources for members to use. My proposed redesign takes advantage of these existing traits and builds upon them to better align with the etic and emic perspectives described above. For example, I advocate for the continued use of bright colors throughout the building, and adding to it with the creation of murals in classrooms and common areas. These colors and images can support learning and student engagement goals of the EF. Additionally, whereas the yard is hidden in the original layout of the EF (due to its location in the back of the house and few—if any—windows looking out onto it), in my final design, the yard is moved to the mid-section of the house and made visible with the addition of sliding glass doors on three sides. A more visible and accessible yard creates another space for learning, events, and informal activities to occur. Because the EF is located in a residential community, I thought it would be important for the new building to retain the current structure's façade and orientation to the street, thereby retaining its current residential character. Therefore, I retained the façade, porch, yard, kitchen, and dining/living room in my new plan.

Though the EF has a sizable collection of books, tapes, and CDs—in French or about French culture—for members to borrow, the majority of these resources are ensconced in the teacher lounge or in recessed or covered shelves and therefore largely inaccessible. In contrast, my design proposal features a number of bookshelves in common seating areas and classrooms, which enables members to engage with materials and teachers to more easily incorporate music (for example) into their classroom activities.

Seating arrangements

Another change I wanted to make at the École Française was the inclusion and integration of informal seating options for individuals and groups. First, the main hallway and staircase are the primary circulatory axes of the first floor of the EF, meaning that the majority of people entering/exiting the space will pass through one or both of those areas. Thus, seating is arranged in relationship to those areas to create a lively feel and invite people to inhabit the space. In addition to seating areas made available for individuals, there are several pairs or groups of chairs, including the group workspace on the second floor, the bistro table and chairs on the patio, and the tables in the kitchen and dining room (which also can be rearranged to meet the needs of the *conversation* and *conference* events). Finally, because the front porch is currently used as an informal social space, I proposed the addition of tables and chairs in that area to help reinforce current patterns of use.

Would members like the new space?

Ultimately, this is the most important question for me to ask in assessing my final plan. Indeed, the cultural information I gained through interviewing Claire guided my final design process and could be used as criteria to evaluate my final plan. In particular, I believe that Claire would welcome the addition of additional seating options and informal, social spaces because she mentioned her desire for members to feel welcome in and use the EF space outside of formal classes and events. Further, my proposed addition of the children's classroom would aid the EF in being able to offer classes to young people, a goal it is not currently able to achieve due to insufficient facilities. Finally, despite calling for a significant renovation of existing space, my final plan does not include any changes to the façade of the building, helping to preserve the home-like feel and sense of identity the École gains from its unique building. For these reasons, I believe both the process and outcome of my design process are respectful of and loyal to Claire's perspective.

BOX 1: LOWER-COST DESIGN IDEAS

- Change location of office and individual study room (see initial redesign in Appendix 2)
- Extend use of colorful paint to the kitchen, office, and individual study room; consider painting a mural on the wall of the stairway
- Change the default furniture configuration of the dining/living room to a couch and smaller round table, rather than the long seminar-style table and chairs that make the space feel formal and cramped
- Rotate materials displayed on bulletin boards and/or invite students to contribute materials, particularly regarding their trips to France, interests, etc.

The only part of my design proposal that I would anticipate resistance to from the EF is my recommendation for a significant structural renovation of the first and second floors, as well as the inclusion of sliding glass doors, both of which I anticipate to be costly additions. The École Française is a non-profit organization and therefore may not be able to obtain sufficient funding for such an endeavor. See Box 1 for lower-cost design solutions to meet the goals articulated above.

Need for education

Robert Sommer emphasizes the need to engage students and teachers in the design process and provide each group with education about the uses and vision for each space.[12] Therefore, an essential aspect of my final design proposal—if adopted by the EF board—would be the structured engagement with members of the École Française to communicate with and educate all stakeholders about the proposed vision and functions of each space.

Conclusion

Though I initially experienced some trepidation about the prospect of identifying and developing rapport with an unknown informant in an unfamiliar location, I quickly discovered how interesting and rewarding ethnographic research can be. On a personal level, I appreciated the opportunity to challenge myself to step outside of my comfort zone by initiating interactions with "strangers" and articulating my academic interests (and doing so in French when I could manage it). It only took a few minutes of asking questions during the first interview to realize how much I enjoy listening to other people talk about their lives. Claire's candor taught me the value of and the unique perspective gained from informant interviews and served as an example of the importance of ethnographic research in eliciting the cultural meanings, activities, and needs that occur in spatial contexts. Soliciting and understanding the user perspective is an important part of architectural practice and research, and the specific methods I used in this project serve as a model for my own future endeavors as well as for architects, researchers, and even building administrators.

As a "non-architecture" student making my way through my first semester in an Architecture PhD program, I greatly valued the opportunity to struggle through the process of envisioning and creating floor plans. The act of drawing a space—rather than merely describing it in words—made my design proposals much more tangible and meaningful for me. In fact, after compiling all of the photos I used to annotate my final design proposal, a process that spanned several days and required many hours of working with, arranging, and manipulating images, I became so invested in the design I had envisioned and drawn that I was momentarily shocked to revisit the EF space and realize that my proposed changes hadn't been made! To me, this is a testament to the power of images to communicate—and even bring to life—spatial concepts and ideas.

Bibliography

Bhattacharjee, Yudhijit. "Why Bilinguals Are Smarter." *New York Times,* March 17, 2012. Retrieved from www.nytimes.com.

Bione, Cecilia. *Cultural Centers: Architecture 1990–2011*. Milan, Italy: Motta, 2009.

Burte, Himanshu. *Space for Engagement: The Indian Artplace and a Habitational Approach to Architecture*. Calcutta: Seagull Books, 2008.

Cataloghi, A. S. *Città di Tornio: New Spaces for Cultural Enjoyment.* Milan, Italy: Editrice Abitare Segesta, 2011.

Cenoz, Jasone, and Durk Gorter. "A holistic approach to multilingual education: Introduction." *The Modern Language Journal* 95, no. 3 (2011): 339–343.

Claire. "Ethnographic Interview: Administrator Micro-culture". Personal Communication. September 17, 2012 and October 8, 2012.

Cranz, Galen. *Ethnography & Space: Architecture 110 Ethnography Workbook*. Berkeley, CA: Copy Central, 2012.

Cranz, Galen, and Eleftherios Pavlides, Eds. *Environmental Design Research: The Body, the City, and the Buildings in Between.* San Diego, CA: Cognella, 2012.

Gilardi, Silvia and Chiara Guglielmetti. "University Life of Non-Traditional Students: Engagement Styles and Impact on Attrition." *The Journal of Higher Education* 82, no. 1 (2011): 33–53.

Graetz, Ken A. "The Psychology of Learning Environments." In *Learning Spaces,* edited by Diana G. Oblinger. Washington DC: Educause, 2006. www.educause.edu/learningspaces.

Groat, Linda, and David Wang. *Architectural Research Methods.* New York: John Wiley & Sons, Inc, 2002.

Higgins, Steve, Elaine Hall, Kate Wall, Pam Woolner, and Caroline McCaughey. "The Impact of School Environments: A Literature Review." University of Newcastle, 2005. Retrieved from: www.designcouncil.org.uk.

Jamieson, Peter, Kenn Fisher, Tony Gilding, Peter G. Taylor, and A. C. F. Trevitt. "Place and space in the design of new learning environments." *Higher Education Research and Development* 19, no. 2 (2000): 221–236.

Kenney, Daniel R., Ricardo Dumont, and Ginger Kinney. *Mission and Place: Strengthening Learning and Community through Campus Design.* Westport, CT: Praeger Publishers, 2005.

Kuk, Linda, James H. Banning, and Marilyn J. Amey. *Positioning Student Affairs for Sustainable Change: Achieving Organizational Effectiveness through Multiple Perspectives*. Sterling, VA: Stylus, 2010.

Matthews, Kelly E., Victoria Andrews, and Peter Adams. "Social learning spaces and student engagement." *Higher Education Research & Development* 30, no. 2 (2011): 105–120.

McCurdy, David W., James P. Spradley, and Dianna J. Shandy. *The Cultural Experience: Ethnography in Complex Society*. 2nd ed. Long Grove, IL: Waveland Press, Inc., 2005.

Monahan, Torin. "Flexible Space and Built Pedagogy: Emerging IT Embodiments." *Inventio* 4, no. 1 (2002): 1–19.

Sommer, Robert. *Personal Space: The Behavioral Basis of Design*. Updated ed. Bristol, UK: Bosko Books, 2007.

Weisman, Jerry. "Evaluating Architectural Legibility: Way-Finding in the Built Environment." *Environment and Behavior* 13, no. 2 (1981): 189–204.
Whyte, William. "Sitting Space." In *The Social Life of Small Urban Spaces*, 24–39. Project for Public Spaces, 1980.
Zeisel, John. *Inquiry by Design: Environment/Behavior/Neuroscience in Architecture, Interiors, Landscape, and Planning*. Revised ed. New York, NY: W. W. Norton & Co, 1981, 2006.

Appendices

Appendix 1: Initial redesign (floor plans based on initial observations; in the original, changes were highlighted in color)

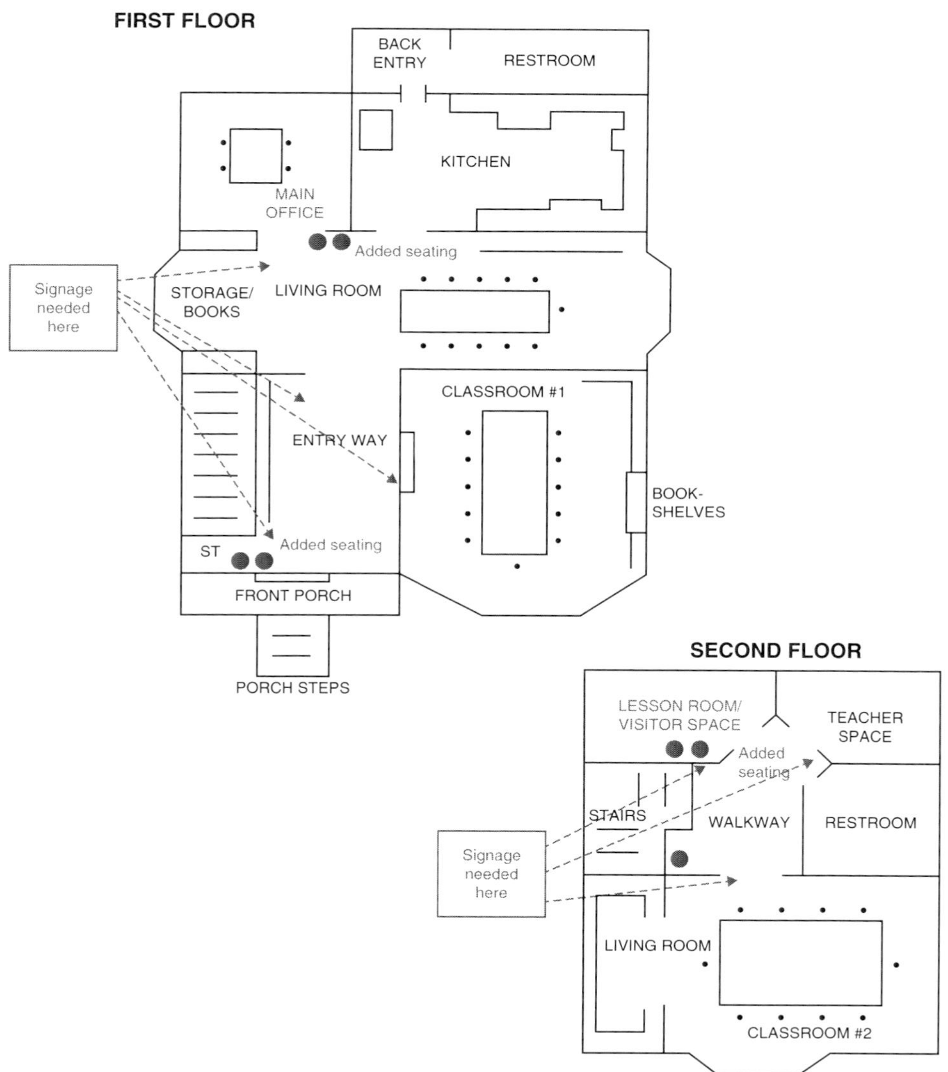

Figure 1 Initial redesign: proposed changes to floors 1 and 2

Appendix 2: Final design proposal

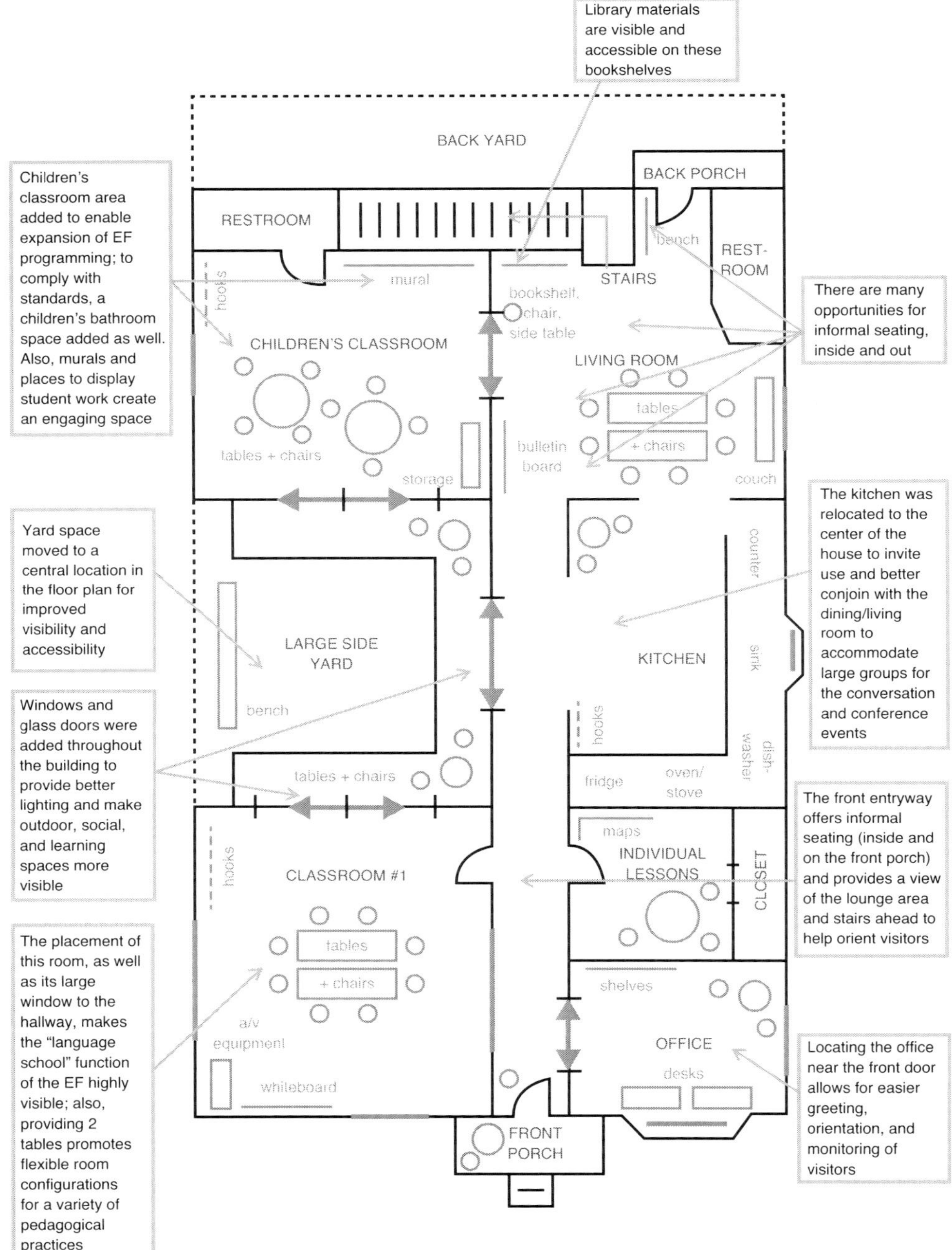

Figure 2 First floor: annotated plan

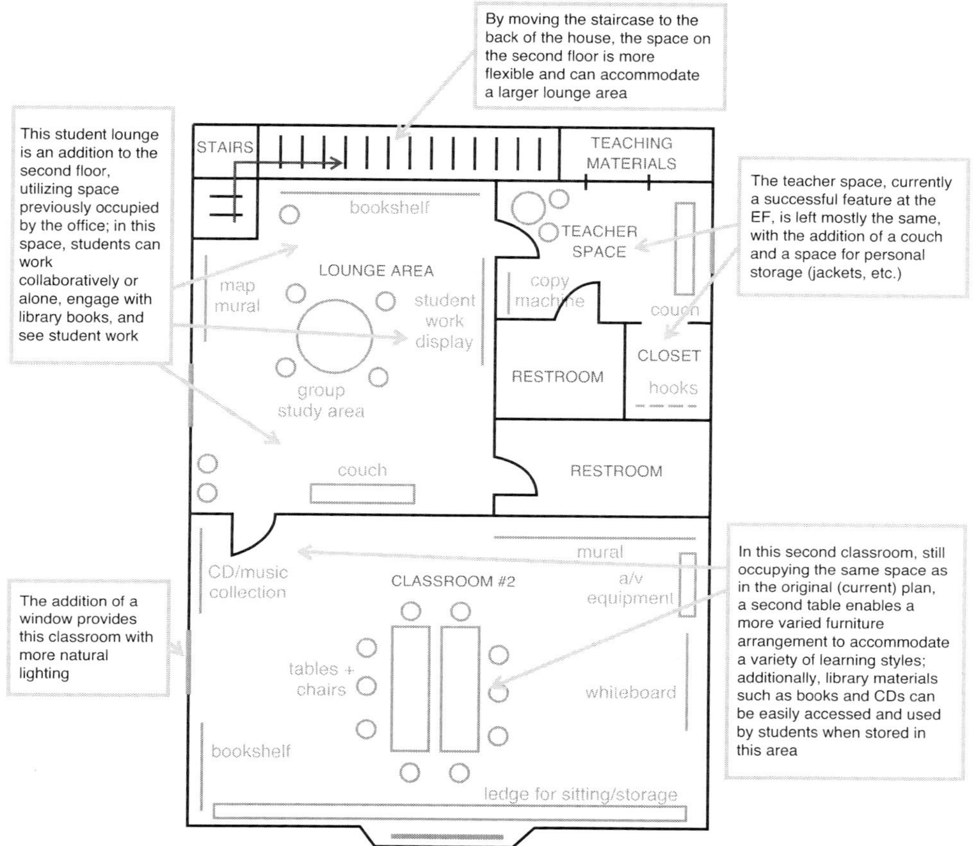

Figure 3 Second floor: annotated plan

Notes

1 George E. Marcus and Dick Cushman, "Ethnographies as Texts." *Annual Review of Anthropology* 11 (1982), p. 38.
2 Galen Cranz. *Ethnography & Space: Architecture 110 Ethnography Workbook*. (Berkeley, CA: Copy Central, 2012), p. 85.
3 Cf. Jerry Weisman, "Evaluating Architectural Legibility: Way-Finding in the Built Environment." *Environment and Behavior* 13, no. 2 (1981): 189–204, and William Whyte, "Sitting Space." In *The Social Life of Small Urban Spaces*, 24–39. Project for Public Spaces, 1980.
4 Cf. Robert Sommer, *Personal Space: The Behavioral Basis of Design*. Updated ed., (Bristol, UK: Bosko Books, 2007) and Steve Higgins et al. "The Impact of School Environments: A Literature Review." University of Newcastle, 2005. Retrieved from: www.designcouncil.org.uk.
5 Higgins et al., "The Impact of School Environments," 2005, p. 7.
6 Daniel R. Kenney, Ricardo Dumont, and Ginger Kinney. *Mission and Place: Strengthening Learning and Community through Campus Design*. (Westport, CT: Praeger Publishers, 2005).
7 Sommer, *Personal Space*, p. 141.
8 Himanshu Burte, *Space for Engagement: The Indian Artplace and a Habitational Approach to Architecture*. (Calcutta: Seagull Books, 2008), p. 18. See also George Kuh, 2001, quoted

in Silvia Gilardi and Chiara Guglielmetti, "University Life of Non-Traditional Students: Engagement Styles and Impact on Attrition." *The Journal of Higher Education* 82, no. 1 (2011): 33–53.

9 Cf. Cecilia Bione, *Cultural Centers: Architecture 1990–2011*, (Milan, Italy: Motta, 2009).

10 Yudhijit Bhattacharjee, "Why Bilinguals Are Smarter," *New York Times*, March 17, 2012. Retrieved from www.nytimes.com.

11 Jasone Cenoz and Durk Gorter. "A holistic approach to multilingual education: Introduction." *The Modern Language Journal* 95, no. 3 (2011), p. 340.

12 Sommer, *Personal Space*, 2007.

RYAN HUNT, "COWORKING," 2013

Introduction

The way people work is changing. Laptop computers and Wi-Fi connectivity have enabled workers to leave the traditional office environment and do their work almost anywhere. Many industries allow their employees to work from home. In the Bay Area, it is not uncommon to find a tech worker working in a coffee shop in the middle of the day. In the early 2000s, a group of these remote workers, missing the camaraderie and social connections fostered by office environments yet enjoying the freedom of freelance work, realized they could afford an office space if they all pitched in. What resulted was the birth of the coworking space, a new building type that has been popping up in different cities all over the world ever since.[1]

The site I chose for this study is a new coworking space in Oakland, CA. The building is a multi-story, historic building along the city's rapidly changing waterfront. The first story of the building houses a newly refurbished restaurant space as well as the lobby of the coworking offices. The second and third stories, also newly renovated, contain several types of workspaces available for rent: private office spaces designed for a team or group work, smaller private offices for a single worker, personal desk and storage spaces in a shared office, or coworking desk spaces in an open, shared area. Coworking spaces such as this offer a number of benefits to renters: first, the terms specified by rental agreements allow small business owners to choose the type of working environment that best suits their needs. Second, such an arrangement assumes that people will share ideas and knowledge despite—or perhaps because of—working in different industries; this access to different creative industries can be particularly advantageous to small businesses.

Location

The Waterfront Workspace is comprised of two buildings, both of which members can access: the main office building and, just around the corner, the Merritt House. My research centered on the Merritt House.

The Merritt House, built around the turn of the 20th Century on a site adjacent to the Transcontinental Railroad terminal, originally housed a restaurant and brothel. According to the 1902 Sanborn Fire Insurance Map, this space also once housed the train depot and waiting room as well as an artificial limb factory.

Today, the space is dedicated to the Waterfront Workspace and a restaurant (see above). The coworking space is used by a number of businesses as well as several independent workers. Collectively, the people who rent workspace come from a range of industries; during the course of my research, I met a music booking agent, lawyers, a web designer, an interior designer, employees of an engineering firm, and others.

Purpose

I chose to study a coworking site because I am interested to see what kind of resources or knowledge are shared between proximate workers, and I also hope to consider the larger implications of this kind of development.

Similar to the historical function of the multi-use industrial complex in which the Waterfront Workspace is situated, coworking itself relies on a somewhat closed commercial community, with firms coming and going regularly and their constituents engaged in productive activity through a network of personal relationships between entrepreneurs. Additionally, the clustering of different businesses offers constituent firms opportunities to take on side work and to learn new skills from other firms in the space. Further, the proximity of the different entrepreneurs in a coworking cluster creates a sense of solidarity that can be especially productive for new companies facing daunting challenges.

Richard Florida refers to young tech workers, designers, artists, musicians and entrepreneurs as the creative class, a group of people whom cities compete to attract and retain. To do so, Florida argues, cities should cultivate a vibrant night life and restaurant scene, encourage art events, and provide outdoor recreational activities. The vibrant urban environment that results eases the transition of young creatives to city life. In fact, Florida continues, creative workers typically first choose where to live (based on the amenities a city offers) and *then* seek to find employment once they arrive. Developing a city attractive to these young workers requires a diverse set of activities for a diverse set of people.[2]

At the same time, businesses have begun looking for ways to both cut costs and retain their best employees. Allowing workers to work remotely is one way businesses can achieve both goals simultaneously. However, in catering services and amenities to these highly valuable, newly mobile workers, Harvey reminds us that others are left behind.[3] This broader theme of inclusion and exclusion—as facilitated by coworking spaces—is one I explore in greater detail below.

Methods

I began my research by contacting the workspace site and requesting a tour. The person who showed me around the facilities agreed to be my informant and allowed me to interview her for this study. Aside from the interview, I also conducted site observations and a literature review about pertinent themes including office culture, coworking, industrial clustering, knowledge sharing, and the office as a social environment.

Informant

My informant, Isabel, is a staff member of the Waterfront Workspace and in charge of the daily operation of the business. I decided that she would be a good informant because she has experience with different coworking spaces and is knowledgeable about the Waterfront Workspace site. During our first meeting, Isabel led me on a tour of the two buildings that comprise the Waterfront Workspace and introduced me to the owner of the business. Because she is familiar with the many tenants who rent offices and coworking space at the site, Isabel also recommended a couple of people for me to talk to in order to learn more about the Workspace from the user perspective.

Interview

My initial interview with Isabel lasted about 15 minutes and was conducted in the lobby of the main office building. Two additional staff members were present, which was a bonus as they would periodically chime in with extra information. The questions I asked were related to the overall function of the Workspace business and how knowledge about people's preferences for different work environments was used to shape the building and business model of the Waterfront Workspace. I was particularly interested to learn more about the Waterfront Workspace's concept of "territorial vs. social people." This phrase, repeated by both Isabel and the owner of the business, relates to people's working preferences and seems to function as a sorting mechanism by which tenants are divided into two categories (and often, spaces). See Appendix for a transcript and analysis of my interview with Isabel.

Findings

Observations and personal perspective

My initial interview and observation revealed several social and organizational sorting mechanisms in place at the Waterfront Workspace. First, due to the different designs of the two buildings, tenants have separated themselves depending on the culture of their business. Business owners who want a more professional environment tend to favor the main office building over the Merritt House. Second, tenants further differentiate themselves through the choice of renting private offices vs. coworking spaces. The doors of all private offices are decorated with the tenants' business logos, which signify that tenants are claiming those spaces as their own. In fact, some of the tenants with private offices have gone so far as to move desks from the coworking space to their own private offices. In contrast, those who rent space in the coworking area, despite not having assigned work areas, tend to share more equitably available conference rooms, private phone booths, and vacant offices as well as the coworking desk spaces.

The private offices at the Merritt House line the edges of the building and each office has one or two windows facing outside, glass walls, and doors that face the central office space or hallway. The 3rd floor of the building is naturally lit by a large skylight and desks in the coworking space are arranged around a spiral staircase in the center of the building. A kitchen is located on the 3rd floor and a small break room is on the 2nd.

The coworking space on the 2nd floor does not have as many desks as that on the 3rd floor, but does include a number of unique workstation configurations, such as standing desks and a work area that mimics a reception station with a curved, standing height ledge on the opposite side of the workstation. To accommodate an increase in renters, the designer of the Waterfront Workspace is planning to add more standing height desks on the 3rd floor and more coworking desk space on the 2nd floor.

I observed the territorial and social dynamics mentioned by my informant. For example, one of the businesses occupying a coworking space has several employees. The owners of this business would sit together working quietly while the rest of their employees would work in one of the available conference rooms or at a nearby desk, but never at the same desk or table as the owners. To me, it seemed like either the employees were consciously separating themselves from the owners or the owners were consciously separating themselves from the employees. This territorial dynamic is probably common in a traditional office setting, but in this case it was interesting to see it play out in the coworking space. In another instance I observed, while one tenant (who is an accountant) was assembling a new desk and chair, another tenant stopped to inquire about which accounting software he should be using for his business. In fact, I have been able to witness many such exchanges between different tenants: business consultants gave advice to retail startups, accountants made book-keeping recommendations, and programmers shared ideas about ways to push software forward. This is an example of one of the benefits of coworking: the opportunity for informal collaboration.

At a larger scale, coworking spaces are a positive element in Oakland because they can add new pull factors to attract new businesses to the city. The civic amenities in Oakland have been increasing in the past few years and include many great bars and restaurants and night life. More people have been moving to the area as the real estate prices in San Francisco keep growing and people are now wanting to live, work, and play in Oakland.

Emic point of view

Coworking is a relatively new way of doing business. It caters to a segment of the workforce that wants to have both a sense of community and collaboration as well as a degree of private space. As an alternative to the traditional office environment, coworking can be a valuable resource for new businesses.

The Waterfront Workspace appears to be doing a lot of things right: they consider the different ways people work, they are conscious of the varied nature of social interaction, they have repurposed old buildings in Oakland, and they facilitate social connections for workers who desire it.

Though this kind of working environment can bring disparate creative workers together, it also acts like a citadel from other kinds of work. Much of the work that is done in coworking environments is divorced from place and doesn't allow other businesses to take advantage of the proximity and creative collaboration enjoyed by coworkers. In other words, in fostering collaboration among workers, coworking spaces also create larger social space of proximate strangers.

Etic point of view

I focused my literature review on the following points: coworking, office space, social factors of work, and the socio-economic context of urban offices. These four points allowed me to look at coworking environments at different scales and helped to broaden my research beyond the office walls. A summary of main findings follows:

- **Coworking:** The concept of coworking is relatively recent and was born out of the rise of freelancers in the workforce who found themselves working at home or in cafés and missed having the social connectedness available in a more traditional office environment. These independent workers initially had very basic needs. They needed Wi-Fi, coffee or tea, desk space, and a pleasant environment. Beyond these benefits, the cooperative workspace also brought the potential for collaboration.[4] This model of collaborative working in fact is attractive to a range of workers. Programmers, entrepreneurs, remote workers, students, and small businesses owners have become increasingly interested in developing (and working in) an environment focused on knowledge sharing, collaboration, openness, and sustainability, all of which are supported by coworking spaces.[5]
- **Office space:** Typical office space designs balance collaboration and sociability with privacy and productivity. Yet health impacts of office settings are a burgeoning area of interest for researchers and designers alike. Beyond the mental stress people can endure at work, recent studies have focused on the physical stress of sitting for long periods of time in front of a keyboard. Yet office designs have long prioritized efficiency over comfort. Another health concern is the cluster of illnesses that began appearing in office workers in the 1960s and now known as Sick Building Syndrome (SBS). SBS is a group of work-related symptoms such as cough, nausea, skin rash, and respiratory infections that occur more commonly in certain types of buildings.[6]
- **Social factors of work:** One of the most common tropes in office design is the open-plan office. This style of office layout is characterized by an arrangement of desks side-by-side with minimal—if any—partitions in-between. The purpose of this layout is to increase the amount of knowledge shared between different workers and to create (the appearance of) a more equal environment for all workers. Yet workers in this type of environment often complain of a lack of privacy, increased distractions and interruptions, and difficulty controlling ambient conditions such as temperature, lighting, and ventilation. Ultimately, this type of layout may harm productivity levels.[7]
- **Socio-economic factors:** Coworking offers an opportunity for real estate developers to repurpose older office spaces for new styles of working. This requires that the developers make design decisions that improve the functions of traditional workspaces. A small minority of the workforce is able to work remotely, and the majority of those who do so are self-employed or contract workers.[8] Some cities see coworking as part of an "innovation cluster" and have included coworking spaces into their city plans. In this way, coworking offers are seen as mechanisms with which to attract new businesses to cities; in fact, New York state identified coworking spaces as means to help economic development.[9] Yet with these benefits come risks: coworking spaces are typically inhabited by industries and new businesses that can fluctuate dramatically. New businesses and entrepreneurial ventures are risky by nature and given the pace of technological change, such investments could be precarious.[10]

Comparison

The Waterfront Workspace faces an important challenge: to live up to the promises of coworking, for both the people who rent space in its buildings and the City of Oakland in which it resides. My informant, Isabel, is tasked with figuring out ways that the workspace can create community and cater to the needs of tenants. Yet she also must balance the management of the facility with the social cohesion of the tenants. To do so involves a mix of marketing, operations management, and curating a client base; regarding the latter, the diversity of clients is an important part of both the marketing of the business and the functioning of the space.

The Waterfront Workspace is able to maintain a diverse collection of tenants, which is one way in which they aim to balance more stable businesses with newer, less stable ventures. As a relatively new business model, coworking benefits from a freelance-based creative class. In the next five years, a predicted 24 million workers will be self-employed; coworking spaces can benefit greatly from this trend. Though some of these workers will choose to work at home, others may choose a coworking space for some part of their work environment.[11]

Redesign

The Merritt House coworking spaces have only been open for three months so the space is undergoing rapid change. Fortunately, the owners had the foresight to use moveable and adjustable furniture for most of the office furniture so the layout is fairly malleable.

Initial redesign

The initial changes or recommendations I proposed were merely functional: I suggested adding a workshop area with 3D printers and CNC machines, a large format print station, design workstations with preinstalled software, a green screen, an equipment/tool library. These resources could help attract a broader range of employees and small businesses whose operations require specialized equipment (but for whom the cost of purchasing these items on their own would be prohibitive).

Final redesign

After conducting interviews and observations at the Waterfront Workspace and reviewing literature on coworking and office environments, I proposed a few changes to the existing workspace (of the Merritt House building) as well as to the restaurant on the 1st floor.

First, I recommend that the Waterfront Workspace abandon its plans to install a slide to connect the 2nd and 3rd floors. While a slide is a clever marketing tool that speaks to startup culture and is evocative of the early dot-com offices in the 1990s, it is neither functional nor practical. The space needed for the slide would require the floor on the 3rd story to be cleared and thus eliminate at least three private offices. Instead of installing the slide, my recommendation is to leave the offices but convert one into a lounge space on the 2nd floor. Though the Merritt House already has a breakroom on the 2nd floor—complete with a ping-pong table—the addition of a second lounge space would offer tenants a quiet space to relax. On the 3rd floor where the entrance to the slide would be, the coworking floor space should be expanded. In lieu of the folding tables that are currently in the coworking space, several rows of either adjustable, standing-height workspaces or pub-height tables could be used. The rationale for these changes is to give the tenants more choice in their active or passive use of the building and to promote health through postural variation.

One thing that is missing in the coworking space is a means of integrating with the surrounding community. Currently the space is closed to the public and access is controlled with magnetic key cards. Only once a month—during an art and street festival—is the space opened to the public. While this event is a nice gesture to the arts community, the festival is not representative of the entire Oakland community.

Just two doors down from the site, a small office houses a nonprofit that works to help young adults in underserved communities complete college and earn degrees. This proximity begs for some kind of collaborative coordination either in the form of free access to meeting rooms or through more structured interaction between the two user groups through classes or tutoring. The restaurant on the 1st floor could be redesigned to facilitate these ideas: first, the restaurant space could be integrated into the coworking business by including meeting rooms in the rear of the restaurant that are available to both the tenants of the Workspace and to the broader public. Second, the integration of the workspace and restaurant would add a casual environment—a "third space"—for further collaboration and information sharing to occur.[12]

Comparison

Initially, the changes that I proposed for this site were mostly functional; for example, adding a large format printer, a green screen, and equipment library. The rationale behind this initial proposal was to expand the tenant possibilities to different types of startup companies that had a need for expensive equipment for their operation. Now that I have a better understanding of how the tenants are curated and the working conditions they are accustomed to, I've proposed more substantive changes to the building. These changes include forgoing the site's current plans to install a slide and adding additional coworking desk options that include more standing desks, a room intended for more passive relaxation, and more active uses in the proposed restaurant on the first floor.

Beyond the obvious differences in the final redesign and the initial redesign, the new changes are aimed both inwardly and outwardly. First, my final proposal gives tenants a variety of choices in both where and how to work, rest, and collaborate. Having the option to work either standing or seated, and being able to choose to either actively rest (e.g., play ping pong or socialize) or to passively rest (e.g., sit or lie down and in a quiet space) will lead to positive outcomes for the tenants. Second, my final proposal, by taking into account the broader environment in which the Workspace is situated, increases the probability of chance encounters and opens up knowledge sharing to a larger audience.

Conclusion

In order for a coworking space to be a successful business, it must focus on the needs of its constituent workers. Coworking spaces are continually expanding and changing according to new needs, so the Waterfront Workspace can serve as a model for other spaces to learn from; additionally, I hope that the analysis and proposals I have offered above can point to new directions for successful growth and change. In particular, in my final proposal, I emphasized the opportunity such spaces have in incorporating other local entities—e.g., the restaurant—into their operation. Additional social spaces outside of the work environment can act as spaces of interaction between the surrounding community and the vibrant coworking environment. I feel strongly that in order for this kind of coworking space to benefit more communities, more porous walls are needed to allow new people in.

All told, the Waterfront Workspace has a strong foundation as a coworking business and thus is a model for other industrial coworking environments. For example, with Oakland's growing food industry, shared kitchens are starting to pop-up and food start-ups are gaining more traction every day. These kinds of cooperative models are good ways for businesses with limited resources to get started and thus have the potential to be diverse economic engines for urban development.

References

"Oakland, CA." Sanborn Fire Insurance Map. 1902.

"The Evolution of Silicon Valley—CHM Revolution." www.computerhistory.org. N.p., n.d. Web. 10 Nov. 2013.

Aguiton, Christophe, and Dominique Cardon. "The Strength of Weak Cooperation: An Attempt to Understand the Meaning of Web 2.0." *Communications & Strategies* 65, 1st Quarter 2007 (2007): 51–65.

Baer, Drake. "Why Everybody's Going Freelance." www.fastcompany.com, n.d. Retrieved December 1, 2013.

Baldry, Chris, Peter Bain, and Phil Taylor. "Sick and Tired? Working in the Modern Office." *Work, Employment & Society* (1997): 519–539.

Becattini, Giacomo. *The Marshallian Industrial District as a Socio-Economic Notion*. (Geneva: International Institute for Labour Studies, 1990).

Brookes, Malcom, and Archie Kaplan. "The Office Environment: Space Planning and Affective Behaviour." *Human Factors: The Journal of Human Factors and Ergonomics Society* 14.5 (1972): 373–391.

Deijl, Claudia. *Two Heads Are Better Than One: A Case Study of the Coworking Community in the Netherlands*. (Rotterdam: Erasmus University, 2001).

Feifer, Jason. "Offices For All! Why Open-Office Layouts Are Bad For Employees, Bosses, And Productivity." www.fastcompany.com, n.d. Retrieved November 29, 2013.

Felstead, Alan, Nick Jewson, and Sally Walters. "The shifting locations of work: new statistical evidence on the spaces and places of employment." *Work, Employment and Society* 19, no. 2 (2005): 415–431.

Florida, Richard. "The Rise of the Creative Class." www.washingtonmonthly.com, n.d. Retrieved December 1, 2013.

Frost, Dan. "They're Working on Their Own, Just Side by Side." *New York Times* (February 20, 2008).

Froth, Marcus. *Urban Informatics, Ubiquitous Computing and Social Media for Healthy Cities*. (Brisbane, Queensland, Australia: Urban Informatics Research Lab, Queensland University of Technology, 2011).

Harvey, David. "Flexible Accumulation Through Urbanization: Reflections on 'Post-Modernism' in the American City." *Antipode* 19.3 (1987): 260–286.

Hedge, Alan. "The Open-Plan Office: A Systematic Investigation of Employee Reactions to Their Work Environment." *Environment and Behavior* 14.5 (1982): 519–542.

Leforestier, Anne. *The Co-Working Space Concept.* (Indian Institute of Management, 2009).

Noennig, Jörg Rainer, and Lars Schlenker. "Atmospheres and Socio-spatial Patterns: Designing Hyperspaces for Knowledge Work." In *Distributed, Ambient, and Pervasive Interactions.* Ed. Norbert Streitz and Constantine Stephanidis. Vol. 8028. (Berlin, Heidelberg: Springer Berlin Heidelberg, 2013), 474–483.

Oldenburg, Ray. *The Great Good Place.* (Cambridge, MA: Da Capo Press, 1989).

Salinger, Jordan Harrison. *Economic Development Policies through Business Incubation and Co-Working: A Study of San Francisco and New York City.* (New York: Columbia University, 2013).

Schwartz, Ariel. "You're Not Alone: Most People Hate Open Offices." www.fastcoexist.com, n.d. Retrieved November 29, 2013.

Spinuzzi, C. "Working Alone Together: Coworking as Emergent Collaborative Activity." *Journal of Business and Technical Communication* 26.4 (2012): 399–441.

Thursfield, D. "The Social Construction of Professionalism among Organizers and Senior Organizers in a UK Trade Union." *Work, Employment & Society* 26.1 (2012): 128–144.

Vivant, Elsa. "Creatives in the City: Urban Contradictions of the Creative City." *City, Culture and Society* 4.2 (2013): 57–63.

Webber, Lauren. "More Workers Choose Independence—At Work." www.WSJ.com. Retrieved December 1, 2013.

Wells, Meredith M. "Office Clutter or Meaningful Personal Displays: The Role of Office Personalization in Employee and Organizational Well-Being." *Journal of Environmental Psychology* 20.3 (2000): 239–255.

Appendix

Table 8.1 Interview transcription and coding

Interview	*Data analysis*	*Vocabulary*
Q: So you've already told me a little bit about the space when I came for the tour last time. But why don't you tell me a little bit about what your day looks like? What's sort of a normal day for you here? A: Making sure there is coffee and the dishes are done is probably the most important thing. Beyond that we have to take care of all the sales and marketing stuff for the building. For instance, we realized that we did not have an events management process for when we have events. So today, I had to start putting that together. Other than that, I set up tours and get leases together for people.	Open offices are available for anyone to use.	Coffee & dishes Sales Marketing Events management
Q: Last time I was here, both you and the owner mentioned that some people were territorial and some were social. What did you mean by that? A: Well, we notice that some people work differently than others. Like, some want to have their own office space, with their own desks and storage, and other are fine with working out in the coworking spaces.	The main office has a more neutral color scheme and was first coworking space in the company. The Merritt House is still being finished and not all of the spaces are occupied yet. A proposed slide would connect the 2nd and 3rd floors.	Territorial vs. social

(Continued)

Table 8.1 continued

Interview	*Data analysis*	*Vocabulary*
Q: Do you notice different people making those kinds of decisions on where they will work in the space? A: Well, if there are unleased offices, the coworkers are free to go work in there so if someone wanted to work in a more private setting, they'd have that option as long as there is an open office. So there is a level of sorting that is involved with that.	Rather than a differentiation between the types of workers who choose to work in the open vs. work in a private office, some differentiation may occur between the decision of which building to work in.	Open Private
Q: So you've showed me both of the buildings. What are the differences between the two? A: The main office, by design, is the cleaner, more professional, mellow space and this building [the Merritt Building] is a more lively, playful environment.	Entry to both buildings is via a magnetic key card. The card will open the doors to both buildings and different leases allow access at different days and times	Cleaner Professional Mellow Lively Playful
Q: Hence the slide . . . A: Yea that's why we have the slide in this building.		Slide
Q: Do you find that people sort themselves by building then? A: Definitely. Between the buildings there is a level of sorting. The people in the main office have long term leases on private spaces and typically have a more professional vibe.		Long Term Leases Private Space Professional Vibe
Q: What sort of hours do people come in? Is it different between the buildings? A: Coworkers usually come in between 10–11 and office tenants usually come in between 8–9.		Coworking vs. Private Office
Q: I noticed that most of the desks are moveable . . . A: Yea, most of the desks are moveable, but they're temporary. Since we are going to have more events, we need to be able to change the space to make room for that. (New tenant comes in to sign a lease; interview ends)		Moveable Desks Temporary Events

Notes

1 Dan Frost, "They're Working on Their Own, Just Side by Side," *New York Times*, February 2008.
2 Richard Florida, "The Rise of the Creative Class." www.washingtonmonthly.com. N.d. Web. Retrieved 1 Dec. 2013.
3 David Harvey, "Flexible Accumulation Through Urbanization: Reflections on 'Post-Modernism' in the American City," *Antipode* 19, no. 3, 1987, 269.
4 Cf: Dan Frost, "They're Working on Their Own, Just Side by Side," 2008; Anne Leforestier, *The Co-Working Space Concept*, Indian Institute of Management, 2009; and Christophe

Aguiton and Dominique Cardon, "The Strength of Weak Cooperation: An Attempt to Understand the Meaning of Web 2.0," *Communications & Strategies* 65 (1st Quarter), 51–65.

5 Claudia Deijl, *Two Heads Are Better Than One: A Case Study of the Coworking Community in the Netherlands*, Erasmus University Rotterdam, 2001.

6 Cf: Chris Baldry, Peter Bain, and Phil Taylor, "Sick and Tired? Working in the Modern Office," *Work, Employment & Society*, 1997, 519–539; and Malcolm Brookes and Archie Kaplan, "The Office Environment: Space Planning and Affective Behaviour," *Human Factors: The Journal of Human Factors and Ergonomics Society,* 14, no.5, 1972, 373–391.

7 Cf: Alan Hedge, "The Open-Plan Office: A Systematic Investigation of Employee Reactions to Their Work Environment" *Environment and Behavior,* 14, no. 5, 1982, 519–542; Ariel Schwartz, "You're Not Alone: Most People Hate Open Offices," www.fastcoexist.com, n.d.; Jason Feifer, "Offices For All! Why Open-Office Layouts Are Bad For Employees, Bosses, And Productivity," www.fastcompany.com, n.d.

8 Alan Felstead, Nick Jewson, and Sally Walters, "The shifting locations of work: new statistical evidence on the spaces and places of employment," *Work, Employment and Society* 19, no. 2, 2005, 415–431.

9 Jordan Harrison Salinger, *Economic Development Policies through Business Incubation and Co-Working: A Study of San Francisco and New York City*, New York: Columbia University, 2013.

10 Elsa Vivant, "Creatives in the City: Urban Contradictions of the Creative City." *City, Culture and Society* 4, no. 2, 2013, 57–63.

11 Cf: Drake Baer, "Why Everybody's Going Freelance," www.fastcompany.com/3017222/leadership-now/why-everybodys-going-freelance, retrieved January 4, 2016, and Lauren Webber, "More Workers Choose Independence—At Work", *Wall Street Journal,* http://blogs.wsj.com/atwork/2013/09/10/more-workers-choose-independence/, retrieved January 4, 2016.

12 Ray Oldenburg, *The Great Good Place*, Cambridge, MA: Da Capo Press, 1989.

MEGAN LANDES, "YOU ARE NOW ENTERING A SCI-FI BOOKSTORE: GETTING LOST IN THE WORLD OF SCIENCE FICTION & FANTASY," 2014

Introduction

This semantic ethnography investigates a space using a combination of observations and semantic interviews to obtain a holistic understanding of a cultural group at a site, and uses this understanding as the foundation of a comprehensive redesign of that space. The resulting redesign proposal is not meant to be purely functional or aesthetic, but rather to follow a more human-centered approach to creating a space that celebrates the micro-culture that uses it. I chose to study the science fiction and fantasy book fanatics who frequent a bookstore called Fantasy Books.

Welcome to Fantasy Books

Founded in 1976, Fantasy Books occupies an unassuming location nestled between a comic book store and a local market; together these shops comprise a single block on one side of a busy street that receives relatively little foot traffic. Though Fantasy Books has faced some economic challenges over the years, it has managed to stay open due to the efforts and loyalty of its regular customers: the sci-fi fanatics of the local area.

One of the reasons I was initially attracted to Fantasy Books was that it was strikingly different from any other bookstore I had ever been to: it felt less like a bookstore and more like a small portal to a time and place far from the quaint shops nearby. I am an avid reader and have always loved the science fiction and fantasy genres. Fantasy Books has an unconventional appearance from the outside, giving it intriguing curb appeal. I run by the store a few times a week, but had never been inside. I was fascinated by the space and eager to learn more about it.

Visiting the space

After selecting Fantasy Books as my site, I conducted an hour-long observation of the bookstore. During this time, I entered the store and did my best not to let it be known that I was conducting an observation so as to not affect the behavior of the people I was observing. I imitated the behavior of the patrons of the bookstore, slowly milling around the bookshelves and taking note both of the objective aspects of the store and my own more subjective impressions.

Description and first impressions

Both the inside and the outside of the shop give the impression that it's perpetually decorated for Halloween. The outside features an enormous inflatable black cat, and the inside is extremely unkempt. It seems as though there is no kind of regular cleaning, nor any kind of system of organization. Packaging supplies set out in a nook in the front of the store look as if someone had been working and abandoned their progress halfway through without having bothered to clean anything up.

Because the store is so cramped with shelves, patrons have nowhere to sit and hardly anywhere to step as they make their way through the store. The small amount of available floor space is shared between people and books. Little toys and games are also sold in the store, and are simply nailed haphazardly into the wood of the bookshelves.

Each of the customers I observed stayed for at least 15 minutes; of the 6 customers in the store during my observation, 4 remained for the entire duration of my stay (~1 hour). Most customers perused the entire store before either leaving or purchasing books. The customers that bought books typically purchased more than one. The shopkeeper didn't offer help to anyone, but was not unfriendly; it seemed as though he simply did not want to disturb them. I found it easy to spend an hour walking through the bookstore and go fairly unnoticed by both the customers and the shopkeeper. My initial impression was that Fantasy Books is an environment that encourages people to get lost in their own world, far from the normal rules and regulations of the outside world. This seemed very fitting for a science fiction bookstore.

Experts say: an insider's perspective

Based on my observations, I deduced that the best informant would be an employee of the bookstore rather than a regular customer. The bookstore occupies an extremely unconventional space, and it seemed more likely that an employee would be able to shed more light on why the bookstore is the way it is than a regular customer would. I chose the owner and founder of the store as my informant, as he is knowledgeable about the history and the inner workings of the bookstore and also bears witness to the everyday happenings of Fantasy Books.

Meeting my informant

I asked the man behind the counter if I could speak to him about the space. He obliged but told me that Tom, the owner, was next door at the comic book shop, which he also owns. I walked next door and asked if I could chat with Tom about Fantasy Books, and he agreed. I explained that I had chosen to study his bookstore for a project because the space had caught my interest.

When I told Tom that I was hoping to be able to conduct a study of how the space was used with the intent of creating a successful redesign, he was enthusiastic about the prospect of making a few informed changes to the site. We walked back to the bookstore to do the interview so he could show me around.

Tom is an excellent source of information because he has spent every day at the store for the last few decades. The original founder of Fantasy Books, Tom is intimately familiar with the history and the culture of the bookstore. Further, given his daily presence at the shop, Tom is also able to discuss the demographics of customers, their patterns of behavior, and the overall performance of the bookstore in terms of the things that work well and the things he would like to improve.

Conducting an interview

To begin our conversation, I asked Tom how he felt about being in the store every day. From there, I asked questions to hone in on specific things Tom mentioned in order to encourage him to further elaborate his perspective and, in so doing, help deepen my understanding of the space. Despite being reserved, Tom was responsive to my questions and quickly began leading the conversation. He even went so far as to lead me around the shop to explain which features he liked and others he thought were noteworthy. Tom works at Fantasy Books seven days a week and was open to my inquiries and curious about my project.

Findings

On the origin of the store

Fantasy Books was born when Tom was just 21. Tom had worked in a sci-fi bookstore while he attended college and opened this store, Fantasy Books, shortly after graduating. After moving the store a number of times, Tom ended up in the current location, where the store has stayed ever since. Tom had originally bought a neighboring space for storage, but when he opened up the comic book store, all of the inventory he had stored in the space had to be moved into Fantasy Books. He explained:

> We moved in kind of in a hurry. We did a lot of things we thought would be temporary that just kind of stayed. Like these clip-on lights that have been here for 20 years.

If Tom finds the bookstore's constant clutter in any way charming, he doesn't show it. To Tom, the massive piles of books that line the walls and the floor of Fantasy Books represent a mountain he has been climbing since he opened the bookstore, yet can never seem to summit. The ever-growing list of things to do and inventory to take stock of is overwhelming to Tom, and he views his bookstore with a strange mix of affectionate loyalty and a constant gnawing anxiety that has caused him to throw up his hands and surrender to the sea of incoming books and the natural yet inconsistent ebb and flow of business. Tom reflected:

> It used to be novel that we were a science fiction bookstore. Nowadays we get enough street cred for just being a bookstore in the first place.

Being overwhelmed is a common feeling for my informant. As the owner of Fantasy Books, Tom is not only in charge of handling customers, but also handles managing the inventory and the finances of the bookstore. This leaves little time for organization or advertising, and because Tom spends so much of his time focusing on things that *must* be done, he has no time to focus on the things he hopes for or that he would like to catch up on.

On inventory

When I had asked if Tom had a system for collecting inventory, Tom shook his head. "It's kind of an ebb and flow," he explained. The number of books keeps growing and growing as new orders combine with the inventory of the books previously stored in the comic book shop, the latter of which are always a surprise, as many are titles he ordered more than twenty years ago.

Given this surplus inventory, books end up piled haphazardly on the floor and on shelves with little apparent order. Tom explained: "I have no idea how many books are here. There's no way for me to know." As the years have gone by, the number of science fiction books has risen significantly:

> We used to just get all the science fiction books. There weren't that many back then. Now there's so many . . . the books have kind of outgrown the store.

Because he lacks the time for adequate research on what is or is not good inventory for Fantasy Books, Tom purchases a broad range of titles and ends up with more books than he has space for or reasonably knows what to do with, all in the hopes that someone will stumble upon the bookstore and the books that live there and will find exactly what they're looking for, or maybe something they didn't know they wanted.

On business

Like the inventory, business is inconsistent. Customers generally hear about the store by word of mouth: people who are into science fiction seek it out and tell their friends, and loyal customers keep coming year after year. Still, others just walk by. Tom explained: "We lose people who are really Type A. They walk in, walk out and never come back again." Fantasy Books' business is highly volatile and depends largely on the loyalty of its customers. The natural ups and downs of business have been a major source of worry for Tom, who takes little comfort in the fact that business has maintained itself just enough to keep the store from closing. He said: "Sometimes business is good. Sometimes it's desperate. But it's always enough to keep us from closing." Fantasy Books has the advantage of being a niche market; it appeals to a certain type of reader who may not find satisfaction in any other kind of bookstore. Regulars come in and spend hours getting lost in the maze of shelves and titles, and usually leave with a sizable pile of books. However, with this comes the consequence that the people who come in with regularity don't come in very often because it takes a considerable amount of time for them to make their way through the books they purchase before returning to purchase more.

On the space

The physical space itself is unconventional: "The building itself is kind of funky. It was built during the WWII era, and they had to use what they could get." Tom's favorite feature of the store is the skylight. He works at Fantasy Books every day, and despite wanting a day off, likes spending so much of his time in the space. "I try to draw people to the back of the store, but it's hard," he says.

Tom has ideas and visions for Fantasy Books that he acknowledges will probably never be realized: he is so preoccupied with keeping the store in business and maintaining the bookstore as it is that he simply does not have the time nor the money to invest in making the changes he would like to see in the bookstore, or to fully carry out the tasks he began when he first opened Fantasy Books:

> I had a vision for the space when we first got here, but it was different from I had thought. It was narrower, and I had thought I could do things with the shelves that I can't. There were a lot of things we just didn't get around to.

Fantasy Books encompasses many features that were meant to be temporary and ended up becoming permanent more or less by accident. On the first day we spoke, Tom pointed out some clip-on lights that had originally been put in place as a sort of makeshift means of lighting the bookshelves (see quote, above). Twenty years later, the same lights are still in the same place. Tom made the store's bookshelves himself, but arranged them without much thought as to how the space would be used. When the store originally opened, the shelves were made out of necessity, because there were none. However, as business got going, Tom never saw an opportune time to reevaluate the use or the placement of the shelves in the bookstore, nor time to correct the shelves that he had put in a way he didn't particularly like. Similarly, the store's inventory organization scheme also was more or less thrown together with the intention of eventually becoming more organized and systematic; yet, as is the case with the other elements of the bookstore, time seemed to get away from Tom and the store's system of organization has stayed more or less unorganized.

Tom finds consolation in that the bookstore is organized in the way that Ray Bradbury, one of the most revered science fiction writers of all time, would have thought appropriate. This is especially fitting because the bookstore gets its name from one of Ray Bradbury's anthologies.

On the people in the space

Many customers are regulars, and a number stumble upon the shop because of sheer curb appeal. Customers are content to come in and get lost in the sea of semi-categorized sci-fi novels, though Tom says he is "surprised people don't sit down and spend the afternoon reading in there." The chair at the front of the shop is little used by customers, perhaps due to its location.

Crowds—and thus events—are difficult to accommodate in the store. "We used to have authors come in and sit there to do book signings," Tom explained. Yet:

> They don't really come anymore [because] the line goes out the door. The space is a little cramped, it's not really ideal for that sort of thing . . . Some bookstores have staging areas for things like that. We would have to buy out the building next door, and that would take a lot of money and a lot of time.

All things considered, Tom knows that there are others who deeply appreciate Fantasy Books, and for this he is grateful. Tom is kind and friendly to all who pass through, whether they are a curious browser or an everyday regular, and is happy to see the same fondness he feels for Fantasy Books reflected in the people he created the store for. This is what keeps him coming back every morning.

For people like Tom and the regulars, Fantasy Books is a haven. They feel comfortable there, spending hours amidst the disarray of books and morbid toys that come with little to no regularity nor reason. It is a place that functions without the rules and order of the outside world, which is only fitting of a store that specializes in science fiction, a genre that characteristically tells of new worlds that work differently than our current one, or the future based on the consequences of our current social structure. It may also explain why people who are so drawn to that genre feel so at home there.

The sense of belonging that Tom feels at Fantasy Books is at odds with the constant pressure he feels to be doing something to better organize and maintain or promote the bookstore. This creates a perpetual sense of conflict: he feels at home in Fantasy Books and at the same time feels like he can't escape it. For Tom, Fantasy Books is both his corner of the universe and a force that holds him hostage: he is at the mercy of the natural ebbs and flows of business and inventory and despite his best efforts, has more or less resigned to the fact that he is powerless against the unpredictable but miraculously always sufficient tides of customers and merchandise. That is not to say that Tom doesn't love his bookstore; he does. He has spent every day there since the day he opened it. "It's my little place in the universe," he explained.

Analysis

After conducting my interview with Tom, I analyzed my notes to identify key words. A diagram of common words and phrases is in Figure 1; these words are arranged taxonomically in Figure 2.

What experts say: the outsider's perspective (literature review)

To further understand this site, I researched what experts had to say about three topics: understanding bookstore challenges and successes, understanding science fiction, and understanding systems of business organization. I felt that these three disciplines would help both broaden and deepen my understanding of the way Fantasy Books works now and how it could become more successful.

Life as a successful independently owned bookstore

Bookstores that succeed in an age where almost everything can be bought on Amazon or downloaded electronically are those that afford their customers an experience that they can't get online.[1] Typically, this looks like the ability to meander through the store, maybe dip in off the street on a whim, and enjoy the experience of book browsing. Fantasy Books does an excellent job at providing any bookworm with an experience they definitely would not be able to find online; the journey of hunting through the thousands of titles is theirs to make on their own.

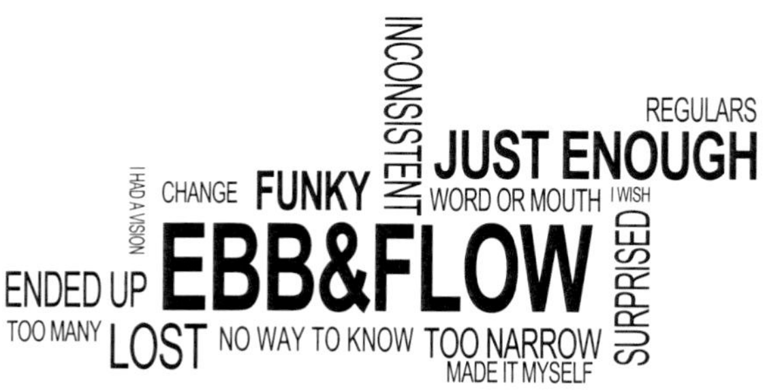

Figure 1 Words and phrases frequently used by Tom to describe Fantasy Books

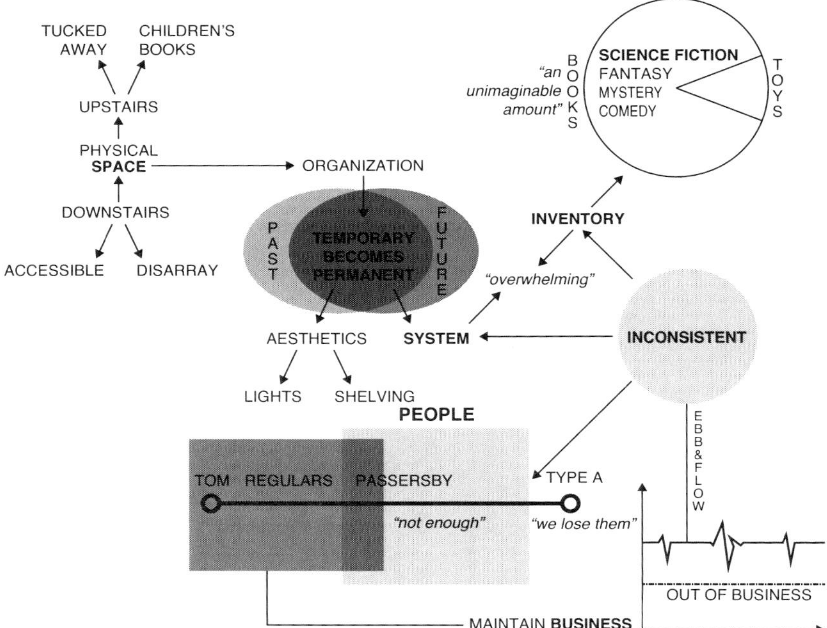

Figure 2 Taxonomy of key terms

Science Fiction and the West

The West, specifically, is especially drawn to science fiction according to a study published in *The Atlantic*.[2] According to the article, a remarkably high percentage of movies about magic or some genre of fantasy top the list of most successful movies in Hollywood. In other major movie industries, this is not so. The theory behind this is that the West has become disenchanted; it is starved for a little bit of magic:

> Because of modern science, a rise in secularism, an impersonal market economy, and government administered through bureaucracies rather than bonds of loyalty, Western societies perceived the world as knowably rational and systematic, leading to a widespread loss of a sense of wonder and magic.[3]

Thus, we fill that gap with science fiction and fantasy and the supernatural. Science fiction has another draw: As humanity and technology become more and more intermixed, science fiction becomes more relevant (relatable) to a broader range of readers.[4]

Being remarkable

Still, Fantasy Books is not for everyone. The store caters to a specific demographic of person: a science-fiction and fantasy lover who is comfortable in chaos. This, however, may not be detrimental to business; in fact, it may actually help. Seth Godin argues that today, businesses that cater to the masses are in danger of being unsuccessful because they become white noise. The way to have a successful business or idea, he argues, is to stand out. He calls this idea being "remarkable," or "worth remarking about." Businesses can do this by catering to a very specific group of people. The specific group of people that business people cater to spreads the word about the business in and among itself and thus perpetuates business.[5] Fantasy Books does a good job of successfully catering to a specific demographic and propagating word of the bookshop to other science fiction fanatics that also feel at home in the maze of sci-fi titles that bring the space to life.

From a business standpoint, a very specific target demographic is also beneficial because it reduces competition and makes it easier to promote the product or service your audience finds appealing.

Personal perspective

Upon entering and taking myself on a quick tour of the store, two things stuck out in my mind: the haphazardness with which the toys and other merchandise were simply nailed to the plain wood of the bookshelves, and the sheer magnitude of books. Because I had never been inside the store, I had thought maybe they were lying on the ground in such great quantities because the store was going through a redesign or a renovation. It was only after speaking with Tom that I came to understand that the disorganized state of the store is fairly constant and that the store is perpetually designing itself.

Speaking with Tom left me more deeply intrigued with the bookstore than I had been even after my initial site visit because of how linked the past is with the present. Fantasy Books is, in many ways, still living in its own past while the present and the future invade the space that was designed for the Fantasy Books of the 1970s.

After observing Fantasy Books I couldn't get it out of my mind. The quiet chaos of the bookstore is somehow magnetic, akin to the experience of getting lost: meandering through the maze of shelves and exploring books that seem placed without any rhyme or reason is a unique experience. I spent most of my time there wondering to myself, "How can it be that a place like this exists and operates and maintains itself?" It's as if the bookstore has a heartbeat and a life force of its own.

As I thought about the redesign, I realized the need to focus not on making the bookstore operate like a more standard store, but rather to find ways to celebrate its idiosyncrasies and to emphasize the already unique experience of hunting for books in Fantasy Books.

The redesign

Initial redesign

Instead of redesigning the space to be more organized, I decided that the idea behind the initial redesign should be to highlight the "lost-in-a-sea-of-science-fiction" feeling that Fantasy Books exudes. Because customers seemed more than content to almost aimlessly browse through the chaos and clutter of books, I thought creating a more maze-like environment would heighten the experience of meandering through the shelves and exploring the thousands of titles. My initial redesign aimed to cater to more stagnant behavior based on the way people had behaved in the space, as opposed to facilitating movement through the space.

Final redesign

Though I did attempt to account for the cultural nuances of Fantasy Books and for the natural movement of people in my initial redesign, my research illuminated the shortcomings of this proposal. Though my first proposal featured a maze-like arrangement of the bookshelves meant to accentuate the feeling of getting lost amidst the seemingly endless science fiction titles that customers seem to enjoy, this design did little to ease Tom's troubled mind, as it arguably would have made keeping track of inventory more chaotic than it already is.

The primary elements of my proposed redesign are as follows:

- **Communicating value:** One of the things that came up in my conversations with Tom was that I found myself reassuring him again and again that the customers do appreciate Fantasy Books for what it is and that they don't expect it to be like other bookstores. In fact, they like it because it isn't like other bookstores. To take steps toward remedying this, I decided to make one of the back walls of the upstairs children's section into a chalkboard wall where people are encouraged to write down book recommendations and scribble or sketch whatever comes to mind. This serves a number of purposes: the first is to draw people upstairs, a long-time goal of Tom's. Second, this resource can help people direct their searches and encourages the buying of books in the bookstore rather than just browsing and then ordering online. If customers feel they are more fully integrated into the bookstore and through this communication with their fellow sci-fi readers, customers may feel more integrated in (and therefore loyal to) Fantasy Books.
- **Maintaining the ecosystem:** A recommendation wall would also allow the bookstore to be slightly more self-maintaining. If customers are recommending books to each other, it helps them navigate through the titles so Tom doesn't have to. Such a system would engage patrons in a new way, meanwhile creating a record to remind Tom that the store is indeed beloved. Further, the chalkboard could be photographed and posted online every day so there is always room for more recommendations, and also allows fans of Fantasy Books to delight in scrolling through past collections of the unique murals that are newly recreated each day, perhaps searching for a new recommendation or a thrill of seeing their own words be immortalized on the internet. The aspect of "shareability" that these pictures would offer also present a potential for advertising, something Fantasy Books does none of now and is another source of stress for Tom.
- **Sittable spaces:** Tom mentioned during our first conversation that he was surprised that almost no one stopped to sit and read in the bookstore despite spending great quantities of time meandering around the store. His comment surprised me: with no places to sit in the bookstore, I wondered where Tom expected people to stop to sit and read. Thus, another aspect of the redesign of Fantasy Books is to take a nod from William Whyte and add sittable spaces throughout the shop.[6] This will be done in two ways: first, by adding reading chairs on both floors, and second, by converting part of the staircase into sittable space.
- **Entering the land of books:** To accommodate the ever-growing inventory of books, I propose adding arched bookshelf doorways; doing so would both create more storage opportunities and heighten the feeling of entering a new place. In my final proposal, I propose the same maze-like layout I envisioned in my original

redesign; yet in this iteration I aim to enhance the feeling of being welcomed to meander around and lose oneself in the shop's vast collection of books.

Conclusion

Learning how to look at a space through perspectives other than my own has brought me closer to understanding what it means to understand a space and the elements that make it successful. Though aesthetics and functionality play a role in making a design successful, perhaps more important is the extent to which these elements symbolically celebrate the culture of the people who use the space.

Studies of spaces similar to Fantasy Books may note that the best solution is not always the most obvious one. The most obvious change that could be made to Fantasy Books is to come up with a better system of organization to clear the clutter off of the floor and other available surfaces, which would also simplify the process of finding books. However, this change would not necessarily be a successful one because it detracts from the culture of the place and could potentially take away the feeling that draws so many to Fantasy Books and keeps them there.

Bookstore and other small business owners might be encouraged by the success of Fantasy Books as a small, independent bookstore in a decidedly digital age. Fantasy Books has demonstrated its ability to coexist with large online retailers like Amazon. In fact, I believe the store's success is due largely to the unique experience it promises each of its visitors, an experience not available online.

Exploring the different facets of Fantasy Books has been extremely rewarding. When I had first observed the site, everything about it seemed fragmented and logistically unsustainable, but still there was something about the bookstore that drew me, and enough consistent customers to stay in business, inside. Because of (not in spite of) its long-standing clutter and sheer lack of organization or efficiency, Fantasy Books has forever won a place in my heart.

References

Bacon-Smith, Camille. *Science Fiction Culture*. (Philadelphia, PA: University of Pennsylvania Press, 2000).

Bukatman, Scott. *Terminal Identity: The Virtual Subject in Postmodern Science Fiction*. Fifth ed. (Durham, NC: Duke University Press, 2002).

D., G. "A Real Cliffhanger." *The Economist*. 27 Feb. 2013.

Hall, Edward T. *The Silent Language*. (Garden City, NY: Doubleday & Co., 1959).

Folch, Christine. "Why the West Loves Sci-Fi and Fantasy: A Cultural Explanation." *The Atlantic*. 13 June 2013.

Godin, Seth. *Purple Cow: Transform Your Business by Being Remarkable*. (New York: Portfolio, 2003).

Leonard, Andrew. "The Independent Bookstore Lives! Why Amazon's Conquest Will Never Be Complete." *Salon*. 4 Apr. 2014.

"Media and Imagination: A Short History of American Science Fiction." *MIT Communications Forum*. Web. 16 Oct. 2014.

Whyte, William. "Sitting Space." In *The Social Life of Small Urban Spaces*. (Project for Public Spaces, 1980), p. 24–39.

Notes

1 G. D., "The Future of the Bookstore: A Real Cliffhanger" *The Economist Newspaper,* 27 Feb. 2013.
2 Christine Folch, "Why the West Loves Sci-Fi and Fantasy: A Cultural Explanation." *The Atlantic,* 13 June 2013.
3 Ibid.
4 Scott Bukatman, *Terminal Identity: The Virtual Subject in Postmodern Science Fiction.* 5th ed. (Durham, NC: Duke UP, 2002).
5 Seth Godin, *Purple Cow: Transform Your Business by Being Remarkable,* (New York: Portfolio, 2003).
6 William Whyte, "Sitting Space." In *The Social Life of Small Urban Spaces.* (Project for Public Spaces, 1980), p. 24–39.

DOUGLAS LOOK, "A MARTIAL ARTS SCHOOL," 1990

Introduction

Because of China's increasing presence on the global stage, Americans have a new awareness of and interest in Chinese culture. One element of Chinese culture whose expression in popular culture has been more fictional than factual is the practice of *kung-fu*. This ancient practice has gained increasing attention in modern popular culture, with the legendary Bruce Lee leading the way, and unfortunately creating a new Asian stereotype in the process: the Chinese superman.

Today in the United States, *kung-fu* schools, studios, or *kwoons*, have become increasingly numerous. These schools can take a range of forms. Some schools, motivated primarily by commercial profit, cater to ever-changing fads in an attempt to increase enrollment of paying students. For example, these schools, noting the rising popularity of *kung-fu* in recent years, have switched the signs outside of their school to advertise karate *and kung-fu*. Other schools, often led by a teacher who is dedicated to promoting his art, emphasize the practice itself, even at the expense of monetary gain.

Martial arts schools draw a diverse range of students who together form a special micro-culture. Though they all share an interest in the art, students enroll in martial arts programs for different reasons. Regardless of their motivations, however, all students of the martial arts must learn new types of vocabulary, both mental and physical.

Site introduction

I chose to study the School of Internal Martial Arts because it seemed to be a school in which the teacher is dedicated to and interested in his students. In fact, the school has only one teacher—or *sifu*—who is considered the master. The teacher, Master C., has studied the martial arts for over 30 years. He has dedicated his life to the mastery and teaching of *kung-fu* and thus has much to offer his students. In addition to his expertise in the martial arts, Master C. also is a painter of Chinese brush painting and calligraphy.

Students are taught at both individual and group levels: classes are held at the group level, but Master C. personally corrects and teaches students one-by-one. The distinguishing factor of this school, as compared to other martial arts schools, is the character and proficiency of Master C. In this school, combat applications are de-emphasized, while philosophical explanations are given for each technique.

This school also emphasizes the integration of both mental and physical aspects of the human body: each is equally important in the practice of *kung-fu*. To me, the possibility to design an environment to accommodate this kind of integrated experience is a welcome challenge.

Entry into the micro-culture

My entry into the site was not too difficult, as I had previously visited the school. My familiarity with the site helped me feel comfortable at the site and also aided me in finding willing informants.

The range of people at the school is notable. One way to group students is by the length of time they have practiced at the school. People who have been at the school since its inception in 1973 are now considered "staff" since they have learned enough to instruct others. Students refer to these people as "assistants." From here down the hierarchy, people are distinguished by how long they have been practicing at the site and by how diligent their practice is.

I wanted to choose an informant who could represent the culture and who could articulate their ideas for me in a clear, concise manner. To better aid my understanding of the site, in addition to conducting focused interviews with my informants, I also took time to talk and socialize more informally with other students. Ultimately, I interviewed three informants.

One informant, Sutton, is a 26-year-old male who has been studying *t'ai chi* for about three years. He is an assistant and also continues to learn from Master C. Another male, Adam, who recently completed a Ph.D. in mathematics, has been practicing *t'ai chi* for approximately nine months. Although Adam has been at the school for a relatively short period of time, he has studied diligently every day and is considered an assistant by students. My third informant, Annie, is a Chinese woman, about 24 years old. Annie has been with the school since it was started. She has been studying *kung-fu* for three or four years. She enjoys the community the school offers.

I initiated conversations with my informants with ease and established a good rapport with each of them. To introduce my project, I simply pointed out that this school was an interesting place and that I would like to propose a redesign based on what I learned from interviewing students. My goal for the design, I explained, would be to envision a space conducive to the needs of students and thus was dependent on how well I could understand their needs. My informants seemed curious to learn about my project and interested in what the final design proposal would look like. Not wanting to ask leading questions, I attempted to be subtle and ask open-ended questions, such as a "grand tour" question. In my opinion, my rapport and entry into this scene were successful, and the conversations I had with my informants felt relaxed. Based on these interviews, I was able to learn a lot of information about the site, its various users and their motivations for attending the school, and the range of activities in which students engage; main findings are summarized in the tables of taxonomies.

Table 1 Different types of martial arts

Internal	*T'ai chi* *Pa kua* *Hsing yee*
External	*Shaolin* White crane Praying mantis

Table 2 Taxonomy of activities

Practicing martial arts	Practicing *t'ai chi* Practicing *shaolin*
Teaching and learning	*t'ai chi* *Shaolin*
Socializing	Talking with friends Attending lectures Potluck dinners Dinners cooked by students Meditation Watching movies

Table 3 Taxonomy of roles

Teacher (*sifu*)	Master C.
Assistants	Students who attend daily; diligent students who have practiced over one year; students with special devotion
Students	Beginning students in new classes Intermediate students Advanced students Assistants
Visitors	People observing People interested in learning Out of curiosity

Table 4 Taxonomy of rooms of the school

Main room	Main entrance Windows Mirrors Opening to small room Room one Stretching bar
Small room	Practice room Room two
Staff room	Toilet Shower Kitchen
Teacher's room	Bedroom Dining

Table 5 Taxonomy of reasons for being here

Physical	Getting in shape Good for you Self defense
Mental	Relaxing Integration of physical and mental aspects Calming, a kind of high
Aesthetic	Form looks nice Looks graceful
Cultural	Learning Chinese culture
Social	Meeting others Feeling like a community Enjoy being part of a group Have friends practicing

Description of the present environment

The school building is divided into four major spaces: the large room, the small room, the staff room, and the teacher's private room (see Figure 1).

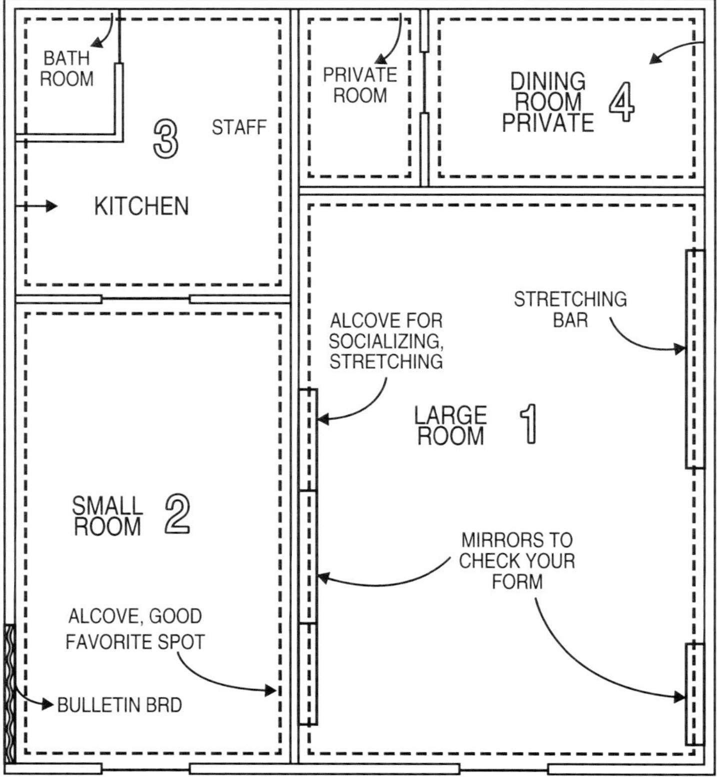

Figure 1 Site plan as-is

The large and small rooms—separate spaces linked by two alcoves in the wall that divides the two—are used as practice areas. Because a wall separates the two rooms, each room is used for a different function, and even the large room is not large enough to comfortably accommodate larger groups.

The staff room's name implies its original planned use: to be limited to certain members of the site. However, because students have no other place to change into their gym clothes aside from the bathroom in the staff area, the space is used by staff and students alike and for a variety of functions. The staff room also includes a kitchen, available to anyone who wants to cook, as long as they keep the place clean. This area should be expanded to better accommodate its many uses.

The teacher's private room consists of both his bedroom and a dining room. This area is private and thus needs to remain separate from the public spaces of the school.

The present environment has made good use of the existing site, yet spatial constraints pose a major challenge. To that end, my initial redesign assumed a larger space (see Figure 2).

Design implications

To guide my final redesign of this space I tried to work with the relationship between spaces, both interior and exterior. My intent was for the spaces to relate well to each other and better accommodate the school's various users and activities. Although the main emphasis of the school is the study and practice of the martial arts, my research indicated an important secondary use: the school as a site of socializing. Besides practicing *kung-fu*, students host pot-luck dinners, lectures, movie nights, and informal conversation. This social function, not anticipated or accounted for in the initial site design, has become an important part of the school and thus needs a spatial correlate; in other words, a space to house these activities.

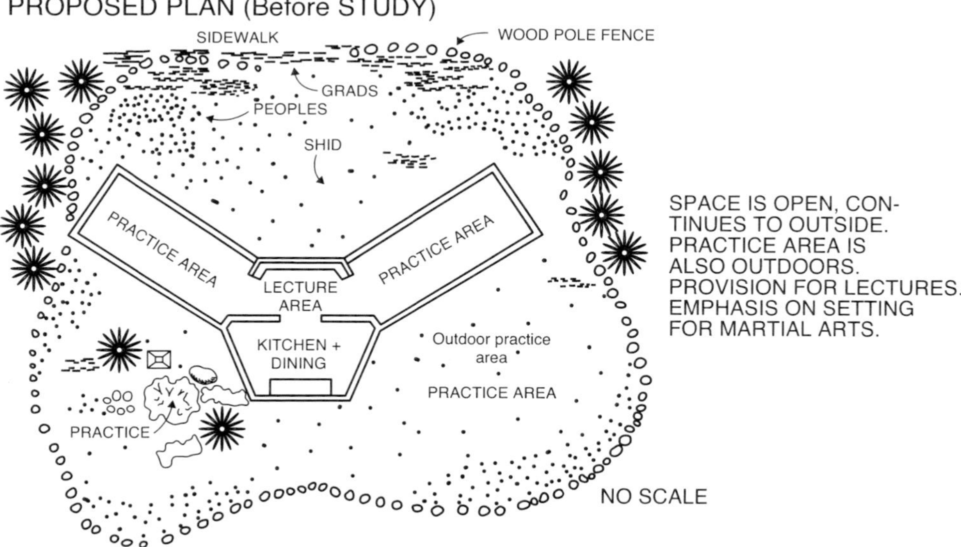

Figure 2 This initial redesign proposal assumes a larger site and extensive use of outdoor spaces

The present environment seems to have maximized the available space. The size of the building and the fact the site is leased (not owned) pose limits for major site changes. I learned in the course of my research that, though many students come from the local area, others come from nearby cities, some more than 10 miles away; thus, the school could (at some point) consider a change to a larger site to better meet the needs of students.

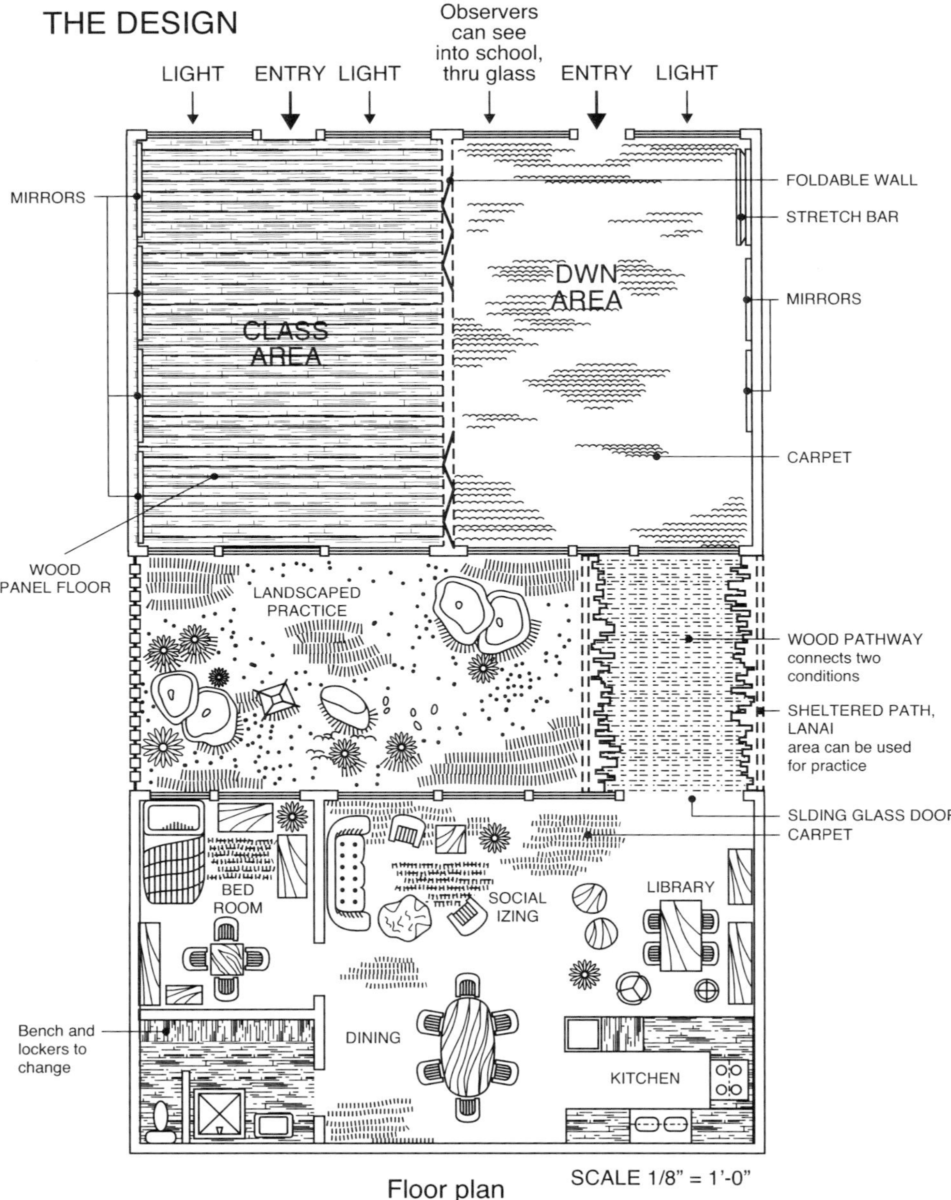

Figure 3 Final redesign proposal

The large and small rooms have become more specialized by use over time: the larger room is used to teach group classes, and the smaller room is reserved for individual practice. Both of these activities must be accounted for in my final redesign.

Finally, my informants explained that when the inside spaces of the school begin to feel too crowded, students go outside to a nearby tennis court for individual practice. The *sifu* encourages this practice because being outside is more invigorating and the air quality is better outside than in. I was inspired by this indoor/outdoor relationship in my final redesign (see Figure 3).

A solution

From the ethnographic data I collected, I identified several unmet needs in the current site design. First, I noted the need for a place in which social activities could be held. In response, I created a large area ("the socializing area") that includes a place to cook, eat, read, or just simply sit down and socialize.

I also proposed the addition of a landscaped area between the two functional parts of the school. This landscaped area provides a nice "change of pace" and a visual contrast with the interior spaces and also can be used for individual practice. This break in the scenery also helps to provide sufficient natural light and ventilation.

One problem with the present school design is that the two practice areas cannot be joined together to create a larger space. Thus, the two spaces are too small to accommodate current enrollment needs. I propose, then, the addition of a "foldable wall" between the two rooms that can be closed off when the two rooms are being used for different purposes or opened to create a unified space.

My design proposal (see Figure 3) is an attempt to unify the school as a whole, yet also be mindful of—and provide specific spaces for—the variety of student needs. In sum, much like *king-fu*'s integration of body and mind, this design solution integrates different functions in its constituent spaces.

Conclusions

As an architecture student I feel that ethnographic research is useful because it encourages designers to understand the position of the user and enables them to obtain direct feedback. Yet an important complement to ethnographic research are the practices of observation and introspection, both of which can illuminate additional insights about the activities and users that define a site.

It is not sufficient, however, to just collect the data: the architect must then translate these ideas into the design of a space. This has direct bearing on the success of the design from the standpoint of its users and also tests a designer's ability to transform abstract ideas into concrete design decisions. Essential to this process is the recognition, by the designer, that she has *translated* the user's ideas into design concepts and thus has engaged in an *interpretive* process. This act of translation is an important and fruitful source of creativity.

MARIANNE MOORE, "FOR WHOM THE BOOTH TOLLS," 1979[1]

Introduction

"New Ethnography" describes a social situation from the point of view of the people in the setting. It is useful for designers in several ways:

1. It takes the point of view of the people who use the environment and thereby balances the tendency to analyze a problem from an outsider's point of view.
2. Semantic ethnography is a distinctive interviewing technique that lends itself to use in ordinary client–designer discussions either in the field or in the office.

This study of the Ocean Bridge Toll Plaza is an example of how the technique can be applied to settings in modern industrial society.

The booths

The toll booths on the Ocean Bridge are small and equipped with a change tray and an axle counting machine. One toll taker sits—facing the oncoming traffic—in each booth. To the left of the toll taker is an open half-door through which she enters and reaches out to take tolls. Behind her are shelves for extra money trays, an electric fan, and a radio. None of the windows open. Consequently, toll takers find it difficult to communicate with each other, yet they engage (over the half-door) with hundreds of patrons each day.

My informant, who has worked at the Ocean Bridge Toll Plaza, said little about the details of her physical work. It's simple: she takes money, counts axles, presses the corresponding button on the axle-counting machine, gives change when necessary, and occasionally issues commute books and passes. The job is monotonous and the booth unremarkable. Instead, according to my informant, the three elements most important to the Toll Plaza are the toll takers, the drivers, and the traffic lanes.

The toll takers

The employees are a diverse group, including Ph.D. candidates in psychology and retired cops. My informant, Sally, who is active in union politics, classifies toll takers according to how they cope with the monotony of the job and how they relate to the public. After the first few months, toll collectors do not have to concentrate much to handle the amazing array of details involved in the job and their work becomes automatic. Sally explains:

> They tell you at the beginning—if you're not sure you've pushed the button on the counting machine after a car has gone by, assume that you have. Assume that it's become so automatic that you did it without thinking.

Toll takers relieve the monotony of the job by listening to the radio—even during rush commute hours when doing so is not allowed—and reading. Sally explains how she finds points of interest:

> There's *always* something to watch, even if it's just things in the back seat or faces. You get to recognize regulars and talk to them too. There's an awful lot of eye contact with one car coming by every three seconds. I try to connect to the people even if it's just to say hello, but it gets exhausting some days. Some of the toll takers won't even acknowledge the customers. They just sit for eight hours taking the money without talking or moving one muscle more than necessary. It's their way of dealing with it.

Most of the toll takers are laid back in their jobs, although some are "eager beavers," according to Sally. A further distinction is friendliness toward drivers; that is, the toll taker's willingness to make human contact with patrons. Sally described her own style:

> Generally, if I'm in a good mood, I try to say something so that people know I'm there. And I won't take money unless they first look at me. I try to be nice, it'd be horrible if I didn't. . . . It may be just for a few seconds, but I see the whole person and can tell a lot from the image they project. But most of all I'm just a hand. It can get you down.

Other toll takers feel they must be emotionally removed from their patrons in order to get through the workday.

Being young and very attractive also affects Sally's relation to her work. Suggestions, invitations, and insinuations are always coming her way. A strong sexual undercurrent underlies her dealings with the customers. Perhaps the briefness of the contact makes such things possible—both Sally and her "fans" know not to expect any follow-up from their exchanges. Sally seems to take this all in stride: "I've got to admit it—I get my feminine ego boosted eight hours a day. How many other jobs can offer you that?"

The nature of the work promotes camaraderie among the collectors. "The people I work with are great," Sally said. "If it wasn't for them I wouldn't be able to last here at all." Considering the barriers against developing strong bonds—no means of communication between booths, segregated break rooms, and strict break schedules—the large numbers of interactions and strong group identity among the toll takers is impressive.

Drivers

Patrons run the gamut from truckers to teenage joy riders and are interchangeably referred to by toll collectors as "easy-riders," "tourists," or "people." Truckers are distinctive because of their large, noisy vehicles, and buses merit a separate category because they drive without stopping to pay the toll.

The vehicle alone is not what distinguishes one driver from thousands of others; whether or not the toll taker recognizes him—the "knowns" and the "unknowns"—also distinguishes one driver from the rest. Among the "knowns" are personal friends and "regulars." Regulars are those drivers who have passed by a toll taker often enough for them to be recognized, visually if not also verbally. The toll taker's work detail is such that they are in a different lane of traffic every day. So it is really quite a feat for a driver to hit the same toll taker's lane often enough to become a regular.

Since Sally's shift (6am to 2pm) encompasses the morning commute rush, she has a large number of "regulars," some of whom even jockey for position to ensure that she will be the one to take their toll. But regulars are in the minority: the vast majority of drivers are faceless entities who just drive by, pay their toll, and move on. They are the ones who make the job so routine, who allow Sally to do her crossword puzzles and plan what to have for dinner while taking tolls.

The strongest distinguishing characteristic of drivers is their ability to give the toll correctly. Toll takers have a preferred manner of being handed the money—car at full stop, arm extended completely and hand turned downward so that the money is placed easily in the toll taker's hand. Any deviation from this procedure is considered a "hassle" of varying degrees. The list of hassles is endless. They are usually caused by lack of experience with paying tolls or inattention to the toll taker, but sometimes they are caused by unprovoked malice. Some notable examples of this maliciousness are drivers who burn the coins with a match before handing them to the toll taker, and the driver who purposely and forcefully throws his coins at the toll taker. "I would definitely say this job has lowered my opinion of people," Sally reflected.

The lanes

The booth itself is not as important as the lane of traffic on which it is located. Each toll taker works a different lane every day, and certain lanes are favored over others. Some booths *are* better than others, particularly when it comes to ventilation. The lanes are designated "commute," "regular auto," "truck," and "bus." Lanes are preferred primarily because of the amount of traffic (and corresponding workload) going through them; secondarily for the types of drivers most likely to use that lane; and lastly for the physical condition of the lane or booth.

Most collectors prefer the commute lane because they do not have to actually take toll, but instead only check to see if three or more people are in each car before waving them on. Other collectors prefer the truck lane because they enjoy talking to the truckers who in most cases are regulars. A few others dislike the truck lanes because of the noise and heavier pollution. From these examples one can see that each lane has its good points and bad points, and toll takers perceive them as good or bad according to individual preference.

Design changes

Improved conditions such as improved ventilation, easier communication between booths, better weather protection, noise dampening, and accident protection would positively affect toll takers (see Figure 1 for proposed changes). However, these changes would not completely solve the basic problems of the toll-taking environment, namely its impersonality and boredom. Far more important than an uncomfortable seat or too much sun is that attitude of the public with whom the toll taker comes into contact. The quality of the social interaction between the driver and toll taker and the quality of the work itself needs improvement as much as the booths do. Two points—that the average driver sees the toll taker as little more than an extension of the state highway system and that the work is extremely dull—came up constantly in my interview with Sally.

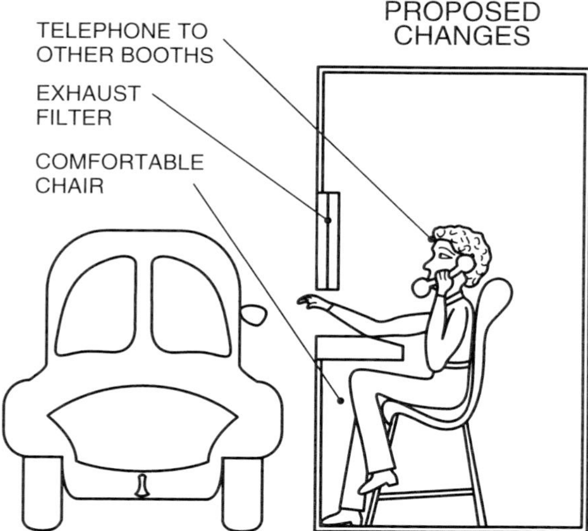

Figure 1 Proposed redesign of the toll booth. Though these design solutions can help to alleviate some of the social and physical stressors faced by toll collectors, the author also suggests broader societal and economic changes

Here I face the quandary of how to better the "spiritual" atmosphere through physical change. I started this project with the objective of redesigning the toll booth and have ended up wanting to change long-held attitudes of the general driving public.

Some physical changes could be implemented to improve the toll taker/driver relations and reduce the impersonality of the contact. For example, lower the toll booth for more eye-to-eye contact. A giant "Love Your Toll Taker" campaign might be more effective, because the contact between drivers and toll takers is so brief that drivers would need to be "preconditioned" with positive attitudes to make those five seconds really pleasant.

I have learned through this project how multi-leveled environmental change is. Physical improvements need to be backed up with attitude changes. And even the changes mentioned would still not solve the problem of the tedium of the job. Upon further reflection, I suggest getting rid of the toll system altogether! Instead, I suggest finding other ways to finance the bridge and relocate the displaced workers into other types of meaningful work.

Note

1 Adapted from Marianne Moore, "For Whom the Booth Tolls," *Concrete*, Vol. 5 No. 3, Feb. 20, 1979.

KAREN OKAZAKI, "A JAPANTOWN HARDWARE STORE," 1982

Introduction

The site I studied is Japantown Hardware, a hardware and appliance store in San Francisco's Japantown. The store is relatively small compared to other buildings on the block, but it carries a great variety of merchandise. Japantown Hardware sells tools, Japanese imports, paint, lumber, patio equipment, household appliances, and much more. The interior consists of three long aisles, a cash register in the middle, an appliance area (with stoves, dryers, refrigerators, and other large appliances), and a small office and storage area upstairs.

Observation and initial redesign

I sat across the street in front of Japantown Hardware, watching the types of people who patronized the store. Tourists frequent Japantown, and a few stopped in front of the store, apparently attracted by the Japanese stone lanterns in the display window. However, not many tourists went into the store. Japantown Hardware is located toward the end of the block and receives few passers-by.

In response to these observations, in my initial redesign I proposed changing the front façade of the store to look more Japanese (for example, with a shingled roof, dark stained lumber, perhaps a small bamboo tree) in order to attract more people—especially tourists—into the store by catching the eye of passers-by.

When I first entered the store I noticed the long, narrow aisles that extended all the way to the rear of the store. The cash register was located in the middle of the store, thereby preventing cashiers from seeing the entire store and its patrons. Given this lack of visibility, I assumed the store had a problem with shoplifting. I decided that moving the cash register to the front of the store and making the floor multi-leveled would

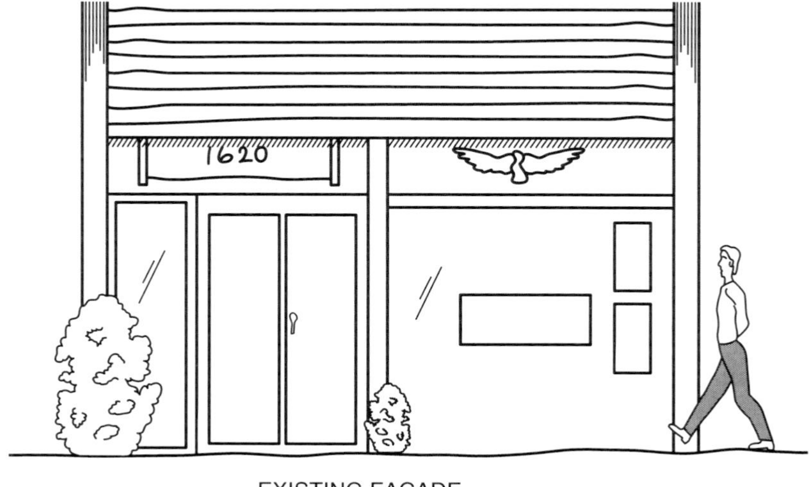

Figure 1 Sketch of façade as-is

Figure 2 Sketch of façade with proposed changes

pose greater barriers to shoplifters trying to evade surveillance. I proposed relocating the cash register to the front of the store, on the first level, where the owner of the store could greet customers. In total, I proposed three levels, each lower than the next, with the cash register at the highest level, looking down at the next two floors.

Additionally, in response to a "buzzing noise" I noticed emanating from the store's fluorescent lights, I proposed to have soft Japanese music playing inside to drown out the noise of the lights.

To summarize, in my first redesign, I proposed to:

- Change the front façade to look more inviting to passers-by (see Figure 2).
- Add Japanese music to mask buzzing noise and also add to the Japantown atmosphere.
- Move the cash register to the front of the store.
- Introduce three levels to discourage potential shoplifters (see Figure 3).

My informant

I selected Mr. Kodama (whom I will refer to as Mr. K.), the owner of Japantown Hardware, as my informant. I decided that he would be the best informant since he has been working at the store for 30 years and therefore knows the most about the activities and user groups that define the store. Mr. K. is approximately 56 years old, not too tall, has "graying" hair, and glasses. He is a very pleasant person. He is always cheerful and greets everyone with a smile and by saying, "How are we doing?" When I asked him to be my informant, he seemed honored and eager to talk.

During my first visit to the store, Mr. K. told me a little about the history of Japantown Hardware. In 1946, he and his three brothers started the business (then called "Kodama Brothers") at a different site in Japantown. In 1962, they moved the business to its present location. Mr. K. became the sole owner of the store in 1967 and changed the name to Japantown Hardware.

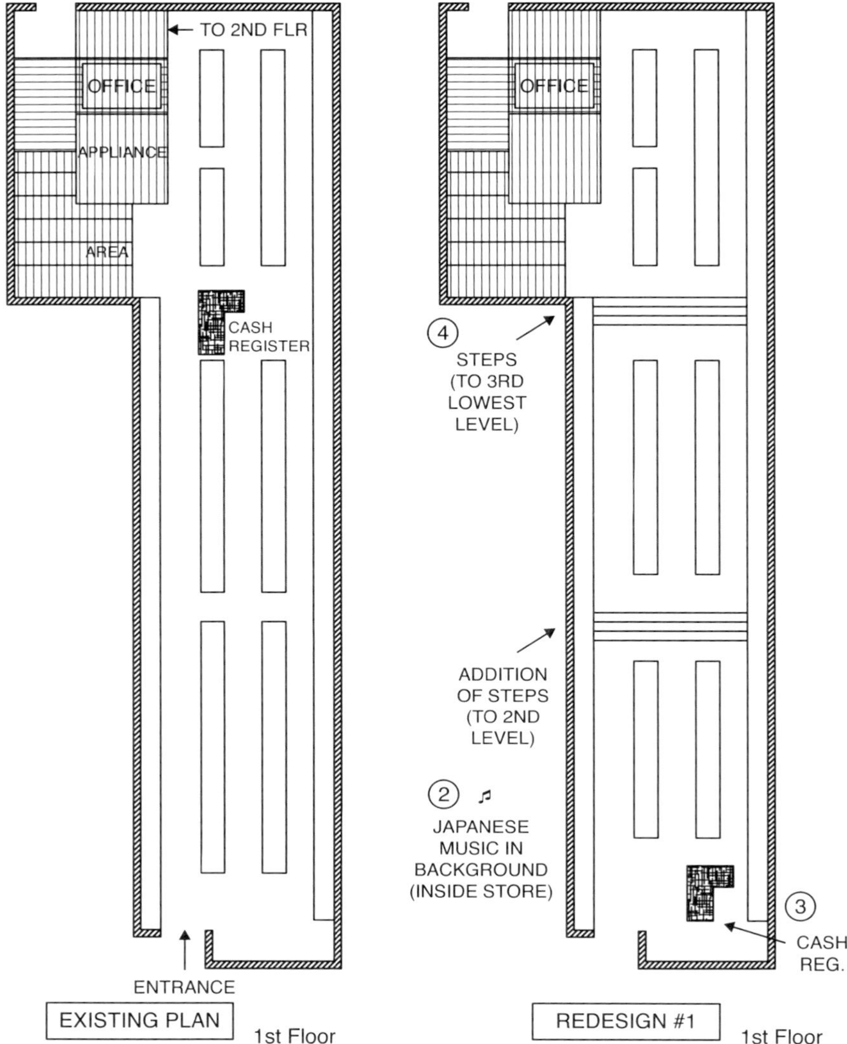

Figure 3 Existing site plan (left) and proposed changes (right)

The interview

I interviewed Mr. K. at his home on a Sunday afternoon. I had previously talked to him very briefly at the store; however, customers kept coming in so I never had the opportunity to talk to him for more than 5 or 10 minutes at a time. Mr. K. suggested that I interview him on one of his days off because he would be more relaxed then and able to give more thought to his answers. This was a gracious offer, though interviewing Mr. K. at home posed unique challenges. At the time I was scheduled to interview Mr. K., he had just finished fixing a broken water pipe in the garage, and he was tired and dirty as a result. Additionally, the L.A./San Antonio game was on T.V. so periodically during the interview he would take a minute off to watch the game.

Despite these minor problems, the interview went well. Below is a summary of what I learned from Mr. K.

Workers

I asked Mr. K. to tell me about the workers in the store. He began by talking a little bit about how a new employee begins his job. Because Japantown Hardware does not have a formal "training program," new workers simply watch others and learn on the job. To Mr. K., observing is the best method of learning.

The eight people who comprise the staff of Japantown Hardware each have specific job duties. First, the two "stock boys"—Jimmy, Mr. K's 20-year-old son and Thai, a 30-year old man who recently arrived from Vietnam—carry new stock upstairs to the storage room and take inventory. "Floor workers" (salespeople) include Mr. K., his older brother, his brother-in-law, and Larry, Mr. K.'s 22-year-old son. "Outside delivery" is done by Kenny, a cheerful 24-year-old. Kenny's job includes delivering and installing large appliances such as washers and dryers in customers' homes. Finally, Cathy, the 27-year-old bookkeeper, was described by Mr. K as being neat and diligent in her work.

Customers

I asked Mr. K. about the types of people who patronize the store. He was hesitant to "label" his customers. However, Larry, who was also in the room at the time, referred to some of the customers as "browsers" and "freeloaders." Regarding the latter remark, Mr. K. gave Larry a disgusted look, but agreed that some customers—mostly tourists—browse the store without buying anything. Mr. K. explained that most customers are "set customers" who have been doing business with Japantown Hardware for many years. He also mentioned a few "big name customers" (famous people) and seemed very proud while doing so. For example, Walter Matthau once came into the store while filming a scene in Japantown for "Laughing Policemen." Tito Fuentes and Willie Mays both bought large household appliances from the store. I asked Mr. K. if most of his customers were Japanese (since his store is located in Japantown) and he estimated that only about 50% were Asian.

Daily activities

Mr. K. says he has encountered only a small number of shoplifters, but he still keeps a sharp look-out for them. "Highlight work" (important tasks) includes ordering new stock through salesmen who come to the store; Mr. K. orders most of his hardware goods through this process. Lunch falls sometime between 11:00am and 2:00pm (depending on the time each worker takes his/her break). Mr. K. usually dines at restaurants in Japantown that are owned by people who do business with his store. This is the way Mr. K. "reciprocates." The main activity of the day is selling. Mr. K. believes that a good salesman is courteous and helpful.

Special services

Mr. K. also mentioned several of the special services offered by his store. For example, customers can purchase items that are in stock on the "floor" or place special orders through catalogues. Home delivery and pick-ups are also services offered by Japantown Hardware. The shop also offers repair service for broken radios, televisions, irons, and other appliances sold in the store.

Business hours

I asked Mr. K. to describe a typical day. At 9:00am or earlier, Mondays through Saturdays, Mr. K. opens the store. To do so, he goes through the "opening up routine" that consists of turning off the alarm, placing the "till" in the register, turning on the lights, opening the front door, and displaying the "open" sign. Customers typically enter within 5 minutes of opening and tend to patronize the store in "spurts" throughout the day. The morning hours are usually busier than other times of day due to the fact that most people tend to start building and repair projects earlier in the day. During "non-busy" times, employees gather around the appliance section and eat doughnuts and drink coffee (Mr. K. brings these refreshments for his employees). The younger workers talk about cars and fishing and the older workers talk about Social Security and tax laws. All of the employees converse with each other and get along very well. At 5:30pm, Mr. K. closes the store: he turns on the alarm, deposits the till, locks the front door, turns off the lights, and flips the sign to "closed."

Summary

After the interview, I was satisfied with the information Mr. K. had provided. During our talk, he continually mentioned the history of the business, especially its growth. Mr. K distinguishes Japantown Hardware from discount hardware stores in that his store aims to be helpful to customers in "setting up" their problem and helping them choose the appropriate tools and materials. In contrast, at discount stores, workers usually only ring up purchases and do not take the time to explain products. Mr. K. is very concerned with the reputation of his store and stresses the importance of friendliness, honesty, and sincerity toward workers, clients, and customers.

Final redesign proposal: abandoning old and creating new ideas

After visiting Japantown Hardware a couple of times—and especially after talking to Mr. K.—I discovered that many of my original redesign proposals were inappropriate for the store. Below, I describe my final redesign proposal and note how my ideas about the site have changed.

Stereotyping customers

Looking back at my first redesign proposal, I became aware that I, not knowing anything about the culture, had stereotyped Japantown Hardware. Because the store is located in Japantown, one block away from the Japanese Cultural Center, I assumed that many tourists frequented the store. Thus, my original proposal included changing the design of the front façade to a Japanese style in order to catch the eye of tourists and draw in more customers. However, Mr. K. told me that tourists do not make up a large percentage of his customers; rather, the majority are "set customers" who have been doing business at Japantown Hardware for many years. Set customers will come to the store regardless of the appearance of the store's façade; thus, I no longer propose investing resources into the redesign of the store's façade.

I also had assumed that shoplifting would be a big problem. According to Mr. K., the problem was not as bad as I thought. I originally proposed to move the cash register to the front of the store and create three different levels to provide Mr. K. with a visual overview of the store. However, Mr. K. did not think that moving the cash register to the front of the store was feasible because many times during the day, the register is left unattended and thus moving it closer to the shop's entrance would be more risky. Though Mr. K. liked the idea of having better visibility in the store, he said that multi-levels would not work due to the need to move heavy boxes and products across the store using hand trucks. Based on Mr. K.'s feedback and needs, I have abandoned my original ideas of moving the cash register and creating a multi-level floor plan.

Final redesign priorities

I decided that because employees spend the most time in the store (selling, cleaning, socializing), my second redesign should make the environment as pleasant and convenient for them as possible. Also, during my interviews with Mr. K., I noticed that his customers mean a lot to him and learned that he places value in being "courteous and helpful." Thus, I concluded that my second redesign should include changes that benefit everyone in the store, employees as well as customers.

Music

I propose the addition of music to the store as a nice gesture for both employees and customers. Mr. K. liked my initial idea of having music, but he did not want Japanese music. He said: "It would sound too much like a sushi bar." I decided that jazz or soft rock music might be more appropriate.

Cluttered atmosphere

One important point I realized is that a hardware store needs a lot of space to accommodate not only tools, but also household appliances, patio furniture, pipes, lumber, and other large items. Japantown Hardware does not have sufficient space. Mr. K. said that "clutteredness" was a problem in his store: employees have a hard time finding store space for new stock and customers have trouble finding what they need because everything is so cluttered. The existing second floor consists of a small storage area and a bathroom; these areas take up only one-third of the store's surface area. Thus, extending the second floor all the way to the front of the store would gain a significant amount of much-needed storage space. This is precisely what I propose: part of the extended second floor area could be used to display large merchandise (stoves, dishwashers, vacuums) and the rest could be dedicated to storage. Since all large items would be moved upstairs, the first floor would have more room and feel less cluttered.

Creating an overview

In order to create more space on the second floor, I propose to move the office to the rear of the store and elevate it about eight feet off of the floor. This solution would save additional ground space and also provide workers in the office an overview of the entire first floor.

Thus, to summarize my final redesign, I propose to:

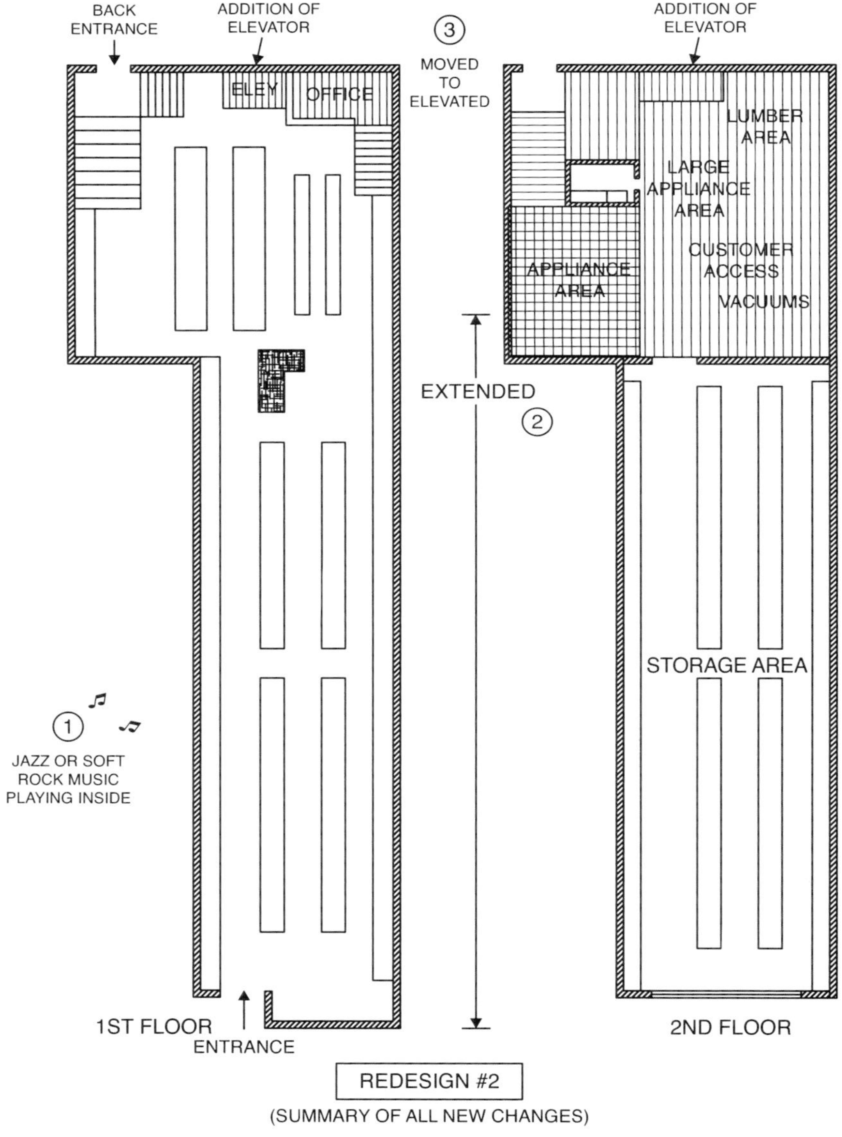

Figure 4 Final proposed redesign

1. Have music inside (soft rock or jazz).
2. Extend the second floor to create more storage and display space.
3. Move and elevate the office to create an overview of the store (see Figure 4).

Conclusion

This project helped me see that ethnography is a useful tool to understand—and design for—a specific culture. Through interviews I gained access to an insider's point of view and was able to understand his preferences and needs, neither of which I would have been able to see through personal observation. Mr. K. also benefitted from this ethnographic project. He liked my idea of providing music and he said he eventually might move the office to the rear of the store. He is also in favor of extending the second floor in order to obtain more space and hopes to be able to do so as soon as the economy improves. I was very happy to hear that he was seriously considering making many of the changes I proposed. Mr. K.'s comments made me feel helpful and made this ethnographic design project even more rewarding.

Glossary of key terms

annotated bibliography One facet of the ***literature review*** process, an annotated bibliography is a bibliographic list of sources that is added to (or annotated) with a short discussion of the relevance of the source to the larger research project (in this case, the ethnography project) as well as a brief evaluation of the trustworthiness of the source. *See section 6.1 and Box 6.1: Skill Spotlight—Conducting and writing a literature review, for additional information on conducting a literature review, and section 6.2 for an example.*

case study A case study is a type of research in which the researcher conducts a detailed study of a specific example—or case—but not others. Therefore, a case study results in a rich description of a single example rather than a comparison of two or more. Your ethnography project is a case study of a particular sited micro-culture and your research for this study employs several methods, all focusing on a single micro-culture within your site.

citation A standardized method of noting the original source of a fact, argument, or other type of information referenced or otherwise utilized in a paper. Though you can select the style of citations you prefer to use in your work (APA, MLA, or Chicago style), the need to cite is not optional. *See Box 6.1: Skill Spotlight—Conducting and writing a literature review, for more information on how and why to cite.*

coding and content analysis ***Content analysis*** is the process of reviewing cultural texts (anything from magazine article titles to interview transcripts) to identify primary themes. This process involves, according to Ryan and Bernard, a number of processes: identifying main themes and sub-themes, prioritizing themes based on relative importance, and tracking and defining themes.[1] In general, the process of identifying themes in a text is referred to as "***coding***." For more see section 5.9.[2]

content and structure (taxonomy) A ***taxonomy*** (or "logical structure of meaning," 5.5) of cultural terms displays both ***content*** (codes, vocabulary, meaning) and ***structure*** (connections and relationships between terms). In other words, taxonomies convey in graphical form the language your informant uses to describe ***cultural terms, cultural categories***, and the relationship between terms. Your task in conducting a semantic ethnography is to discover the content and structure of your informant's cultural knowledge. *See section 5.5 for additional information about the structure and content of cultural knowledge including descriptions of terms, elements, and connections.*

conventional vs. deep programming The ***program*** of a building is a technical description of its main functions and the planned use of the space by building occupants. Whereas a ***conventional*** program for a staff lounge might specify the (minimal behavioral) need for seating for 15, a microwave, a room of at least 15' × 24', cupboards, a sink, and a refrigerator, we encourage students to aim for a ***deeper program***, wherein the social and cultural activities of the people who use the space would be accounted for. A deep program for the staff lounge might specify the need for a space for a surprise birthday party, nostalgic music, a cake, balloons, presents, and games. *See section 7.2 for more on this example as well as a discussion of the difference between conventional vs. deep programming.*

cover terms See ***cultural terms***.

cultural categories Cultural categories comprise the underlying structure that gives significance and meaning to the cultural terms used by your informant. When conducting an interview, try to listen for—and ask questions about—the ways in which single terms are classified and the means by which your informant describes the similarities or differences between terms.[3] For example, if your informant talks about the importance of a fireplace in the home, you will need to determine the underlying cultural category in which fireplace fits to accurately understand your informant's worldview: is the fireplace a way to keep warm? Or is it a social space, a prop for romantic ambience, a place of family togetherness, or signifier of social class? In semantic ethnography, you must identify not only the definition of cultural terms, but the categorization or structure of cultural knowledge to accurately understand the worldview of your informant. *See the Preface for the original usage of this example as well as sections 5.1–5.3 for more information.*

cultural knowledge We define ***culture*** as shared knowledge that is learned by members of a group and used to organize behavior and ascribe meaning. Cultural knowledge is organized; thus, through ***semantic ethnographic*** methods, you can learn to understand the information you obtain from your informant as a series of ***cultural categories*** that give ***terms*** and ***objects*** meaning. *See sections 3.2 and 5.2 for more information.*

cultural practice The "information and ideas people use to guide their everyday behavior," including beliefs, values, and worldview of a culture (1.1). Our belief is that all designs should be based on a profound understanding of and respect for cultural practice.

cultural terms Cultural terms are the words your informant uses to describe his cultural knowledge (the setting, beliefs, behaviors, and any other aspect of her culture). Though the terms can be defined in and of themselves, their meaning is more significantly and accurately defined by the ***categories*** into which they are divided. Indeed, ***cultural knowledge*** is structured, and the terms that describe larger ***cultural categories*** are known as ***cover terms***. *For additional information, see the Preface and section 5.5.*

culture Culture is a complex term, often described as the whole way of life of a group of people, including the sum of their material, intellectual, and linguistic ways of life. However, for the purposes of this project, we define culture in more restrictive terms. We conceive of culture as the system of meanings shared by a group; in other words, the knowledge of rules and meanings that guide behavior. *For more on different definitions of culture and their relationship to **semantic ethnography**, see 3.1.*

McCurdy, Spradley, and Shandy distinguish between tacit and explicit culture. ***Tacit culture*** is "the ***cultural knowledge*** people don't put into words."[4] The classic example of tacit knowledge is Edward T. Hall's study of *proxemics*, or the "bubbles" of space—intimate, personal, social, and public—that people in a culture define and maintain through their actions with and responses to others. Though Hall coined a term to describe this phenomenon, the people he studied did not express this practice with words. In contrast, ***explicit culture*** refers to the "cultural categories . . . coded in language," meaning the parts of your informant's cultural knowledge that can be talked about and expressed verbally using names, labels, terms, and cover terms. Note that different research methods are required to learn about explicit and implicit aspects of a culture: what is implicit—such as Hall's *proxemics*—cannot be articulated and therefore must be observed; what is explicit can be articulated through informant interviews.[5]

data collection The systematic process of collecting information for a research project. Different methods of data collection you will use in your ethnography include ***observation*** and ***semantic interviews***. To select the proper method of data collection for any research project, the researcher must be attentive to the type of information needed and the possible sources of that data. In the case of your ethnography project, you will want to learn about the range of activities that occur in the site you are studying (data collection method: observation) as well as their cultural significance (data collection method: semantic interviews). Yet you also want to learn about what others external to your site have said about similar cultural or environmental contexts; therefore, you will engage a third data collection method: a ***literature review***.

deductive vs. inductive Elsewhere in this text we have described ethnography as a "discovery science," meaning that ethnography does not start out with a guiding hypothesis or generalization, but rather *produces* or helps to form a theory or hypothesis through the detailed study of a cultural group. This type of research is called ***inductive***, which is distinctive from more common, ***deductive*** approaches to scientific inquiry that focus on hypothesis-testing. *See Preface for more information.*

definitions (of cultural terms) One of your tasks as a semantic ethnographer will be to define—in the words of your informant—each of the cultural terms she uses. These definitions will help you infer the deeper meaning of terms and construct a taxonomic representation of your informant's cultural knowledge. However, note that cultural terms can be defined in a number of ways (*see 5.7 for additional information*).

Perceptual definitions rely on sensorial experiences—pointing to something and saying "there's one," smelling a "good" or "bad" smell, or even describing the experiential "feeling of a place"—to define the essence of an object or idea.

Nominal definitions use names to define and distinguish items from one another. To obtain a nominal definition, you might ask your informant: "What do you call *that?*"

Though common, **dictionary definitions** are only one type of meaning and should not be seen as the definitive source of definitions. Dictionary definitions are descriptive statements about an object or term.

A **taxonomic definition** is distinct in its focus on relational terms; in other words, the relationship or degree of contrast—high or low—between different concepts or terms. Another taxonomic type of definition is one that states something in terms of something else; for example, a garage is a type of building, just as two-car garages and multi-story parking garages are types of garages. Notice how these statements resemble the ***taxonomy*** of ***cultural terms*** you will create.

Finally, **componential definitions** articulate the characteristics of a particular ***cultural category*** and, in so doing, enumerate the subtleties in meaning of the category.

elevation A building elevation is a common type of architectural drawing that depicts a building or structure as seen from one side or façade. This type of drawing is used to convey the outward appearance of a site. Figure 1 demonstrates the use of elevation drawings in a student ethnography project.

emic and etic Recognizing our definition of ***culture*** as a system of shared knowledge, we make an important distinction between an insider's (or cultural group member's) knowledge and that of an outsider. Anthropologists use the terms ***emic*** (insider) and ***etic*** (outsider) to convey these distinct points of view. These terms stem from linguistic terminology wherein *phonetic* refers to the sound of a word (or what an outsider might hear) and *phonemic* connotes its meaning (a type of group member knowledge). *For more on emic and etic perspectives, see section 3.2.*

empirical An empirical study is based on observable, verifiable experience and evidence (rather than, say, pure theory or logic). In your ethnography project, you are collecting empirical data from a number of sources, for example through behavioral observation and semantic interviews.

environmental determinism The idea that something in the built environment *causes* behaviors, beliefs, feelings, etc. In fact, given the complexity of human experience—of which person–environment relationships are just a part—at most we can say that the environment may facilitate or make easier certain behaviors or activities and evoke emotional responses but do not cause (or determine) either. We also need to recognize that people modify their environments and make thoughtful, intentional decisions regarding their behavior within environments. Instead, we may say that the range of possible activities might be limited by the

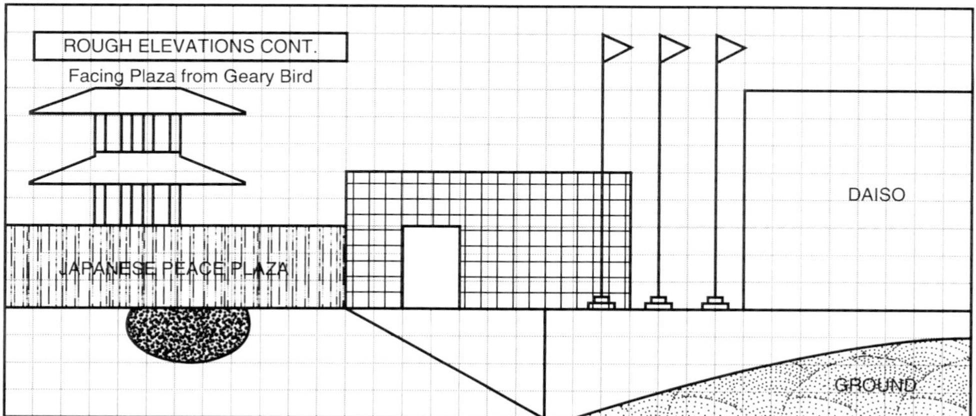

Figure 1 Adrienne Ito sketched this elevation of her site while conducting her initial observation. (Adrienne Ito, "Japantown Peace Plaza," 2012)

environment and, considering the ***symbolic meanings and cues*** conveyed within an environment, behavior may be influenced by the norms or feeling of a space. Regarding the latter, communication theory—of which symbolism and cues are a part—offers ways to think about the person–environment relationship and sidestep the issue of environmental determinism. *For more about environmental determinism in the context of your ethnographic study, see the Preface and 3.2.*

ethnocentrism Though our own cultural background will always influence our perception of the environment, we must beware of and avoid the personal bias of ***ethnocentrism***, the "deeply engrained attitude that our own culture is superior to others" (2.4), which compromises objectivity. *For tips on how to avoid, or at least reduce the impact of, ethnocentrism, see 2.4.*

ethnographic design project The goal of the architectural ethnography project we assign in an undergraduate course at UC Berkeley is to employ a specific social science research method, ***semantic ethnography***, to understand the cultural use of and needs for a specific site. By learning from the users of a space, we hope to encourage students—and eventually, architects—to design places that welcome and celebrate cultural practices. Additionally, we see this project as easily modifiable to fit other courses as well as architectural and other design practices (see section 2.1). *Chapter 2 provides a comprehensive summary of each facet of the ethnographic design project this book outlines. Additionally, the rationale for the use of ethnographic methods in design is articulated in Chapter 1.*

ethnography Ethnography is both a theory and a method; it is an interpretive and ***inductive*** practice that aims to describe a culture. Etymologically, *ethnography* means *ethno* (people) and *graphy* (to write), or to write about people. Though most ethnographic practice relies on ***participant observation*** methodologies, ***semantic ethnography*** is a distinct approach in which researchers carefully listen for cultural terms and their meaning through informant interviews. In this way, semantic ethnography emphasizes the learned knowledge of a group and its impact on behavior. *For more, see the Preface and section 1.2.*

evidence-based design Evidence-based design is "a process for the conscientious, explicit, and judicious use of current best evidence from research and practice in making critical decisions, together with an informed client, about the design of each individual and unique project."[6] Research of all kinds can—and should—be a source of inspiration for designers. Designs based on reliable research are more likely to accommodate user needs.

fieldwork Doing research at the site itself—"in the field," in the terms of anthropology— is called ***fieldwork.*** Fieldwork can be an important component of the ethnographic method. *For more, see section 1.4.*

floor plan A floor plan is a common type of architectural drawing that shows from above the relationship between the rooms, spaces, and other physical objects (such as stairs or furniture or even trees and outdoor pathway) that comprise a site. Plans are akin to maps of a site. Figures 2 and 3 are two examples of plans from previous ethnography projects.

future implications In the conclusion of your final report, you might consider ***reflecting on*** the future implications of your work, meaning your thoughts on the contribution your work might make to other areas of study and the future design of similar spaces.

grand tour question We recommend that you begin your interview with a specific

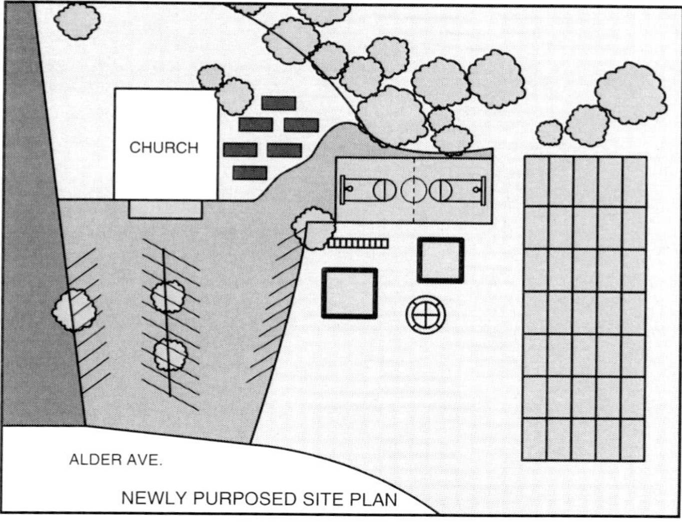

Figure 2 Wesley Tran drew this site plan to depict the proposed redesign of the outdoor spaces surrounding a community church. (Wesley Tran, "Ethnography: A Community Christian Church," 2007)

type of open-ended question called a ***grand tour question***. The goal of this type of question is to elicit abundant, descriptive information from your informant without taking anything for granted. By starting with a general question such as "can you tell me about a typical day here?" your informant is then free to tell you about anything she feels is interesting, relevant, or important. From there, you can ask follow-up questions to learn more about specific aspects of the activities, people, or places your informant mentioned. *For more about grand tour questions, see 5.4.*

informant (cultural informant) A cultural informant is a member of a culture who serves, for the purposes of your study, as the representative of his cultural group. As the term implies, an informant will inform you about the cultural knowledge of the group and help you cultivate a sense of ***emic*** understanding about the ***sited micro-culture*** you are studying. A good informant is someone who is knowledgeable about the culture and is willing to talk openly with you. *Chapter 4 is dedicated to finding, developing rapport with, and interviewing cultural informants; in particular, see 4.1 and 4.6–4.8.*

literature In research, the term literature refers to a body of work that has been published or written about a particular topic. A ***literature review*** is the systematic search, study, and written assessment of a body of work. *For more on conducting a literature review, see Box 6.1: Skill Spotlight—Conducting and writing a literature review.*

literature review A literature review refers both to the process of searching, reading, and analyzing a body of work (the ***literature*** that has been written about a specific topic) *and* the written summary of the findings, outcomes or relevance, and limitations of the body of work as it pertains to a larger research project. Below is an excerpt from Trisha Saavedra Cabantac, who describes her approach

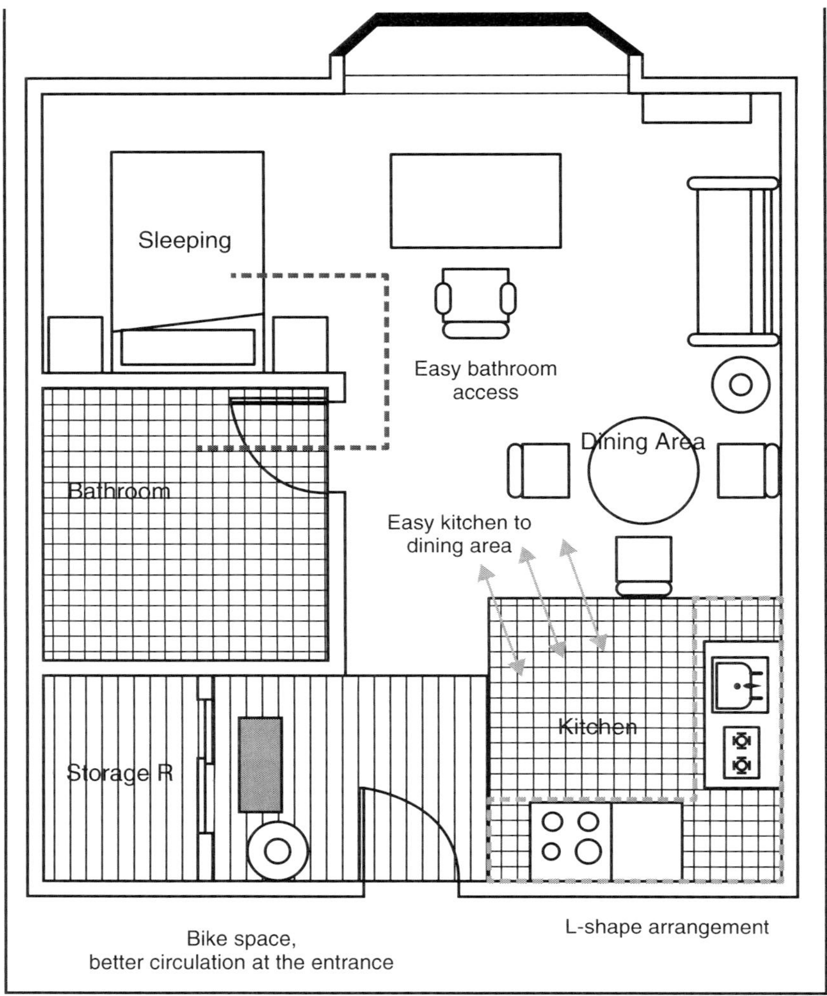

Figure 3 Zheng Zhong created and annotated this plan to propose a new layout for a senior studio. From: (Zheng Zhong, "A Senior Studio Redesign," 2012)

to conducting a literature review to learn more about the ***etic perspective*** of her site of study: a restaurant in Oakland, CA.

> In order to understand the ***etic*** perspective on [my site] I gathered different articles and books regarding the sociology [of] restaurants, the interior design of bars, and the culture of South Boston, the neighborhood that influenced the style of the restaurant. I also found [customer] reviews, which reiterated the initial conception and style of the restaurant already provided by [my informant].[7]

For more on conducting a literature review, see Box 6.1: Skill Spotlight—Conducting and writing a literature review.

observation A particular type of social science research methodology, observation is defined as the act of systematically watching and recording the physical features (or *physical traces*), types of activities, and/or *behaviors* that comprise or occur in a given space.[8] Make a distinction, when taking notes and reflecting on what you observe, between what *actually* happens ("one person sat on the bench") and what you *perceive or interpret* ("man sitting alone must be lonely"). Observational techniques are helpful in conveying the range of activities and behaviors in a given location, but do not, however, explain the *meaning* of any of these aspects. For this reason, it is often helpful to conduct observations in tandem with other research methods such as interviews or surveys.[9] *For more on conducting observations, see Box 2.4: Skill Spotlight—Conducting behavioral observations.*

operationalization A common practice in scientific research—including the social sciences—is that of *operationalizing concepts*. To operationalize means to define a concept in terms that allow for empirical observation, measurement, and distinct and comparable data. Articulating such *operational definitions* is essential not only to scientific inquiry, but also to translating cultural knowledge into design. *For more on operationalizing concepts, see Box 7.1: Skill Spotlight—Concepts: operational definitions and translation into design.*

participant observation Participant observation is a specific, participatory type of ***observation*** in which the researcher becomes part of the community and therefore can speak for it. Anthropologists—in particular, ethnographers—are participant observers in the cultures they study, often spending a year or so conducting fieldwork. Because participant observation is so time consuming, for the purposes of our architectural ethnography project, we use a ***semantic ethnography*** methodology (rather than participant observation) to learn about the ***cultural knowledge*** of a group by carefully listening to and interviewing an informant. *More on participant observation can be found in the Preface and section 1.2.*

person–environment relations This term refers to the broad category of interdisciplinary research concerned with the relationship between people and their built and natural environments. Related disciplines include (but are not limited to): environmental psychology, cultural geography, sociology, and anthropology. Common examples of person–environment concepts are privacy, community, territoriality, density, and identity. It is likely that your ethnography project will touch upon issues from this field; thus, you may find it helpful to familiarize yourself with the Environmental Design Research Association as well as scholars we have mentioned elsewhere in this text, such as William H. Whyte, Edward T. Hall, and Robert Sommer for additional insight into the primary concerns, methodologies, and findings from the field of person–environment studies.

personal perspective In addition to the ***emic*** (inside) and ***etic*** (outside) perspectives you will research through informant interviews and a literature review, respectively, you will bring a third perspective to your ethnography project: your ***personal perspective***, based on your initial observations and impressions of the site you are studying. In order to maintain clarity about the data obtained from each of these perspectives, we recommend that you keep a notebook divided into three sections, one each for your personal observations and impressions, information from your informant interviews (emic), and data you obtain from your literature review (etic). Recognizing the ways in which personal experiences can influence our perception of places, try to be cognizant of your own ***subjectivity*** and to try to be as ***objective*** as possible; *for suggestions on how to do so, see 2.3–2.4.*

perspective drawings Perspective drawings are a common type of architectural drawing used to convey the volumetric dimensions of a building as seen by the eye. One notable characteristic of perspective drawings is the use of vanishing points, wherein items appear to get smaller the farther away they recede from the observer. The examples in Figures 4 and 5 are taken from student ethnography projects.

physical traces In addition to observing the behaviors and activities of people, you can also observe the physical traces, or the material artifacts or visual evidence of activity and use, of a site. For more about how to observe physical traces, see Zeisel's *Inquiry by Design*; for examples of physical traces observation in use, see Rathje's "The Garbage Decade" or *Rubbish! The Archaeology of Garbage* and Banning's use of physical traces to assess the ethical climate of college campuses.[10]

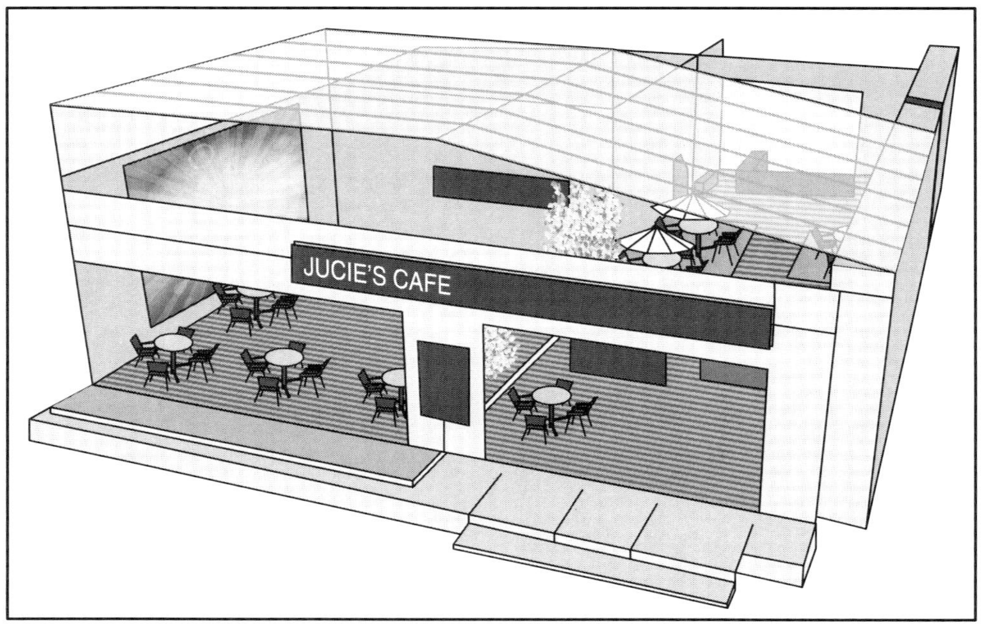

Figure 4 Aline Tanelian, "A Café," 2013

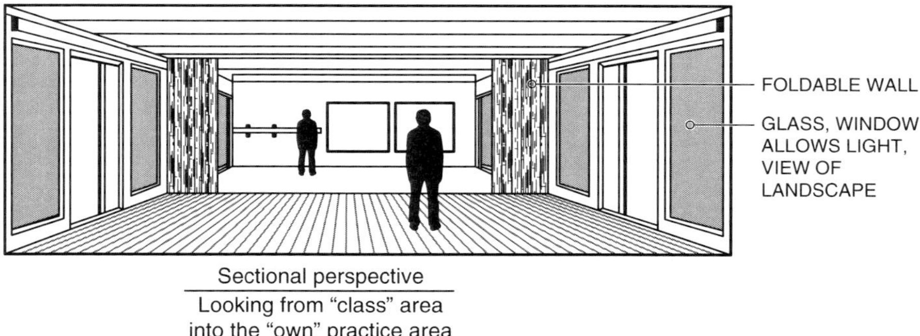

Figure 5 Douglas Look, "A Martial Arts School," 1990; note how Douglas annotated his perspective drawing to highlight important elements

plan See ***floor plan***, above.

post-occupancy evaluation (POE) The practice of evaluating the performance, use, and efficacy of a building after it is built and occupied. The data obtained from POEs can (and should) be used in a number of ways: to identify changes that need to be made on site, to inform future projects, and to build a body of literature regarding certain building types and the efficacy of various designs. Often, POEs focus on occupant satisfaction and comfort, but the assessment you conducted of your site also is a form of POE, since you investigate the ways in which the built environment supports or hinders the activities and beliefs of the micro-culture you studied.[11]

programming See ***conventional vs. deep programming*** above.

programming vs. evaluation research Architectural research can take two forms: programming and evaluation research. ***Programming research*** is concerned with the purpose of a building and is conducted during the initial stages of a project. The program of a building specifies the size and arrangement of interior spaces as well as the planned uses of the site (see section 1.3). ***Evaluation research*** occurs after the building is constructed (and occupied) and seeks to evaluate the extent to which the building succeeds in meeting the expressed goals of its designer and needs of its clients (users).

questions (ethnographic interviews) In ethnographic interviews, you might ask three different types of questions. The first type of question (with which you should begin an interview) is the ***grand tour question*** (see above for definition).

In order to assist in the construction of your ***taxonomy***, you can ask ***structural questions***, which will help you determine the cover term of a category and associated terms therein. Examples of structural questions include: "What are all of the items included on the menu?" or "are there different types of menus?" In other words, structural questions help you discover similarities between terms and create categories to group like items together. *For additional information and examples, see 5.6.*

A third type of question, ***attribute questions***, seeks to discover differences between terms; in other words, the information or qualities that cultural group members use to distinguish one thing from another. To obtain this information, you can ask attribute questions such as: "What is the difference between a brunch menu and a regular menu?" *For more information and examples, see 5.8.*

reflections In the conclusion of your final report, you should reflect on your experiences over the course of the project. To reflect is to offer a thoughtful self-assessment of your experiences and, in the context of this project, personal thoughts about what you have learned.

section drawings Section drawings (or cross-sections) are a type of architectural drawing that depicts a vertical cut through a building and therefore shows the height, volume, and relationship (or height) of floors of a building. Just as a ***plan*** is a rendering of a horizontal cut through a building, a ***section*** is the vertical rendering of an object or building. Often plans, sections, and elevations are used in tandem to articulate the feeling and dimensions of a building. Figure 6 demonstrates how a section drawing can complement a ***plan*** by giving more detail about the vertical relationships within a space.

Yet another way to demonstrate the spatial relationships within a building is to use a three-dimensional rendering technique such as isometric or axonometric

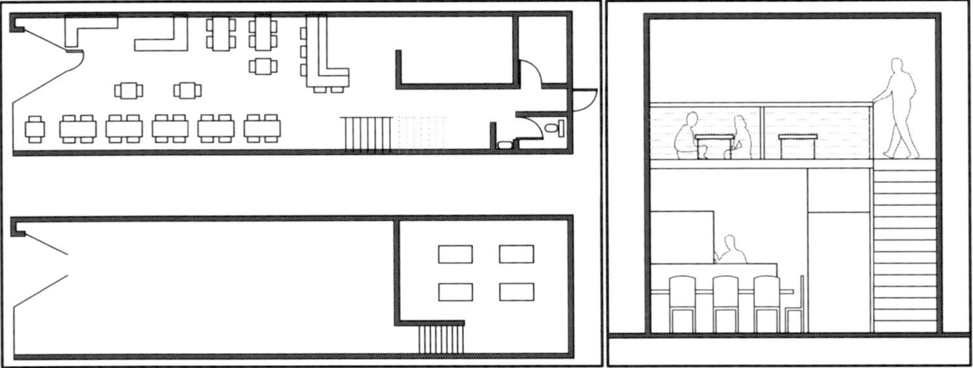

Figure 6 To depict his final proposal for the redesign of a restaurant, Kyle Yamamoto created *both* plan *and* section renderings of the space, the latter of which was particularly helpful to show his proposed addition of a lofted dining space. (Kyle Yamamoto, "A Japanese Restaurant," 2012)

drawings. These drawings enable you to convey the ***plan*** and ***section*** simultaneously. Figures 7 and 8 are examples of each from previous student ethnography projects.

semantic ethnography See ***ethnography***, above.

semantic interviews The interviews you conduct with your informant, as part of your ***semantic ethnography*** project, are called semantic interviews. Once you complete your interview, we recommend that you ***transcribe*** and ***code*** your dialog to help you identify, define, and analyze the ***content*** and ***structure*** of your informant's ***cultural knowledge***.

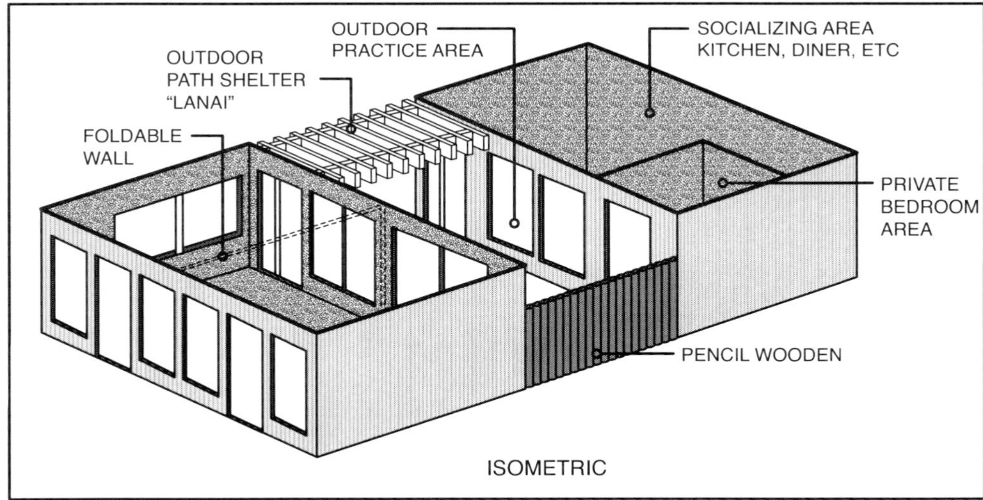

Figure 7 Douglas Look drew an isometric version of the same site depicted above (see Figure 3), a martial arts school. (Douglas Look, "A Martial Arts School," 1990)

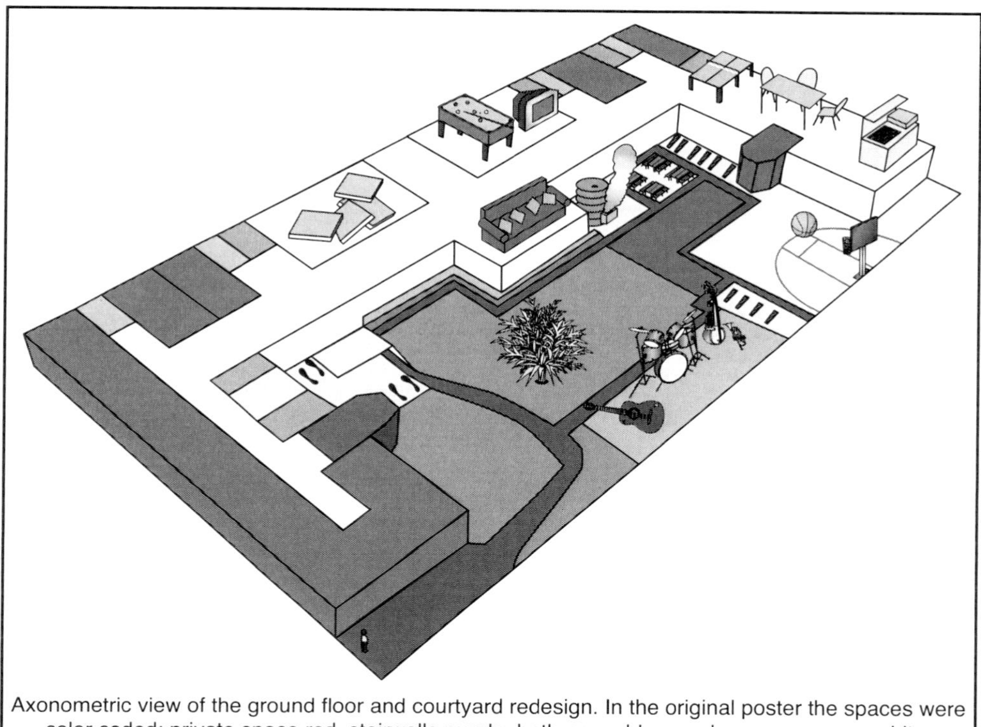

Axonometric view of the ground floor and courtyard redesign. In the original poster the spaces were color coded: private space red, stairwells purple, bathrooms blue, and common space white.

Figure 8 In his study of a cooperative residence, Kevin Hui created this color-coded axonometric rendering of his site to depict programmatic and spatial relationships. (Kevin Hui, "A Campus Cooperative," 2009)

If you chose to record your interview, listen to the recording and then ***transcribe***—or write down, verbatim—all that was said, including all casual dialog, the questions you asked, and of course your informant's answers. If you were unable to record your interview, *immediately* after your conversation, write down everything you remember—especially key terms and definitions your informant described—and integrate your transcription with any notes you took during the interview. Two examples of interview transcriptions are given in Figures 9 and 10.

Once you have transcribed the interview, your next step is to analyze or ***code*** the text. You should look for ***cultural terms*** and any words your informant used to describe their meaning. Then, re-read the transcript several times to try to organize the list of cultural terms into a format that conveys both the ***content*** and ***structure*** of your informant's cultural knowledge. Though this process may be time consuming, it is a necessary and helpful first step in creating a ***taxonomy***. Using the same examples above, we can see how Daniel and Caitlin coded their transcribed interviews in Figures 11 and 12.

sited culture/sited micro-culture Spradley and McCurdy offer the term ***micro-culture*** to refer to a small community within a larger culture; in other words, a subculture or sub-sub-culture. This scale makes an ethnographic study such as ours practical: to study an entire, singular culture such as the "American interview summary

Q: Who uses the bart station?
A: people who live around the area mostly.
El Cerrito / Kensignton / Richmond / Albany / some of Berkeley
Q: like?
A: kids, students, "older folks", commuters, biciclists people wearing suit / dont sit / stay clean.
– el cerrito / kensignton / albany / richmond
Q: what kind of students?
A: high school/ middle/college-> cal/comm. colleges
Q: what kind of commuters?
bart riders /bus/ cabs/ bike
Q: What do they do in the bart station?
A: they either just take transportation or hang out
Q: what do you mean by hang out?
A: "fool" around / have lunch / dance / fight / drugs (group competitions) --> often get in fights

Figure 9 Excerpt from Daniel Malagon, "BART Station Ethnography," 2009

C: The **teachers** have to pay membership too, or the teachers are members?
AF: Well, teachers are members.
C: It sounds like a lot of different groups that use this place. Lots of different age groups. How do the different people interact with the Alliance?
AF: We don't offer **classes** to children, because, actually, this space doesn't work that well for children or even for sometimes, we've had a few adolescent classes in the past but it didn't work out. So it's adults. So different levels of **French language** learning is offered . . . a **theatre group** has used the space.
C: Oh, cool.
AF: There's also one of the, um, requirements is that is that it has something to do with the **French** culture and language. So this group is actually in **French**, the **French theatre** group.

Figure 10 Excerpt from Caitlin DeClercq, "L'École Française," 2012

culture," one could argue, isn't even possible given the diversity of perspectives within that cultural group. For the purposes of our study, we add an additional layer of specificity to our unit of study: recognizing the uses and experiences of a particular place, we use the term sited micro-culture to emphasize the relationship of a micro-culture to a physical place. Several different micro-cultures may share a single location; thus, a single place or social situation may have several different definitions or interpretations according to the various micro-cultures that interact with the space. *For more information (including examples of sited micro-cultures), see 2.6 and 3.3–3.4.*

interview summary	data analysis	vocabulary
Q: who uses the bart station? A: people who live around the area mostly. El Cerrito / Kensignton / Richmond / Albany / some of Berkeley Q: like? A: kids, students, "older folks", commuters, bicyclists people wearing suit / dont sit / stayclean. - el cerrito / kensignton / albany / richmond Q: what kind of students? A: high school / middle/college -> cal/ comm. colleges Q: what kind of commuters? bart riders / bus / cabs / bike	**"older folks":** harji site serves the LOCAL refers to non-high **community** (serves nearby school / teenage cities) people: seniors / parents / adults / people on suit (- assumption of professional jobs, therefore a higher level of maturity. Students: -2 High schools near by / Albany and Richmond - 1 middle school two categories: **younger crowd long term (time):** from 2–3 hours -(students category) **older crowd short term** (time): 1 – 30 minutes -(Commuters)	older folks local community younger crowd older crowd long term users short term users commuters pedestrians bikers

Figure 11 Notice how Daniel Malagon identified key vocabulary words and analyzed each using descriptions and definitions given by his informant. (Daniel Malagon, "BART Station Ethnography," 2009)

C: The **teachers** have to pay membership too, or the teachers are members? **AF:** Well, teachers are members **C:** It sounds like a lot of different groups that use this place. Lots of different age groups. How do the different people interact with the Alliance? **AF:** We don't offer **classes** to children, because, actually, this space doesn't work that well for children or even for sometimes, we've had a few adolescent classes in the past but it didn't work out. So it's	Now we are talking about more **People** at the school, namely, the **members.** The different categories of members pay different fee levels. • Vocab: **members, teacher, student** These categories of **People** (**members**) all interact with the school in slightly different ways; **Programming** is more available to adults than children and adolescents.

Figure 12 Notice how Caitlin DeClercq offers a narrative summary of the interview (the general themes of conversation) as well as a list of key vocabulary words, highlighted to the right as well as in-text. (Caitlin DeClercq, "L'École Française," 2012)

social research methods Methods are standard, agreed upon conventions for collecting data; for example, ***ethnography*** is a research method often used in the social sciences, and in particular, anthropology (though, it should be noted, other disciplines and professions make use of ethnographic techniques—indeed, we argue that semantic ethnography can and should be used in the architectural profession). In the course of your architectural ethnography project you will utilize a number of ***social science research methods*** including: ***observation***, ***semantic interviews***, and a ***literature review***.

symbolic meanings and cues Buildings impact behavior in many ways. Buildings, as with any other cultural artifact, are imbued with and communicate ***symbolic meaning***. Columns, more than the structural function they play in buttressing an overhang, are a symbol of classical cultures and, in the present, convey official, civic meaning. ***Cues*** refer to the subtle—yet impactful—messages communicated about the proper way to act and move within a space, often conveyed through the size, shape, proximities, and materiality of furnishings within. Think of a classroom: even if you were unfamiliar with the class itself, the arrangement of desks would likely tell you that you, the student, are to sit in a particular place while the instructor sits (or stands) elsewhere; in a similar fashion, you also might learn that students are supposed to sit while learning, a more passive stance than teachers who are expected to take in the classroom. *For more about how buildings communicate with and impact people, see Preface and sections 1.1 and 1.6.*

taxonomy Simply put, a taxonomy is a graphical organization of concepts (5.5) comprised of a series of ***categories*** and constituent ***concepts***. Creating a taxonomy of ***cultural terms*** is a way to structure the wealth of information you obtain from your informant into a logical structure of meaning and to represent your findings in graphical or diagrammatic terms. Taxonomies must include *both* cultural terms and the connections between them. This information can take several forms, including tree charts, tables, and outlines, but must include all cultural terms. The taxonomies in Figures 13 and 14 demonstrate the variety of formats

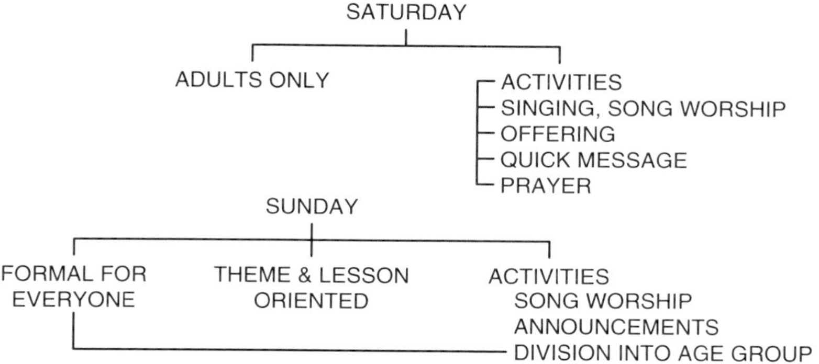

Figure 13 This taxonomy uses a simple format to convey the temporal structure of a community church's activities. (Wesley Tran, "Ethnography: A Community Christian Church," 2007)

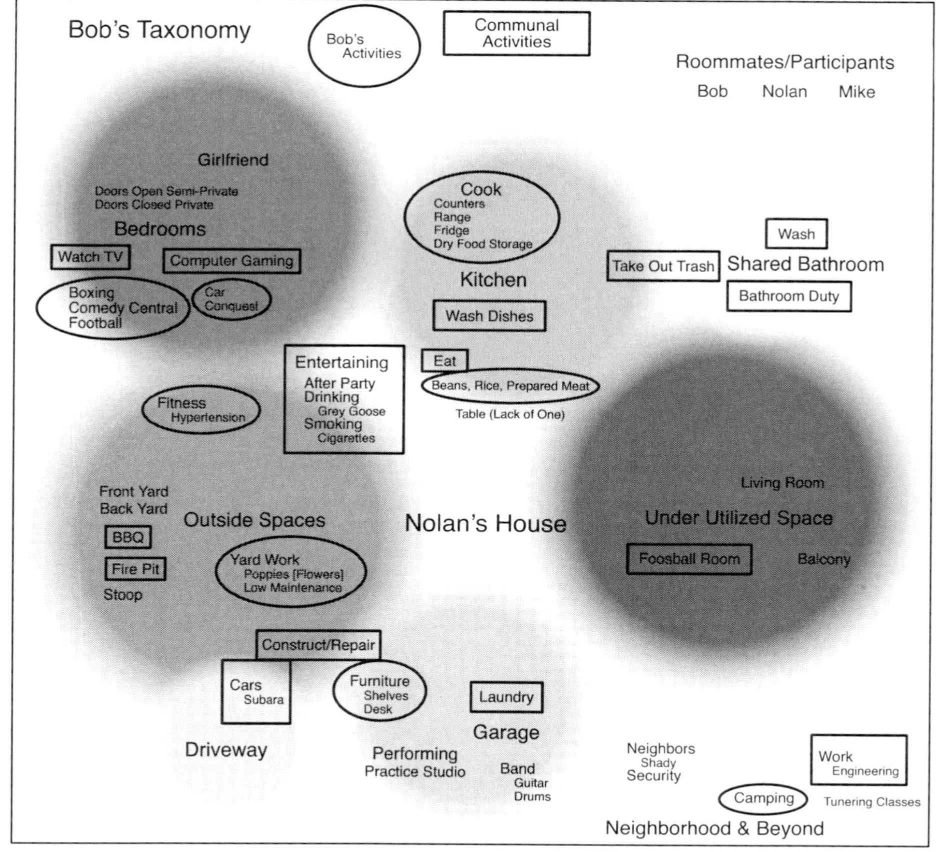

Figure 14 In his ethnography of a private residence, Edward Samaniego added shapes and colors to a cluster diagram format to denote the spatial relationships (colors), social relationships (circles and squares). (Edward Samaniego, "Bob's House," 2009)

and graphical representations that can be used in taxonomies. *For additional information and sample taxonomies, see 5.5.*

Notes

1 Ryan and Bernard, "Techniques to Identify Themes," 2003.
2 For an example of an article that makes use of the content analysis methodology, see Galen Cranz and Michael Boland, "Defining the Sustainable Park: A Fifth Model for Urban Parks," *Landscape Journal* 23, no. 2 (2004).
3 Spradley and McCurdy, *The Cultural Experience,* 1972, 3.
4 McCurdy, Spradley, and Shandy, *The Cultural Experience*, 2005, 8.
5 Ibid.
6 D. Kirk Hamilton and David H. Watkins, *Evidence-Based Design for Multiple Building Types* (Hoboken, NJ: John Wiley, 2009), 9.
7 Trisha Saavedra Cabantac, "The Sandwich Shop" (Fall 2012).
8 Zeisel, *Inquiry by Design,* 2006.
9 See Pavlides and Cranz,"Ethnographic Methods in Support of Architectural Practice," 2012.
10 Zeisel, *Inquiry by Design*, 2006; William L. Rathje, "The Garbage Decade," *American Behavioral Scientist* 28, no. 1 (1984); James H. Banning, "Assessing the Campus' Ethical Climate: A Multi-Dimensional Approach," *New Directions for Student Services* 77 (1997).
11 For an example of a Post-Occupancy Evaluation, see Galen Cranz and Eunah Cha, "Body-Conscious Design in a Teen Space: Post-Occupancy Evaluation in an Innovative Public Library," *Public Libraries* (November/December, 2006): 48–56.

Bibliography

AIA/ACSA "Teachers Seminar Program Notes." *Journal of Architectural Education* 28, no. 1/2, Part 1. (1976): 4–9.

Andrade, Roy. "A Cognitivist's View of the Units Debate in Cultural Anthropology." *Cross-Cultural Research* 35, no. 2 (May 2001): 242–57.

Arnould, Eric J. and Melanie Wallendorf. "Market-Oriented Ethnography: Interpretation Building and Market Strategy Formulation." *Journal of Marketing Research* 31 (November 1994).

Banning, James H. "Assessing the Campus' Ethical Climate: A Multi-Dimensional Approach." *New Directions for Student Services* 77 (1997).

Becker, Franklin D. *Housing Messages*. Stroudsburg, PA: Dowden, Hutchinson & Ross, 1977.

Bissell, Janice Marie. "Teachers' Construction of Space and Place: A Study of School Architectural Design as a Context of Secondary School Teachers' Work." Ph.D. diss., University of California, Berkeley, 2002.

Bray, David. *Social Space and Governance in Urban China: The Danwei System from Origins to Reform*. Stanford, CA: Stanford University Press, 2005, Chap. 1.

Bristol, Katharine G. "The Pruitt-Igoe Myth." *Journal of Architectural Education* 44, no. 3 (1991): 163–71.

Bruner, Jerome, Jacqueline J. Goodnow, and George A. Austin. *A Study of Thinking*. New York: Wiley, 1956.

Castells, Manuel. *The Informational City: Information Technology, Economic Restructuring, and the Urban–Regional Process*. Oxford: Basil-Blackwell, 1989.

Cayla, Julien and Eric J. Arnould. "Ethnographic Stories for Market Learning." *Journal of Marketing*, 77, no. 4 (2013): 1–16.

Chiesi, Leonardo. *Il Doppio Espazio dell'architettura: Ricerca sociologica e progettazione*. Naples, Italy: Liguori Editions, 2010.

Conklin, Harold C. "Lexicographical Treatment of Folk Taxonomies." In *Problems in Lexicography*, edited by F. W. Householder and S. Saporta. Indiana University Research Center in Anthropology, Folklore and Linguistics Publication, 21: 119–41, 1962.

Cranz, Galen. *The Politics of Park Design: A History of Urban Parks in America*. Cambridge, MA: The MIT Press, 1982.

———. Keynote address. Environmental Design Research Association conference, Chicago, 1993.

———. *The Chair: Rethinking Culture, Body, and Design*. New York: W. W. Norton, 2000.

Cranz, Galen, and Michael Boland. "Defining the Sustainable Park: A Fifth Model for Urban Parks." *Landscape Journal* 23, no. 2 (2004).

Cranz, Galen, and Eunah Cha. "Body-Conscious Design in a Teen Space: Post-Occupancy Evaluation in an Innovative Public Library." *Public Libraries* (November/December 2006): 48–56.

Crosier, Scott. "John Snow: The London Cholera Epidemic of 1854." (Center for Spatially

Integrated Social Science, n.d.). Accessed June 29, 2015 from www.csiss.org/classics/content/8/.

Csikzentmihali, Mihali, and Eugene Rochberg-Halton. *The Meaning of Things: Domestic Symbols and the Self*. Cambridge: Cambridge University Press, 1981.

Davis, Sam. *The Architecture of Affordable Housing*. Berkeley: University of California Press, 1995.

Denzin, Norman K. *Interpretive Ethnography: Ethnographic Practices for the 21st Century*. Thousand Oaks, CA: Sage, 1997.

Dragoman, Lina. "An Empathetic Lens." Policy X Design Blog, Public Policy Lab, 2012. Retrieved from http://publicpolicylab.org/2013/03/an-empathetic-lens.

Freire, Paolo. *Pedagogy of the Oppressed*. New York: Bloomsbury, 1970, 2012.

Freidrichs, Chad. Director. *The Pruitt-Igoe Myth*. Unicorn Stencil Films, 2011.

Gehl, Jan. *Life between Buildings: Using Public Space*. Third Edition. Translated by Jo Koch. Copenhagen: Arkitektens Forlag, 1996.

Gieryn, Thomas F. "A Space for Place in Sociology." *Annual Review of Sociology* 26 (2000): 463–96.

Groat, Linda, and David Wang. *Architectural Research Methods*. New York: John Wiley, 2002.

Gutman, Robert, Ed., *People and Buildings*. New York: Basic Books, 1972.

Hall, Edward T. *The Silent Language*. New York: Anchor Press/Doubleday, 1959.

———. *The Hidden Dimension*. New York: Doubleday, 1966.

Halle, David. *Inside Culture: Art and Class in the American Home*. Chicago, IL: University of Chicago Press, 1993.

Hamilton, D. Kirk, and David H. Watkins. *Evidence-Based Design for Multiple Building Types*. Hoboken, NJ: John Wiley, 2009.

Haraway, Donna. "Situated Knowledges: The Science Question in Feminism and the Privilege of Partial Perspective." *Feminist Studies* 14, no. 3 (1998): 575–99.

Holl, Steven. *Tripleness*. Bellevue, WA: Bellevue Art Museum, 2001.

Jackson, Laura E. "The Relationship of Urban Design to Human Health." *Landscape and Urban Planning* 64 (2003).

Jencks, Charles. *The Language of Post-modern Architecture*. New York: Rizzoli, 1987.

Jones, Alice. "The Psychology of Sustainability: What Planners Can Learn from Attitude Research." *Journal of Planning Education and Research* 16 (1996): 56–65.

Jones, Paul. *The Sociology of Architecture*. Liverpool: Liverpool University Press, 2011.

Kelly, Donna and Michael Gibbons. "Marketing Methodologies Ethnography: The Good, the Bad, and the Ugly." *Journal of Medical Marketing*, 8, no. 279 (2008).

Levinson, Nancy. "Critical Beats." *Places*. (March 6, 2010). Accessed from http://places.designobserver.com/feature/critical-beats/12948.

Lin, Maya Ying. *Boundaries*. New York: Simon and Schuster, 2000.

Lopez, Sarah Lynn. "The Remittance House: Architecture of Migration in Rural Mexico." *Buildings and Landscapes* 17, no. 2 (2010).

McCurdy, David W., James P. Spradley, and Dianna J. Shandy. *The Cultural Experience: Ethnography in a Complex Society*. Second Edition. Long Grove, IL: Waveland Press, 2005.

Matthews, Kevin. *The Great Buildings Collection*, CD-ROM. Artifice, 2001.

Mazumdar, Sanjoy. "How Programming Can Become Counterproductive: An Analysis of Approaches to Programming." *Journal of Environmental Psychology* 12 (1992).

Montgomery, Roger. "Pruitt-Igoe: Policy Failure or Societal Symptom." In *The Metropolitan Midwest: Policy Problems and Prospects for Change*, edited by Barry Checkoway and Carl V. Patton. Champaign: University of Illinois Press, 1985.

Newman, Oscar. *Defensible space: Crime prevention through urban design*. New York: Collier books, 1973.

Oldenburg, Ray. *The Great Good Place*. Cambridge, MA: Da Capo Press, 1989.

Pavlides, Eleftherios. "Vernacular Architecture in its Social Context: A Case Study of Eressos, Greece." Ph.D. diss., University of Pennsylvania, 1985.

Pavlides, Eleftherios, and Jana E. Hesser. "Vernacular Architecture as an Expression of Its Social Context in Eressos, Greece." In *Housing, Culture and Design: A Comparative Perspective*, edited by S. Low and E. Chambers, 357–74. Philadelphia: University of Pennsylvania Press, 1989.

Pavlides, Eleftherios, and Galen Cranz. "Three Theoretical Assumptions Needed to Create Useful Applied Social Science Research for Architecture." *International Journal of Interdisciplinary Social Sciences*, 4, no. 10 (2009): 191–201.

Pavlides, Eleftherios, and Galen Cranz. "Ethnographic Methods in Support of Architectural Practice." In *Enhancing Building Performance*, edited by Shauna Mallory-Hill, Wolfgang F. E. Preiser, and Chris Watson. Chichester: Wiley-Blackwell, 2012.

Portigal, Steve. *Interviewing Users: How to Uncover Compelling Insights*. Brooklyn, NY: Rosenfeld Media, 2013.

Price, John A. "The Field Course in Anthropology." Paper presented at the American Anthropological Association Meeting in New Orleans, November 1969.

Rathje, William L. "The Garbage Decade." *American Behavioral Scientist* 28, no. 1 (1984).

Rathje, William L., and Cullen Murphy. *Rubbish! The Archaeology of Garbage*. Tucson: University of Arizona Press (2001).

Ryan, Gery W. and H. Russell Bernard. "Techniques to Identify Themes." *Field Methods* 15, no. 1 (February 2003).

Salvador, Tony, Genevieve Bell, and Ken Anderson. "Design Ethnography." *Design Management Journal* 10, no. 4 (1999).

Seamon, David. Ed. *Architectural and Environmental Phenomenology Newsletter* (Manhattan: Kansas State University), Cumulative Index (Volumes 1–25, 1990–2015).

Sorrells, Kathryn. "Gifts of Wisdom: An Interview with Dr. Edward T. Hall." In *The Edge*, http://people.umass.edu/~leda/comm494r/The%20Edge%20Interview%20Hall.htm.

Sommer, Robert, and Helge Olsen. "The Soft Classroom." *Environment and Behavior* 12, no. 1 (1980).

Sommer, Robert, and Barbara Sommer. *A Practical Guide to Behavioral Research: Tools and Techniques*. Fifth Edition. New York: Oxford University Press, 2002.

Spradley, James. *You Owe Yourself a Drunk: Adaptive Strategies of Urban Nomads*. Boston, MA: Little Brown, 1970.

———.*The Ethnographic Interview*. New York: Holt, Rinehart, and Winston, 1979.

Spradley, James, and David W. McCurdy. *The Cultural Experience: Ethnography in Complex Societies*. Chicago, IL: Science Research Associates, 1972.

Spradley, James, and Brenda Mann. *The Cocktail Waitress*. New York, NY: John Wiley, 1975.

Strauss, Anselm, and Juliet Corbin. "Grounded Theory Methodology: An Overview." In *Handbook of Qualitative Research*, edited by Norman K. Denzin and Yvonna S. Lincoln, 273–85. Thousand Oaks, CA: Sage, 1994.

Wallace, Anthony F. C. *Culture and Personality*. Second Edition. New York: Random House, 1970.

Watson, Donald and Kenneth Labs. *Climatic Design: Energy-Efficient Building Principles and Practices*. New York: McGraw Hill, 1983.

Watson, Richard, and Patty Jo Watson. *Man and Nature: An Anthropological Essay in Human Ecology*. New York: Harcourt Brace Jovanovich, 1969.

Williams, Raymond. *Keywords: A Vocabulary of Culture and Society*. New York: Oxford University Press, 1976.

Whyte, William H. "Sitting Space." In *The Social Life of Small Urban Spaces*, 24–39. New York: Project for Public Spaces, 1980.

Zeisel, John. *Inquiry by Design: Environment/Behavior/Neuroscience in Architecture, Interiors, Landscape, and Planning*. Revised Edition. New York: W. W. Norton, 1981, 2006.

Zimring, Craig and Thierry Rosenheck. "Post-Occupancy Evaluations and Organizational Learning." In *Learning from Our Buildings: A State-of-the-Practice Summary of Post-Occupancy Evaluation*, 42–53. Washington, DC: National Academies Press, 2002.

Zubrzycki, Jaclyn. "Building toward a Positive School Climate." Education Week 32, no. 15 (January 10, 2013).

Cited Student Projects

Alter, Emily. "Fast, Slow Food: A Gourmet Fast Food Restaurant." Fall 2008.

Baldwin, Annallee. "A Sea Explorer's Base." Spring 1996.

Becker, Leslie. "First Time Mothers and Babies." Spring 2004.

Borden, Danielle. "A Mediterranean Restaurant." Fall 2006.

Burgos, Oracio. "A Sex Shop." Spring 1997.

Cabantac, Trisha Saavedra. "The Sandwich Shop." Fall 2012.

Carvalho, Flávia. "An Irish Pub." Fall 2004.

Cha, Eunah. "A Feminist Bookstore: Books, Gifts, Events, and More for Women." Spring 2004.

Chen, Annie. "A Hardware Store in Berkeley." Fall 2013.

Chen, Justin. "An Assisted Living and Alzheimer's Community." Fall 2004.

Cheng, Janet. "Rio, A Food Cart." 1998.

Chong, Kevin. "Recipe for an Engaging Farmers' Market." 2014.

Cohn-Martin, Elizabeth Leah. "Community Sustenance: Sunday Brunch at a Thai Buddhist Temple." Fall 2008.

DeClercq, Caitlin. "L'École Française: Education, Engagement, and the French Language and Culture." Fall 2012.

Doan, Andrew. "A Campus Café." Fall 2006.

Feliciano, Selena. "Choosing Informant and Interview Summary." Fall 2014.

Hoffman, Junius. "A Second-hand Store." Spring 1977.

Horiuchi, Myra. "The Adventure Playground." (no date)

Hui, Kevin. "A Campus Cooperative." Fall 2009.

Hunt, Ryan. "Coworking." Fall 2013.

Inaba, Jeff. "An Architectural Redesign Based on Ethnographic Research." Spring 1982.

Irving, Shelly. "A North Berkeley Senior Center." Spring 2001.

Ito, Adrienne. "Japantown Peace Plaza: Preserving an Ethnic Community and Cultural Identity." Fall 2012.

Kao, Michael. "A Montessori Pre-school." Spring 1996.

Kwok, Eva. "A Chinese Food Kiosk." Spring 1996.

Landes, Megan. "You Are Now Entering a Sci-Fi Bookstore: Getting Lost in the World of Science Fiction & Fantasy." Fall 2014.

Lin, Kenneth. "Bus Driver." Spring 1980.

Look, Douglas. "A Martial Arts School." Fall 1990.

Malagon, Daniel. "BART Station Ethnography." Fall 2009.

Mattson, Mark. "Chiropractor's Office." Fall 2008.

Mazgub, Sholeh. "Movie Theater." 2005.

Medrano, Sarah. "Driving Range." No date.

Mehta, Ami. "Indian Restaurant." Spring 2001.

Miller, Vanessa. "Boathouse." Spring 1998.

Moore, Marianne. "For Whom the Booth Tolls." *Concrete* 5, no. 3, February 20, 1979.

Nakamura, Nori. "A Neighborhood Bar." Spring 2001.

Nguyen, Tu Tuan. "The Play-yards at a Campus Day-care Center." Spring 1997.
Okazaki, Karen. "A Japantown Hardware Store." Spring 1982.
Palfreyman, Sam. "Goodwill Taxonomy." Fall 2009.
Phumzile, Mazeko. "A Taxi Co-op." Spring 1996.
Rönnerfalk, Malin. "The Small Café on 12th and Oak." Fall 2013.
Russell, Emily. "The Children's Library." Fall 2007.
Samaniego, Edward. "Bob's House." Fall 2009.
Smith, Talon. "Bring the Beat In: An Iconic Music Store." Fall 2013.
Stuckett, Nissa. "A Recovery Room." Spring 1997.
Sutherland, Junge, "A Prison AIDS Prevention Center." Spring 1997.
Tanelian, Aline. "A Café." Fall 2013.
Thongbenjamas, Thi thi. "Commuters on the Ferry." 1996.
To, Christin. "Developing a Program for Design: A University Tennis Complex." Fall 2005.
Tran, Wesley. "A Community Christian Church." Fall 2007.
Traverso, Pablo. "Skateboarding." Fall 2007.
Treetipbut. "A San Francisco Hotel." 2004.
Tressler, William. "A University Computer Lab." No date.
Wang, Wei-hsiang. "The Pizza Collective." No date.
Witanto, Grace. "The Music Store and Café." Fall 2013.
Yamamoto, Kyle. "A Japanese Restaurant." Fall 2012.
Zhong, Zheng. "A Senior Studio Redesign." Fall 2012.

Suggested Readings Not Cited

Agar, Michael H. *The Professional Stranger: An Informal Introduction to Ethnography*. San Diego, CA: Academic Press, 1996.

Atkinson, Paul. *The Ethnographic Imagination: Textual Constructions of Reality*. London: Routledge, 1990.

———. *Understanding Ethnographic Texts*. London: Sage, 1992.

Bean, Lowell and Sylvia B. Vane, "Ethnography and the NPS: Opportunities and Obligations." *CRM Bulletin: A National Park Service Technical Bulletin* 10, no. 1 (1987): 34–6.

Bell, Diane. *Gendered Fields: Men, Women and Ethnography*. London: Routledge, 1993.

Boas, Franz. *A Franz Boas Reader: The Shaping of American Anthropology, 1883–1911*. Edited by George W. Stocking Jr. Chicago, IL: University of Chicago Press, 1974.

Boas, Franz, and others. *General Anthropology*. Boston, MA: D.C. Heath, 1938.

Boissevain, Jeremy. *A Village in Malta*. New York: Holt, Rinehart and Winston, 1980.

Brown, Stephen Gilbert, and Sidney I. Dobrin, Eds. *Ethnography Unbound: From Theory Shock to Critical Praxis*. Albany: State University of New York Press, 2004.

Buroway, Michael, Ed. *Ethnography Unbound: Power and Resistance in the Modern Metropolis*. Berkeley: University of California Press, 1991.

———. *Global Ethnography*. Berkeley: University of California Press, 2000.

Buzard, James. "On Auto-Ethnographic Authority." *Yale Journal of Criticism* 16, no.1 (2003): 61–91.

Campbell, Marie, and Frances Gregor. *Mapping Social Relations: A Primer in Doing Institutional Ethnography*. Walnut Creek, CA: Altamira, 2004.

Clifford, James. *The Predicament of Culture: 20th-century Ethnography, Literature and Art*. Cambridge: Harvard University Press, 1988.

Coles, Alex, Ed. *Site Specificity: The Ethnographic Turn*. London: Black Dog Press, 2000.

Crespi, M. "Ethnography and the N. P. S.: A Growing Partnership." *CRM Bulletin* 10, no. 1 (1987): 1–4.

Davies, Charlotte Aull. *Reflexive Ethnography: A Guide to Researching Selves and Others*. Cardiff: University of Wales Press, 2003.

Denzin, Norman K. *Performance Ethnography: Critical Pedagogy and the Politics of Culture*. Thousand Oaks, CA: Sage, 2003.

Dexter, Lewis Anthony. *Elite and Specialized Interviewing*. Evanston, IL: Northwestern University Press, 1970.

Dixon, Beverly R., Gary D. Bouma, and G. B. J. Atkinson. *A Handbook of Social Science Research*. Oxford: Oxford University Press, 1987.

Dorst, John Darwin. *Written Suburb, American Site: An Ethnographic Dilemma*. Philadelphia: University of Pennsylvania Press, 2000.

Ellis, Carolyn and Arthur P. Bochner, Eds. *Composing Ethnography: Alternate Forms of Qualitative Writing*. Walnut Creek, CA: Altamira, 1996.

Emerson, Robert M. *Writing Ethnographic Fieldnotes*. Chicago, IL: University of Chicago Press, 1995.

Ethnografeast, Proceedings of the 2002 UC Berkeley Conference on Ethnography.

Evans-Pritchard, E. E. *The Nuer: A Description of the Modes of Livelihood and the Political Institutions of a Nilotic People*. Oxford: Oxford University Press, 1940.

Fonow, Mary Margaret, and Judith A. Cook. *Beyond Methodology: Feminist Scholarship as Lived Research*. Bloomington: Indiana University Press, 1991.

Geertz, Clifford, Ed. *Myth, Symbol and Culture*. New York: Norton, 1971.

———. *The Interpretation of Cultures*. New York: Basic Books, 1973.

Geertz, Clifford, and George E. Marcus, Eds. *Writing Culture: The Poetics and Politics of Ethnography*. Berkeley: University of California Press, 1986.

Hall, Edward T. *Beyond Culture*. New York: Anchor Press/Doubleday, 1976.

Hammersley, Martyn. *Reading Ethnographic Research: A Critical Guide*. London: Longman, 1991.

———. *What's Wrong with Ethnography?* London: Routledge, 1992.

Hebdige, Dick. *Subculture: The Meaning of Style*. London: Routledge, 1979.

Hebert, Ernest. *The Dogs of March*. Lebanon, NH: Hardscrabble Books, 1995.

Hine, Christine. *Virtual Ethnography*. London: Sage, 2000.

James, Allison, Jenny Hockey, and Andrew Dawson, Eds. *After Writing Culture: Epistemology and Praxis in Contemporary Anthropology*. London: Routledge, 1997.

Jones, Michael Owen. *Studying Organizational Symbolism: What, How, Why?* Thousand Oaks, CA: Sage, 1996.

Low, Setha. "Social Science Methods and Landscape Architecture Design." *Landscape Planning* 3 (1982): 137–48.

Low, Setha, Dana Taplin, and Suzanne Scheld. *Rethinking Urban Parks: Public Space and Cultural Diversity*. Austin: University of Texas Press, 2005.

Marcus, George E. *Ethnography through Thick and Thin*. Princeton, NJ: Princeton University Press, 1998.

Malinowski, Bronislaw. *Argonauts of the Western Pacific*. New York: Dutton, 1961.

———. *A Diary in the Strict Sense of the Term*. New York: Harcourt, Brace and World, 1967.

Naples, Nancy A. *Feminism and Method: Ethnography, Discourse Analysis and Activist Research*. New York: Routledge, 2003.

Punch, Maurice. *The Politics and Ethics of Fieldwork*. London: Sage, 1986.

Reed-Danahay, Deborah E., Ed. *Auto-Ethnography: Writing the Self and the Social*. Oxford: Berg, 1997.

Rohner, Ronald P., Ed. *The Ethnography of Franz Boas*. Chicago, IL: University of Chicago Press, 1969.

Saukko, Paula. *Doing Research in Cultural Studies: An Introduction to Classical and New Methodological Approaches*. London: Sage, 2003.

Schaap, Frank. *The Words That Took Us There: Ethnography in a Virtual Reality*. Amsterdam: Aksant Academic Publishers, 2002.

Sommer, Robert. *Social Design: Creating Buildings with People in Mind*. Englewood Cliffs, NJ: Prentice-Hall, 1983.

———. *Personal Space: The Behavioral Basis of Design*. Updated Edition. Bristol: Bosko Books, 2007.

Spindler, George, Ed. *Doing the Ethnography of Schooling: Educational Anthropology in Action*. New York: Holt, Rinehart and Winston, 1982.

Suchman, Lucille Alice. *Plans and Situated Actions: The Problem of Human–Machine Communication*. Cambridge: Cambridge University Press, 1987.

Strauss, Anselm. *Basics of Qualitative Research: Grounded Theory Procedures and Techniques*. Newbury Park, CA: Sage, 1990.

Thomas, Jim. *Doing Critical Ethnography*. London: Sage, 1993.

Von Maanen, John. *Tales of the Field: On Writing Ethnography*. Chicago, IL: University of Chicago Press, 1988.

———. *Representation in Ethnography*. Thousand Oaks, CA: Sage, 1995.

Index

Page numbers in **bold** indicate a Box or Table, in *italics* indicate illustrations